Timothy Daniel Sullivan

Speeches from the dock

Protests of Irish patriotism. 23rd Dublin Edition

Timothy Daniel Sullivan

Speeches from the dock
Protests of Irish patriotism. 23rd Dublin Edition

ISBN/EAN: 9783337124212

Printed in Europe, USA, Canada, Australia, Japan

Cover: Foto ©ninafisch / pixelio.de

More available books at **www.hansebooks.com**

"Guilty, or not Guilty?"

SPEECHES FROM THE DOCK,
OR
PROTESTS OF IRISH PATRIOTISM.

The Manchester Tragedy and the Cruise of the Jackmell Packet.

"THE WEARING OF THE GREEN,"
OR
THE PROSECUTED FUNERAL PROCESSION, &c.

BY

T. D. SULLIVAN, A. M. SULLIVAN, AND D. B. SULLIVAN

CONTAINING,

WITH INTRODUCTORY SKETCHES AND BIOGRAPHICAL NOTICES,

SPEECHES DELIVERED IN THE DOCK

BY

THEOBALD WOLFE TONE
WILLIAM ORR
THE BROTHERS SHEARES
ROBERT EMMET
THOMAS RUSSELL
JOHN MITCHELL
JOHN MARTIN [1848]
WILLIAM SMITH O'BRIEN
THOMAS FRANCIS MEAGHER
TERENCE BELLEW M'MANUS
WILLIAM P. ALLEN
MICHAEL LARKIN
MICHAEL O'BRIEN
THOMAS C. LUBY
JOHN O'LEARY
CHARLES J. KICKHAM
J. O'DONOVAN ROSSA
COLONEL THOMAS F. BURKE
CAPTAIN JOHN M'AFFERTY
STEPHEN J. MEANY
EDWARD DUFFY
CAPTAIN JOHN M'CLURE
JOHN EDWARD KELLY
COLONEL JOHN WARREN
AUGUSTINE E. COSTELLO
CAPTAIN MACKAY
A. M. SULLIVAN
JOHN MARTIN [1868].

TWENTY-THIRD DUBLIN EDITION,
AND
FIRST AMERICAN EDITION.

PROVIDENCE, R. I.:
HENRY McELROY,
MURPHY AND McCARTHY.
1878.

PART I.

SPEECHES FROM THE DOCK;

OR,

PROTESTS OF IRISH PATRIOTISM.

SPEECHES DELIVERED AFTER CONVICTION,

BY

THEOBALD WOLFE TONE,	TERENCE BELLEW M'MANUS,
WILLIAM ORR,	JOHN MITCHEL,
THE BROTHERS SHEARES,	THOMAS C. LUBY,
ROBERT EMMET,	JOHN O'LEARY,
JOHN MARTIN (1848),	CHARLES J. KICKHAM,
WILLIAM SMITH O'BRIEN,	COLONEL THOMAS F. BURKE,
THOMAS FRANCIS MEAGHER.	CAPTAIN MACKAY.

"Freedom's battle, once begun,—
Bequeath'd from bleeding sire to son,—
Though baffled oft, is ever won."

PROVIDENCE, R. I.:
HENRY McELROY,
MURPHY AND McCARTHY.
1878.

PREFACE.

During their many years in the book business, the publishers have received numerous orders for the present work. But, as the book had never been published in America, the orders could only be filled at great expense. These facts, together with the daily increasing Irish national spirit among Irishmen, and their descendants in this country, have decided them to undertake the task of supplying, at a reasonable price, a want that has long been felt. They ardently hope that their endeavor may haply contribute toward arousing, to an even higher enthusiasm, the aspirations of their fellow-countrymen. That the "Speeches from the Dock" may reëcho through every lyceum, college and household, fanning into a blaze the glowing embers of that patriotic spirit of Irish national independence, is their most earnest desire.

PROVIDENCE, R. I.,
    May-day, 1878.

TABLE OF CONTENTS.

PART I.

	BY	PAGE
Introductory	D. B. S.	7
Theobald Wolfe Tone	T. D. S.	14
William Orr	D. B. S.	28
Henry and John Sheares	D. B. S.	32
Robert Emmet	T. D. S.	39
Thomas Russell	D. B. S.	54
John Mitchel	T. D. S.	72
John Martin	D. B. S.	93
W. S. O'Brien	D. B. S.	107
T. F. Meagher	D. B. S.	133
Kevin Izod O'Doherty	D. B. S.	144
Terence Bellew MacManus	D. B. S.	148
Thomas Clarke Luby	T. D. S.	152
John O'Leary	T. D. S.	163
J. O'Donovan (Rossa)	T. D. S.	171
Brian Dillon, John Lynch, and others	T. D. S.	174
Charles J. Kickham	T. D. S.	184
Thomas F. Burke	D. B. S.	188
John M'Afferty	T. D. S.	200
Edward Duffy, S. J. Meany, and John M'Clure	T. D. S.	204
Edward Kelly and Captain Mackey	T. D. S.	219

PART II.

	BY	PAGE
The Dock and the Scaffold	A. M. S. and D. B. S.	3
The Cruise of the " Jackmel" (Colonel Warren, Augustine E. Costello, General W. Halpin)	T. D. S.	61

PART III.

	BY	PAGE
The Wearing of the Green ; or, The Prosecuted Funeral Procession.	A. M. S.	3

SPEECHES FROM THE DOCK.

INTRODUCTORY.

To the lovers of Ireland—to those who sympathize with her sufferings and resent her wrongs, there can be few things more interesting than the history of the struggles which sprang from devotion to her cause, and were consecrated by the blood of her patriots. The efforts of the Irish race to burst the fetters that foreign force and native dissensions imposed on them, and elevate their country from bondage and degradation to a place amongst free nations, fill a page in the world's history which no lover of freedom can read without emotion, and which must excite wonder, admiration, and regret in the mind of every man with whom patriotism is not a reproach, and who can sympathize with a cause ennobled by fidelity and sacrifice, and sanctified by the blood and tears of a nation. "How hands so vile could conquer hearts so brave," is the question which our national poet supposes to arise in the mind of the stranger, as he looks on the spectacle of Ireland in her decay; but another question will suggest itself to those who study the history of our country: it is, how a feeling so deeply rooted as the love of independence is in the hearts of the Irish people—an aspiration so warmly and so widely entertained—which has been clung to with so much persistency—which has survived through centuries of persecution—for which generations have arisen, and fought and bled, and dashed themselves against the power of England with a succession as unbroken as that of the waves upon our shores—a cause so universally loved, so deeply reverenced, and so unflinchingly supported by a brave and intrepid race, should never have attained the blessing of success. A more signal instance than that which Ireland can supply of the baffling of a nation's hope, the prolonged frustration of a people's will, is not on record; and few even of those who most condemn the errors and weakness by which Irishmen themselves have retarded the national object, will hesitate to say that they have given to mankind the noblest proof they possess of the vitality of the principles of freedom, and the indestructibility of national sentiment.

It is for us, however, Irish of the Irish, that the history of the struggle for Ireland's rights possesses most attractions. We live amidst the scenes where the battles against the stranger were fought, and where the men who waged them lived and died. The bones of the patriots who labored for Ireland, and of those who died for her, repose in the graveyards around us; and we have still amongst us the inheritors of their blood, their name, and their spirit. It was to make us free—to render independent and prosperous the nation to which we belong—that the pike was lifted and the green flag raised; and it was in furtherance of this object, on which the hearts of Irishmen are still set, that the men whose names shine through the pages on which the story of Ireland's struggles for national existence is written, suffered and died. To follow out that mournful but absorbing story is not, however, the object aimed at in the following pages. The history of Ireland is no longer a sealed volume to the people; more than one author has told it truthfully and well, and the list of books devoted to it is every day receiving valuable accessions. Nor has it even been attempted, in this little work, though trenching more closely on its subject, to trace the career and sketch the lives of the men who fill the foremost places in the ranks of Ireland's political martyrs. In the subjoined pages little more will be found than a correct report of the addresses delivered, under certain peculiar circumstances, by the group of Irishmen whose names are given on the titlepage. A single public utterance from the lips of each of these gentlemen is all that we have printed, though it would be easy to supplement them, in nearly every case, by writings and speeches owning a similar authorship, equally eloquent and equally patriotic. But the speeches given here are associated with facts which give them peculiar value and significance, and were spoken under circumstances which lend to them a solemn interest and impressiveness which could not otherwise be obtained. They reach us—these dock speeches, in which nobility of purpose and chivalrous spirit is expressed—like voices from the tomb, like messages from beyond the grave, brimful of lessons of dignity and patriotism. We can see the men who spoke them standing before the representatives of the government whose oppression had driven them to revolt, when the solemn farce of trying them for a crime which posterity will account a virtue had terminated, and when the verdict of "guilty" had gladdened the hearts of their accusers. The circumstances under which they spoke might well cause a bold man to falter. They were about parting forever from all that makes life dear to man; and, for some of them, the sentence which was to cut short the thread of their existence, to consign them to a bloody and ignominious death, to leave their bodies mutilated corpses, from which the rights of Christian burial were to be withheld—which was to assign them the death of a dog, and to follow them with persecuting hand into the valley of death—was about to fall from the lips of the judges whom they addressed. Against others a fate less repulsive, perhaps, to the feelings of humanity, but certainly not more merciful, and hardly less painful and appalling, was about to be decreed. Recent revelations have thrown some light on the horrors endured by the Irish political prisoners who languish within the prison pens of England; but it needs far more than a stray letter, a half-stifled cry from the dungeon depths, to enable the public to realize the misery, the wretchedness, and the degradation attached to the condition to which England reduces her political convicts. Condemned to associate with the vilest of the scoundrels bred by the immorality and godlessness of England—exposed, without possibility of redress, to the persecutions of brutal, coarse-minded men, accustomed to deal only with ruffians than whom beasts are less ferocious and unreclaimable—

restricted to a course of discipline which blasts the vigor of the body, and under whose influence reason herself totters upon her throne—the Irish rebel, against whom the doom of penal servitude has been pronounced, is condemned to the most hideous and agonizing punishments to which men of their class could be exposed. It was with such terrors staring them in the face, that the men whose words are recorded in this little work delivered their speeches from the dock. It is surely something for us, their countrymen, to boast of, that, neither in their bearing nor in their words, was there manifested the slightest trace of weakness, the faintest exhibition of any feeling which could show that their hearts were accessible to the terror which their situation was so well calculated to inspire. No cheek grew pale, no eyes lost their light—their tones were unbroken, and their manner undaunted as ever, as these men uttered the words we purpose recording. Their language tells of minds which persecution could not subdue, and for which death itself possessed no sting; and the manner in which it was expressed showed that, in their case, elevation of sentiment was allied with unconquerable firmness and resolution. Never were lessons so noble more boldly preached. It is in courts of justice, after all, declares a great English authority, that the lessons of morality are best taught; and in Ireland the truthfulness of the assertion is established. But it is not from the bench or the jury-box that the words have fallen in which the cause of morality and justice has been vindicated; venality, passion, and prejudice have but too often swayed the decisions of both: and it is to the dock we must turn when we seek for honor, integrity, and patriotism.

We owe it to the men who suffered so unflinchingly in the cause of our country, and who have left us so precious a heritage in the speeches in which they hurled a last defiance at their oppressors, that their names should not be forgotten, or the recollection of their acts suffered to grow cold. The noblest incentive to patriotism, as it is the highest reward which this world can offer those who dare and suffer for fatherland, is the gratitude, the sympathy, and the applause of the people for whom they labored. We owe it to the brave men whose patriotism is attested in the addresses comprised in this volume, that the memory of their noble deeds shall not pass away, and that their names shall remain enshrined in the hearts of their countrymen. They failed, it is true, to accomplish what they attempted, and the battle to which they devoted themselves has yet to be won; but we know that they, at least, did their part courageously and well; and, looking back now upon the stormy scenes of their labors, and contrasting the effects of their sacrifices with the cost at which they were made, the people of Ireland are still prepared to accept the maxim that—

> "'Tis better to have fought and lost,
> Than never to have fought at all."

While such men can be found to suffer as they have suffered for Ireland, the ultimate triumph of her aspirations cannot be doubted; nor can the national faith be despaired of while it has martyrs so numerous and so heroic. It is by example that the great lessons of patriotism can best be conveyed; and if the national spirit burn brightly to-day in Ireland—if the spirit of her children be still defiant and unsubdued—if, at home and in the far West, the hearts of the Irish people still throb with the emotions that prompted Emmet and Wolfe Tone —if their eyes are still hot to see the independence of their country, their arms still ready to strike, and their spirit ready to sacrifice for the accomplishment of that object, we owe the result largely to the men whose names are inscribed in this little work, and whose memory it is intended to perpetuate.

We have commenced our series with the speech of Theobald Wolfe Tone, and our record stretches no further back than the memorable insurrection of 1798. If our object were to group together the Irishmen who are known to have struggled for the independence of their country, and who suffered for their attachment to her cause, we might go much further back into history, and indefinitely increase the bulk of this publication.

We fix the insurrection of '98 as the limit of our collection, chiefly because it was at that time trials for high treason in Ireland assumed the precise meaning and significance which they now possess; and there is consequently, in the speeches which follow, such a unity of purpose and sentiment as renders them especially suitable for presentation in a single volume. Only seventy years have elapsed since Wolfe Tone spoke to the question why sentence should not be pronounced on him—only two-thirds of a century since Emmet vindicated the cause of his country from the Green-street dock,—and already what a host of imitators and disciples have they had! There is not a country in Europe, there is not a nationality in the world, can produce such another collection as that which we to-day lay before the people of Ireland. We live under a government which claims to be just, liberal, and constitutional, yet against no other government in Christendom have the same number of protests been made within the same space of time. Not Poland, not Hungary, not Venetia, can point to such an unbroken succession of political martyrs. The pages of history contain nothing to compare with the little volume we to-day place in the hands of our countrymen; and we know of no more powerful and eloquent condemnation of the system on which Ireland is governed, than that contained in the simple fact that all those speeches were spoken, all those trials carried out, all those sentences decreed, within the lifetime of a single generation. It is idle to think of subduing a people who make so many sacrifices, and who are undaunted still; it is vain to think of crushing a spirit which survives so much persecution. The executioner and the gaoler, the gibbet, the block, and the dungeon, have done their work in the crusade against Irish Nationality, and we know what the result is to-day. The words of the last political convict whose name appears in these pages are as uncompromising and as bold as those of the first of his predecessors; and, studying the spirit which they have exhibited, and marking the effect of their conduct on the bulk of their countrymen, it is impossible to avoid the conclusion that so much persistent resolution and heroism must one day eventuate in success, and that Ireland, the country for which so many brave men have suffered with such unfaltering courage, is not destined to disprove the rule that—

> "Freedom's battle once begun,—
> Bequeath'd from bleeding sire to son,—
> Though baffled oft, is ever won."

THEOBALD WOLFE TONE.

No name is more intimately associated with the national movement of 1798 than that of Theobald Wolfe Tone. He was its main-spring, its leading spirit. Many men connected with it possessed, as he did, brilliant talents, unfailing courage and determination, and an intense devotion to the cause; but the order of his genius raised him above them all, and marked him out from the first as the head and front of the patriot party. He was one of the original founders of the Society of United Irishmen, which was formed in Belfast in the year 1791. In its early days this society was simply a sort of reform association, a legal and constitutional body, having for its chief object the removal of the frightful oppressions by which the Catholic people of Ireland were tortured and disgraced; but in the troubled and portentous condition of home and foreign politics, the society could not long retain this character. The futility of seeking a redress of the national grievances by parliamentary means was becoming apparent to every understanding. The system of outrage and injustice towards the Catholics, unabating in its severity, continued to exasperate the actual sufferers, and to offend all men of humane feelings and enlightened principles; and, at the same time, the electric influence of the American War of Independence and the French Revolution was operating powerfully in every heart, evoking there the aspiration for Irish freedom, and inspiring a belief in its possible attainment. In the midst of such exciting circumstances the society could not continue to stand on its original basis. In the year 1794, after a debate among the members, followed by the withdrawal of the more moderate or timid among them from its ranks, it assumed the form and character of a secret revolutionary organization; and Tone, Thomas Addis Emmet, Samuel Neilson, Thomas Russell, James Napper

THEOBALD WOLFE TONE.
From a Portrait by his Daughter-in-law Mrs. Sampson Tone.

Tandy, with a number of other patriotic gentlemen in Belfast, Dublin, and other parts of the country, soon found themselves in the full swing of an insurrectionary movement, plotting and planning for the complete overthrow of British power in Ireland. Thenceforward, for some time, the organization went on rapidly extending through the province of Ulster, in the first instance, and subsequently over most of the midland and southern counties.

Such was the state of affairs when, in the early part of 1794, an emissary from the French government arrived in Ireland, to ascertain to what extent the Irish people were likely to coöperate with France in a war against England. This individual was the Rev. William Jackson, an Irish Protestant clergyman, who had for some years been resident in France, and had become thoroughly imbued with democratic and republican principles. Unfortunately, he was not one of the most prudent of envoys. He revealed his mission to an acquaintance of his, an English attorney, named Cockayne, who repaid his confidence by betraying his secrets to the government. Cockayne was immediately employed as a spy upon Jackson's further proceedings, in which capacity he accompanied his unsuspecting victim to Ireland, and acquired cognizance of most of his negotiations. On the 28th of April, 1794, Jackson was arrested on a charge of high treason. He was brought to speedy trial, was found guilty, but was not sentenced, for, on the day on which the law's award was to have been announced to him, he contrived, before entering the court, to swallow a dose of poison, from the effects of which he expired in the dock. Tone, with whom Jackson was known to have been in confidential communication, was placed by those events in a very critical position: owing, however, to some influence which had been made with the government on his behalf, he was permitted to exile himself to America. As he had entered into no engagement with the government regarding his future line of conduct, he made his expatriation the means of forwarding, in the most effective manner, the designs he had at heart. He left Dublin for Philadelphia on the 20th of May, 1795. One of his first acts, after arriving, was to present to the French Minister there resident a memorial on the state of Ireland. During the remaining months of the year letters from his old friends came pouring in on him, describing the brightening prospects of the cause at home, and urging him to proceed to the French capital, and impress upon the Directory the policy of despatching at once an expedition to insure the success of the Irish revolutionary movement.

Tone was not the man to disregard such representations. He had at the time a fair prospect of securing a comfortable independence in America, but, with the full concurrence of his heroic wife, who had accompanied him across the Atlantic, he sacrificed those chances and resumed the perilous duties of an Irish patriot. On the 1st of January, 1796, he left New York for Paris, to try what he could do as a diplomatist for the cause of Ireland. Arrived at the French capital, he had his business communicated to the Directory through the medium of an Irish gentleman, named Madgett, and also by memorial, representing always that the landing of a force of 20,000 men in Ireland, with a supply of arms for the peasantry, would insure the separation of Ireland from England. Not satisfied with the slow progress he was thus achieving, he went on the 24th of February direct to the Luxemburg Palace, and sought and obtained an interview with the War Minister, the celebrated Carnot, the "organizer of victory." The Minister received him well, listened attentively to his statements, discussed his project with him, and appeared much impressed with the prospects it presented. The result was that, on the 16th of December in the same year, a splendid expedition sailed from Brest for Ireland. It consisted of seventeen sail of the line, thirteen frigates and fifteen transports, with some smaller craft, and had on board 15,000 troops, with a large supply of arms for the Irish patriots. Tone himself, who had received the rank of Adjutant-General in the French service, was on board one of the vessels. Had this force been disembarked on the shores of Ireland, it is hardly possible to doubt that the separation of this country from England would have been effected. But the expedition was unfortunate from the outset. It was scattered on the voyage during a gale of wind, and the admiral's vessel, with Iloche the commander on board, was separated from the others. A portion of the expedition entered the magnificent Bay of Bantry, and waited there several days, in expectation of being rejoined by the vessel containing the admiral and commander; but they waited in vain. Tone vehemently urged that a landing should be effected with the forces then at hand—some 6,500 men; but the officers procrastinated, time was lost, the wind which had been blowing from the east (that is out the harbor) rose to a perfect hurricane, and on the 27th and 28th of the month the vessels cut their cables and made the best of their way for France.

This was a terrible blow to the hopes of the Irish organizer. Rage and sadness filled his heart by turns as the fierce storm blew his vessel out of the bay and across the sea to the land which he had left under such favorable auspices. But yet he did not resign himself to despair. As the patient spider renews her web again and again after it has been torn asunder, so did this indefatigable patriot set to work to repair the misfortune that had occurred, and to build up another project of assistance for his unfortunate country. His perseverance was not unproductive of results. The Batavian or Dutch Republic, then in alliance with France, took up the project that had failed in the Bay of Bantry. In the month of July, 1797, they had assembled in the Texel an expedition for the invasion of Ireland, nearly, if not quite, as formidable in men and ships as that which had left Brest in the previous year. Tone was on board the flagship, even more joyous and hopeful than he had been on the preceding occasion. But again, as if by some extraordinary fatality, the weather interposed an obstacle to the realization of the design. The vessels were ready for sea, the troops were on board, nothing was wanted but a slant of wind to enable the fleet to get out. But for five weeks it continued to blow steadily in the adverse direction. The supplies ran low; the patience of the officers and of the government became exhausted—the troops were disembarked, and the project abandoned! The second failure in a matter of such weight and importance was a heavy blow to the heart of the brave Tone. Elaborate and costly efforts like those which had ended so poorly, he felt, could not often be repeated; the drift of the war was cutting out other work for the fleets and armies of France and her allies, and the unwelcome conviction began to settle darkly on his mind that never again would he see such a vision of hope for dear Ireland as that which had shone before him on those two occasions, and vanished in doubt and gloom.

Yet there was no need to despair. Assurances reached Tone every day that the defeat and humiliation of England was a settled resolve of the French government, one which they would never abandon. And for a time everything seemed to favor the notion that a direct stroke at the heart of England was intended. In the latter part of 1797, the Directory ordered the formation of "The Army of England," the command of which was given to General Buonaparte. Tone's heart again beat high with hope, for now matters looked more promising than ever. He was in constant communication with some of the chief officers of the expedition, and in the month of December he had several interviews with Buonaparte himself, which, however, he could hardly consider of a satisfactory nature. On the 20th of May, 1798, General Buonaparte embarked on board the fleet at Toulon and sailed off—not for Ireland or England, but for Egypt.

On the Irish leaders at home these repeated disappointments fell with terrible effect. The condition of the country was daily growing more critical. The government, now thoroughly roused and alarmed, and persuaded that the time for "vigorous measures" had arrived, was grappling with the conspiracy in all directions. Still those men would, if they could, have got the people to possess their souls in patience and wait for aid from abroad before unfurling the banner of insurrection; for they were constant in their belief that, without the presence of a disciplined army on Irish soil to consolidate their strength and direct it, a revolutionary effort of the Irish people could end only in disaster. But the government had reasons of their own for wishing to set an Irish rebellion afoot at this time, and they took measures to precipitate the rising. The arrest of the delegates at the house of Oliver Bond in Dublin, and the capture of Lord Edward Fitzgerald, contributed to this end; but these things the country might have peaceably endured, if no more dreadful trial had been put upon it. What could not be endured was the system of riot and outrage and murder, to which the unfortunate peasantry were then given over. Words fail to describe its cruelty and its horrors. It was too much for human nature to bear. On the 23d of May, three days after Buonaparte had sailed from Toulon for Alexandria, the Irish insurrection broke out. The news of the occurrence created the most intense excitement among the Irish refugees then in Paris. Tone rushed to and fro to the Directory and to the generals, pleading for the despatch of some assistance to his struggling countrymen. Various plans were suggested and taken into consideration, but, while time was being wasted in this way, the military forces of the British government were rapidly suppressing the insurrection of the unarmed and undisciplined Irish peasantry. In this condition of affairs a gallant, but rash and indiscreet French officer, General Humbert, resolved that he would commit the Directory to action, by starting at once with a small force for the coast of Ireland. Towards the middle of August, calling together the merchants and magistrates of Rochelle, " he forced them to advance a small sum of money, and all that he wanted, on military requisition; and embarking on board a few frigates and transports with 1,000 men, 1,000 spare muskets, 1,000 guineas, and a few pieces of artillery, he compelled the captains to set sail for the most desperate attempt which is, perhaps, recorded in history." Three Irishmen were on board the fleet—Matthew Tone, brother to Theobald, Bartholomew Teeling, and Sullivan, an officer in the French service, who was enthusiastically devoted to the Irish cause, and had rendered much aid to his patriotic countrymen in France. Humbert landed at Killala, routed with his little handful of men a large force of the royal troops, and held his ground until General Lake, with 20,000 men, marched against him. After a resistance sufficient to maintain the honor of the French arms, Humbert's little force surrendered as prisoners of war. The Irish who had joined his standard were shown no mercy. The peasantry were cruelly butchered. Of those who had accompanied him from France, Sullivan, who was able to pass as a Frenchman, escaped; Teeling and Matthew Tone were brought in irons to Dublin, tried, and executed. The news of Humbert's expedition, and the temporary success that had attended it, created much excitement in France, and stirred up the Directory to attempt something for Ireland more worthy of the fame and power of the French nation, and more in keeping with their repeated promises to the leaders of the Irish movement. But their fleet was at the time greatly reduced, and their resources were in a state of disorganization. They mustered for the expedition only one sail of the line and eight small frigates, commanded by Commodore Bompart, conveying 5,000 men under the leadership of General Hardy. On board the admiral's vessel, which was named the *Hoche*, was the heroic Theobald Wolfe Tone. He knew this expedition had no chance of success, but he had all along declared that, "if the government sent only a corporal's guard, he felt it his duty to go along with them." The vessels sailed on the 20th of September, 1798; it was not till the 11th October that they arrived off Lough Swilly—simultaneously with an English squadron that had been on the look-out for them. The English ships were about equal in number to the French, but were of a larger class, and carried a much heavier armament. The French admiral directed some of his smaller craft to endeavor to escape by means of their light draught of water, and he counselled Tone to transfer himself to that one of them which had the best chance of getting away. The Frenchmen, he observed, would be made prisoners of war, but for the Irish rebel a worse fate was reserved, if he should fall into the hands of his enemies. But to this suggestion the noble-hearted Tone declined to accede. "Shall it be said," he replied, "that I fled while the French were fighting the battles of my country?" In a little time the *Hoche* was surrounded by four sail of the line and one frigate, which poured their shot into her upon all sides. During six hours she maintained the unequal combat, fighting "till her masts and rigging were cut away, her scuppers flowed with blood, her wounded filled the cockpit, her shattered ribs yawned at each new stroke, and let in five feet of water in the hold, her rudder was carried off, and she floated a dismantled wreck on the water; her sails and cordage hung in shreds, nor could she reply with a single gun from her dismounted batteries to the unabating cannonade of the enemy." During the action Tone commanded one of the batteries "and fought with the utmost desperation, as if he was courting death." But, as often has happened in similar cases, death seemed to shun him, and he was reserved for a more tragic fate.

The French officers who survived the action, and had been made prisoners of war, were, some days subsequently, invited to breakfast with the Earl of Cavan, who commanded in the district in which they had been landed. Tone, who, up to that time, had escaped recognition, was one of the party, and sat undistinguished among them, until Sir George Hill, who had been a fellow-student of his in Trinity College, entered the room and accosted him by his name. This was done, not inadvertently, but with the intention of betraying him. In a moment he was in the hands of a party of military and police, who were in waiting for him in the next room. Seeing that they were about to put him in fetters, he complained indignantly of the offering of such an insult to the uniform which he wore, and the rank—that of *Chef de Brigade*—which he bore in the French army. He cast off his regimentals, protesting that they should not be so sullied, and then, offering his limbs to the irons, exclaimed: "For the cause which I have embraced, I feel prouder to wear these chains, than if I were decorated with the Star and Garter of England." He was hurried off to Dublin, and, though the ordinary tribunals were sitting at the time, and the military tribunals could have no claim on him, as he had never belonged to the English army, he was put on his trial before a court-martial. This was absolutely an illegal proceeding, but his enemies were impatient for his blood, and would not brook the chances and the delays of the ordinary procedure of law. On the 10th of November, 1798, his trial, if such it might be called, took place in one of the Dublin barracks. He appeared before the Court, "dressed," says the *Dublin Magazine* for November, 1798, "in the French uniform: a large cocked hat, with broad gold lace and the tri-colored cockade; a blue uniform coat, with gold-embroidered collar and two large gold epaulets; blue pantaloons, with gold-laced garters at the knees; and short boots, bound at the tops with gold lace." In his bearing there was no trace of excitement. "The firmness and cool serenity of his whole deportment," writes his son, "gave to the awe-struck assembly the measure of his soul." The proceedings of the Court are detailed in the following report which we copy from the "Life of Tone," by his son, published at Washington, U. S., in 1826:—

The members of the court having been sworn, the Judge Advocate called on the prisoner to plead guilty or not guilty to the charge of having acted traitorously and hostilely against the King. Tone replied:—
"I mean not to give the court any useless trouble, and wish to spare them the idle task of examining witnesses. I admit all the facts alleged, and only request leave to read an address which I have prepared for this occasion."
COLONEL DALY:—"I must warn the prisoner that, in acknowledging those *facts*, he admits, to his prejudice, that he has acted *traitorously* against his Majesty. Is such his intention?"
TONE:—" Stripping this charge of the technicality of its terms, it means, I presume, by the word traitorously, that I have been found in arms against the soldiers of the King in my native country. I admit this accusation in its most extended sense, and request again to explain to the court the reasons and motives of my conduct."
The court then observed they would hear his address, provided he kept himself within the bounds of moderation.
Tone rose, and began in these words:—"Mr. President and Gentlemen of the Court-Martial, I mean not to give you the trouble of bringing judicial proof to convict me legally of having acted in hostility to the government of his Britannic Majesty in Ireland. I admit the fact. From my earliest youth I have regarded the connection between Great Britain and Ireland as the curse of the Irish

nation, and felt convinced that, whilst it lasted, this country could never be free nor happy. My mind has been confirmed in this opinion by the experience of every succeeding year, and the conclusions which I have drawn from every fact before my eyes. In consequence, I was determined to employ all the powers which my individual efforts could move, in order to separate the two countries. That Ireland was not able of herself to throw off the yoke, I knew; I therefore sought for aid wherever it was to be found. In honorable poverty I rejected offers which, to a man in my circumstances, might be considered highly advantageous. I remained faithful to what I thought the cause of my country, and sought in the French Republic an ally to rescue three millions of my countrymen from—"

The President here interrupted the prisoner, observing that this language was neither relevant to the charge, nor such as ought to be delivered in a public court.

A Member said it seemed calculated only to inflame the minds of a certain description of people (the United Irishmen), many of whom might be present, and that the court could not suffer it.

The JUDGE ADVOCATE said:—"If Mr. Tone meant this paper to be laid before his Excellency in the way of *extenuation*, it must have quite a contrary effect, if the foregoing part was suffered to remain."

The President wound up by calling on the prisoner to hesitate before proceeding further in the same strain.

TONE then continued:—" I believe there is nothing in what remains for me to say which can give any offence, I mean to express my feelings and gratitude towards the Catholic body, in whose cause I was engaged."

PRESIDENT:—"That seems to have nothing to say to the charge against you, to which you are only to speak. If you have anything to offer in defence or extenuation of the charge, the court will hear you, but they beg you will confine yourself to that subject."

TONE:—" I shall, then, confine myself to some points relative to my connection with the French army. Attached to no party in the French Republic—without interest, without money, without intrigue—the openness and integrity of my views raised me to a high and confidential rank in its armies. I obtained the confidence of the Executive Directory, the approbation of my generals, and, I will venture to add, the esteem and affection of my brave comrades. When I review these circumstances, I feel a secret and internal consolation which no reverse of fortune, no sentence in the power of this court to inflict, can deprive me of, or weaken in any degree. Under the flag of the French Republic I originally engaged with a view to save and liberate my own country. For that purpose I have encountered the chances of war amongst strangers; for that purpose I repeatedly braved the terrors of the ocean, covered, as I knew it to be, with the triumphant fleets of that power which it was my glory and my duty to oppose. I have sacrificed all my views in life; I have courted poverty; I have left a beloved wife unprotected, and children whom I adored, fatherless. After such a sacrifice in a cause which I have always considered—conscientiously considered—as the cause of justice and freedom, it is no great effort, at this day, to add the sacrifice of my life. But I hear it said that this unfortunate country has been a prey to all sorts of horrors. I sincerely lament it. I beg, however, it may be remembered that I have been absent four years from Ireland. To me these sufferings can never be attributed. I designed, by fair and open war, to procure the separation of the two countries. For open war I was prepared, but, instead of that, a system of private assassination has taken place. I repeat, whilst I deplore it, that it is not chargeable on me. Atrocities, it seems, have been committed on both sides. I do not less deplore them. I detest them from my heart; and to those who know my character and sentiments, I may safely appeal for the truth of this assertion: with them I need no justification. In a case like this, success is everything. Success, in the eyes of the vulgar, fixes its merits. Washington succeeded, and Kosciusko failed. After a combat nobly sustained—a combat which would have excited the respect and sympathy of a generous enemy—my fate has been to become a prisoner, to the eternal disgrace of those who gave the orders. I was brought here in irons like a felon. I mention this for the sake of others; for me, I am indifferent to it. I am aware of the fate which awaits me, and scorn equally the tone of complaint and that of supplication. As to the connection between this country and Great Britain, I repeat it—all that has been imputed to me (words, writings, and actions), I here deliberately avow. I have spoken and acted with reflection and on principle, and am ready to meet the consequences. Whatever be the sentence of the court, Its members will surely discharge their duty—I shall take care not to be wanting in mine."

The court having asked if he wished to make any further observation,

TONE said:—"I wish to offer a few words relative to one single point—the mode of punishment. In France our *emigrés*, who stand nearly in the same situation in which I now stand before you, are condemned to be shot. I ask that the court shall adjudge me the death of a soldier, and let me be shot by a platoon of grenadiers. I request this indulgence, rather in consideration of the uniform I wear—the uniform of a *Chef de Brigade* in the French army—than from any personal regard to myself. In order to evince my claim to this favor, I beg that the court may take the trouble to peruse my commission and letters of service in the French army. It will appear from these papers that I have not received them as a mask to cover me, but that I have been long and *bona fide* an officer in the French service."

JUDGE ADVOCATE:—"You must feel that the papers you allude to will serve as undeniable proof against you."

TONE:—"Oh, I know they will. I have already admitted the facts, and I now admit the papers as full proof of conviction."

[The papers were then examined: they consisted of a brevet of *Chef de Brigade* from the Directory, signed by the Minister of War, of a letter of service granting to him the rank of Adjutant-General, and of a passport.]

GENERAL LOFTUS:—"In these papers you are designated as serving in the army of England."
TONE :—"I did serve in that army, when it was commanded by Buonaparte, by Dessaix, and by Kilmaine, who is, as I am, an Irishman ; but I have also served elsewhere."
The court requested if he had anything further to say.
He said that nothing more occurred to him, except that the sooner his Excellency's approbation of the sentence was obtained the better.

This is Tone's speech, as reported in the public prints at that time, but the recently-published " Correspondence" of Lord Cornwallis—Lord-Lieutenant in those days—supplies a portion of the address which was never before published, the court having forbade the reading of it at the trial. The passage contains a noble outburst of gratitude towards the Catholics of Ireland. Tone himself, as every reader is aware, was a Protestant, and there can have been no reason for its suppression except the consideration that it was calculated to still more endear the prisoner to the hearts of his countrymen. We now reprint it, and thus place it, for the first time, before the people for whom it was written :—

" I have labored to create a people in Ireland, by raising three millions of my countrymen to the rank of citizens. I have labored to abolish the infernal spirit of religious persecution, by uniting the Catholics and Dissenters. To the former I owe more than ever can be repaid. The services I was so fortunate as to render them, they rewarded munificently; but they did more. When the public cry was raised against me—when the friends of my youth swarmed off and left me alone—the Catholics did not desert me; they had the virtue even to sacrifice their own interests to a rigid principle of honor; they refused though strongly urged, to disgrace a man who, whatever his conduct towards the government might have been, had faithfully and conscientiously discharged his duty towards them; and in so doing, though it was in my own case, I will say they showed an instance of public virtue of which I know not whether there exists another example."

The sad sequel of those proceedings is soon told. The request of the prisoner to receive a military execution was refused by the Viceroy, Lord Cornwallis, and Tone was sentenced to die " the death of a traitor," within forty-eight hours from the time of his conviction. But he—

influenced, it must be confessed, by a totally mistaken feeling of pride, and yielding to a weakness which every Christian heart should be able to conquer—resolved that, rather than allow his enemies to have the satisfaction of dangling his body from a gibbet, he would become his own executioner. On the night of the 11th of November he contrived, while lying unobserved in his cell, to open a vein in his neck with a penknife. No intelligence of this fact had reached the public, when, on the morning of the 12th, the intrepid and eloquent advocate, John Philpot Curran, made a motion in the Court of King's Bench for a writ of *Habeas Corpus* to withdraw the prisoner from the custody of the military authorities, and transfer him to the charge of the civil power. The motion was granted immediately, Mr. Curran pleading that, if delay were made, the prisoner might be executed before the order of the court could be presented. A messenger was at once despatched from the court to the barrack with the writ. He returned to say that the officers in charge of the prisoner would obey only their military superiors. The Chief Justice issued his commands peremptorily:— " Mr. Sheriff, take the body of Tone into custody; take the Provost Marshal and Major Sandys into custody, and show the order of the court to General Craig." The Sheriff sped away, and soon returned with the news that Tone had wounded himself on the previous evening, and could not be removed. The Chief Justice then ordered a rule suspending the execution. For the space of seven days afterwards did the unfortunate gentleman endure the agonies of approaching death; on the 19th of November, 1798, he expired. No more touching reference to his last moments could be given than the following pathetic and noble words traced by a filial hand, and published in the memoir from which we have already quoted:—

" Stretched on his bloody pallet in a dungeon, the first apostle of Irish union and most illustrious martyr of Irish independence counted each lingering hour during the last seven days and nights of his slow and silent agony. No one was allowed to approach him. Far from his adored family, and from all those friends whom he loved so dearly, the only forms which flitted before his eyes were those of the grim jailor and his rough attendants—the only sound which fell on his dying ear the heavy tread of the sentry. He retained, however, the calmness of his soul and the possession of his faculties to the last. And the consciousness of dying for his country, and in the cause of justice and liberty, illumined like a bright halo his later moments and kept up his fortitude to the end. There is no situation under which those feelings will not support the soul of a patriot."

Tone was born in Stafford-street, Dublin, on the 20th of June, 1764. His father was a coachmaker who carried on a thriving business; his grandfather was a comfortable farmer who held land near Naas, county Kildare. In February, 1781, Tone entered Trinity College, Dublin; in January, 1787, he entered his name as a law student on the books of the Middle Temple, London, and in 1789 he was called to the bar. His mortal remains repose in Bodenstown churchyard, county Kildare, whither parties of patriotic young men from the metropolis and the surrounding districts often proceed to lay a green wreath on his grave. His spirit lives, and will live forever, in the hearts of his countrymen.

WILLIAM ORR.

TWELVE months before Wolfe Tone expired in his prison cell, one of the bravest of his associates paid with his life the penalty of his attachment to the cause of Irish independence. In the subject of this sketch, the United Irishmen found their first martyr; and time has left no darker blot on the administration of English rule than the execution of the high-spirited Irishman whose body swung from the gallows of Carrickfergus on the 14th of October, 1797.

William Orr was the son of a farmer and bleach-green proprietor, of Ferranshane, in the county of Antrim. The family were in comfortable circumstances, and young Orr received a good education, which he afterwards turned to good account in the service of his country. We know little of his early history, but we find him, on growing up to manhood, an active member of the Society of United Irishmen, and remarkable for his popularity amongst his countrymen in the north. His appearance, not less than his principles and declarations, was calculated to captivate the peasantry amongst whom he lived; he stood six feet two inches in height, was a perfect model of symmetry, strength, and gracefulness, and the expression of his countenance was open, frank, and manly. He was always neatly and respectably dressed—a prominent feature in his attire being a green necktie, which he wore even in his last confinement.

One of the first blows aimed by the government against the United Irishmen was the passing of the Act of Parliament (36 George III), which constituted the administration of their oath a capital felony. This piece of legislation, repugnant in itself to the dictates of reason and justice, was intended as no idle threat; a victim was looked for to suffer under its provisions, and William Orr, the champion of the northern Presbyterian patriots, was doomed to serve the emergency.

He was arraigned, tried, and convicted at Carrickfergus on a charge of having administered the United Irishman's oath to a soldier named Wheatly. The whole history of the operations of the British law courts in Ireland contains nothing more infamous than the record of that trial. We now know, as a matter of fact, that the man who tendered the oath to Wheatly was William M'Keever, a well-known member of the society, who subsequently made his escape to America. But this was not a case, such as sometimes happens, of circumstantial evidence pointing to a wrong conclusion. The only evidence against Orr was the unsupported testimony of the soldier Wheatly; and after hearing Curran's defence of the prisoner, there could be no possible doubt of his innocence. But Orr was a doomed man—the government had decreed his death beforehand; and in this case, as in every other, the bloodthirsty agents of the crown did not look in vain for Irishmen to coöperate with them in their infamy.

At six o'clock in the evening the jury retired to consider their verdict. The scene that followed in the jury-room is described in the sworn affidavits of some of its participators. The jury were supplied with supper by the crown officials; a liberal supply of intoxicating beverages, wines, brandy, etc., being included in the refreshments. In their sober state several of the jurymen—amongst them Alexander Thompson, of Cushendall, the foreman—had refused to agree to a verdict of guilty. It was otherwise, however, when the decanters had been emptied, and when threats of violence were added to the bewildering effects of the potations in which they indulged. Thompson was threatened by his more unscrupulous companions with being wrecked, beaten, and "not left with sixpence in the world," and similar means were used against the few who refused with him to return a verdict of guilty. At six in the morning, the jury, not a man of whom by this time was sober, returned into court with a verdict of guilty, recommending the prisoner, at the same time, in the strongest manner, to mercy. Next day Orr was placed at the bar, and sentenced to death by Lord Yelverton, who, it is recorded, at the conclusion of his address, burst into tears. A motion was made by Curran in arrest of judgment, chiefly on the grounds of the drunkenness of the jury, but the judges refused to entertain the objection. The following is the speech delivered by William Orr after the verdict of the jury had been announced :—

"My friends and fellow-countrymen :—In the thirty-first year of my life I have been sentenced to die upon the gallows, and this sentence has been in pursuance of a verdict of twelve men, who should have been indifferently and impartially chosen. How far they have been so, I leave to that country from which they have been chosen, to determine ; and how far they have discharged their duty, I leave to their God and to themselves. They have, in pronouncing their verdict, thought proper to recommend me as an object of humane mercy. In return, I pray to God, if they have erred, to have mercy upon them. The judge who condemned me humanely shed tears in uttering my sentence. But whether he did wisely in so highly commending the wretched informer who swore away my life, I leave to his own cool reflection, solemnly assuring him and all the world, with my dying breath, that that informer was foresworn.

"The law under which I suffer is surely a severe one—may the makers and promoters of it be justified in the integrity of their motives and the purity of their own lives ! By that law I am stamped a felon, but my heart disdains the imputation.

"My comfortable lot and industrious course of life, best refuted the charge of being an adventurer for plunder ; but if to have loved my country, to have known its wrongs, to have felt the injuries of the persecuted Catholics, and to have united with them and all other religious persuasions in the most orderly and least sanguinary means of procuring redress,—if those be felonies, I am a felon, but not otherwise. Had my counsel (for whose honorable exertions I am indebted) prevailed in their motions to have me tried for high treason, rather than under the insurrection law, I should have been entitled to a full defence, and my actions have been better vindicated ; but that was refused, and I must now submit to what has passed.

"To the generous protection of my country I leave a beloved wife, who has been constant and true to me, and whose grief for my fate has already nearly occasioned her death. I have five living children, who have been my delight. May they love their country as I have done, and die for it, if needful !

"Lastly, a false and ungenerous publication having appeared in a newspaper, stating certain alleged confessions of guilt on my part, and thus striking at my reputation, which is dearer to me than life, I take this solemn method of contradicting the calumny. I was applied to by the high-sheriff, and the Rev. William Bristow, sovereign of Belfast, to make a confession of guilt, who used entreaties to that effect : this I peremptorily refused. If I thought myself guilty, I would freely confess it, but, on the contrary, I glory in my innocence.

"I trust that all my virtuous countrymen will bear me in their kind remembrance, and continue true and faithful to each other as I have been to all of them. With this last wish of my heart—nothing doubting of the success of that cause for which I suffer, and hoping for God's merciful forgiveness of such offences as my frail nature may have at any time betrayed me into—I die in peace and charity with all mankind."

Hardly had sentence of death been passed on William Orr, when compunction seemed to seize on those who had aided in securing that result. The witness Wheatly, who subsequently became insane, and is believed to have died by his own hand, made an affidavit before a magistrate, acknowledging that he had sworn falsely against Orr. Two of the jury made depositions setting forth that they had been induced to join in the verdict of guilty while under the influence of drink; two others swore that they had been terrified into the same course by threats of violence.

These depositions were laid before the viceroy, but Lord Camden, the then Lord-Lieutenant, was deaf to all appeals. Well might Orr exclaim within his dungeon that the government "had laid down a system having for its object murder and devastation." The prey was in the toils of the hunters, on whom all appeals of justice and humanity were wasted.

Orr was hung, as we have said, in the town of Carrickfergus, on the 14th of October, 1797. It is related that the inhabitants of the town, to express their sympathy with the patriot about being murdered by law, and to mark their abhorrence of the conduct of the government towards him, quitted the town *en masse* on the day of his execution.

His fate excited the deepest indignation throughout the country; it was commented on in words of fire by the national writers of the period, and through many an after year the watchword and rallying cry of the United Irishmen was—

"REMEMBER ORR."

HENRY AND JOHN SHEARES.

AMONG the many distinguished Irishmen who acted prominent parts in the stormy events of 1798, and whose names come down to us hallowed by the sufferings and sacrifices inseparable in those dark days from the lot of an Irish patriot, there are few whose fate excited more sympathy, more loved in life, more honored in death, than the brothers, John and Henry Sheares. Even in the days of Emmet and Wolfe Tone, of Russell and Fitzgerald, when men of education, talent, and social standing were not few in the national ranks, the Sheareses were hailed as valuable accessions to the cause, and were recognized by the United Irishmen as heaven-destined leaders for the people. It is a touching story, the history of their patriotic exertions, their betrayal, trial, and execution; but it is by studying such scenes in our history that Irishmen can learn to estimate the sacrifices which were made in bygone days for Ireland, and attach a proper value to the memory of the patriots who made them.

Henry and John Sheares were sons of John Sheares, a banker in Cork, who sat in the Irish parliament for the borough of Clonakilty. The father appears to have been a kindly-disposed, liberal-minded man, and numerous stories are told of his unostentatious charity and benevolence. Henry, the elder of the two sons, was born in 1753, and was educated in Trinity College, Dublin. After leaving college he purchased a commission in the 51st regiment of foot; but the duties of a military officer were ill suited to his temperament and disposition, and the young soldier soon resigned his commission to pursue the more congenial occupation of law student. He was called to the bar in 1790; his brother John, his junior by three years, who had adopted the same profession, obtained the rank of barrister-at-law two years previously.

The brothers differed from each other widely in character and disposition. Henry was gentle in manners, modest and unassuming, but firmly attached to his principles, and unswerving in his fidelity to the cause which he adopted; John was bold, impetuous, and energetic, ready to plan and to dare, fertile of resources, quick of resolve, and prompt of execution. To John the elder brother looked for guidance and example, and his gentle nature was ever ruled by the more fiery and impulsive spirit of his younger brother. On the death of the father Henry Sheares came in for property to the value of £1,200 per annum, which his rather improvident habits soon diminished by one-half. Both brothers, however, obtained large practice at their profession, and continued in affluent circumstances up to the day of their arrest.

In 1792 the two brothers visited Paris, and this excursion seems to have formed the turning-point of their lives and fortunes. The French Revolution was in full swing, and in the society of Roland, Brissot, and other republican leaders, the young Irishmen imbibed the love of freedom, and impatience of tyranny and oppression, which they clung to so faithfully, and which distinguished them so remarkably during the remainder of their lives. On returning to Ireland in January, 1793, the brothers joined the ranks of the United Irishmen. John at once became a prominent member of the society, and his signature appears to several of the spirited and eloquent addresses by which the Dublin branch sought from time to time to arouse the ardor and stimulate the exertions of their compatriots. The Society of United Irishmen looked for nothing more at this period than a thorough measure of parliamentary reform, household suffrage being the leading feature in their programme; but when the tyranny of the government drove the leaguers into more violent and dangerous courses; when republican government and separation from England were inscribed on the banners of the society instead of electoral reform, and when the selfish and the wavering had shrunk aside, the Sheareses still remained true to the United Irishmen, and seemed to grow more zealous and energetic in the cause of their country according as the mists of perplexity and danger gathered around it.

To follow out the history of the Sheareses' connection with the United Irishmen would be foreign to our intention and to the scope of this work. The limits of our space oblige us to pass over the ground at a rapid pace, and we shall dismiss the period of the Sheareses' lives comprised in the years between 1793 and 1798, by saying that, during that period, while practising their profession with success, they devoted themselves, with all the earnestness of their nature, to the furtherance of the objects of the United Irishmen. In March, 1798, the affairs of the organization became critical; the arrest of the Directory at Oliver Bond's deprived the party of its best and most trusted leaders, besides placing in the hands of the government a mass of information relative to the plans and resources of the conspirators. To fill the gap thus caused, John Sheares was soon appointed a member of the Directory, and he threw himself into the work with all the ardor and energy of his nature. The fortunes of the society had assumed a desperate phase when John Sheares became its ruling spirit. Tone was in France; O'Connor was in England; Russell, Emmet, and Fitzgerald were in prison. But Sheares was not disheartened; he directed all his efforts towards bringing about the insurrection for which his countrymen had so long been preparing, and the 23d of May, 1798, was fixed on by him for the outbreak. He was after visiting Wexford and Kildare, and making arrangements in those counties for the rising, and was on the verge of starting for Cork on a similar mission, when the hand of treachery cut short his career, and the gates of Kilmainham Prison opened to receive him.

Amongst all the human monsters who filled the ranks of the government informers in that dark and troubled period, not one appears to merit a deeper measure of infamy than Captain Warnesford Armstrong, the entrapper and betrayer of the Sheareses. Having obtained an introduction to John, he represented himself as a zealous and hard-working member of the organization, and soon wormed himself completely into the confidence of his victims. He paid daily visits to the house of the Sheareses in Baggot-street, chatted with their families, and fondled the children of Henry Sheares upon his knee. We have it on his own testimony that each interview with the men whose confidence he was sharing was followed by a visit to the Castle. We need not go through the sickening details of this vile story of treachery and fraud. On the 21st of May the Sheareses were arrested and lodged in prison, and on the 12th of the following month Armstrong appeared against them in the witness box. The trial was continued through the night—Toler, of infamous memory, who had been created attorney-general expressly for the occasion, refusing Curran's request for an adjournment; and it was eight o'clock in the morning of the 13th when the jury, who had been but seventeen minutes absent, returned into court with a verdict of guilty against both prisoners.

After a few hours' adjournment the court reassembled to pass sentence. It was then that John Sheares, speaking in a firm tone, addressed the court as follows:—

"My Lords:—I wish to offer a few words before sentence is pronounced, because there is a weight pressing on my heart much greater than that of the sentence which is to come from the court. There has been, my lords, a weight pressing on my mind from the first moment I heard the indictment read upon which I was tried; but that weight has been more peculiarly pressing upon my heart when I found the accusation in the indictment enforced and supported upon the trial. That weight would be left insupportable if it were not for this opportunity of discharging it: I shall feel it to be insupportable since a verdict of my country has stamped that evidence as well founded. Do not think, my lords, that I am about to make a declaration against the verdict of the jury or the persons concerned with the trial; I am only about to call to your recollection a part of the charge at which my soul shudders, and, if I had no opportunity of renouncing it before your lordships and this auditory, no courage would be sufficient to support me. The accusation of which I speak, while I linger here yet a minute, is that of holding out to the people of Ireland a direction to give no quarter to the troops fighting for its defence! My lords, let me say thus, that if there be any acquaintances in this crowded court—I do not say my intimate friends, but acquaintances—who do not know what I say is truth, I shall be reputed the wretch which I am not; I say, if any acquaintance of mine can believe that *I* could utter a recommendation of giving no quarter to a yielding and unoffending foe, it is not the death that I am about to suffer that I deserve—no punishment could be adequate to such a crime. My lords, I can not only acquit my soul of such an intention, but I declare, in the presence of that God before whom I must shortly appear, that the favorite doctrine of my heart was, *that no human being should suffer death but when absolute necessity required it*. My lords, I feel a consolation in making this declaration, which nothing else can afford me, because it is not only a justification of myself, but, where I am sealing my life with that breath which cannot be suspected of falsehood, what I say may make some impression upon the minds of men not holding the same doctrine. I declare to God I know of no crime but assassination which can eclipse or equal that of which I am accused. I discern no shade of guilt between that and taking away the life of a foe, by putting a bayonet to his heart when he is yielding and surrendering. I do request the bench to believe that of me—I do request my country to believe that of me—I am sure God will think that of me. Now, my lords, I have no favor to ask of the court; my country has decided I am guilty, and the law says I shall suffer—it sees that I am ready to suffer. But, my lords, I have a favor to request of the court that does not relate to myself. My lords, I have a brother whom I have even loved dearer than myself: but it is not from any affection for him alone that I am induced to make the request. He is a man, and therefore, I would hope, prepared to die if he stood as I do—though I do not stand unconnected; but he stands more dearly connected. In short, my lords, to spare your feelings and my own, I do not pray that that *I* should not die, but that the husband, the father, the son—all comprised in one person—holding these relations dearer in life to him than any other man I know—for such a man I do not pray a pardon—for that is not in the power of the court—but I pray a respite for such time as the court in its humanity and discretion shall think proper. You have heard, my lords, that his private affairs require arrangement. When I address myself to your lordships, it is with the knowledge you will have of all the sons of our aged mother being gone. Two have perished in the service of the King—one very recently. I only request that, disposing of me with what swiftness either the public mind or justice requires, a respite may be given to my brother, that the family may acquire strength to bear it all. That is all I wish; I shall remember it to my last breath, and I shall offer up my prayers for you to that Being who has endued us all with the sensibility to feel. That is all I ask. I have nothing more to say."

It was four o'clock, P.M., when the judge proceeded to pass sentence, and the following morning was appointed for the double execution. At midday on Saturday, July 14th, the hapless men were removed to the room adjoining the place of execution, where they exchanged a last embrace. They were then pinioned, the black caps put over their brows, and holding each other by the hand, they tottered out on the platform. The elder brother was somewhat moved by the terrors of his situation, but the younger bore his fate with unflinching firmness. They were launched together into eternity—the same moment saw them dangling lifeless corpses before the prison walls. They had lived in affectionate unity, inspired by the same motives, laboring for the same cause, and death did not dissolve the tie. "They died hand in hand, like true brothers."

When the hangman's hideous office was completed, the bodies were taken down, and the executioner, in accordance with the barbarous custom of the time, proceeded to sever the heads from the bodies. It is said, however, that only on the body of Henry Sheares was that horrible act performed. While the arrangements for the execution were in progress, Sir Jonah Barrington had been making intercession with Lord Clare on their behalf, and beseeching at least a respite. His lordship declared that the life of John Sheares could not be spared, but said that Henry might possibly have something to say which would induce the government to commute his sentence; he furnished Sir Jonah with an order to delay the execution one hour, and told him to communicate with Henry Sheares on the subject. "I hastened," writes Sir Jonah, "to Newgate, and arrived at the very moment that the executioner was holding up the head of my old college friend, and saying, 'Here is the head of a traitor.'" The fact of this order having been issued by the government may have so far interrupted the bloody work on the scaffold as to save the remains of the younger Sheares from mutilation. The bodies of the patriots were interred on the night of execution in the vaults of St. Michan's church, where, enclosed in oaken coffins, marked, in the usual manner, with the names and ages of the deceased, they still repose. Many a pious visit has since been paid to those dim chambers— many a heart filled with love and pity, has throbbed above those coffin-lids—many a tear has dropped upon them. But it is not a feeling of grief alone that is inspired by the memory of those martyrs to freedom; hope, courage, constancy, are the lessons taught by their lives, and the patriotic spirit that ruled their career is still awake and active in Ireland.

ROBERT EMMET.

ROBERT EMMET.

In all Irish history there is no name which touches the Irish heart like that of Robert Emmet. We read, in that eventful record, of men who laid down their lives for Ireland amid the roar and crash of battle; of others who perished by the headsman's axe or the halter of the hangman; of others whose eyes were closed forever in the gloom of English dungeons, and of many whose hearts broke amid the sorrows of involuntary exile; of men, too, who, in the great warfare of mind, rendered to the Irish cause services no less memorable and glorious. They are neither forgotten nor unhonored. The warrior figure of Hugh O'Neill is a familiar vision to Irishmen; Sarsfield expiring on the foreign battle-field with that infinitely pathetic and noble utterance on his lips—" Would that this were for Ireland"—is a cherished remembrance, and that last cry of a patriotic spirit dwells forever about our hearts; Grattan battling against a corrupt and venal faction, first to win and then to defend the independence of his country, astonishing friends and foes alike by the dazzling splendor of his eloquence; and O'Connell on the hill-side pleading for the restoration of Ireland's rights, and rousing his countrymen to a struggle for them, are pictures of which we are proud— memories that will live in song and story while the Irish race has a distinct existence in the world. But in the character of Robert Emmet there was such a rare combination of admirable qualities, and in his history there are so many of the elements of romance, that the man stands before our mental vision as a peculiarly noble and loveable being, with claims upon our sympathies that are absolutely without a parallel. He had youth, talent, social position, a fair share of fortune, and bright prospects for the future on his side when he embarked in the defeat and ruin. Courage, genius, enthusiasm were his, high hopes and strong affections, all based upon and sweetened by a nature utterly free from guile. He was an orator and a poet; in the one art he had already achieved distinction, in the other he was certain to take a high place, if he should make that an object of his ambition. He was a true patriot, true soldier, and true lover. If the story of his political life is full of melancholy interest, and calculated to awaken profound emotions of reverence for his memory, the story of his affections is not less touching. Truly, "there's not a line but hath been wept upon." So it is, that of all the heroic men who risked and lost everything for Ireland, none is so frequently remembered, none is thought of so tenderly as Robert Emmet. Poetry has cast a halo of light upon the name of the youthful martyr, and some of the sweetest strains of Irish music are consecrated to his memory.

Robert Emmet was born on the 4th of March, 1778. He was the third son of Doctor Robert Emmet, a well-known and highly respectable physician of Dublin. Thomas Addis Emmet, already mentioned in these pages, the associate of Tone, the Sheareses, and other members, of the United Irish organization, was an elder brother of Robert, and his senior by some sixteen years. Just about the period when the United Irishmen were forming themselves into a secret revolutionary society, young-Emmet was sent to receive his education in Trinity College. There the bent of the lad's political opinions was soon detected; but among his fellow-students he found many and amongst them older heads than his own, who not only shared his views, but went beyond them in the direction of liberal and democratic principles. In the Historical Society—composed of the *alumni* of the college, and on whose books at this time were many names that subsequently became famous—those kindred spirits made for themselves many opportunities of giving expression to their sentiments, and showing that their hearts beat in unison with the great movement for human freedom which was then agitating the world. To their debates Emmet brought the aid of a fine intellect and a fluent utterance, and he soon became the orator of the patriot party.

So great was the effect created by his fervid eloquence and his admirable reasoning, that the heads of the college thought it prudent on several occasions to send one of the ablest of their body to take part in the proceedings, and assist in refuting the argumentation of the "young Jacobin." And to such extremeties did matters proceed at last that Emmet, with several of his political friends, was expelled the college, others less obnoxious to the authorities were subjected to a severe reprimand, and the society, thus terrorized and weakened, soon ceased to exist. Our national poet, Thomas Moore, the fellow-student and intimate friend of young Emmet, witnessed many of those displays of his abilities, and in his "Life and Death of Lord Edward Fitzgerald," speaks of him in terms of the highest admiration. "Were I," he says, "to number the men among all I have ever known who appeared to me to combine in the greatest degree pure moral worth with intellectual power, I should, among the highest of the few, place Robert Emmet." "He was," writes the same authority, "wholly free from the follies and frailties of youth—though how capable he was of the most devoted passion events afterwards proved." Of his oratory he says, "I have heard little since that appeared to me of a loftier, or what is a far more rare quality in Irish eloquence, purer character." And the appearance of this greatly gifted youth, he thus describes: "Simple in all his habits, and with, a repose of look and manner indicating but little movement within, it was only when the spring was touched that set his feelings, and through them his intellect in motion, that he at all rose above the level of ordinary men. No two individuals indeed could be much more unlike to each other than was the same youth to himself before rising to speak and after; the brow that had appeared inanimate and almost drooping, at once elevating itself to all the consciousness of power, and the whole countenance and figure of the speaker assuming a change as of one suddenly inspired."

The expulsion of Emmet from the college occurred in the month of February, 1798. On the 12th of the following month his brother, Thomas Addis Emmet, was arrested. The manner in which this noble-hearted gentleman took the oath of the United Irish Society, in the year 1795, is so remarkable that we cannot omit mention of it here. His services as a lawyer having been engaged in the defense of some persons who stood charged with having sworn in members of the United Irish organization—the crime for which William Orr was subsequently tried and executed—he, in the course of the proceedings, took up the oath and read it with remarkable deliberation and solemnity. Then, taking into his hand the prayer book that lay on the table for the swearing of witnesses, and looking to the bench and around the court, he said aloud—

"My Lords—Here, in the presence of this legal court, this crowded auditory—in the presence of the Being that sees and witnesses, and directs this judicial tribunal—here, my lords, I, myself, in the presence of God, declare I take this oath."

The terms of the oath at this time were, in fact, perfectly constitutional, having reference simply to attainment of a due representation of the Irish nation in parliament—still, the oath was that of a society declared to be illegal, and the administration of it had been made a capital offence. The boldness of the advocate in thus administering it to himself in open court appeared to paralyze the minds of the judges. They took no notice of the act, and what was even more remarkable, the prisoners, who were convicted, received a lenient sentence.

But to return to Robert Emmet—the event of 1798, it might be supposed, had a powerful effect on the feelings of the enthusiastic young patriot, and he was not free of active participation with the leaders of the movement in Dublin. He was, of course, an object of suspicion to the government, and it appears marvellous that they did not immediately take him into their safe keeping under the provisions of the *Habeas Corpus* Suspension Act. Ere long, however, he found that prudence would counsel his concealment, or his disappearance from the country, and he took his departure for the Continent, where he met with a whole host of the Irish refugees; and, in 1802, was joined by his brother and others of the political prisoners who had been released from the confinement to which—in violation of a distinct agreement between them and the government—they had been subjected in Fort George, in Scotland. Their sufferings had not broken their spirit. There was hope still, they thought, for Ireland; great opportunities were about to dawn upon that often defeated, but still unconquerable nation, and they applied themselves to the task of preparing the Irish people to take advantage of them.

At home the condition of affairs was not such as to discourage them. The people had not lost heart; the fighting spirit was still rife amongst them. The rebellion had been trampled out, but it had been sustained mainly by a county or two, and it had served to show that a general uprising of the people would be sufficient to sweep every vestige of British power from the land. Then they had in their favor the exasperation against the government which was caused by that most infamous transaction, the passage of the Act of Union. But they found their chief encouragement in the imminence of another war between France and England. Once more, the United Irishmen put themselves into communication with Buonoparte, then First Consul, and again they received flattering promises of assistance. Robert Emmet obtained an interview with that great man, and learned from him that it was his settled purpose on the breaking out of hostilities, which could not long be deferred, to effect an invasion of England. Full of high hopes, Emmet returned to Dublin in October, 1802; and as he was now in very heart of a movement for another insurrection, he took every precaution to avoid discovery. He passed under feigned names, and moved about as little as possible. He gathered together the remnants of the United Irish organization, and with some money of his own, added to considerable sums supplied to him by a Mr. Long, a merchant, residing at No. 4 Crow-street, and other sympathizers, he commenced the collection of an armament and military stores for his followers. In the month of May, 1803, the expected war between France and England broke out. This event of course raised still higher his hopes, and gave a great stimulus to his exertions. To and fro he went from one to another of the depots which he had established for the manufacture and storage of arms in various parts of the city, cheering, directing and assisting his men at their work. Pikes were got ready by the thousand, and ingeniously stowed away until they should be wanted; rockets, handgrenades, and other deadly missiles were carefully prepared; but an accidental explosion, which occurred, on the 16th of July, in one of these manufactories situated in Patrick-street, was very near leading to the discovery of the entire business, and had the effect of precipitating the outbreak. The government at this time had undoubtedly got on the scent of the movement, and the leaders considered that no time was to be lost in bringing matters to a crisis. Emmet now took up his abode in the Marshalsea-lane depot, snatching his few hours of sleep "on a mattress, surrounded by all the implements of death." There he made a final arrangement of his plans, and communicated his instructions to his subordinates, fixing the 23d of July as the date for the rising.

The history of that unfortunate attempt need not here be written. Suffice it to say that the arrangements miscarried in nearly every particular. The men in the numbers calculated upon did not assemble at the appointed time or in the appointed places, and the whole force that turned out in Thomas-street for the attack on the Castle did not number a hundred insurgents. They were joined by a riotous and noisy rabble; and their unfortunate leader soon perceived that his following was, as had previously been said of the king's troops, "formidable to every one but the enemy." They had not proceeded far on their way when a carriage, in which were Lord Kilwarden, Chief Justice of the King's Bench, his daughter, and his nephew, the Rev. Mr. Wolfe, drove into the street. The vehicle was stopped, and the Chief Justice was immediately piked by a man in the crowd whose son he had some time previously condemned to execution. The clergyman also was pulled out of the carriage and put to death. To the lady no violence was offered, and Emmet himself, who had heard of the deplorable tragedy, rushing from the head of his party, bore her in his arms to an adjoining house   No attack on the Castle took place, the insurgent party scattered and melted away, even before the appearance of military on the scene; and in little more than an hour from the time of his setting out on his desperate enterprise, Robert Emmet was a defeated and ruined man, a fugitive, with the whole host of British spies and bloodhounds employed to hunt him to the death.

Yet he might have foiled them and got clear out of the country if his personal safety was all on earth he cared for. But in that noble heart of his there was one passion coexistent with his love of Ireland, and not unworthy of the companionship, which forbade his immediate flight. With all that intensity of affection of which a nature so pure and so ardent as his was capable, he loved a being in every way worthy of him—a lady so gentle, and good, and fair, that, even to a less poetic imagination than his own, she might seem to be a fitting personification of his beloved Erin; and by her he was loved and trusted in return. Who is it that has not heard her name?—who has not mourned over the story of Sarah Curran? In the ruin that had fallen on the hopes and fortunes of the patriot chief, the happiness of this amiable lady was involved. He would not leave without an interview with her—no! though a thousand deaths should be the penalty. The delay was fatal to his chances of escape. For more than a month he remained in concealment, protected by the fidelity of friends, many of whom belonged to the humbler walks of life, and one of whom in particular—the heroic Anne Devlin, from whom neither proffered bribes nor cruel tortures could extort a single hint as to his place of abode—should ever be held in grateful remembrance by Irishmen. At length, on the 25th of August, the ill-fated young gentleman was arrested in the house of a Mrs. Palmer, at Harold's-cross. On the 19th of September he was put on his trial in the court-house, Green-street, charged with high treason. He entered on no defence, beyond making a few remarks in the course of the proceedings with a view to the moral and political justification of his conduct. The jury, without leaving their box, returned a verdict of guilty against him; after which, having been asked in due form why sentence of death should not be pronounced upon him, he delivered this memorable speech, every line of which is known and dear to the hearts of the Irish race:—

"MY LORDS—I am asked what have I to say why sentence of death should not be pronounced on me, according to law. I have nothing to say that can alter your predetermination, nor that it will become me to say, with any view to the mitigation of that sentence which you are to pronounce, and I must abide by. But I have that to say which interests me more than life, and which you have labored to destroy. I have much to say why my reputation should be rescued from the load of false accusation and calumny which has been cast upon it. I do not imagine that, seated where you are, your mind can be so free from prejudice as to receive the least impression from what I am going to utter. I have no hopes that I can anchor my character in the breast of a court constituted and trammelled as this is. I only wish, and that is the utmost that I expect, that your lordships may suffer it to float down your memories untainted by the foul breath of prejudice, until it finds some more hospitable harbor to shelter it from the storms by which it is buffetted. Was I only to suffer death, after being adjudged guilty by your tribunal, I should bow in silence, and meet the fate that awaits me without a murmur; but the sentence of the law which delivers my body to the executioner will, through the ministry of the law, labor in its own vindication to consign my character to obloquy; for there must be guilt somewhere: whether in the sentence of the court, or in the catastrophe, time must determine. A man in any situation has not only to encounter the difficulties of fortune, and the force of power over minds which it has corrupted or subjugated, but the difficulties of established prejudice. The man dies, but his memory lives. That mine may not perish, that it may live in the respect of my countrymen, I seize upon this opportunity to vindicate myself from some of the charges alleged against me. When my spirit shall be wafted to a more friendly port—when my shade shall have joined the bands of those martyred heroes who have shed their blood on the scaffold and in the field in the defence of their country and of virtue, this is my hope—I wish that my memory and name may animate those who survive me, while I look down with complacency on the destruction of that perfidious government which upholds its domination by blasphemy of the Most High—which displays its power over man, as over the beasts of the forest —which sets man upon his brother, and lifts his hand, in the name of God, against the throat of his fellow who believes or doubts a little more or a little less than the government standard—a government which is steeled to barbarity by the cries of the orphans, and the tears of the widows it has made."

[Here Lord Norbury interrupted Mr. Emmet, saying, "that the mean and wicked enthusiasts who felt as he did, were not equal to the accomplishment of their wild designs.")

"I appeal to the immaculate God—I swear by the throne of Heaven, before which I must shortly appear—by the blood of the murdered patriots who have gone before me—that my conduct has been, through all this peril, and through all my purposes, governed only by the conviction which I have uttered, and by no other view than that of the emancipation of my country from the superinhuman oppression under which she has so long and too patiently travailed; and I confidently hope that, wild and chimerical as it may appear, there is still union and strength in Ireland to accomplish this noblest of enterprises. Of this I speak with confidence of intimate knowledge, and with the consolation that appertains to that confidence. Think not, my lords, I say this for the petty gratification of giving you a transitory uneasiness. A man who never yet raised his voice to assert a lie will not hazard his character with posterity, by asserting a falsehood on a subject so important to his country, and on an occasion like this. Yes, my lords, a man who does not wish to have his epitaph written until his country is liberated, will not leave a weapon in the power of envy, or a pretence to impeach the probity which he means to preserve, even in the grave to which tyranny consigns him."

[Here he was again interrupted by the court.]

"Again I say, that what I have spoken was not intended for your lordship, whose situation I commiserate rather than envy—my expressions were for my countrymen. If there is a true Irishman present, let my last words cheer him in the hour of his affliction."

[Here he was again interrupted. Lord Norbury said he did not sit there to hear treason.]

"I have always understood it to be the duty of a judge, when a prisoner has been convicted, to pronounce the sentence of the law. I have also understood that judges sometimes think it their duty to bear with patience and to speak with humanity; to exhort the victim of the laws, and to offer, with tender benignity, their opinions of the motives by which he was actuated in the crime of which he was adjudged guilty. That a judge has thought it his duty so to have done, I have no doubt; but where is the boasted freedom of your institutions—where is the vaunted impartiality, clemency, and mildness of your courts of justice, if an unfortunate prisoner, whom your policy, and not justice, is about to deliver into the hands of the executioner, is not suffered to explain his motives sincerely and truly, and to vindicate the principles by which he was actuated? My lords, it may be a part of the system of angry justice to bow a man's mind by humiliation to the purposed ignominy of the scaffold ; but worse to me than the purposed shame or the scaffold's terrors, would be the shame of such foul and unfounded imputations as have been laid against me in this court. You, my lord, are a judge; I am the supposed culprit. I am a man; you are a man also. By a revolution of power we might change places, though we never could change characters. If I stand at the bar of this court and dare not vindicate my character, what a farce is your justice ! If I stand at this bar and dare not vindicate my character, how dare you calumniate it? Does the sentence of death, which your unhallowed policy inflicts on my body, condemn my tongue to silence and my reputation to reproach? Your executioner may abridge the period of my existence; but while I exist, I shall not forbear to vindicate my character and motives from your aspersions; and, as a man, to whom fame is dearer than life, I will make the last use of that life in doing justice to that reputation which is to live after me, and which is the only legacy I can leave to those I honor and love, and for whom I am proud to perish. As men, my lords, we must appear on the great day at one common tribunal; and it will then remain for the Searcher of all hearts to show a collective universe, who was engaged in the most virtuous actions, or swayed by the purest motive—my country's oppressors, or——"

[Here he was interrupted, and told to listen to the sentence of the law.]

"My lords, will a dying man be denied the legal privilege of exculpating himself in the eyes of the community from an undeserved reproach, thrown upon him during his trial, by charging him with ambition, and attempting to cast away for a paltry consideration the liberties of his country? Why did your lordships insult me? Or rather, why insult justice, in demanding of me why sentence of death should not be pronounced against me? I know, my lords, that form prescribes that you should ask the question. The form also presents the right of answering. This, no doubt, may be dispensed with, and so might the whole ceremony of the trial, since sentence was already pronounced at the Castle before the jury were empanelled. Your lordships are but the priests of the oracle, and I insist on the whole of the forms."

[Here Mr. Emmet paused, and the court desired him to proceed.]

"I am charged with being an emissary of France. An emissary of France! and for what end? It is alleged that I wished to sell the independence of my country ; and for what end? Was this the object of my ambition? And is this the mode by which a tribunal of justice reconciles contradiction? No; I am no emissary; and my ambition was to hold a place among the deliverers of my country, not in power nor in profit, but in the glory of the achievement. Sell my country's independence to France ! and for what?

Was it a change of masters? No, but for my ambition. Oh, my country! was it personal ambition that could influence me? Had it been the soul of my actions, could I not, by my education and fortune, by the rank and consideration of my family, have placed myself amongst the proudest of your oppressors? My country was my idol. To it I sacrificed every selfish, every endearing sentiment; and for it I now offer up myself, O God! No, my lords; I acted as an Irishman, determined on delivering my country from the yoke of a foreign and unrelenting tyranny, and the more galling yoke of a domestic faction, which is its joint partner and perpetrator in the patricide, from the ignominy existing with an exterior of splendor and a conscious depravity. It was the wish of my heart to extricate my country from this doubly rivetted despotism—I wished to place her independence beyond the reach of any power on earth. I wished to exalt her to that proud station in the world. Connection with France was, indeed, intended, but only as far as mutual interest would sanction or require. Were the French to assume any authority inconsistent with the purest independence, it would be the signal for their destruction. We sought their aid—and we sought it as we had assurance we should obtain it—as auxiliaries in war, and allies in peace. Were the French to come as invaders or enemies, uninvited by the wishes of the people, I should oppose them to the utmost of my strength. Yes! my countrymen, I should advise you to meet them upon the beach with a sword in one hand, and a torch in the other. I would meet them with all the destructive fury of war. I would animate my countrymen to immolate them in their boats, before they had contaminated the soil of my country. If they succeeded in landing, and if forced to retire before superior discipline, I would dispute every inch of ground, burn every blade of grass, and the last entrenchment of liberty should be my grave. What I could not do myself, if I should fall, I should leave as a last charge to my countrymen to accomplish; because I should feel conscious that life, any more than death, is unprofitable when a foreign nation holds my country in subjection. But it was not as an enemy that the succors of France were to land. I looked, indeed, for the assistance of France; but I wished to prove to France and to the world that Irishmen deserved to be assisted—that they were indignant at slavery, and ready to assert the independence and liberty of their country; I wished to procure for my country the guarantee which Washington procured for America—to procure an aid which, by its example, would be as important as its valor; disciplined, gallant, pregnant with science and experience; that of a people who would perceive the good, and polish the rough points of our character. They would come to us as strangers, and leave us as friends, after sharing in our perils and elevating our destiny. These were my objects: not to receive new taskmasters, but to expel old tyrants. It was for these ends I sought aid from France; because France, even as an enemy, could not be more implacable than the enemy already in the bosom of my country."

[Here he was interrupted by the court.]

"I have been charged with that importance in the emancipation of my country as to be considered the keystone of the combination of Irishmen; or, as your lordship expressed it, 'the life and blood of the conspiracy.' You do me honor over much: you have given to the subaltern all the credit of a superior. There are men engaged in this conspiracy who are not only superior to me, but even to your own conceptions of yourself, my lord—men before the splendor of whose genius and virtues I should bow with respectful deference, and who would think themselves disgraced by shaking your blood-stained hand."

[Here he was interrupted.]

"What, my lord, shall you tell me, on the passage to the scaffold, which that tyranny (of which you are only the intermediary executioner) has erected for my murder, that I am accountable for all the blood that has and will be shed in this struggle of the oppressed against the oppressor—shall you tell me this, and must I be so very a slave as not to repel it? I do not fear to approach the Omnipotent Judge to answer for the conduct of my whole life; and am I to be appalled and falsified by a mere remnant of mortality here? By you, too, although, if it were possible to collect all the innocent blood that you have shed in your unhallowed ministry in one great reservoir, your lordship might swim in it."

[Here the judge interfered.]

"Let no man dare, when I am dead, to charge me with dishonor; let no man attaint my memory, by believing that I could have engaged in any cause but that of my country's liberty and independence; or that I could have become the pliant minion of power, in the oppression and misery of my country. The proclamation of the Provisional Government speaks for our views; no inference can be tortured from it to countenance barbarity or debasement at home, or subjection, humiliation, or treachery from abroad. I would not have submitted to a foreign oppressor, for the same reason that I would resist the foreign and domestic oppressor. In the dignity of freedom, I would have fought upon the threshold of my country, and its enemy should enter only by passing over my lifeless corpse. And am I, who lived but for my country, and who have subjected myself to the dangers of the jealous and watchful oppressor, and the bondage of the grave, only to give my countrymen their rights, and my country her independence,—am I to be loaded with calumny, and not suffered to resent it? No; God forbid!"

Here Lord Norbury told Mr. Emmet that his sentiments and language disgraced his family and his education, but more particularly his father, Dr. Emmet, who was a man, if alive, that would not countenance such opinions. To which Mr. Emmet replied:—

"If the spirits of the illustrious dead participate in the concerns and cares of those who were dear to them in this transitory life, O ever dear and venerated shade of my departed father! look down with scrutiny upon the conduct of your suffering son, and see if I have, even for a moment, deviated from those principles of morality and patriotism which it was your care to instil into my youthful mind, and for which I am now about to offer up my life. My lords, you are impatient for the sacrifice. The blood which you seek is not congealed by the artificial terrors which surround your victim—it circulates warmly and unruffled through the channels which God created for noble purposes, but which you are now bent to destroy, for purposes so grievous that they cry to heaven. Be yet patient! I have but a few more words to say—I am going to my cold and silent grave—my lamp of life is nearly extinguished—my race is run—the grave opens to receive me, and I sink into its bosom. I have but one request to ask at my departure from this world: it is—THE CHARITY OF ITS SILENCE. Let no man write my epitaph; for, as no man who knows my motives dare now vindicate them, let not prejudice or ignorance asperse them. Let them and me rest in obscurity and peace; and my tomb remain uninscribed, and my memory in oblivion, until other times and other men can do justice to my character. When my country takes her place among the nations of the earth, *then* and *not till then*, let my epitaph be written. I have done."

This affecting address was spoken—as we learn from the painstaking and generous biographer of the United Irishmen, Dr. Madden—"in so loud a voice as to be distinctly heard at the outer doors of the court-house; and yet, though he spoke in a loud tone, there was nothing boisterous in his manner; his accents and cadence of voice, on the contrary, were exquisitely modulated. His action was very remarkable; its greater or lesser vehemence corresponded with the rise and fall of his voice. He is described as moving about the dock, as he warmed in his address, with rapid, but not ungraceful motions—now in front of the railing before the bench, then retiring, as if his body, as well as his mind, were swelling beyond the measure of its chains. His action was not confined to his hands; he seemed to have acquired a swaying motion of the body when he spoke in public, which was peculiar to him, but there was no affectation in it."

At ten o'clock, P. M., on the day of his trial, the barbarous sentence of the law—the same that we have so recently heard passed on prisoners standing in that same dock, accused of the same offence against the rulers of this country—was passed on Robert Emmet. Only a

few hours were given him in which to withdraw his
thoughts from the things of this world, and fix them on the
next. He was hurried away, at midnight, from Newgate
to Kilmainham Jail, passing through Thomas-street, the
scene of his attempted insurrection. Hardly had the
prison van driven through, when workmen arrived and
commenced the erection of the gibbet from which his
body was to be suspended. About the hour of noon, on
the 20th of September, he mounted the scaffold with a
firm and composed demeanor; a minute or two more
and the lifeless remains of one of the most gifted of
God's creatures hung from the crossbeams—strangled
by the enemies of his country—cut off in the bloom of
youth, in the prime of his physical and intellectual
powers, because he had loved his own land, hated her
oppressors, and striven to give freedom to his people.
But not yet was English vengeance satisfied. While the
body was yet warm it was cut down from the gibbet,
the neck placed across a block on the scaffold, and the
head severed from the body. Then the executioner held
it up before the horrified and sorrowing crowd that
stood outside the lines of soldiery, proclaiming to them—
"This is the head of a traitor!" A traitor! It was a
false proclamation. No traitor was he, but a true and
noble gentleman. No traitor, but a most faithful heart
to all that was worthy of love and honor. No traitor,
but a martyr for Ireland. The people who stood agonized
before his scaffold, tears streaming from their eyes, and
their hearts bursting with suppressed emotion, knew
that for them and for Ireland he had offered up his
young life. And when the deed was finished, and the
mutilated body had been taken away, and the armed
guards had marched from the fatal spot, old people and
young moved up to it to dip their handkerchiefs in the
blood of the martyr, that they might then treasure up the
relics forever. Well has his memory been cherished in
the Irish heart from that day to the present time. Six
years ago a procession of Irishmen, fifteen thousand
strong, bearing another rebel to his grave, passed by the
scene of that execution, every man of whom reverently

uncovered his head as he reached the hallowed spot. A few months ago, a banner borne in another Irish insurrection displayed the inscription—

"REMEMBER EMMET."

Far away "beyond the Atlantic foam," and "by the long wash of Australasian seas," societies are in existence bearing his name, and having for their object to cherish his memory and perpetuate his principles. And wherever on the habitable globe a few members of the scattered Irish race are to be found, there are hearts that are thrilled by even the faintest allusion to the uninscribed gravestone and the unwritten epitaph.

THOMAS RUSSELL.

When Emmet was dead, and the plan to which he devoted his fortune, his talents, and his life, had sunk in failure, the cause of Irish independence appeared finally lost, and the cry, more than once repeated in after times, that " now, indeed, the last bolt of Irish disaffection has been sped, and that there would never again be an Irish rebellion," rung loudly from the exulting enemies of Ireland. The hearts of the people seemed broken by the weight of the misfortunes and calamities that overwhelmed them. The hopes which had brightened their stormy path, and enabled them to endure the oppression to which they were subjected by expectations of a glorious change, flickered no longer amidst the darkness. The efforts of the insurgents were everywhere drowned in blood; the hideous memories of '98 were brought up anew; full of bitter thoughts, exasperated, humiliated, and despondent, the people brooded over their wretched fate, and sullenly submitted to the reign of terror which was inaugurated amongst them. Little had the Irish patriots to look forward to in that dark hour of suffering and disappointment. A nightmare of blood and violence weighed down the spirits of the people; a stupor appeared to have fallen on the nation; and though time might be trusted to arouse them from the trance, they had suffered another loss, not so easily repaired, in the death and dispersion of their leaders. Where now should they find the Moses to lead them from the land of captivity? Tone, Fitzgerald, Emmet, Bond, M'Cracken, the Sheareses—all were dead. M'Nevin, Neilson, and O'Connor were in exile. Heavily and relentlessly the arm of vengeance had fallen on them one by one; but the list was not even then completed. There was yet another victim to fall before the altar of liberty; and the sacrifice which commenced with Orr did not conclude until Thomas Russell had perished on the gallows of Downpatrick.

The importance of the part which Thomas Russell fills in the history of the United Irishmen, the worth of his character, the purity and nobility of his sentiments, and the spirit of uncompromising patriotism displayed in his last address, would render unpardonable the omission of his name from such a work as this. "I mean to make my trial," said Russell, "and the last of my life, if it is to close now, as serviceable to the cause of liberty as I can:" and he kept his word. To-day, we try in some slight way to requite that fidelity which endured unto death, by rescuing Thomas Russell's name from oblivion, and recalling his services and virtues to the recollection of his countrymen.

He was born at Betsborough, Dunnahane, in the parish of Kilshanick, county Cork, on the 21st November, 1767. His father was an officer in the British army, who had fought against the Irish Brigade in the memorable battle of Fontenoy, and who died in a high situation in the Royal Hospital at Kilmainham. Thomas, the youngest of his three sons, was educated for the Protestant Church; but his inclinations sought a different field of action, and at the age of fifteen he left for India as a volunteer, where he served with his brother Ambrose, whose gallantry in battle called down commendation from the English king. Thomas Russell quitted India after five years' service, and his return is ascribed to the disgust and indignation which filled him on witnessing the extortions, the cruelties, the usurpations, and brutalities, which were carried out and sanctioned by the government under which he served. He left Ireland burdened with few fixed political principles and little knowledge of the world; he returned a full-grown man, imbued with the opinions which he never afterwards abandoned. He was then, we are told, a model of manly beauty, one of those favored individuals whom we cannot pass in the street without being guilty of the rudeness of staring in the face while passing, and turning round to look at the receding figure. Though more than six feet high, his majestic stature was

scarcely observed, owing to the exquisite symmetry of his
form. Martial in his gait and demeanor, his appearance
was not altogether that of a soldier. His dark and steady
eye, compressed lip, and somewhat haughty bearing,
were occasionally strongly indicative of the camp; but
in general the classic contour of his finely-formed head,
the expression of sweetness that characterized his smile,
and the benevolence that beamed in his fine countenance,
seemed to mark him out as one that was destined to be
the ornament, grace, and blessing of private life. His
manners were those of the finished gentleman, combined
ith that native grace which nothing but superiority of
intellect can give; he was naturally reserved and retiring
in disposition, and his private life was distinguished by
eminent purity and an unostentatious devotion to the
precepts of religion.

Such was Thomas Russell when he made the acquaintance of Theobald Wolfe Tone in Dublin. There is no
doubt that the views and opinions of Tone made a profound impression on young Russell; it is equally certain,
on the other hand, that Tone learned to love and esteem
his new friend, whose sentiments were so much in accordance with his own. Throughout Tone's journal we find
constant references to Thomas Russell, whom he always
places with Thomas Addis Emmet at the head of his list
of friends. Early in 1791 Russell proceeded to Belfast
to join the 64th regiment, in which he had obtained a
commission; before leaving Dublin, he appears to have
become a member of the Society of United Irishmen,
and in Belfast he soon won the friendship and shared
the councils of the patriotic men who were laboring for
Ireland in that city.

While in Belfast, Russell fell into pecuniary embarrassments. His generous and confiding nature induced
him to go bail for a false friend, and he found himself
one morning obliged to meet a claim for £200, which he
had no means of discharging except by the sale of his
commission. Russell sold out and retired to Dungannon,
where he lived for some time on the residue of the
money thus obtained, and during this period he was

appointed a justice of the peace for the county of
Tyrone. After a short experience of "Justices' justice"
in the North, he retired from the bench through motives
alike creditable to his head and heart. "I cannot reconcile it to my conscience," he exclaimed one day, "to
sit on a bench where the practice exists of inquiring
what religion a person is before investigating the charge
against him." Russell returned, after taking this step,
to Belfast, where he was appointed to a situation in the
public library of the town, and where he became a regular contributor to the organ of the Ulster patriots, the
Northern Star.

In 1796 he was appointed by the United Irishmen to
the supreme military command in the county Down, a
post for which his military experience, not less than his
personal influence, fitted him; but his political career was
soon afterwards interrupted by his arrest on the 26th of
September, 1796. Russell was removed to Dublin, and
lodged in Newgate Prison. His arrest filled the great
heart of Tone, who was then toiling for his country in
France, with sorrow and dismay. "It is impossible,"
he says in his journal, "to conceive the effect this misfortune has on my mind. If we are not in Ireland in
time to extricate him, he is lost; for the government will
move heaven and earth to insure his condemnation.
Good God!" he adds, "if Russell and Neilson fall, where
shall I find two others to replace them?" During the
eventful months that intervened between the date of his
arrest and the 19th of March, 1799, poor Russell remained chafing, his imprisoned soul filled with patriotic
passion and emotion, in his prison cell in Kilmainham.
On the latter date, when the majority of his associates
were dead, and their followers scattered and disheartened,
he was transferred to Fort George in Scotland, where he
spent three years more in captivity. The government
had no specific charge against him, but they feared his
influence and distrusted his intentions, and they determined to keep him a prisoner while a chance remained
of his exerting his power against them. No better illustration of Russell's character and principles could be

afforded than that supplied in the following extract from one of the letters written by him during his incarceration in Fort George:—"To the people of Ireland," he writes, addressing an Irish friend and sympathizer, "I am responsible for my actions; amidst the uncertainties of life this may be my valedictory letter; what has occasioned the failure of the cause is useless to speculate on—Providence orders all things for the best. *I am sure the people will never abandon the cause; I am equally sure it will succeed.* I trust men will see," he adds, referring to the infidel views then unhappily prevalent, "that the only true basis of liberty is morality, and the only stable basis of morality is religion."

In 1802 the government, failing to establish any distinct charge against Russell, set him at liberty, and he at once repaired to Paris, where he met Robert Emmet, who was then preparing to renew the effort of Fitzgerald and Wolfe Tone. Time had not changed, nor suffering damped, the patriotic impulses of Thomas Russell; he entered heartily into the plans of young Emmet, and, when the latter left for Ireland in November, 1802, to prosecute his hazardous enterprise, it was with the full understanding that Russell would stand by his side in the post of danger, and with him perish or succeed. In accordance with this arrangement, Russell followed Robert Emmet to Dublin, where he arrived so skilfully disguised that even his own family failed to recognize him. Emmet's plans for the outbreak in Dublin were matured when Russell, with a trusty companion, was despatched northwards to summon the Ulster men to action. Buoyant in spirit, and filled with high expectation, he entered on his mission, but he returned to Dublin, a week later, prostrate in spirit and with a broken heart. One of his first acts on arriving in Belfast was to issue a proclamation, in which, as "General-in-Chief of the Northern District," he summoned the people of Ulster to action.

The North, however, refused to act. It was the old, old story. Belfast resolved on waiting "to see what the South would do," and the South waited for Belfast.

Disgusted and disappointed, Russell quitted the northern capital and proceeded to Antrim, where at least he thought he might expect to find cordial coöperation; but fresh disappointments awaited him, and with a load of misery at his heart, such as he had never felt before, Russell returned to Dublin, where he lived in seclusion, until arrested by Major Sirr and his myrmidons on the 9th of September, 1803. A reward of £1,500 had been offered for his apprehension. We learn on good authority that the ruffianly town-major, on arresting him, seized the unfortunate patriot rudely by the neck-cloth, whereupon, Russell, a far more powerful man than his assailant, flung him aside, and drawing a pistol, exclaimed—" I will not be treated with indignity." Sirr parleyed for a while; a file of soldiers was meanwhile summoned to his aid, and Russell was borne off in irons a prisoner to the Castle. While undergoing this second captivity, a bold attempt was made by his friends to effect his liberation by bribing one of the gaolers; the plot, however, broke down, and Russell never breathed the air of freedom again. While awaiting his trial—that trial which he knew could have but one termination, the death of a felon—Russell addressed a letter to one of his friends outside, in which the following noble passage, the fittest epitaph to be engraved on his tombstone, occurs:—" I mean to make my trial," he writes, " and the last of my life, if it is to close now, as serviceable to the cause of liberty as I can. *I trust my countrymen will ever adhere to it:* I know it will soon prosper. When the country is free," he adds—that it would be free, he never learned to doubt—" I beg they may lay my remains with my father in a private manner, and pay the few debts I owe. I have only to beg of my countrymen to remember that the cause of liberty is the cause of virtue, *which I trust they will never abandon.* May God bless and prosper them, and, when power comes into their hands, I entreat them to use it with moderation. May God and the Saviour bless them all."

Russell was taken to Downpatrick, escorted by a strong force of cavalry, where he was lodged in the governor's rooms, preparatory to being tried in that town by a Special Commission. While in prison in Downpatrick, he addressed a letter to Miss M'Cracken, a sister of Henry Joy M'Cracken, one of the insurgent leaders of 1798, in which he speaks as follows : " Humanly speaking, I expect to be found guilty and immediately executed. As this may be my last letter, I shall only say that I did my best for my country and for mankind. I have no wish to die; but, far from regretting its loss in such a cause, had I a thousand lives, I would willingly risk or lose them in it. Be assured, liberty will in the midst of those storms be established, and God will wipe the tears from all eyes."

The sad anticipations expressed by Russell were but too fully borne out. There was short shrift in those days for Irishmen accused of treason, and the verdict of guilty, which he looked forward to with so much resignation, was delivered before the last rays of the sun which rose on the morning of the trial had faded in the gloaming. It was sworn that he had attended treasonable meetings and distributed green uniforms; that he asked those who attended them, " if they did not desire to get rid of the Sassanaghs;" that he spoke of 30,000 stands of arms from France, but said, if France should fail them, " forks, spades, shovels, and pickaxes," would serve that purpose. It was useless to struggle against such testimony, palpably false and distorted as it was in some parts, and Russell decided on cutting short the proceedings. "I shall not trouble my lawyers," he said, "to make any statement in my case. There are but three possible modes of defence—firstly, by calling witnesses to prove the innocence of my conduct; secondly, by calling them to impeach the credit of opposite witnesses, or by proving an *alibi*. As I can resort to none of those modes of defence without involving others, I consider myself precluded from any." Previous to the judge's charge, the prisoner asked, "if it was not permitted to persons in his situation to say a few words, as he wished to give his valedictory advice to his countrymen in as concise a manner as possible, being well convinced how speedy the transition was from that vestibule of the grave to the scaffold." He was told in reply, "that he would have an opportunity of expressing himself;" and, when the time did come, Russell advanced to the front of the dock, and spoke in a clear, firm tone of voice, as follows:—

"Before I address myself to this audience, I return my sincere thanks to my learned counsel for the exertions they have made, in which they displayed so much talent. I return my thanks to the gentlemen on the part of the crown for the accommodation and indulgence I have received during my confinement. I return my thanks to the gentlemen of the jury for the patient investigation they have afforded my case; and I return my thanks to the court for the attention and politeness they have shown me during my trial. As to my political sentiments, I shall, in as brief a manner as possible (for I do not wish to engross the time of the court), say a few words. I look back to the last thirteen years of my life, the period with which I have interfered with the transactions of Ireland, with entire satisfaction; though for my share in them I am now about to die—the gentlemen of the jury having, by their verdict, put the seal of truth on the evidence against me. Whether, at this time, and the country being situated as it is, it be safe to inflict the punishment of death upon me for the offence I am charged with, I leave to the gentlemen who conduct the prosecution. My death, perhaps, may be useful in deterring others from following my example. It may serve, on the other hand, as a memorial to others, and, on trying occasions, it may inspire them with courage. I can now say, as far as my judgment enabled me, I acted for the good of my country and of the world. It may be presumptuous for me to deliver my opinions here as a statesman: but, as the government have singled me out as a leader, and given me the appellation of "General," I am in some degree entitled to do so. To me it is plain that all things are verging towards a change, when we shall be of one opinion. In ancient times, we read of great empires having their rise and their fall; and yet do the old governments proceed as if all were immutable. From the time I could observe and reflect, I perceived that there were two kinds of laws—the laws of the State and the laws of God—frequently clashing with each other; by the latter kind, I have always endeavored to regulate my conduct; but that laws of the former kind do exist in Ireland, I believe no one that hears me can deny. That such laws have existed in former times, many and various examples clearly evince. The Saviour of the world suffered by the Roman laws—by the same laws His Apostles were put to the torture, and deprived of their lives in His cause. By my conduct I do not consider that I have incurred any moral guilt. I have committed no moral evil. I do not want the many and bright examples of those gone before me;

but did I want this encouragement, the recent example of a youthful hero—a martyr in the cause of liberty—who has just died for his country, would inspire me. I have descended into the vale of manhood. I have learned to estimate the reality and delusions of this world; *he* was surrounded by everything which could endear this world to him—in the bloom of youth, with fond attachments, and with all the fascinating charms of health and innocence; to his death I look back, even in this moment, with rapture. I have travelled much and seen various parts of the world, and I think the Irish are the most virtuous nation on the face of the earth; they are a good and a brave people, and, had I a thousand lives, I would yield them in their service. If it be the will of God that I suffer for that with which I stand charged, I am perfectly resigned to His holy will and dispensation. I do not wish to trespass much more on the time of those who hear me; and did I do so, an indisposition which has seized on me since I came into court, would prevent my purpose. Before I depart from this to a better world, I wish to address myself to the landed aristocracy of this country. The word 'aristocracy,' I do not mean to use as an insulting epithet, but in the common sense of the expression.

"Perhaps, as my voice may now be considered as a voice crying from the grave, what I now say may have some weight. I see around me many, who, during the last years of my life, have disseminated principles for which I am now to die. Those gentlemen, who have all the wealth and the power of the country in their hands, I strongly advise, and earnestly exhort, to pay attention to the poor—by the poor, I mean the laboring class of the community, their tenantry and dependents. I advise them for their good to look into their grievances, to sympathize in their distress, and to spread comfort and happiness around their dwellings. It might be that they may not hold their power long, but at all events to attend to the wants and distresses of the poor is their truest interest. If they hold their power, they will thus have friends around them; if they lose it, their fall will be gentle, and I am sure, unless they act thus, they can never be happy. I shall now appeal to the right honorable gentleman in whose hands the lives of the other prisoners are, and entreat that he will rest satisfied with my death, and let that atone for those errors into which I may have been supposed to have deluded others. I trust the gentleman will restore them to their families and friends. If he shall do so, I can asure him that the breeze which conveys to him the prayers and blessings of their wives and children will be more grateful than that which may be tainted with the stench of putrid corpses, or carrying with it the cries of the widow and the orphan. Standing as I do in the presence of God and of man, I entreat him to let my life atone for the faults of all, and that my blood alone may flow.

"If I am then to die. I have therefore two requests to make. The first is, that, as I have been engaged in a work possibly of some advantage to the world, I may be indulged with three days for its completion; secondly, that, as there are those ties which even death cannot sever, and as there are those who may have some regard for what will remain of me after death, I request that my remains, disfigured as they will be, may be delivered after the execution of the sentence to those dear friends, that they may be conveyed to the ground where my parents are laid, and where those faithful few may have a consecrated spot over which they may be permitted to grieve. I have now to declare, when about to pass into the presence of Almighty God, that I feel no enmity in my mind to any being, none to those who have borne testimony against me, and none to the jury who have pronounced the verdict of my death."

The last request of Russell was refused, and he was executed twelve hours after the conclusion of the trial. At noon, on the 21st of October, 1803, he was borne pinioned to the place of execution. Eleven regiments of soldiers were concentrated in the town, to overawe the people and defeat any attempt at rescue; yet, even with this force at their back, the authorities were far from feeling secure. The interval between the trial and execution was so short that no preparation could be made for the erection of a scaffold, except the placing of some barrels under the gateway of the main entrance to the prison, with planks placed upon them as a platform, and others sloping up from the ground, by which it was ascended. On the ground hard by, were placed a sack of sawdust, an axe, a block, and a knife. After ascending the scaffold, Russell gazed forward, through the archway, towards the people, whose white faces could be seen glistening outside, and again expressed his forgiveness of his persecutors. His manner, we are told, was perfectly calm, and he died without a struggle.

A purer soul, a more blameless spirit, than Thomas Russell, never sunk on the battle-field of freedom. Fixed in principle, and resolute in danger, he was nevertheless gentle, courteous, unobtrusive, and humane; with all the modesty and unaffectedness of childhood, he united the zeal of a martyr and the courage of a hero. To the cause of his country he devoted all his energies and all his will; and when he failed to render it prosperous in life, he illumined it by his devotion and steadfastness in death. The noble speech given above, and the passages from his letters which we have quoted, are sufficient in themselves to show how chivalrous was the spirit, how noble the motives, of Thomas Russell. The predictions which he uttered with so much confidence have not indeed been fulfilled, and the success which he looked forward to so hopefully has never been won. But his advice, so often repeated in his letters, is still adhered to; his countrymen have not yet learned to abandon the cause in which he suffered, and they still cherish the conviction which he so touchingly expressed—"that liberty will, in the midst of these storms, be established, and that God will yet wipe off the tears of the Irish nation."

Russell rests in the churchyard of the Protestant church of Downpatrick. A plain slab marks the spot where he is laid, and there is on it this single line—

"THE GRAVE OF RUSSELL."

WE have now closed our reference to the portion of Irish history comprised within the years 1798 and 1803, and as far as concerns the men who suffered for Ireland in those disastrous days, our "Speeches from the Dock" are concluded. We leave behind us the struggle of 1798, and the men who organized it; we turn from the records of a period reeking with the gore of Ireland's truest sons, and echoing with the cries and curses of the innocent and oppressed; we pass without notice the butcheries and outrages that filled the land, while our countrymen were being sabred into submission; and we leave behind us, too, the short-lived insurrection of 1803, and the chivalrous young patriot who perished with it. We turn to more recent events, less appalling in their general aspect, but not less important in their consequences, or less interesting to the present generation, and take up the next link in the unbroken chain of protests against British rule in Ireland, with the lives and the fortunes of the patriots of 1848. How faithfully the principles of freedom have been handed down—how nobly the men of our own times have imitated the patriots of the past—how thoroughly the sentiments expressed from the Green-street dock nineteen years ago coincide with the declarations of Tone, of Emmet, and of Russell—our readers will shortly have an opportunity of judging. They will see how all the sufferings and all the calamities that darkened the path of the martyrs of '98 were insufficient to deter others, as gifted, as earnest, and as chivalrous as they, from following in their footsteps; and how, unquenchable and unending as the altar light of the fire-worshipper, the generous glow of patriotic enthusiasm was transmitted through generations, unaffected by the torrents of blood in which it was sought to extinguish it.

The events of our own generation—the acts of contemporary patriots—now claim our attention; but we are reluctant as yet to turn over the page, and drop the curtain on the scenes with which we have hitherto been dealing, and which we feel we have inadequately described. We have spoken of the men whose speeches from the dock are on record, but we still linger over the history of the events in which they shared, and of the men who were associated with them in their endeavors. The patriots whose careers we have glanced at are but a few out of the number of Irishmen who suffered during the same period, and in the same cause, and whose actions recommend them to the admiration and esteem of posterity. Confining ourselves strictly to those whose speeches after conviction have reached us, the list could not well be extended; but there are many who acted as brave a part, and whose memories are inseparable from the history of the period. We should have desired to speak, were the scope of our labors more extended, of the brave Lord Edward Fitzgerald, the gallant and the true, who sacrificed his position, his prospects, and his life, for the good old cause, and whose arrest and death contributed more largely, perhaps, than any other cause that could be assigned, to the failure of the insurrection of 1798. Descended from an old and noble family, possessing in a remarkable degree all the attributes and embellishments of a popular leader; young and spirited, eloquent and wealthy, ardent, generous, and brave, of good address, and fine physical proportions, it is not surprising that Lord Edward Fitzgerald became the idol of the patriot party, and was appointed by them to a leading position in the organization. Lord Edward Fitzgerald was born in October, 1763; being the fifth son of James Duke of Leinster, the twentieth Earl of Kildare. He grew up to manhood, as a recent writer has observed, when the drums of the volunteers were pealing their marches of victory; and under the stirring events of the period his soul burst through the shackles that had long bound down the Irish aristocracy in servile dependence. In his early years he served, in the American War of Independence, on the side of despotism and oppression—a circumstance which in after years caused him poignant sorrow. He joined the United Irishmen about the time that Thomas Addis Emmet entered their ranks, and the young nobleman threw himself into the movement with all the ardor and energy of his nature. He was appointed commander-in-chief of the national forces in the South, and labored with indefatigable zeal in perfecting the plans for the outbreak on the 23d of May. The story of his arrest and capture is too well known to need repetition. Treachery dogged the steps of the young patriot, and, after lying for some weeks in concealment, he was arrested on the 19th day of May, 1798, two months after his associates in the direction of the movement had been arrested at Oliver Bond's. His gallant struggle with his captors, fighting, like a lion at bay, against the miscreants who assailed him; his assassination, his imprisonment, and his death, are events to which the minds of the Irish nationalists perpetually recur, and which, celebrated in song and story, are told with sympathizing regret wherever a group of Irish blood are gathered around the hearthstone. His genius, his talents, and his influence, his unswerving attachment to his country, and his melancholy end, cast an air of romance around his history; and the last ray of gratitude must fade from the Irish heart before the name of the martyred patriot, who sleeps in the vaults of St. Werburgh, will be forgotten in the land of his birth.

In less than a fortnight after Lord Edward expired in Newgate, another Irish rebel, distinguished by his talents, his fidelity, and his position, expiated with his life the crime of "loving his country above his king." It is hard to mention Thomas Russell and ignore Henry Joy M'Cracken—it is hard to speak of the Insurrection of '98 and forget the gallant young Irishman who commanded at the battle of Antrim, and who perished, a few weeks subsequently, in the bloom of his manhood, on the scaffold in Belfast. Henry Joy M'Cracken was one of the first members of the Society of United Irishmen, and he was one of the best. He was arrested, owing to private information received by the government, on the 10th of October, 1796—three weeks after Russell, his friend and confidant, was flung into prison— and lodged in Newgate Jail, where he remained until the 8th of September in the following year. He was then liberated on bail, and immediately, on regaining his liberty, returned to Belfast, still bent on accomplishing at all hazards the liberation of his country. Previous to the outbreak in May, '98, he had frequent interviews with the patriot leaders in Dublin, and M'Cracken was appointed to the command of the insurgent forces in Antrim. Filled with impatience and patriotic ardor, he heard of the stirring events that followed the arrest of Lord Edward Fitzgerald; he concentrated all his energies in preparing the Northern patriots for action, but circumstances delayed the outbreak in that quarter, and it was not until the 6th of June, 1798, that M'Cracken had perfected his arrangements for taking the field, and issued the following brief proclamation, "dated the first year of liberty, 6th June, 1798," addressed to the Army of Ulster:—

"To-morrow we march on Antrim. Drive the garrison of Randalstown before you. and hasten to form a junction with your commander-in-chief."

Twenty-one thousand insurgents were to have rallied at the call of M'Cracken, but not more than seven thousand responded to the summons. Even this number, however, would have been sufficient to strike a successful blow, which would have filled the hearts of the gallant Wexford men, then in arms, with exultation, and effected incalculable results on the fate of Ireland, had not the curse of the Irish cause, treachery and betrayal, again come to the aid of its enemies. Hardly had the plans for the attack on Antrim been perfected, when the secrets of the conspirators were revealed to General Nugent, who commanded the British troops in the North, and the defeat of the insurgents was thus secured. M'Cracken's forces marched to the attack on Antrim with great regularity, chorusing the Marseillaise Hymn as they charged through the town. Their success at first seemed complete, but the English general, acting on the information which had treacherously been supplied him, had taken effective means to disconcert and defeat them. Suddenly, and as it seemed, in the flush of victory, the insurgents found themselves exposed to a galling fire from a force posted at either end of the town; a gallant resistance was offered, but it was vain. The insurgents fled from the fatal spot, leaving 500 of their dead and dying behind them, and at nightfall Henry Joy M'Cracken found himself a fugitive and a ruined man. For some weeks he managed to baffle the bloodhounds on his track, but he was ultimately arrested and tried by court-martial, in Belfast, on the 17th July, 1798. On the evening of the same day he was executed. We have it on the best authority that he bore his fate with calmness, resolution, and resignation. It is not his fault that a "Speech from the Dock" under his name is not amongst our present collection. He had actually prepared one, but his brutal judges would not listen to the patriot's exculpation. He was hung, amidst the sobs and tears of the populace, in front of the Old Marketplace of Belfast, and his remains were interred in the graveyard now covered by St. George's Protestant church.

Later still, in the same year, two gallant young officers of Irish blood shared the fate of Russell and M'Cracken. They sailed with Humbert from Rochelle; they fought at Castlebar and Ballinamuck; and when the swords of their French allies were sheathed, they passed into the power of the foes. Matthew Tone was one of them; the other was Bartholomew Teeling. The latter filled the rank of *Etat-major* in the French army; and a letter from his commanding officer, General Humbert, was read at his trial, in which the highest praise was given to the young officer for the humane exertions which he made throughout his last brief campaign in the interest of mercy. " His hand," he said, " was ever raised to stay the useless effusion of blood, and his protection was afforded to the prostrate and defenceless." But his military judges paid little heed to those extenuating circumstances, and Teeling was condemned to die on the day of his trial. He perished on the 24th September, 1798, being then in his twenty-fourth year. He marched with a proud step to the place of execution on Arbor Hill, Dublin, and he died, as a soldier might, with unshaken firmness and unquailing mien. No lettered slab marks the place of his interment; and his bones remain in unhallowed and unconsecrated ground. Hardly had his headless body ceased to palpitate, when it was flung into a hole at the rear of the Royal Barracks. A few days later the same unhonored spot received the mortal remains of Matthew Tone. " He had a more enthusiastic nature than any of us," writes his brother, Theobald Wolfe Tone, " and was a sincere republican, capable of sacrificing everything for his principles." His execution was conducted with infamous cruelty and brutality, and the life-blood was still gushing from his body when it was flung into "The Croppy's Hole." " The day will come," says Dr. Madden, " when that desecrated spot will be hallowed ground—consecrated by religion—trod lightly by pensive patriotism—and decorated by funeral trophies in honor of the dead whose bones lie there in graves that are now neglected and unhonored."

There are others of the patriot leaders who died in exile, far away from the land for which they suffered, and whose graves were dug on alien shores by the heedless hands of the stranger. This was the fate of Addis

Emmet, of Neilson, and of M'Nevin. In Ireland they were foremost and most trusted amongst the gifted and brilliant throng that directed the labors and shaped the purposes of the United Irishmen. They survived the reign of terror that swallowed up the majority of their compatriots, and, when milder councils began to prevail, they were permitted to go forth from the dungeon which confined them, into banishment. The vision of Irish freedom was not permitted to dawn upon them in life; from beyond the sandy slopes washed by the Western Atlantic they watched the fortunes of the old land with hopeless, but enduring, love. Their talents, their virtues, and their patriotism were not unappreciated by the people amongst whom they spent their closing years of life. In the busiest thoroughfare of the greatest city of America, there towers over the heads of the by-passers the monument of marble which grateful hands have raised to the memory of Addis Emmet. In the centre of Western civilization, the home of republican liberty, the stranger reads, in glowing words, of the virtues and the fame of the brother of Robert Emmet, sculptured on the noble pillar erected in Broadway, New York, to his memory. Nor was he the only one of his party to whom such an honor was accorded. A stone-throw from the spot where the Emmet monument stands, a memorial, not less commanding in its proportions and appearance, was erected to William James M'Nevin; and the American citizen, as he passes through the spacious streets of that city which the genius of liberty has rendered prosperous and great, gazes proudly on those stately monuments, which tell him that the devotion to freedom which England punished and proscribed found in his own land the recognition which it merited from the gallant and the rfee.*

---

* The inscriptions on the Emmet monument are in three languages—Irish, Latin, and English. The Irish inscription consists of the following lines:—

Do mbiannaich se ardmáth
Cum tir a breith
Do thug se clu a's fuair se moladh
An deig a buis.

The following is the English inscription:

In Memory of
THOMAS ADDIS EMMET.
Who exemplified in his conduct,
And adorned by his integrity,
The policy and principles of the
UNITED IRISHMEN—
" To forward a brotherhood of affection,
A community of rights, an identity of interests, and a union of power
Among Irishmen of every religious persuasion,
As the only means of Ireland's chief good,
An impartial and adequate representation
IN AN IRISH PARLIAMENT."
For this (mysterious fate of virtue) exiled from his native land,
In America, the land of Freedom,
He found a second country,
Which paid his love by reverencing his genius.
Learned in our laws, and in the laws of Europe,
In the literature of our times, and in that of antiquity,
All knowledge seemed subject to his use.
An orator of the first order, clear, copious, fervid.
Alike powerful to kindle the imagination, touch the affections,
And sway the reason and will;
Simple in his tastes, unassuming in his manners,
Frank, generous, kind-hearted, and honourable,
His private life was beautiful,
As his public course was brilliant.
The name and example of such a man,
Alike illustrious by his genius, his virtues, and his fate;
Consecrated to their affections by his sacrifices, his perils,
And the deeper calamities of his kindred,
IN A JUST AND HOLY CAUSE;
His sympathizing countrymen
Erected this Monument and Cenotaph.

JOHN MITCHEL.

SUBSEQUENT to the melancholy tragedy of 1803, a period of indescribable depression was experienced in Ireland. Defeat, disaster, ruin, had fallen upon the national cause; the power on whose friendly aid so much reliance had been placed was humbled, and England stood before the world in the full blaze of triumph and glory. Her fleet was undisputed mistress of the ocean, having swept off all hostile shipping, and left to the enemy little more than the small craft that sheltered in narrow creeks and under the guns of well-defended harbors. Her army, if not numerically large, had proved its valor on many a well-fought field, and shown that it knew how to bring victory to light upon its standards; and, what was not less a matter of wonder to others, and of pride to herself, the abundance of her wealth and the extent of her resources were shown to be without a parallel in the world. Napoleon was an exile on the rock of St. Helena; the "Holy Alliance"—as the European sovereigns blasphemously designated themselves—were lording it over the souls and bodies of men by "right divine;" the free and noble principles in which the French Revolution had its origin were now sunk out of sight, covered with the infamy of the Reign of Terror and the responsibility of the series of desolating wars which had followed it, and no man dared to speak for them. Those were dark days for Ireland. Her parliament was gone, and in the blighting shade of the provincialism to which she was reduced, genius and courage seemed to have died out from the land. Thousands of her bravest and most devoted children had perished in her cause—some on the scaffold, and others on the field of battle; and many, whose presence at home would have been invaluable to her, were obliged to seek safety in exile. So Eriu, the crownless Queen, sat in the dust with fetters on her limbs, her

JOHN O'LEARY.   CHARLES J. KICKHAM.   THOMAS CLARK LUBEY.

broken sword fallen from her hand, and with mournful memories lying heavy on her heart. The feelings of disappointment and grief then rankling in every Irish breast are well mirrored in that plaintive song of our national poet, which opens with these tristful lines:—

> "'Tis gone, and for ever, the light we saw breaking,
> Like heaven's first dawn o'er the sleep of the dead,
> When man, from the slumber of ages awaking,
> Looked upward and blessed the pure ray ere it fled.
> 'Tis gone, and the gleams it has left of its burning
> But deepen the long night of bondage and mourning,
> That dark o'er the kingdoms of earth is returning,
> And darkest of all, hapless Erin, o'er thee."

In this gloomy condition of affairs there was nothing for Irish patriotism to do except to seek for the removal, by constitutional means, of some of the cruel grievances that pressed on the people. Emancipation of the Catholics from the large remainder of the penal laws that still degraded and despoiled them, was one of the baits held out by Mr. Pitt when playing his cards for the Union; but not long had the Irish parliament been numbered with the things that were, when it became evident that the minister was in no hurry to fulfil his engagement, and it was found necessary to take some steps for keeping him to his promise. Committees were formed, meetings were held, speeches were made, resolutions were adopted, and all the machinery of parliamentary endeavor was put in motion. The leaders of the Catholic cause in this case, like those of the national cause in the preceding years, were liberal-minded Protestant gentlemen; but, as time wore on, a young barrister from Kerry, one of the old race and the old faith, took a decided lead amongst them, and soon became its recognized champion, the elect of the nation, the "man of the people." Daniel O'Connell stood forth, with the whole mass of his Catholic countrymen at his back, to wage, within the lines of the constitution, this battle for Ireland. He fought it resolutely and skilfully; the people supported him with an unanimity and an enthusiasm that were wonderful; their spirit rose and strengthened to that degree, that the probability of another civil war began to loom up in the near future. Inquiries instituted by the government resulted in the discovery that the Catholics serving in the army, and who constituted at least a third of its strength, were in full sympathy with their countrymen on this question, and could not be depended on to act against them: the ministry recognized the critical condition of affairs, saw that there was danger in delay, yielded to the popular demand—and Catholic Emancipation was won.

The details of that brilliant episode of Irish history cannot be told within the limits of this work, but some of its consequences concern us very nearly. The triumph of the constitutional struggle for Catholic Emancipation confirmed O'Connell in the resolution he had previously formed, to promote an agitation for a Repeal of the Union, and encouraged him to lay the proposal before his countrymen. The forces that had wrung the one measure of justice from an unwilling parliament were competent, he declared, to obtain the other. He soon succeeded in impressing his own belief on the minds of his countrymen, whose confidence in his wisdom and powers was unbounded. The whole country responded to his call, and soon "the Liberator," as the emancipated Irish Catholics loved to call him, found himself at the head of a political organization, which, in its mode of action, its extent, and its ardor, was "unique in the history of the world." Every city and great town in Ireland had its branch of the Repeal Association; every village had its Repeal reading-room—all deriving hope and life, and taking direction from the headquarters in Dublin, where the great Tribune himself "thundered and lightened" at the weekly meetings. All Ireland echoed with his words. Newspapers, attaining thereby to a circulation never before approached in Ireland, carried them from one extremity of the land to the other—educating, cheering, and inspiring the hearts of the long down-trodden people. Nothing like this had ever occurred before. The eloquence of the patriot orators of the Irish parliament had not been brought home to the masses of the population; and the United Irishmen could only speak to them secretly, in whispers. But here were addresses glowing, and bold, and tender, brimful of native humor, scathing in their sarcasms, terrible in their denunciations, ineffably beautiful in their pathos—addresses that recalled the most glorious as well as the saddest memories of Irish history, and presented brilliant vistas of the future—addresses that touched to its fullest and most delicious vibration every chord of the Irish heart—here they were being sped over the land in an unfailing and ever-welcome supply. The peasant read them to his family by the fireside when his hard day's work was done; and the fisherman, as he steered his boat homeward, reckoned as not the least of his anticipated pleasures, the reading of the last report from Conciliation Hall. And it was not the humbler classes only who acknowledged the influence of the Repeal oratory, sympathized with the movement, and enrolled themselves in the ranks. The priesthood, almost to a man, were members of the Association and propagandists of its principles; the professional classes were largely represented in it; of merchants and traders it could count up a large roll; and many of the landed gentry, even though they held her Majesty's Commission of the Peace, were amongst its most prominent supporters. In short, the Repeal Association represented the Irish nation, and its voice was the voice of the people. The "Monster Meetings" of the year 1843 put this fact beyond the region of doubt or question. As popular demonstrations, they were wonderful in their numbers, their order, and their enthusiasm. O'Connell, elated by their success, fancied that his victory was as good as won. He knew that things could not continue to go on as they were going—either the government or the Repeal Association should give way, and he believed the government would yield. For, the Association, he assured his countrymen, was safe within the limits of the law, and not a hostile hand could be laid upon it without violating the constitution. His countrymen had nothing to do but obey the law and support the Association, and a Repeal of the Union within a few months was, he said, inevitable. In all this he had allowed his own heart to deceive him; and his mistake was clearly shown when, in October, 1843, the government, by proclamation and a display of military force, prevented the intended monster meeting at Clontarf. It was still more fully established in the early part of the following year, when he, with a number of his political associates, was brought to trial for treasonable and seditious practices, found guilty, and sentenced to twelve months' imprisonment. The subsequent reversal of the verdict by the House of Lords was a legal triumph for O'Connell; but, nevertheless, his prestige had suffered by the occurrence, and his policy had begun to pall upon the minds of the people.

After his release the business of the Association went on as before, only there was less of confidence and of defiance in the speeches of the Liberator, and there were no more monster meetings. He was now more emphatic than ever in his advocacy of moral-force principles, and his condemnation of all warlike hints and allusions. The weight of age—he was then more than seventy years—was pressing on his once buoyant spirit; his prison experience had damped his courage; and he was haunted night and day by a conviction—terrible to his mind—that there was growing up, under the wing of the Association, a party that would teach the people to look to an armed struggle as the only sure means of obtaining the freedom of their country. The writings of the *Nation*—then a new light in the literature and politics of Ireland—had a ring in them that was unpleasant to his ears, a sound as of clashing steel and the explosion of gunpowder. In the articles of that journal much honor was given to men who had striven for Irish freedom by other methods than those in favor at Conciliation Hall; and the songs and ballads which it was giving to the youth of Ireland—who received them with delight, treasuring every line "as if an angel spoke"—were bright with the spirit of battle, and taught any doctrine except the sinfulness of fighting for liberty. The Liberator grew fearful of that organ and of the men by whom it was conducted. He distrusted that quiet-faced, thoughtful, and laborious young man, whom they so loved and reverenced—the founder, the soul, and the centre of their party. To the keen glance of the aged leader it appeared that for all that placid brow, those calm grey eyes and softly curving lip of his, the man had no horror of blood-spilling in a righteous cause, and was capable not only of deliberately inciting his countrymen to rise in arms against English rule, but also of taking a foremost place in the struggle. And little less to be dreaded than Thomas Davis, was his friend and *collaborateur*, Charles Gavan Duffy, whose sharp and active intellect and resolute spirit were not in the least likely to allow the national cause to rest forever on the peaceful platform of Conciliation Hall. Death removed Davis early from the scene; but in John Mitchel, who had taken his place, there was no gain to the party of moral force. Then there was that other young firebrand—that dapper, well-built, well-dressed, curled and scented young gentleman from the *Urbs Intacta*—whose wondrous eloquence, with the glow of its thought, the brilliancy and richness of its imagery, and the sweetness of its cadences, charmed and swayed all hearts—adding immensely to the dangers of the situation. O'Brien, too, staid and unimpulsive as was his character, deliberate and circumspect as were his habits, was evidently inclined to give the weight of his name and influence to this "advanced" party. And there were many less prominent, but scarcely less able men giving them the aid of their great talents in the press and on the platform—not only men, but women too. Some of the most inspiriting of the strains that were inducing the youth of the country to familiarize themselves with steel blades and rifle barrels, proceeded from the pens of those fair and gifted beings. Day after day, as this party sickened of the stale platitudes, and timid counsels, and crooked policy of the Hall, O'Connell, his son John, and other leading members of the Association, insisted more and more strongly on their doctrine of moral force, and indulged in the wildest and most absurd denunciations of the principle of armed resistance to tyranny. "The liberty of the world," exclaimed O'Connell, "is not worth the shedding of one drop of human blood." Notwithstanding the profound disgust which the utterance of such sentiments caused to the bolder spirits in the Association, they would have continued within its fold, if those debasing principles had not been actually formulated into a series of resolutions, and proposed for the acceptance of the Society. Then they rose against the ignoble doctrine which would blot the fair fame of all who ever fought for liberty in Ireland or elsewhere, and rank the noblest men the world ever saw in the category of fools and criminals. Meagher, in a brilliant oration, protested against the resolutions, and showed why he would not "abhor and stigmatize the sword.' Mr. John O'Connell interrupted and interfered with the speaker. It was plain that freedom of speech was to be had no longer on the platform of the Association, and that men of spirit had no longer any business there. Meagher took up his hat and left the Hall, and amongst the crowd that accompanied him, went William Smith O'Brien, Thomas Devin Reilly Charles Gavan Duffy, and John Mitchel.

After this disruption, which occurred on the 28th of July, 1846, came the formation of the "Irish Confede ration" by the seceders. In the proceedings of the new society Mr. Mitchel took a more prominent part than he had taken in the business of the Repeal Association. And he continued to write in his own terse and forcible style in the *Nation*. But his mind travelled too fast in the direction of war for either the journal or the society with which he was connected. The desperate condition of the country, now a prey to all the horrors of famine, for the awfully fatal effects of which the government was clearly responsible—the disorganization and decay of the Repeal party, consequent on the death of O'Connell—the introduction of Arms' Acts and other coercive measures by the government, and the growing ardor of the Confederate Clubs, were to him as signs and tokens unmistakable that there was no time to be lost in bringing matters to a crisis in which the people should hold their own by force of arms. Most of his political associates viewed the situation with more patience; but Mr. Mitchel was resolved that, even if he stood alone, he would speak out his opinions to the people. In the latter part of December, 1847, he withdrew from the *Nation*. On the 5th of February, 1848, at the close of a debate, which had lasted two days, on the merits of his policy of immediate resistance to the collection of rates, rents, and taxes, and the division on which was unfavorable to him, he, with a number of friends and sympathizers, withdrew from the Confederation. Seven days afterwards, he issued the first number of a newspaper, bearing the significant title of *The United Irishman*, and having for its motto the following aphorism, quoted from Theobald Wolfe Tone: " Our independence must be had at all hazards. If the men of property will not support us, they must fall; we can support ourselves by the aid of that numerous and respectable class of the community, the men of no property."

The *Nation* had been regarded as rather an outspoken journal, and not particularly well affected to the rulers of the country. But it was mildness, and gentleness, and loyalty itself, compared to the new-comer in the field of journalism. The sudden uprising of a most portentous comet sweeping close to this planet of ours could hardly create more unfeigned astonishment in the mind of people in general, than did the appearance of this wonderful newspaper, brimful of open and avowed sedition, crammed with incitements to insurrection, and with diligently prepared instructions for the destruction of her Majesty's troops, barracks, stores, and magazines. Men rubbed their eyes, as they read its articles and correspondence, scarcely believing that any man in his sober senses would venture, in any part of the Queen's dominions, to put such things in print. But there were the articles and the letters, nevertheless, on fair paper and in good type, published in a duly registered newspaper, bearing the impressed stamp of the Customs—a sign to all men that the proprietor was bound in heavy sureties to the government against the publication of "libel, blasphemy, or sedition!"—couched, moreover, in a style of language possessing such grace and force, such delicacy of finish, and yet such marvellous strength, rich with so much of quiet humor, and bristling with such rasping sarcasm and penetrating invective, that they were read as an intellectual luxury even by men who regarded as utterly wild and wicked the sentiments they conveyed. The first editorial utterance in this journal consisted of a letter from Mr. Mitchel to the Viceroy, in which that functionary was addressed as "The Right Hon. the Earl of Clarendon, Englishman, calling himself her Majesty's Lord Lieutenant-General and General Governor of Ireland." The purport of the document was to declare, above-board, the aims and objects of the *United Irishman*—a journal with which, wrote Mr. Mitchel, "your lordship and your lordship's masters and servants are to have more to do than may be agreeable either to you or me." That that purpose was to resume the struggle which had been waged by Tone and Emmet, or, as Mr. Mitchel put it, "the Holy War, to sweep this island clear of the English name and nation." "We differ," he said, "from the illustrious conspirators of '98, not in principle—no, not an *iota*—but, as I shall presently show you, materially as to the mode of action." And the difference was to consist in this—that, whereas the revolutionary organization in Ninety-eight was a secret one, which was ruined by spies and informers, that of Forty-eight was to be an open one, concerning which informers could tell nothing that its promoters would not willingly proclaim from the housetops. "If you desire," he wrote, "to have a Castle detective employed about the *United Irishman* office in Trinity-street, I shall make no objection, provided the man be sober and honest. If Sir George Grey or Sir William Somerville would like to read our correspondence, we make him welcome for the present—only let the letters be forwarded without losing a post." Of the fact that he would speedily be called to account for his conduct in one of her Majesty's courts of law, the writer of this defiant language was perfectly cognizant; but he declared that the inevitable prosecution would be his opportunity of achieving a victory over the government. "For, be it known to you," he wrote, "that in such a case you shall either publicly, boldly, notoriously *pack a jury*, or else see the accused rebel walk a free man out of the court of Queen's Bench—which will be a victory only less than the rout of your lordship's red-coats in the open field." In case of his defeat, other men would take up the cause and maintain it, until at last England would have to fall back on her old system of courts-martial, and triangles, and free quarters, and Irishmen would find that there was no help for them "in franchises, in votings, in spoutings, in shoutings, and toasts drank with enthusiasm—nor in anything in this world, save the *extensor* and *contractor* muscles of their right arms, in these and the goodness of God above." The conclusion of this extraordinary address to her Majesty's representative was in the following terms:—

"In plain English, my Lord Earl, the deep and irreconcilable disaffection of this people to all British laws, lawgivers, and law administrators, shall find a voice. That holy Hatred of foreign dominion which nerved our noble predecessos fifty years ago for the dungeon, the field, or the gallows (though of late years it has worn a vile *nisi prius* gown, and snivelled somewhat in courts of law and on spouting platforms) still lives, thank God! and glows as fierce and hot as ever. To educate that holy Hatred, to make it know itself, and avow itself, and, at least, fill itself full, I hereby devote the columns of the *United Irishman*."

After this address to the Lord Lieutenant, Mr. Mitchel took to addressing the farming classes; and it is really a study to observe the exquisite precision, the clearness, and the force of the language he employed to convey his ideas to them. In his second letter he supposes the case of a farmer who has the entire produce of his land in his haggard, in the shape of six stacks of corn; he shows that three of these ought, in all honor and conscience, to be sufficient for the landlord and the government to seize upon, leaving the other three to support the family of the man whose labor had produced them. But what are the facts?—the landlord and the government sweep *all* away, and the peasant and his family starve by the ditch sides. As an illustration of this condition of things, he quotes from a southern paper an account of an inquest held on the body of a man named Boland, and on the bodies of his two daughters, who, as the verdict declared, had "died of cold and starvation," although occupants of a farm of over twenty acres in extent. On this melancholy case the comment of the editor of the *United Irishman* was as as follows:—

"Now what became of poor Boland's twenty acres of crop? Part of it went to Gibraltar, to victual the garrison; part to South Africa, to provision the robber army; part went to Spain, to pay for the landlord's wine; part to London, to pay the interest of his honor's mortgage to the Jews. The English ate some of it; the Chinese had their share; the Jews and the Gentiles divided it amongst them—and there was *none* for Boland."

As to the manner in which the condition and fate of poor Boland were to be avoided, abundant instructions were given in every number. The anti-tithe movement was quoted as a model to begin with; but, of course, that was to be improved upon. The idea that the people would not venture on such desperate movements, and had grown enamored of the Peace policy and of " Patience and Perseverance," Mr. Mitchell refused to entertain for a moment:—

"I will not believe that Irishmen are so degraded and utterly lost as this. The Earth is awakening from sleep; a flash of electric fire is passing through the dumb millions. Democracy is girding himself once more like a strong man to run a race; and slumbering nations are arising in their might, and 'shaking their invincible locks.' Oh! my countrymen, look up, look up! Arise from the death-dust where you have long been lying, and let this light visit your eyes also, and touch your souls. Let your ears drink in the blessed words, 'Liberty! Fraternity! Equality!' which are soon to ring from pole to pole! Clear steel will, ere long, dawn upon you in your desolate darkness; and the rolling thunder of the People's cannon will drive before it many a heavy cloud that has long hidden from you the face of heaven. Pray for that day; and preserve life and health that you may worthily meet it. Above all, let the man amongst you who has no gun sell his garment and buy one."

So Mr. Mitchell went on for some weeks, preaching in earnest and exciting language the necessity of preparation for an immediate grapple with "the enemy." In the midst of his labors came the startling news of another revolution in France, Louis Philippe in full flight, and the proclamation of a Republic. Yet a few days more and the Berliners had risen and triumphed, only stopping short of chasing their king away because he conceded all they were pleased to require of him; then came insurrection in Sicily, insurrection in Lombardy, insurrection in Milan, insurrection in Hungary—in short, the revolutionary movement became general throughout Europe, and thrones and principalities were tumbling and tottering in all directions. Loud was the complaint in the *United Irishman* because Dublin was remaining tranquil. It was evident, however, that the people and their leaders were feeling the revolutionary impulse, and that matters were fast hurrying towards an outbreak. John Mitchel knew that a crisis was at hand, and devoted all his energies to making the best use of the short time that his newspaper had to live. His writing became fiercer, more condensed, and more powerful than ever. Lord Clarendon was now addressed as "Her Majesty's Executioner-General and General Butcher of Ireland," and instructions for street warfare and all sorts of operations suitable for an insurgent populace occupied a larger space than ever in his paper. But the government were now resolved to close with their bold and clever enemy. On Tuesday, the 21st of March, 1848, Messrs. O'Brien, Meagher, and Mitchel were arrested, the former for seditious speeches uttered at a meeting of the Confederation held on the 15th of that month, the latter for three seditious articles published in the *United Irishman*. All were released on bail, and when the trials came on, in the month of May, disagreements of the jury took place in the cases of O'Brien and Meagher. But before the trial of Mr. Mitchel could be proceeded with, he was arrested on a fresh charge of "treason-felony"—a new crime, which had been manufactured by act of Parliament a few weeks before. He was, therefore, fast in the toils, and with but little chance of escape. Little concern did this give the brave-hearted patriot, who only hoped and prayed that at last the time had come when his countrymen would launch out upon the resolute course of action which he had so earnestly recommended to them. From his cell in Newgate, on the 16th of May, he addressed to them one of his most exciting letters, of which the following are the concluding passages :—

"For me, I abide my fate joyfully; for I know that, whatever betide me, my work is nearly done. Yes; Moral Force and 'Patience and Perseverance' are scattered to the wild winds of heaven. The music my countrymen now love best to hear is the rattle of arms and the ring of the rifle. As I sit here and write in my lonely cell, I hear, just dying away, the measured tramp of ten thousand marching men—my gallant confederates, unarmed and silent, but with hearts like bended bow, waiting till *the time* comes. They have marched past my prison windows, to let me know there are ten thousand fighting men in Dublin—'felons' in heart and soul.

"I thank God for it. The game is afoot at last. The liberty of Ireland may come sooner or later, by peaceful negotiation or bloody conflict—but it is *sure;* and wherever between the poles I may chance to be, I will hear the crash of the downfall of the thrice-accursed British Empire."

On Monday, May 22d, 1848, the trial of Mr. Mitchel commenced in the Commission Court, Green-street, before Baron Lefroy. He was eloquently defended by the veteran lawyer and uncompromising patriot, Robert Holmes, the brother-in-law of Robert Emmet. The mere law of the case was strong against the prisoner, but Mr. Holmes endeavored to raise the minds of the jury to the moral views of the case, upon which English juries have often acted regardless of the letter of the Act of Parliament. With a jury of Irishmen impartially chosen it would have been a good defence, but the Castle had made sure of their men in this case. At five o'clock on the evening of the 26th, the case went to the jury, who, after an absence of two hours, returned into court with a verdict of "Guilty."

That verdict was a surprise to no one. On the day the jury was empanelled, the prisoner and every one else knew what it was to be. It was now his turn

to have a word to say for himself, and he spoke, as was
his wont, in plain terms, answering thus the question
that had been put to him:—

"I have to say that I have been found guilty by a packed jury—
by the jury of a partisan sheriff—by a jury not empanelled even
according to the law of England. I have been found guilty by a
packed jury obtained by a juggle—a jury not empanelled by a
sheriff, but by a juggler."

This was touching the high sheriff on a tender place,
and he immediately called out for the protection of the
court. Whereupon Baron Lefroy interposed, and did
gravely and deliberately, as is the manner of judges,
declare that the imputation which had just been made on
the character of that excellent official, the high sheriff,
was most "unwarranted and unfounded." He adduced,
however, no reason in support of that declaration—not a
shadow of proof that the conduct of the aforesaid official
was fair or honest—but proceeded to say that the jury
had found the prisoner guilty on evidence supplied by
his own writings, some of which his lordship, with a
proper expression of horror on his countenance, proceeded to read from his notes. In one of the prisoner's
publications, he said, there appeared the following passage: "There is now growing on the soil of Ireland a
wealth of grain, and roots, and cattle, far more than
enough to sustain in life and comfort all the inhabitants
of the island. That wealth must not leave us another
year, not until every grain of it is fought for in every
stage, from the tying of the sheaf to the loading of the
ship; and the effort necessary to that simple act of self-
preservation will, at one and the same blow, prostrate
British dominion and landlordism together." In reference to this piece of writing, and many others of a
similar nature, his lordship remarked that no effort had
been made to show that the prisoner was not responsible
for them; it was only contended that they involved no
moral guilt. But the law was to be vindicated; and it
now became his duty to pronounce the sentence of the
court, which was—that the prisoner be transported

beyond the seas for a term of fourteen years. The severity of the sentence occasioned general surprise; a general suspiration and low murmur were heard through the court. Then there was a stillness as of death, in the midst of which the tones of John Mitchel's voice rang out clearly, as he said:—

"The law has now done its part, and the Queen of England, her crown and government in Ireland, are now secure, pursuant to act of parliament. I have done my part also. Three months ago I promised Lord Clarendon and his government in this country, that I would provoke him into his courts of justice, as places of this kind are called, and that I would force him publicly and notoriously to pack a jury against me to convict me, or else that I would walk a free man out of this court, and provoke him to a contest in another field. My lord, I knew I was setting my life on that cast, but I knew that in either event the victory should be with me, and it is with me. Neither the jury, nor the judges, nor any other man in this court presumes to imagine that it is a criminal who stands in this dock."

Here there were murmurs of applause, which caused the criers to call out for "Silence!" and the police to look fiercely on the people around them. Mr. Mitchel resumed:—

"I have shown what the law is made of in Ireland. I have shown that her Majesty's government sustains itself in Ireland by packed juries, by partisan judges, by perjured sheriffs."

Baron Lefroy enterposed. The court could not sit there to hear the prisoner arraign the jurors, the sheriffs, the courts, and the tenure by which England holds this country. Again the prisoner spoke:—

"I have acted all through this business, from the first, under a strong sense of duty. I do not repent anything that I have done, and I believe that the course which I have opened is only commenced, The Roman who saw his hand burning to ashes before the tyrant, promised that three hundred should follow out his enterprise. Can I not promise for one, for two, for three, aye for hundreds?"

As he uttered these words, Mr. Mitchel looked proudly into the faces of the friends near him, and around the court. His words and his glance were immediately responded to by an outburst of passionate voices from all parts of the building, exclaiming—"For me! for me! promise for me, Mitchel! and for me!" And then came a clapping of hands and a stamping of feet, that sounded loud and sharp as a discharge of musketry, followed by a shout like a peal of thunder. John Martin, Thomas Francis Meagher, and Devin Reilly, with other gentlemen who stood close by the dock, reached over it to grasp the hand of the new-made felon. The aspect of affairs looked alarming for a moment. The policemen laid violent hands on the persons near them, and pulled them about. Mr. Meagher and Mr. Doheny were taken into custody. Baron Lefroy, in a high state of excitement, cried out—"Officer! remove Mr. Mitchel!" and then, with his brother judges, retired hurriedly from the bench. The turnkeys who stood in the dock with Mr. Mitchel motioned to him that he was to move; he took a step or two down the little stairs under the flooring of the court-house, and his friends saw him no more.

He was led through the passages that communicated with the adjoining prison, and ushered into a dark and narrow cell, in which, however, his detention was of but a few hours' duration. At four o'clock in the evening of that day—May 27th, 1848—the prison van, escorted by a large force of mounted police and dragoons, with drawn sabres, drove up to the prison gate. It was opened, and forth walked John Mitchel—*in fetters*. A heavy chain was attached to his right leg by a shackle at the ankle; the other end was to have been attached to the left leg, but, as the jailors had not time to effect the connection when the order came for the removal of the prisoner, they bade him take it in his hand, and it was in this plight, with a festoon of iron from his hand to his foot, he passed from the prison into the street—repeating, mayhap, to his own heart the words uttered by Wolfe Tone in circumstances not dissimilar:—"For the cause which I have embraced, I feel prouder to wear these chains, than if I were decorated with the star and garter of England." Four or five police inspectors assisted him to step into the van, the door was closed after him, the word was given to the escort, and off went the cavalcade at a thundering pace to the North-wall, where a government steamer, the *Shearwater*, was lying with her steam up, in readiness to receive him. He clambered the side-ladder of the steamer with some assistance; on reaching the dock, the chains tripped him and he fell forward. Scarcely was he on his feet again, when the paddles of the steamer were beating the water, and the vessel was moving from the shores of that "Isle of Destiny," which he loved so well, and a sight of which has never since gladdened the eyes of John Mitchel.

The history of Mr. Mitchel's subsequent career, which has been an eventful one, does not rightly fall within the scope of this work. Suffice it to say that on June the 1st, 1848, he was placed on board the *Scourge* man-of-war, which then sailed off for Bermuda. There Mr. Mitchel was retained on board a penal ship, or "hulk," until April 22d, 1849, when he was transferred to the ship *Neptune*, on her way from England to the Cape of Good Hope, whither she was taking a batch of British convicts. Those convicts the colonists at the Cape refused to receive into their country, and a long struggle ensued between them and the commander of the *Neptune*, who wished to deposit his cargo according to instructions. The colonists were willing to make an exception in the case of Mr. Mitchel, but the naval officer could not think of making any compromise in the matter. The end of the contest was that the vessel, with her cargo of convicts on board, sailed on February 19th, 1850, for Van Diemen's Land, where she arrived on April 7th of the same year. In consideration of the hardships they had undergone by reason of their detention at the Cape, the government granted a conditional pardon to all the criminal convicts on their arrival at Hobart Town. It set them free on the condition that they should not return to the "United Kingdom." Mr. Mitchel and the other political convicts were less mercifully treated. It was not until the year 1854 that a similar amount of freedom was given to these gentlemen. Some months previous to the arrival of Mr. Mitchel at Hobart Town, his friends, William Smith O'Brien, John Martin, Thomas F. Meagher, Kevin Izod O'Doherty, Terence Bellew MacManus, and Patrick O'Donoghue, had reached the same place, there to serve out the various terms of transportation to which they had been sentenced. All, except Mr. O'Brien, who had refused to enter into these arrangements, were at that time on parole—living, however, in separate and limited districts, and no two of them nearer than thirty or forty miles. On his landing from the *Neptune*, Mr. Mitchel, in consideration of the delicate state of his health, was allowed to reside with Mr. Martin in the Bothwell district.

In the summer of the year 1853, a number of Irish gentlemen in America took measures to effect the release of one or more of the Irish patriots from Van Diemen's Land, and Mr. P. J. Smyth sailed from New York on that patriotic mission. Arrived in Van Diemen's Land, the authorities, who seemed to have suspicion of his business, placed him under arrest, from which he was released after three days' detention. The friends soon managed to meet and come to an understanding as to their plan of future operations, in conformity with which, Mr. Mitchel penned the following letter to the governor of the island:—

"Bothwell, 8th June, 1853.

"SIR—I hereby resign the 'comparative liberty,' called 'ticket-of-leave,' and revoke my parole of honor. I shall forthwith present myself before the police magistrate of Bothwell, at his police office, show him this letter, and offer myself to be taken into custody. I am, sir, your obedient servant,

"JOHN MITCHEL."

On the next day, June the 9th, Mr. Mitchel and Mr. Smyth went to the police office, saw the magistrate with his attending constables; handed him the letter, waited until he had read its contents, addressed to him a verbal statement to the same effect, and, while he appeared to be paralyzed with astonishment, and uncertain what to do, touched their hats to him and left the office. Chase after them was vain, as they had mounted a pair of fleet steeds after leaving the presence of his worship; but it was not until six weeks afterwards that they were able to get shipping and leave the island. On the 12th of October, 1853, Mr. Mitchel was landed safe in California —to the intense delight of his countrymen throughout the American States, who celebrated the event by many joyful banquets.

Since then, Mr. Mitchel has occupied himself mainly with the press. He started the *Citizen* in New York, and subsequently, at Knoxville, Tennessee, the *Southern Citizen*. As editor of the *Richmond Examiner* during the American civil war, he ably supported the Southern cause, to which he gave a still stronger pledge of his attachment in the services and the lives of two of his brave sons. One of these gentlemen, Mr. William Mitchel, was killed at the battle of Gettysburg; the other, Captain John Mitchel, who had been placed in command of the important position of Fort Sumter, was shot, on the parapet of that work, on July 19th, 1864. Shortly after the close of the war, Mr. John Mitchel was taken prisoner by the Federal government; but after undergoing an imprisonment of some months his release was ordered by President Johnson, acting on the solicitation of a large and influential deputation of Irishmen. In the latter part of the year 1867, turning to the press again, he started the *Irish Citizen* at New York, and in that journal, at the date of this writing, he continues to wield his trenchant pen on behalf of the Irish cause. To that cause, through all the lapse of time, and change of scene, and vicissitude of fortune which he has known, his heart has remained for ever true. He has suffered much for it; that he may live to see it triumphant, is a prayer which finds an echo in the hearts of all his fellow-countrymen.

We have written of Mr. Mitchel only in reference to his political career; but we can, without trenching in any degree on the domain of private life, supply some additional and authentic details which will be of interest to Irish readers. The distinguished subject of our memoir was born at Camnish, near Dungiven, in the county of Derry, on the 3d of November, 1815.

His father was the Rev. John Mitchel, at that time Presbyterian Minister of Dungiven, and a good patriot, too, having been—as we learn from a statement casually made by Mr. Mitchel in Conciliation Hall—one of the United Irishmen of 1798. The maiden name of his mother, who also came of a Presbyterian and county Derry family, was Mary Haslitt. At Newry, whither the Rev. Mr. Mitchel removed in the year 1823, and where he continued to reside till his death in 1843, young John Mitchel was sent to the school of Dr. David Henderson, from which he entered Trinity College, Dublin, about the year 1830 or 1831. He did not reside within the college, but kept his terms by coming up from the country to attend the quarterly examinations. Though he did not distinguish himself in his college course, and had paid no more attention to the books prescribed for his studies than seemed necessary for passing his examinations respectably, John Mitchel was known to his intimate friends to be a fine scholar and possessed of rare ability. While still a college student, he was bound apprentice to a solicitor in Newry. Before the completion of his apprenticeship, in the year 1835, he married Jane Verner, a young lady of remarkable beauty, and only sixteen years of age at the time, a daughter of Captain James Verner. Not long after his marriage he entered into partnership in his profession, and in conformity with the arrangements agreed upon, went to reside at Banbridge, a town ten miles north of Newry, where he continued to practise as a solicitor until the death of Thomas Davis in 1845. He had been an occasional contributor to the *Nation* almost from the date of its foundation; its editors recognized at once his splendid literary powers, and when the "Library of Ireland" was projected, pressed him to write one of the volumes, suggesting as his subject the Life of Hugh O'Neill. How ably he fulfilled the task is known to his countrymen, who rightly regard the volume as one of the most valuable of the whole series. When death removed the amiable and gifted Thomas Davis from the scene of his labors, Mr. Duffy invited John Mitchel, as the man most worthy of all in Ireland, to take his place. Mr. Mitchel regarded the invitation as the call of his country. He gave up his professional business in Banbridge, removed with his wife and family to Dublin, and there, throwing himself heart and soul into the cause, fought it out boldly and impetuously until the day when, bound in British chains, "the enemy" bore him off from Ireland.

JOHN MARTIN.

WHEN the law had consummated its crime, and the doom of the felon was pronounced against John Mitchel, there stood in the group that pressed round him in the dock and echoed back the assurances which he flung as a last defiance at his foes, a thoughtful, delicate-looking, but resolute young Irishman, whose voice perhaps was not the loudest of those that spoke there, but whose heart throbbed responsively to his words, and for whom the final message of the unconquerable rebel possessed a meaning and significance that gave it the force of a special revelation. "Promise for me, Mitchel," they cried out, but he had no need to join in that request; he had no need to intimate to Mr. Mitchel his willingness to follow out the enterprise which that fearless patriot had so boldly commenced. On the previous day, sitting with the prisoner in his gloomy cell, John Martin of Loughorne had decided on the course which he would take in the event of the suppression of the *United Irishman* and the transportation of its editor. He would start a successor to that journal, and take the place of his dear friend at the post of danger. It was a noble resolve, deliberately taken, and resolutely and faithfully was it carried out. None can read the history of that act of daring, and of the life of sacrifice by which it has been followed, and not agree with us that, while the memories of Tone, of Emmet, and of Russell, are cherished in Ireland, the name of John Martin ought not to be forgotten.

A few days subsequent to that memorable scene in Green-street court-house, John Martin quitted his comfortable home and the green slopes of Loughorne, separated himself from the friends he loved and the relatives who idolized him, and entered on the stormy career of a national leader and journalist, at a time when to advocate the principles of nationality was to incur the ferocious hostility of a government whose thirst for vengeance was only whetted by the transportation of John Mitchel. He knew the danger he was braving; he knew that the path on which he entered led down to suffering and ruin; he stood in the gap from which Mitchel had been hurled, with a full consciousness of the perils of the situation; but unflinchingly and unhesitatingly as the martyr goes to his death, he threw himself into the thinning ranks of the patriot leaders; and when the event that he anticipated arrived, and the prison gates opened to receive him—then, too, in the midst of indignities and privations—he displayed an imperturbable firmness and contempt for physical suffering, that showed how powerless persecution is to subdue the spirit that self-conscious righteousness sustains.

His history, previous to the conviction of his friend and school-fellow, John Mitchel, if it includes no events of public importance, possesses for us all the interest that attaches to the early life of a good and remarkable man. John Martin was born at Loughorne, in the lordship of Newry, Co. Down, on the 8th of September, 1812; being the eldest son of Samuel Martin and Jane Harshaw, both natives of that neighborhood, and members of Presbyterian families settled there for many generations. About the time of his birth, his father purchased the fee-simple of the large farm which he had previously rented, and two of his uncles having made similar investments, the family became proprietors of the townland on which they lived. Mr. Samuel Martin, who died in 1831, divided his attention between the management of the linen business—a branch of industry in which the family had partly occupied themselves for some generations—and the care of his land. His family consisted of nine children, of whom John Martin—the subject of our sketch—was the second-born. The principles of his family, if they could not be said to possess the hue of nationality, were at least liberal and tolerant. In '98, the Martins of Loughorne were stern opponents of the United Irishmen; but in '82, his father and uncles were enrolled amongst the volunteers, and the Act of Union was opposed by them as a national calamity. It was from his good mother, however, a lady of refined taste and remarkable mental culture, that young John derived his inclination for literary pursuits, and learned the maxims of justice and equality that swayed him through life. He speedily discarded the prejudices against Catholic Emancipation which were not altogether unknown amongst his family, and which even found some favor with himself in the unreflecting days of boyhood. The natural tendency of his mind, however, was as true to the principles of justice as the needle to the pole; and the quiet rebuke that one day fell from his uncle—" What! John, would you not give your Catholic fellow-countrymen the same rights that you enjoy yourself?"—having set him a-thinking for the first time on the subject, he soon formed opinions more in consonance with liberality and fair play.

When about twelve years of age, young Martin was sent to the school of Dr. Henderson at Newry, where he first became acquainted with John Mitchel, then attending the same seminary as a day scholar. We next find John Martin an extern student of Trinity College, and a year after the death of his father he took out his degree in Arts. He was now twenty years old, and up to this time had suffered much from a constitutional affection, being subject from infancy to fits of spasmodic asthma. Strange to say, the disease which troubled him at frequent recurring intervals at home, seldom attacked him when away from Loughorne, and partly for the purpose of escaping it, he took up his residence in Dublin in 1833, and devoted himself to the study of medicine. He never meditated earning his living by the profession, but he longed for the opportunity of assuaging the sufferings of the afflicted poor. The air of the dissecting-room, however, was too much for Martin's delicate nervous organization; the kindly encouragement of his fellow-students failed to induce him to breathe its fetid atmosphere a second time, and he was forced to content himself with a theoretical knowledge of the profession. By diligent study and with the assistance of lectures, anatomical plates, etc., he managed to conquer the difficulty; and he had obtained nearly all the certificates necessary for taking out a medical degree, when he was recalled in 1835 to Loughorne, by the death of his uncle John, whose house and lands he inherited.

During the four years following he lived at Loughorne, discharging the duties of a resident country gentleman as they are seldom performed in Ireland, and endearing himself to all classes, but particularly to the poor, by his gentle disposition, purity of mind, and benevolence of heart. In him the afflicted and the poverty-stricken ever found a sympathizing friend; and if none of the rewards which the ruling faction were ready to shower on the Irishman of his position who looked to the Castle for inspiration, fell to his share, he enjoyed a recompense more precious in the prayers and the blessings of the poor. The steps of his door were crowded with the patients who flocked to him for advice, and for whom he prescribed gratuitously—not without some reluctance, however, arising from distrust of his own abilities and an unwillingness to interfere with the practice of the regular profession. But the diffidence with which he regarded his own efforts was not shared by the people of the district. Their faith in his professional skill was unbounded, and perhaps the confidence which they felt in his power contributed in some measure to the success that attended his practice.

In 1839 Mr. Martin sailed from Bristol to New York, and travelled thence to the extreme west of Upper Canada, to visit a relative who had settled there. On that occasion he was absent from Ireland nearly twelve months, and during his stay in America he made some tours in Canada and the Northern States, visiting the Falls, Toronto, Montreal, Philadelphia, New York, Washington, Pittsburg, and Cleveland. In 1841 he made a brief continental tour, and visited the chief points of attraction along the Rhine. During this time Mr. Martin's political ideas became developed and expanded, and though, like Smith O'Brien, he at first withheld his sympathies from the Repeal. agitation, in a

short time he became impressed with the justice of the
national demand for independence. His retiring disposition kept him from appearing very prominently before
the public; but the value of his adhesion to the Repeal
Association was felt to be great by those who knew his
uprightness, his disinterestedness, and his ability.

When the suicidal policy of O'Connell drove the Confederates from Conciliation Hall, John Martin was not
a silent spectator of the crisis, and in consequence of
the manly sentiments he expressed with reference to the
treatment to which the Young Ireland party had been
subjected, he ceased to be a member of the Association.
There was another cause, too, for his secession. A standing taunt in the mouth of the English press was, that
O'Connell pocketed the peoples' money and took care to
let nobody know what he did with it. To put an end
to this reproach, Mr. Martin asked that the accounts of
the Association should be published. "Publish the accounts!" shrieked the well-paid gang that marred the
influence and traded in the politics of O'Connell,—"monstrous!" and they silenced the troublesome purist by
suppressing his letters and expelling him from the Association. In the ranks of the Confederates, however,
Martin found more congenial society; amongst them he
found men as earnest, as sincere, and as single-minded
as himself, and by them the full worth of his character
was soon appreciated. He frequently attended their
meetings, and he it was who filled the chair during the
prolonged debates that ended with the temporary withdrawal of Mitchel from the Confederation. When the
United Irishman was started he became a contributor to
its columns, and he continued to write in its pages up to
the date of its suppression, and the conviction of its
editor and proprietor.

There were many noble and excellent qualities which
the friends of John Martin knew him to possess. Rectitude of principle, abhorrence of injustice and intoler-
ance, deep love of country, the purity and earnestness
of a saint, allied with the kindliness and inoffensiveness of childhood; amiability and disinterestedness,

together with a perfect abnegation of self, and total freedom from the vanity which affected a few of his compatriots—these they gave him credit for; but they were totally unprepared for the lionlike courage, the boldness, and the promptitude displayed by him, when the government, by the conviction of Mitchel, flung down the gauntlet to the people of Ireland. Hastily settling up his worldly accounts in the North, he returned to Dublin, to stake his fortune and his life in the cause which he had promised to serve. The *United Irishman* was gone, but Martin had undertaken that its place in Irish journalism should not be vacant; and a few weeks after the office in Trinity-street was sacked, he reoccupied the violated and empty rooms, and issued therefrom the first number of the *Irish Felon*. There was no halting-place in Irish journalism then. The *Nation* had already flung peace and conciliation and "balmy forgiveness" to the winds, and advocated the creed of the sword. The scandalous means used to procure a verdict of guilty against Mitchel tore to tatters the last rag of the constitution in Ireland. It was idle to dictate observance of the law which the government themselves were engaged in violating, and the *Nation* was not the journal to brook the tyranny of the authorities. With a spirit that cannot be too highly praised, it called for the overthrow of the government that had sent Mitchel in chains into banishment, and summoned the people of Ireland to prepare to assert their rights by the only means now left them—the bullet and the pike. And the eyes of men whose hearts were "weary waiting for the fray," began to glisten as they read the burning words of poetry and prose in which the *Nation* preached the gospel of liberty. It was to take its side by that journal, and to rival it in the boldness of its language and the spirit of its arguments, that the *Irish Felon* was established; and it executed its mission well. "I do not love political agitation for its own sake," exclaimed Martin, in his opening address in the first number. "At best I regard it as a necessary evil; and if I were not convinced that my countrymen are determined on

vindicating their rights, and that they really intend to
free themselves, I would at once withdraw from the
struggle and leave my native land forever. I could not
live in Ireland and derive my means of life as a member
of the Irish community, without feeling a citizen's re-
sponsibilities in Irish public affairs. Those responsi-
bilities involve the guilt of national robbery and murder
—of a system which arrays the classes of our people
against each other's prosperity and very lives, like beasts
of prey, or rather like famishing sailors on a wreck—
of the debasement and moral ruin of a people endowed
by God with surpassing resources for the attainment of
human happiness and human dignity. I cannot be loyal
to a system of meanness, terror, and corruption, although
it usurp the title and assume the form of a 'government.' So long as such a 'government' presumes to
injure and insult me, and those in whose prosperity I
am involved, I must offer to it all the resistance in my
power. But if I despaired of successful resistance, I
would certainly remove myself from under such a
'government's'. actual authority ; that I do not exile
myself is a proof that I hope to witness the overthrow,
and assist in the overthrow, of the most abominable
tyranny the world now groans under—the British Imperial system. To gain permission for the Irish people
to care for their own lives, their own happiness and dignity—to abolish the political conditions which compel
the classes of our people to hate and to murder each
other, and which compel the Irish people to hate the very
name of the English—to end the reign of fraud, perjury,
corruption, and 'government' butchery, and to make
law, order, and peace possible in Ireland, the *Irish Felon*
takes its place amongst the combatants in the holy war
now waging in this island against foreign tyranny. In
conducting it my weapons shall be—*the truth, the whole
truth, and nothing but the truth, so help me God!*"

Such "open and avowed treason" as this could not
long continue to be published. Before the third number of
the *Felon* saw the light, a warrant for Mr. Martin's arrest
was in the hands of the detectives, and its fifth was its

last. On Saturday, July 8th, Mr. Martin surrendered himself into custody, having kept out of the way for a few days to prevent his being tried, under the "gagging act," at the Commission sitting when the warrant was issued, and which adjourned until August—the time fixed for the insurrection—in the interim. On the same day, Duffy, Williams, and O'Doherty were arrested. Martin was imprisoned in Newgate, but he continued to write from within his cell for the *Felon*, and its last number, published on July 22d, contains a spirited letter signed with his initials, which formed portion of the indictment against him on his trial. In this letter, Martin calls on his countrymen in impassioned words to "stand to their arms!" "Let them menace you," he writes from his dungeon, "with the hulks or the gibbet for daring to speak or write your love to Ireland. Let them threaten to mow you down with grape-shot, as they massacred your kindred with famine and plague. Spurn their brutal 'Acts of Parliament'—trample upon their lying proclamations—fear them not!"

On Tuesday, August 15th, John Martin's trial commenced in Green-street court-house, the indictment being for treason-felony. "Several of his tenantry," writes the special correspondent of the London *Morning Herald*, "came up to town to be present at his trial, and, as they hoped, at his escape; for they could not bring themselves to believe that a man so amiable, so gentle, and so pious, as they had so long known him, could be"—this is the Englishman's way of putting it—"an inciter to bloodshed. It is really melancholy," added the writer, "to hear the poor people of the neighborhood of Loughorne speak of their benefactor. He was ever ready to administer medicine and advice gratuitously to his poor neighbors and all who sought his assistance; and according to the reports I have received, he did an incalculable amount of good in his way. As a landlord, he was beloved by his tenantry for his kindness and liberality, while, from his suavity of manner and excellent qualities, he was a great favorite with the gentry around him."

At eight o'clock, P. M., on Thursday, August 17th, the jury came into court with a verdict of guilty against the prisoner, recommending him to mercy, on the grounds that the letter on which he was convicted was written from the prison, and penned under exciting circumstances. On the following day, Mr. Martin was brought up to receive sentence, and asked, after the usual form, whether he had anything to say against the sentence being pronounced? The papers of the time state that he appeared perfectly unmoved by the painful position in which he was placed—that he looked around the courthouse in a calm, composed, dignified manner, and then spoke the following reply in clear, unfaltering tones:—

"My lords:—1 have no imputation to cast upon the bench, neither have I anything to charge the jury with, of unfairness towards me. I think the judges desired to do their duty honestly as upright judges and men; and that the twelve men who were put into the box, as I believe, not to try, but to convict me, voted honestly, according to their prejudices. I have no personal enmity against the sheriff, sub-sheriff, or any of the gentlemen connected with the arrangement of the jury-panel—nor against the attorney-general, nor any other person engaged in the proceedings called my trial; *but, my lords, I consider that I have not been yet tried.* There have been certain formalities carried on here for three days regarding me, ending in a verdict of guilty : *but I have not been put upon my country*, as the constitution said to exist in Ireland requires. Twelve of my countrymen, 'indifferently chosen,' have not been put into that jury-box to try me, but twelve men who, I believe, have been selected by the parties who represent the crown, for the purpose of convicting and not of trying me. I believe they were put into that box, because the parties conducting the prosecution knew their political sentiments were hostile to mine, and because the matter at issue here is a political question—a matter of opinion, and not a matter of fact. I have nothing more to say as to the trial, except to repeat that, having watched the conduct of the judges, I consider them upright and honest men. I have this to add, that as to the charge I make with respect to the constitution of the panel and the selection of the jury, I have no legal evidence of the truth of my statement; but there is no one who has a moral doubt of it. Every person knows that what I have stated is the fact; and I would represent to the judges, most respectfully, that they, as upright and honorable men and judges, and as citizens, ought to see that the administration of justice in this country is above suspicion. I have nothing more to say with regard to the trial; but I would be thankful to the court for permission to say a few words in vindication of my character and motives, after sentence is passed."

Baron Pennefather:—"No; we will not hear anything from you after sentence."

Chief Baron:—"We cannot hear anything from you after sentence has been pronounced."

Mr. Martin:—"Then, my lords, permit me to say that, admitting the narrow and confined constitutionl doctrines which I have heard preached in this court to be right, *I am not guilty of the charge according to this act*. I did not intend to devise or levy war against the Queen, or to depose the Queen. In the article of mine on which the jury framed their verdict of guilty, which was written in prison, and published in the last number of my paper, what I desired to do was this—to advise and encourage my countrymen to keep their arms, because that is their inalienable right, which no act of parliament, no proclamation, can take away from them. It is, I repeat, their inalienable right. I advised them to keep their arms; and further, I advised them to use their arms, in their own defence, against all assailants—even assailants that might come to attack them, unconstitutionally and improperly using the Queen's name as their sanction. My object in all my proceedings has been simply to assist in establishing the national independence of Ireland, for the benefit of all the people of Ireland—noblemen, clergymen, judges, professional men—in fact, all Irishmen. I have sought that object: first, because I thought it was our right—because I think national independence is the right of the people of this country;' and secondly, I admit that, being a man who loved retirement, I never would have engaged in politics did I not think it was necessary to do all in my power to make an end of the horrible scenes that this country presents—the pauperism, starvation, and crime, and vice, and hatred of all classes against each other. I thought there should be an end to that horrible system, which, while it lasted, gave me no peace of mind; for I could not enjoy anything in my native country so long as I saw my countrymen forced to be vicious— forced to hate each other—and degraded to the level of paupers and brutes. That is the reason I engaged in politics. I acknowledge, as the solicitor-general has said, that I was but a weak assailant of the English power. I am not a good writer, and I am no orator. I had only two weeks' experience in conducting a newspaper until I was put into jail; but I am satisfied to direct the attention of my countrymen to everything I have written and said, and to rest my character on a fair and candid examination of what I have put forward as my opinions. I shall say nothing in vindication of my motives but this—that every fair and honest man, no matter how prejudiced he may be, if he calmly considers what I have written and said, will be satisfied that my motives were pure and honorable. I have nothing more to say."

Then the judge proceeded to pass sentence. In the course of his remarks he referred to the recommendation to mercy which came from the jury, whereupon Mr. Martin broke in. "I beg your lordship's pardon," he said, "I cannot condescend to accept 'mercy' where I believe I have been morally right; I want justice—not mercy." But he looked for it in vain.

"Transportation for ten years beyond the seas" is spoken by the lips of the judge, and the burlesque of justice is at an end. Mr. Martin heard the sentence with perfect composure and self-possession, though the faces of his brothers and friends standing by showed signs of the deepest emotion. "Remove the prisoner," were the next words uttered, and then John Martin, the pure-minded, the high-souled, and the good, was borne off to the convict's cell in Newgate.

Amongst the friends who clustered round the dock in which the patriot leader stood, and watched the progress of his trial with beating hearts, was Mr. James Martin, one of the prisoner's brothers. During the three long weary days occupied by the trial, his post had been by his brother's side, listening to the proceedings with the anxiety and solicitude which a brother alone can feel, and revealing by every line of his countenance the absorbing interest with which he regarded the issue. The verdict of the jury fell upon him with the bewildering shock of an avalanche. He was stunned, stupefied, amazed; he could hardly believe that he had heard the fatal words aright, and that "guilty" had been the verdict returned. *He* guilty! he whose life was studded by good deeds, as stars stud the wintry sky; *he* guilty, whose kindly heart had always a throb for the suffering and the unfortunate, whose hand was ever extended to shield the oppressed, to succor the friendless, and to shelter the homeless and the needy; *he* "inspired by the devil," whose career had been devoted to an attempt to redress the sufferings of his fellow-countrymen, and whose sole object in life seemed to be to abridge the sufferings of the Irish people, to plant the doctrines of peace and good-will in every heart, and to make Ireland the home of harmony and concord, by rendering her prosperous and free! It was a lie, a calumny, a brutal fabrication!

It was more than his sense of justice could endure: it was more than his hot Northern blood could tolerate. Beckoning a friend, he rushed with him into the street, and drove direct to the residence of Mr. Waterhouse, the foreman of the jury. The latter had barely returned from court, when he was waited upon by Mr. Martin, who indignantly charged him with having bullied the jury into recording a verdict of guilty—an accusation which current report made against him—and challenged the astonished juryman to mortal combat. Mr. Waterhouse was horror-struck by the proposal, to which he gasped out in response a threat to call in the police. He never heard of anything so terribly audacious. He, a loyal Castle tradesman, who had "well and truly" tried the case, according to the recognised acceptance of the words, and who had "true deliverance made," after the fashion in favor with the crown; he whose "perspicuity, wisdom, impartiality," etc., had been appealed to and reminded so often by the attorney-general, to be challenged to a hostile meeting, which might end, by leaving a bullet lodged in his invaluable body. The bare idea of it fairly took his breath away, and with the terrible vision of pistols and bloodshed before his mind, he rushed to the police office and had his indignant visitor arrested. On entering the Green-street courthouse next day, Mr. Waterhouse told his woful story to the judge. The judge was appalled by the disclosure; Mr. Martin was brought before him and sentenced to a month's imprisonment, besides being bound over to keep the peace towards Mr. Waterhouse and everyone else for a period of seven years.

A short time after Mr. John Martin's conviction, he and Kevin Izod O'Doherty were shipped off to Van Dieman's Land on board the *Elphinstone*, where they arrived in the month of November, 1849. O'Brien, Meagher, MacManus, and O'Donoghue had arrived at the same destination a few days before. Mr. Martin resided in the district assigned to him until the year 1854, when a pardon, on the condition of their not returning to Ireland or Great Britain, was granted to himself, O'Brien,

and O'Doherty, the only political prisoners in the country
at that time—MacManus, Meagher, O'Donoghue, and
Mitchel having previously escaped. Mr. O'Brien and Mr.
Martin sailed together in the *Norna* from Melbourne
for Ceylon, at which port they parted, Mr. O'Brien turning northward to Madras, while Mr. Martin came on *via*
Aden, Cairo, Alexandria, Malta, and Marseilles, to Paris,
where he arrived about the end of October, 1854. In
June, 1856, the government made the pardon of Messrs.
Martin, O'Brien, and O'Doherty, unconditional, and Mr.
Martin then hastened to pay a visit to his family from
whom he had been separated during eight years. After
a stay of a few months he went back to Paris, intending
to reside abroad during the remainder of his life, because
he could not voluntarily live under English rule in Ireland. But the death of a near and dear member of his
family, in October, 1858, imposed on him duties which
he could only discharge by residence in his own home,
and compelled him to terminate his exile. Living since
then in his own land, he has taken care to renew and continue his protests against the domination of England in
Ireland. In January, 1864, acting on the suggestion of
many well-known nationalists, he established in Dublin
a Repeal Association called "The National League."
The peculiar condition of Irish politics at the time was
unfavorable to any large extension of the society: but,
notwithstanding this circumstance, the League, by its
meetings and its publications, rendered good service to
the cause of Irish freedom. Mr. Martin has seen
many who once were loud and earnest in their professions of patriotism lose heart and grow cold in the service
of their country, but he does not weary of the good
work. Patiently and zealously he still continues to
labor in the national cause; his mission is not ended
yet; and with a constancy which lapse of years and
change of scene have not affected, he still clings to the
hope of Ireland's regeneration, and with voice and pen
supports the principles of patriotism for which he suffered.
The debt that Ireland owes to him will not easily be
acquitted; and if the bulk of his co-religionists are no

longer to be found within the national camp, we can almost forgive them their shortcomings, when we remember that, within our own generation, the Presbyterians of Ulster have given to Ireland two such men as John Martin and John Mitchel.

Mr. Martin's name will reappear farther on, in another portion of this work; for the occasion of which we have here treated was not the only one on which his patriotic words and actions brought upon him the attention of "the authorities," and subjected him to the troubles of a state prosecution.

WILLIAM S O'BRIEN.
JOHN MITCHEL.   JOHN MARTIN

W. S. O'BRIEN.

LOUDLY across the dark-flowing tide of the Liffey rolled the cheers of welcome and rejoicing that burst from Conciliation Hall on that memorable day in January, '44, when William Smith O'Brien first stood beneath its roof, and presided over a meeting of Repealers. Many a time had the walls of that historic building given back the cheers of the thousands who gathered there to revel in the promises of the Liberator; many a time had they vibrated to the enthusiasm of the Irishmen who met there to celebrate the progress of the movement which was to give freedom and prosperity to Ireland; but not even in those days of monster meetings and popular demonstrations had a warmer glow of satisfaction flushed the face of O'Connell, than when the descendant of the Munster Kings took his place amongst the Dublin Repealers. "I find it impossible," exclaimed the great Tribune, "to give adequate expression to the delight with which I hail Mr. O'Brien's presence in the Association. He now occupies his natural position—the position which, centuries ago, was occupied by his ancestor, Brian Boru. Whatever may become of *me*, it is a consolation to remember that Ireland will not be without a friend such as William Smith O'Brien, who, combining all the modern endowments of a highly-cultured mind, with intellectual gifts of the highest order, nervous eloquence, untiring energy, fervid love of country, and every other high qualification of a popular leader, is now where his friends would ever wish to see him—at the head of the Irish people." Six weeks before, a banquet had been given in Limerick to celebrate O'Brien's adhesion to the national cause, and on this occasion, too, O'Connell bore generous testimony to the value and importance of his accession. "His presence," said the Emancipator, in proposing Mr. O'Brien's health, "cannot prevent me here from expressing, on behalf of the universal people of Ireland, their admiration and delight at his conversion to their cause. Receive the benefactor of Ireland, as such a benefactor should be received. It is certain that our country will never be deserted as long as she has William Smith O'Brien as one of her leaders."

There was much to account for the tumult of rejoicing which hailed Smith O'Brien's entry within the ranks of the popular party. His lineage, his position, his influence, his stainless character, his abilities, and his worth, combined to fit him for the place which O'Connell assigned him, and to rally round him the affection and allegiance of the Irish people. No monarch in the world could trace his descent from a longer line of illustrious men; beside the roll of ancestry to which he could point, the oldest of European dynasties were things of a day. When the towering Pyramids that overlook the Nile were still new; before the Homeric ballads had yet been chanted in the streets of an Eastern city; before the foundations of the Parthenon were laid on the Acropolis; before the wandering sons of Æneas found a home in the valley of the Tiber, the chieftains of his house enjoyed the conqueror's fame, and his ancestors swayed the sceptre of Erin. Nor was he unworthy of the name and the fame of the O'Briens of Kincora. Clear-sighted and discerning; deeply endowed with calm sagacity and penetrating observance; pure-minded, eloquent, talented and chivalrous, he comprised within his nature the truest elements of the patriot, the scholar, and the statesman. Unfaltering attachment to the principles of justice, unswerving obedience to the dictates of honor, unalterable loyalty to rectitude and duty,—these were the characteristics that distinguished him; and these were the qualities that cast their redeeming light round his failings and his errors, and wrung from the bitterest of his foes the tribute due to suffering worth. If nobility of soul, if earnestness of heart and singleness of purpose, if unflinching and self-sacrificing patriotism, allied to zeal, courage, and ability, could have redeemed the Irish cause, it would not be left to us to mourn for it to-day; and instead of the melancholy story we have now to relate, it might be given to us to chronicle the regeneration of the Irish nation.

William Smith O'Brien was born at Dromoland, county Clare, on the 17th of October, 1803. He was the second son of Sir Edward O'Brien, and, on the death of his kinsman, the last Marquis of Thomond, his eldest brother became Baron of Inchiquin. He was educated at Harrow and Trinity College, Cambridge; but his English education, however much it might have colored his views during boyhood, did not seriously affect his innate love of justice, or warp the patriotic feelings which were developed in his earliest years. The associations into which he was cast, the tone of the society in which he moved, the politics of his family, and the modern traditions of his house, combined to throw him into the ranks of the people's enemies; and that these influences were not altogether barren of results is proved by the fact that O'Brien entered Parliament in 1826 as an anti-Repealer, and exerted himself to prevent the return of O'Connell at the memorable election for Clare. But O'Brien was no factious opponent of the national interests; even while he acted thus, he had the welfare of his country sincerely at heart; he steered according to his lights, and when time and experience showed the falseness of his views, he did not hesitate to renounce them. To this period of his political career Mr. O'Brien often adverted in after life, with the frankness and candor that distinguished him. "When the proposal to seek for a Repeal of the Act of Union was first seriously entertained," said O'Brien, "I used all the influence I possessed to discountenance the attempt. I did not consider that the circumstances and prospects of Ireland then justified the agitation of this question. Catholic Emancipation had been recently achieved, and I sincerely believed that from that epoch a new course of policy would be adopted towards Ireland. I persuaded myself that thenceforth the statesmen of Great Britain would spare no effort to repair the evils produced by centuries of misgovernment—that the Catholic and Protestant would be admitted to share on equal terms in all the advantages resulting from our constitutional form of government—that all traces of an ascendancy of race or creed would be effaced—that the institutions of Ireland would be gradually moulded so as to harmonize with the opinions of its inhabitants, and that, in regard of political rights, legislation for both kingdoms would be based upon the principle of perfect equality."

Fourteen years had elapsed from the date of Catholic Emancipation, when O'Brien startled the aristocrats of Ireland by renouncing his allegiance to their party, and throwing himself heart and soul into the vanguard of the people. He told his reasons for the change, in bold, convincing words. He had seen that his expectations of justice were false and delusive. "The feelings of the Irish nation," he said, "have been exasperated by every species of irritation and insult; every proposal tending to develop the sources of our industry—to raise the character and improve the condition of our population, has been discountenanced, distorted, or rejected. Ireland, instead of taking its place as an integral portion of the great empire which the valor of her sons has contributed to win, has been treated as a dependent tributary province; and at this moment, after forty-three years of nominal union, the affections of the two nations are so entirely alienated from each other, that England trusts for the maintenance of their connection, not to the attachment of the Irish people, but to the bayonets which menace our bosoms, and the cannon which she has planted in all our strongholds."

The prospects of the Repeal movement were not at their brightest when O'Brien entered Conciliation Hall. In England, and in Ireland too, the influence of O'Connell was on the wane, and with the dispersion of the multitudes that flocked on that Sunday morning in October, 1843, to listen to the Liberator on the plains of Clontarf, the peaceful policy which he advocated received its death-blow. Over O'Connell himself, and some of the most outspoken of his associates, a state prosecution was impending; and the arm of the government was already stretched out to crush the agitation whose object they detested, and whose strength they had begun to fear. The accession of O'Brien, however, the prestige of his name, and the influence of his example, was expected to do much towards reviving the drooping fortunes of the Association. Nor was the anticipation illusory. From the day on which O'Brien became a Repealer, down to the date of the secession, the strongest prop of Conciliation Hall was his presence and support; he failed, indeed, to counteract the corrupt influences that gnawed at the vitals of the Association and ultimately destroyed it; but while he remained within its ranks, the redeeming influence of his genius, his patriotism, and his worth, preserved it from the extinction towards which it was hastening.

At an early date the penetrating mind of O'Brien detected the existence of the evil which was afterwards to transform Conciliation Hall into a market for place-hunters. " I apprehend," said he, in a remarkable speech delivered in January, '46, " more danger to Repeal from the subtle influence of a Whig administration, than from the coercive measures of the Tories." And he was right. Day by day, the subtle influence which he dreaded did its blighting work; and the success of those who sought the destruction of the Repeal Association through the machinery of bribes and places was already apparent, when, on the 27th of July, 1846, O'Brien, accompanied by Mitchel, Meagher, Duffy, and others, arose in sorrow and indignation, and quitted the Conciliation Hall forever.

Six months later the Irish Confederation held its first meeting in the Round Room of the Rotundo. Meagher, Mitchel, Doheny, O'Brien, O'Gorman, Martin, and M'Gee were amongst the speakers; and amidst the ringing cheers of the densely thronged meeting, the establishment was decreed of the Irish Confederation, for the purpose—as the resolution declared—" of protecting our national interests, and obtaining the Legislative Independence of Ireland by the force of opinion, by the combination of all classes of Irishmen, and by the exercise of all the political, social, and moral influence within our reach." It will be seen that the means by which the Confederates proposed to gain their object, did not differ materially from the programme of the Repeal Association. But there was this distinction. Against place-hunting, and everything savoring of trafficking with the government, the Confederates resolutely set their faces; and in the next place, while prescribing to themselves nothing but peaceful and legal means for the accomplishment of their object, they scouted the ridiculous doctrine, that "liberty was not worth the shedding of a single drop of blood," and that circumstances might arise under which resort to the arbitration of the sword would be righteous and justifiable. In time, however, the Confederates took up a bolder and more dangerous position. As early as May, 1846, Lord John Russell spoke of the men who wrote in the pages of the *Nation*, and who subsequently became the leaders of the Confederation, "as a party looking to disturbance as its means, and having separation from England as its object." The description was false at the time, but, before two years had elapsed, its application became more accurate. A few men there were like Mitchel, who, from the birth of the Confederation, and perhaps before it, abandoned all expectation of redress through the medium of constitutional agitation; but it was not until the flames of revolution had wrapped the nations of the Continent in their fiery folds—until the barricades were up in every capital from Madrid to Vienna—and until the students' song of freedom was mingled with the pæan of victory on many a field of death—that the hearts of the Irish Confederates caught the flame, and that revolution, and revolution alone, became the goal of their endeavors. When Mitchel withdrew from the Confederation in March, 1848, the principles of constitutional action were still in the ascendancy; when he rejoined it a month later, the cry, "To the registries," was superseded by fiery appeals summoning the people to arms. In the first week of April, the doctrine which John Mitchel had long been propounding, found expression in the leading columns of the *Nation :*—" Ireland's necessity," said Duffy, "demands the desperate remedy of revolution." A few weeks later, the same declaration was made in the very citadel of the enemy's power. It was O'Brien who spoke, and his audience was the British House of Commons. With Messrs. Meagher and Hollywood, he had visited Paris to present an address of congratulation on behalf of the Irish people to the republican government; and on taking his seat in the House of Commons after his return, he found himself charged by the Ministers of the Crown with having gone to solicit armed intervention from France on behalf of the disaffected people of Ireland. O'Brien replied in a speech such as never was heard before or since within the walls of the House of Commons. In the midst of indescribable excitement and consternation, he proceeded to declare in calm, deliberate accents—" that if he was to be arraigned as a criminal, he would gladly endure the most ignominious death that could be inflicted on him rather than witness the sufferings and indignities he had seen inflicted by the British legislature on his countrymen. If it is a treason," he exclaimed, "to profess disloyalty to this House and to the government of Ireland, by the parliament of Great Britain—if that be treason, I avow it. Nay, more, I say it shall be the study of my life to overthrow the dominion of this parliament over Ireland." The yells and shouts with which these announcements were received shook the building in which he stood, and obliged him to remain silent for several moments after the delivery of each sentence; but when the uproar began to subside, the ringing tones of O'Brien rose again upon the air, and with the stoicism of a martyr, and the imperturbable courage of a hero, he proceeded. " Irish freedom," he said, "must be won by Irish courage. Every statesman in the civilized globe looks upon Ireland as you look upon Poland, and upon your connection as entirely analogous to that of Russia with Poland. I am here to night to tell you that, if you refuse our claims to legislative independence, you will have to encounter, during the present year, the chance of a Republic in Ireland."

O'Brien returned to Ireland, more endeared than ever to the hearts of his countrymen. And now the game was fairly afoot. Government and people viewed each other with steady and defiant glare, and girded up their loins for the struggle. On the one side, the Confederate clubs were organized with earnestness and vigor, and the spirit of the people awakened by a succession of stirring and glowing appeals. "What if we fail?" asked the *Nation;* and it answered the question by declaring unsuccessful resistance under the circumstances preferable to a degrading submission. "What if we *don't* fail?" was its next inquiry, and the answer was well calculated to arouse the patriots of Ireland to action. On the other hand, the authorities were not idle. Arms' Bills, Coercion Acts, and prosecutions followed each other in quick succession. Mitchel was arrested, convicted, and sent to Bermuda. Duffy, Martin, Meagher, Doheny, O'Doherty, and M'Gee were arrested—all of whom, except Duffy and Martin, were shortly afterwards liberated. Duffy's trial was fixed for August, and this was the time appointed by the Confederates for the outbreak of the insurrection. There were some who advocated a more prompt mode of action. At a meeting of the Confederates held on July 19th, after the greater portion of the country had been proclaimed, it was warmly debated whether an immediate appeal to arms should not be counselled. O'Brien and Dillon advocated delay; the harvest had not yet been reaped in; the clubs were not sufficiently organized throughout the country, and the people might easily conceal their arms until the hour arrived for striking a decisive blow. Against this policy a few of the more impetuous members protested. "You will wait," exclaimed Joe Brennan, "until you get arms from heaven, and angels to pull the triggers." But his advice was disregarded; and the meeting broke up with the understanding that, with the first glance of the harvest sun, the fires of insurrection were to blaze upon the hill-tops of Ireland, and that meanwhile organization and preparation were to engross the attention of the leaders. On Friday, July 21st, a war directory—consisting of Dillon, Reilly, O'Gorman, Meagher, and Father Kenyon—was appointed; and on the following morning O'Gorman started for Limerick, Doheny for Cashel, and O'Brien for Wexford, to prepare the people for the outbreak.

It was war to the knife, and every one knew it. The forces of the government in Ireland were hourly increased in Dublin—every available and commanding position was occupied and fortified. "In the Bank of Ireland," says one who watched the progress of affairs with attentive gaze, "soldiers as well as cashiers were ready to settle up accounts. The young artists of the Royal Hibernian Academy and Royal Dublin Society had to quit their easels to make way for the garrison. The squares of old Trinity College resounded with the tramp of daily reviews; the Custom House at last received some occupation by being turned into a camp. The Linen Hall, the Rotundo, Holmes' Hotel, Alborough House, Dycer's Stables, in Stephen's-green—every institution, literary, artistic, and commercial, was confiscated to powder and pipe-clay. The barracks were provisioned as if for a siege; cavalry horses were shod with plates of steel, to prevent their being injured and thrown into disorder by broken bottles, iron spikes, or the like; and the infantry were occupied in familiarizing themselves with the art of fusillading footpaths and thoroughfares. Arms were taken from the people, and the houses of loyal families stocked with the implements of war."

But the national leaders had calculated on the preparations of the government; they knew the full measure of its military power, and were not afraid to face it; but there was one blow which they had not foreseen, and which came on them with the shock of a thunderbolt. On the very morning that O'Brien left for Wexford, the news reached Dublin that a warrant had been issued for his arrest, and that the suspension of the *Habeas Corpus* Act was resolved on by the government. "It appears strangely unaccountable to me," was Meagher's reflection in after years, "that, whilst a consideration of our

position, our project, and our resources, was taking place;
whilst the stormy future on which we were entering
formed the subject of the most anxious conjecture, and
the danger of it fell like wintry shadows around us,—it
seems strangely unaccountable to me that not an eye was
turned to the facilities for the counteraction of our designs
which the government had at their disposal; that not a
word was uttered in anticipation of that bold, astounding
measure—the suspension of the *Habeas Corpus* Act—the
announcement of which broke upon us so suddenly.
The overlooking of it was a fatal inadvertence. Owing
to it we were routed without a struggle, and were led
into captivity without glory. We suffer not for a rebellion,
but a blunder."

The few of the Confederate leaders at large in Dublin
at the time—Duffy, Martin, Williams, and O'Doherty
were in Newgate—held a hurried council, and their plans
were speedily formed. They were to join Smith O'Brien
at once, and commence the insurrection in Kilkenny.
On the night of Saturday, July 22d, M'Gee left for
Scotland, to prepare the Irishmen of Glasgow for action;
and Meagher, Dillon, Reilly, MacManus, O'Donoghue, and
Leyne started southwards, to place themselves in communication with O'Brien. A week later, the last of the
national papers was suppressed, and the *Nation* went
down, sword in hand as a warrior might fall, with the
words of defiance upon its lips, and a prayer for the good
old cause floating upwards with its latest breath.

O'Brien was in bed when Meagher and Dillon arrived
at Balinkeele where he was stopping. The news of the
suspension of the *Habeas Corpus* Act, and of the plans
formed by the Confederates, were speedily communicated
to him. O'Brien manifested no surprise at the intelligence. He quietly remarked that the time for action
had arrived; and that every Irishman was now justified
in taking up arms against the government; dressed himself and set out, without losing an hour, to inaugurate
his hazardous enterprise at Enniscorthy. As the train
drove along, the three friends occupied themselves with
the important question where should they begin the out-

break. Wexford was mentioned, but the number of Confederates enrolled there were few, and the people were totally unprepared for a sudden appeal to arms; New Ross and Waterford were ruled against, because of the effectual assistance the gunboats stationed in the river could render the garrison of those towns. Against Kilkenny none of those objections applied; and the more they discussed the subject, the more convinced did they become that the most fitting cradle for the infant genius of Irish liberty was the ancient "city of the Confederates." " Perfectly safe from all war steamers, gunboats, and floating batteries; standing on the frontiers of the three best fighting counties in Ireland—Waterford, Wexford, and Tipperary—the peasantry of which could find no difficulty in pouring to its relief; possessing from three to five thousand Confederates, most of whom were understood to be armed; the most of the streets being narrow, and presenting on this account the greatest facilities for the erection of barricades; the barracks lying outside the town, and the line of communication between the powerful portions of the latter and the former being intercepted by the old bridge over the Nore, which might be easily defended, or, at the most, very speedily demolished; no place," says Meagher, "appeared to us to be better adapted for the first scene of the revolution."

Towards Kilkenny they therefore took their way, haranguing the people in soul-stirring addresses as they proceeded. At Enniscorthy and at Graigue-na-mana their appeals were responded to with fervent enthusiasm; they called on the people to form themselves into organized bodies, and prepare to coöperate with the insurgents who were shortly to unfurl their banner beneath the shadow of St. Canice's; and the crowds who hung on their words vowed their determination to do so. But in Kilkenny, as in every town they visited, the patriot leaders found the greatest disinclination to take the initiative in the holy war. There, as elsewhere, the people felt no unwillingness to fight; but they knew they were ill prepared for such an emergency, and fancied the first blow might be struck more effectively elsewhere. "Who will draw the first blood?" asked Finton Lalor in the last number of the *Felon;* and the question was a pertinent one: there was a decided reluctance to draw it. It is far from our intention to cast the slightest reflection on the spirit or courage of the nationalists of 1848. We know that it was no selfish regard for their own safety made the leaders in Wexford, Kilkenny, and elsewhere, shrink from counselling an immediate outbreak in their localities; the people, as the men who led them, looked forward to the rising of the harvest moon, and the cutting of their crops, as the precursors of the herald that was to summon them to arms. Their state of organization was lamentably deficient; anticipating a month of quiet preparation, they had neglected to procure arms up to the date of O'Brien's arrival, and a few weeks would at least be required to complete their arrangements. In Kilkenny, for instance, not one in every eight of the clubmen possessed a musket, and even their supply of pikes was miserably small. But they were ready to do all that in them lay; and when O'Brien, Dillon, and Meagher quitted Kilkenny on Monday, July 24th, they went in pursuance of an arrangement which was to bring them back to the city of the Nore before the lapse of a week. They were to drive into Tipperary, visit Carrick, Clonmel, and Cashel, and summon the people of those towns to arms. Then, after the lapse of a few days, they were to return at the head of their followers to Kilkenny, call out the clubs, barricade the streets, and from the council chambers of the Corporation issue the first revolutionary edict to the country. They hoped that a week later the signal fires of insurrection would be blazing from every hill-top in Ireland; and that the sunlight of freedom, for which so many generations of patriots had yearned, would soon flood glebe and town, the heather-clad mountains, and pleasant vales of Innisfail. *Diis aliter visum;* the vision that glittered before their longing eyes melted away with the smoke of the first insurgent shot; and instead of the laurel of the conqueror they were decked with the martyr's palm.

On arriving in Callan, the travellers were received with every demonstration of sympathy and welcome. The streets were blocked with masses of men that congregated to listen to their words. A large procession, headed by the temperance band, escorted them through the town, and a bonfire was lit in the centre of the main street. They told the people to provide themselves at once with arms, as in a few days they would be asked to march with the insurgent forces on Kilkenny—an announcement that was received with deafening applause. After a few hours' delay the three compatriots quitted Callan, and pursued their road to Carrick-on-Suir, where they arrived on the same evening and received a most enthusiastic reception. They addressed the excited multitude in impassioned words, promised to lead them to battle before many days, and called on them to practise patience and prudence in the interval. On the following day they quitted Carrick, and took their way to Mullinahone, when the people gathered in thousands to receive them. The number of men who assembled to meet them was between three and four thousand, of whom about three hundred were armed with guns, pistols, old swords, and pitchforks. The gathering was reviewed and drilled by the Confederates; and O'Brien, who wore a plaid scarf across his shoulders, and carried a pistol in his breast pocket, told them that Ireland would have a government of her own before many weeks.

On the evening of Tuesday, July 25th, the Confederate leaders arrived in Mullinahone, where they slept. On the following morning they addressed the people, who flocked into the town on hearing of their arrival. And here it was that O'Brien himself dealt the death-blow of the movement. The peasantry, who came from their distant homes to meet him, were left the whole day long without food or shelter. O'Brien himself gave what money he had to buy them bread; but he told them in future they should provide for themselves, as he could allow no one's property to be interfered with. Hungry and exhausted, the men who listened to him returned at night to their homes; they were sensible enough to perceive that insurrection within the lines laid down by their leaders was impossible; the news that they were expected to fight on empty stomachs was spread amongst the people, and from that day forward the number of O'Brien's followers dwindled away.

On July 26th, O'Brien and his party first visited the village of Ballingarry, where he was joined by MacManus, Doheny, Devin Reilly, and other prominent members of the Confederation. They took a survey of the village and its neighborhood; addressed the crowd from the piers of the chapel gate, and slept in the house of one of the village shopkeepers. Next day they returned to Mullinahone and thence to Killenaule, where they were received with every demonstration of welcome and rejoicing. Bouquets fell in showers upon O'Brien; addresses were read, and the fullest and warmest cooperation was freely promised by the excited crowds that congregated in the streets.

The exact position which the Confederates had now assumed towards the Crown and government is deserving of a moment's attention. Up to the last they carefully distinguished between resisting the acts of the government and disputing the sovereignty of the Queen. They regarded the suspension of the *Habeas Corpus* Act as unconstitutional in itself; and when O'Brien told her Majesty's Ministers in the House of Commons that it was they who were the traitors to the country, the Queen, and the Constitution, he did but express the opinions that underlay the whole policy of the Confederation. Even the passing of the *Habeas Corpus* Suspension Act was not quite sufficient to exhaust their patience; in order to fill the measure of the government's transgressions and justify a resort to arms against them, it was necessary, in the opinion of O'Brien and his associates, that the authorities should attempt to carry into operation the iniquitous law they had passed; the arrest of O'Brien was to be the signal for insurrection; meanwhile, they were satisfied with organizing their forces for the fray, and preparing for offering an effective resistance to the execution of the warrant, whenever it should make its appearance.

It was therefore that, when at Kilenaule, a small party of dragoons rode up to the town, they were suffered to proceed unmolested; at the first notice of their coming, the people rushed to the streets and hastily threw up a barricade to intercept them. Dillon commanded at the barricade; beside him stood Patrick O'Donoghue, and a young man whose career as a revolutionist was destined to extend far beyond the scenes in which he was then sharing; and whose name was one day to become first a terror to the government of England, and afterwards a by-word and a reproach amongst his countrymen. O'Donoghue and Stephens were both armed, and when the officer commanding the dragoons rode up to the barricade and demanded a passage, Stephens promptly covered him with his rifle, when his attention was arrested by a command from Dillon to ground his arms. The officer pledged his honor that he did not come with the object of arresting O'Brien; the barricade was taken down, and the dragoons passed scatheless through the town. Another opportunity had been lost, and the hearts of the most resolute of O'Brien's colleagues sunk lower than ever.

On Friday, O'Brien and his followers returned to Ballingarry, where they held a council on the prospects of the movement. It was clear that the case was a desperate one, that the chance of successful resistance was inevitably lost, and that nothing now awaited them—should they persist in their enterprise—but ruin and death. Only a couple of hundred men, wretchedly armed or not armed at all, adhered to their failing fortunes; and throughout the rest of the country the disaffected gave no sign. But O'Brien was unmovable; he would do his duty by his country, let the country answer for its duty towards him.

The collision came at last. On Saturday morning, July 29th, the constabulary of Thurles, Kilkenny, Cashel, and Callan, received orders to march on the village of Ballingarry, for the purpose of arresting Smith O'Brien. On the previous day the government had issued a proclamation, declaring him guilty of treasonable practices, by appearing in arms against the Queen, and offering a reward of £500 for his apprehension ; on the same day, £300 was offered for the arrest of Meagher, Dillon, and Doheny. Fired with the ambition of capturing the rebel party with his own forces, and winning for himself a deathless fame, Sub-inspector Trant marched out in hot haste from Callan, at the head of forty-six policemen, and directed his steps towards Ballingarry, where it was known to him that O'Brien was still stopping. Between twelve and one o'clock they arrived at Farrenrory, within three miles of the village of Ballingarry. On arriving at this point, the police found that effective measures had been adopted to dispute their further progress. Across the road before them a barricade had been thrown up, and behind it was arrayed a body of men numbering from three to four hundred. Fearing to face the insurgent forces, the police turned off to the right, and rushed towards a slate house which they saw in the distance. The people saw the object of the movement, and at once gave chase ; but the police had the advantage of a long start, and they succeeded in reaching the house and barring the door by which they entered, before their pursuers came up.

The die was cast, and the struggle, so long watched for and sighed for, had come at last. But it came not as it had been depicted by the tribune and poet; the vision that had flashed its radiancy before the eager eyes that hungered for the redemption of Ireland, differed sadly from the miserable reality. The serried ranks of glittering steel, the files of gallant pikemen, the armed columns of stalwart peasants, pouring through gap and river course, the glimmering camp fires quivering through the mist, the waving banners, and the flashing swords— where were they now? Where were the thousands of matchless mould, the men of strength and spirit, whose footfalls woke the echoes one month before in a hundred towns as they marched to the meetings at which they swore to strike down the oppressor? Only a few months had passed since two thousand determined men had passed in review before O'Brien at Cork ; scarcely six weeks since, similar sights were witnessed from the city of the Shannon to the winding reaches of the Boyne.

Everywhere there were strength and numbers, and resolution: where were they now in the supreme hour of the country's agony? A thousand times it had been sworn by tens of thousands of Irishmen, that the tocsin of battle would find them clustered round the good old flag to conquer or die beneath its shadow. And now, the hour had come, the flag of insurrection so often invoked was raised; but the patriot that raised it was left defenceless; he at least kept his word, but the promises on which he relied had broken like dissolving ice beneath his feet.

Around O'Brien there clustered, on that miserable noontide, about four hundred human beings—a weak, hungry and emaciated-looking throng for the most part; their half-naked forms, browned by the sun, and hardened by the winter winds—a motley gathering; amongst whom there were scores of fasting men, and hundreds through whose wretched dwellings the wind and rain found free ingress. They were poor, they were weak, they were ignorant, they were unarmed! but there was one thing at least which they possessed—that quality which Heaven bestowed on the Irish race, to gild and redeem their misfortunes. Of courage and resolution they had plenty: they understood little of the causes which led to the outbreak in which they participated; of Smith O'Brien or his associates, few of them had heard up to their appearance at Ballingarry; but they knew that it was against the forces of the British government and on behalf of Ireland's independence they were called on to fight, and in this cause they were ready to shed their blood. Such was the party whom O'Brien gazed upon, with a troubled mind, on that eventful day. Even the attached companions who had so far attended him were no longer by his side; MacManus, O'Donoghue, and Stephens were still there; but Meagher, Dillon, Doheny and O'Gorman had left at break of day to raise the standard of insurrection in other quarters. Of the men around him not more than twenty possessed firearms, about twice that number were armed with pikes and pitchforks; the remainder had but their naked hands and the stones they could gather by the wayside.

On the other side were forty-seven disciplined men splendidly armed, and ensconced, moreover, in a building possessing for the purpose of the hour the strength of a fortress. It stood on the brow of a hill overlooking the country in every direction ; it consisted of two stories with four windows in each, in front and rear ; each gable being also pierced by a pair of windows. There were six little children in the house when the police entered it. Their mother, the Widow M'Cormick, arrived on the spot immediately after the police had taken possession of her domicile, and addressing O'Brien, she besought him to save her little ones from danger. On O'Brien's chivalrous nature the appeal was not wasted. Heedless of the danger to which he exposed himself, he walked up to the window of the house. Standing at the open window with his breast within an inch of the bayonets of the two policemen who were on the inside, he called on them to give up their arms, and avoid a useless effusion of blood. "We are all Irishmen, boys," he said ; " I only want your arms and I'll protect your lives." The reply was a murderous volley poured on the gathering outside. Some half-drunken person in the crowd, it appears, had flung a stone at one of the windows, and the police needed no further provocation. The fire was returned by the insurgents, and O'Brien, seeing that his efforts to preserve peace were futile, quitted the window and rejoined his companions. For nearly two hours the firing continued ; the police, well sheltered from the possibility of injury, fired in all about 220 rounds, killing two men and wounding a number of others, amongst them James Stephens, who was shot in the thigh. Long before an equal number of shots were fired from without, the ammunition of the insurgents was exhausted, and they could only reply to the thick-falling bullets with the stones which the women present gathered for them in their aprons. It was clear that the house could not be stormed in this way ; and MacManus, with half-a-dozen resolute companions, rolled a cartload of hay up to the kitchen door with the intention of setting fire to it, and burning down the house. But O'Brien would not permit it ; there were children in the house, and their innocent lives should not be sacrificed. In vain did MacManus entreat him for permission to fire his pistol into the hay and kindle the ready flames. O'Brien was inexorable; and the first and last battle of the insurrection was lost and won. The Rev. Mr. Fitzgerald, the priest of the parish, and his curate, Father Maher, now appeared on the spot, and naturally used their influence to terminate the hopeless struggle. A large force of constabulary from Cashel soon after were seen approaching, and the people, who now saw the absolute uselessness of further resistance, broke away to the hills. The game was up; the banner of Irish independence had again sunk to the dust; and O'Brien, who had acted throughout with preternatural coolness, and whose face gave no more indications of emotion than if it had been chiselled in marble, turned from the scene with a broken heart. For a length of time he resisted the entreaties of his friends and refused to leave the spot; at last their solicitations prevailed, and mounting a horse taken from one of the police, he rode away.

From that fatal day down to the night of Saturday, August 5th, the police sought vainly for O'Brien. He slept in the peasant's hut on the mountain and he shared his scanty fare; a price which might well dazzle the senses of his poverty-stricken entertainers was on his head, and they knew it; over hillside and valley swarmed the host of spies, detectives, and policemen placed on his track; but no hand was raised to clutch the tempting bribe, no voice whispered the information for which the government proferred its gold. Amongst those, too, who took part in the affray at Ballingarry, and who subsequently were cast in shoals into prison, there were many from whom the government sought to extract information. Bribes and promises of pardon were held up before their eyes, menaces were freely resorted to, but amongst them the government sought vainly for an informer. Many of them died in captivity or in exile; their homes were broken up; their wives and children left destitute and friendless; but the words that would give them liberty and wealth, and terminate the sufferings of themselves and their families, were never spoken. Had O'Brien chosen to escape from the country like Doheny, O'Gorman, Dillon and others of his friends, it is probable he might have done so. He resolved, however, on facing the consequence of his acts, and sharing the fate of the Irish rebel to the bitter end.

The rain fell cold and drearily in the deserted streets of Thurles on the night which saw the arrest of William Smith O'Brien. Away over the shadowy mountains in the distance, the swimming vapors cast their shroud, wrapping in their chilling folds the homes of the hunger-stricken, prostrate race that sat by their fireless hearths. The autumn gale swept over the desolate land as if moaning at the ruin and misery that cursed it, and wailing the dirge of the high hopes and ardent purposes that a few short weeks before had gladdened the hearts of its people. Calmly and deliberately with folded arms O'Brien walked through the streets, and entered the Thurles railway station. He wore a black hat, a blue boat cloak, in which he was rather tightly muffled, and a light plaid trowsers; in his hand he carried a large black stick. He walked to the ticket office and paid his fare to Limerick; then wrapping himself up in his cloak and folding his arms, again he walked slowly along the platform awaiting the arrival of the train. He had resolved on surrendering himself for trial, but he wished to pay one last visit to his home and family. That gratification, however, was denied him, he was recognized by an Englisman named Hulme, a railway guard; in an instant he was surrounded by police and detectives, and torn off with brutal violence to gaol. That same night an express train flashed northwards through the fog and mist, bearing O'Brien a prisoner to Dublin. In the carriage in which he was placed sat General M'Donald, a Sub-inspector of constabulary and four policemen. On entering the train a pistol was placed at O'Brien's head, and he was commanded not to speak on peril of his life. Disregarding the injunction, he turned to M'Donald and asked him why he was so scandalously used. The general "had a duty to perform," and "his orders should be obeyed." " I have played the game and lost," said O'Brien, " and I am ready to pay the penalty of having failed; I hope that those who accompanied me may be dealt with in clemency; I care not what happens to myself."

On Thursday, September 28th, he was arraigned before a Special Commission, on a charge of high treason, at Clonmel. The trial lasted ten days, and ended in a verdict of guilty. It excited unprecedented interest throughout the country, and there are many of its incidents deserving of permanent record. Among the witnesses brought forward by the crown, was John O'Donnell, a comfortable farmer, who resided near Ballingarry. " I won't be sworn," he said on coming on the table, "or give evidence under any circumstances. You may bring me out and put a file of soldiers before me, and plant twenty bullets in my breast, but while I have a heart there, I will never swear for you." He expiated his patriotism by a long imprisonment. Nor was this a solitary instance of heroism; Richard Shea, a fine-looking young peasant, on being handed the book, declared that " he would not swear against such a gentleman," and he, too, was carried off to pass years within a British dungeon. But their sacrifices were unavailing; of evidence there was plenty against O'Brien; the police were overflowing with it, and the eloquence and ability of Whiteside were powerless to save him from a verdict of guilty.

The papers of the time are full of remarks on the firmness and self-possession displayed by O'Brien throughout the trial. Even the announcement of the verdict failed to disturb his composure, and when the usual question was asked, he replied with calmness and deliberation:

"My lords, it is not my intention to enter into any vindication of my conduct, however much I might have desired to avail myself of this opportunity of so doing. I am perfectly satisfied with the consciousness that I have performed my duty to my country—that I have done only that which, in my opinion, it was the duty of every Irishman to have done; and I am now prepared to abide the consequences of having performed my duty to my native land. Proceed with your sentence."

A deep murmur, followed by a burst of applause, filled the court as the noble patriot ceased speaking. Stepping back a pace, and folding his arms on his breast, O'Brien looked fixedly at the judge, and awaited the sentence of the court. Amidst the deepest sensation, Chief Justice Blackburne proceeded to discharge his task. O'Brien was sentenced to be hanged, beheaded, and quartered. "During the delivery of the sentence," says a writer of the period, "the most profound agitation pervaded the court; as it drew towards the close, the excitement became more marked and intense; but when the last barbarous provisions of the sentence were pronounced, the public feeling could only manifest itself by stifled sobs and broken murmurs of sympathy for the heroic man, who, alone, was unmoved during this awful scene, whose lips alone did not quiver, whose hand alone did not tremble, but whose heart beat with the calm pulsation of conscious guiltlessness and unsullied honor."

Nine months later (July 29th, 1849), the brig *Swift* sailed from Kingstown harbor, bearing O'Brien, Meagher, MacManus, and O'Donoghue into exile. In the month of November the vessel reached Hobart Town, where "tickets of leave" were offered to those gentlemen on condition of their residing each one within a certain district marked out for him, and giving their parole to make no attempt at escape while in possession of the ticket. Messrs. Meagher, MacManus, and O'Donoghue accepted these terms; Mr. O'Brien refused them, and was consequently sent to an island off the coast called Maria Island, where he was placed in strict custody and treated with great severity. The news of the indignities and the sufferings to which he was subjected, outraged the feelings of the Irish people in the neighboring country, and ere long his sympathizers in Tasmania laid a plan for his escape. They hired a vessel to lie off the coast on a particular day, and send a boat on shore to take off the prisoner, who had been informed of the plot, and had arranged to be in waiting for his deliverers. This design would unquestionably have succeeded but for the treachery of the captain of the ship, who, before sailing to the appointed spot, had given the government information of the intended escape and the manner of it. What occurred on the arrival of the vessel we shall relate in the words of Mr. Mitchel, who tells the story in his "Jail Journal" as he heard it from Mr. O'Brien himself:

"At last as he wandered on the shore and had almost given up all hope of the schooner, the schooner hove in sight. To give time for her approach, he walked into the woods for a space, that he might not alarm his guardian constable by his attention to her movements. Again he sauntered down towards the point with apparent carelessness, but with a beating heart. San Francisco was to be his first destination; and beyond that golden gate lay the great world, and home, and children, and an honorable life. The boat was coming, manned by three men; and he stepped proudly and resolutely to meet them on the shore. To be sure there was, somewhere behind him, one miserable constable with his miserable musket, but he had no doubt of being able to dispose of that difficulty with the aid of his allies, the boatmen. The boat could not get quite close to the beach, because they had to run her into a kind of cove where the water was calm and unencumbered with large tangled weeds. O'Brien, when he reached the beach, plunged into the water to prevent delay, and struggled through the thick, matted seaweed to the boat. The water was deeper than he expected, and when he came to the boat he needed the aid of the boatmen to climb over the gunwale. Instead of giving him this aid the rascals allowed him to flounder there, and kept looking to the shore, where the constable had by this time appeared with his musket. The moment he showed himself, the three boatmen cried out together, "We surrender!" and invited him on board; where he instantly took up a hatchet—no doubt provided by the ship for that purpose—and stove the boat. O'Brien saw he was betrayed, and on being ordered to move along with the constable and boatmen towards the station, he refused to stir—hoping, in fact, by his resistance, to provoke the constable to shoot him. However, the three boatmen seized on him, and lifted him up from the ground, and carried him wherever the constable ordered. His custody was thereafter made more rigorous, and he was shortly after removed from Maria Island to Port Arthur Station."

To this brief narrative the following "note" is appended in the work from which we have just quoted :—

" Ellis, the captain of the schooner, was some months after seized at San Francisco by Mr. MacManus and others, brought by night out of his ship, and carried into the country to undergo his trial under a tree, whereupon, if found guilty, he was destined to swing. MacManus set out his indictment ; and it proves how much Judge Lynch's method of administering justice in those early days of California excelled anything we know of law or justice in Ireland—that Ellis, for want of sufficient and satisfactory evidence then producible, was acquitted by that midnight court, under that convenient and tempting tree."

Port Arthur station, to which Mr. O'Brien was removed from Maria Island, was a place of punishment for convicts, who, while serving out their terms of transportation, had committed fresh offences against the law. After a detention there for some time, Mr. O'Brien, whose health was rapidly sinking under the rigors of his confinement, was induced, by letters from his political friends, to accept the ticket-of-leave, and avail of the comparative liberty which they enjoyed. The government, on his acceptance of their terms, placed him first in the district of New Norfolk, and subsequently in that of Avoca, where he remained until the conditional pardon, already mentioned in these columns, was granted in 1854. He then left Australia, went on to Madras, where he made a stay of about a month ; from thence he went to Paris and on to Brussels, where he was joined by his wife and children. He next made a tour in Greece, and was in that country when the unconditional pardon, which permitted him to return to his native land, was granted in the month of May, 1856, immediately after the close of the Crimean War. On Tuesday,

July 8th, 1856, Mr. O'Brien stood once more upon his native soil, after an exile of eight years. The news of his arrival was joyfully received by his fellow-countrymen, who welcomed him with every mark of respect and affection whenever he appeared among them. Thenceforward Mr. O'Brien took no active part in Irish politics, but he frequently offered advice and suggestions to his countrymen through the medium of letters and addresses in the *Nation*. In February, 1859, Mr. O'Brien made a voyage to America, and during the ensuing months travelled through a great portion of that country. After his return to Ireland he delivered, in November, 1859, an interesting series of lectures on his tour, in the Mechanics' Institute, Dublin. On July 1st, 1863, he lectured in the Rotundo, Dublin, for the benefit of a fund which was being raised for the relief of the wounded and destitute patriots of the Polish insurrection. In the early part of the year, 1864, the health of the illustrious patriot began rapidly to fail, and he was taken by his friends to England for a change of air. But the weight of many years of care and suffering was on him, and its effects could not be undone. On the 16th of June, 1864, at Bangor, the noble-hearted patriot breathed his last. His family had the honored remains brought to Ireland for interment in the old burial-ground of his fathers. On Thursday morning, at an early hour, they reached Dublin on board the *Cambria* steamer. It was known that his family wished that no public demonstration should be made at his funeral, but the feelings of the citizens who desired to pay a tribute of respect to his memory could not be repressed. In the grey hours of the morning the people in thousands assembled on the quays to await the arrival of the remains, and two steamers, which had been chartered for the purpose, proceeded, with large numbers on board, some distance into the harbor to meet the approaching vessel. All along the way, from the North Wall to the Kingsbridge railway station, the hearse bearing the patriot's body was accompanied by the procession of mourners, numbering about 15,000 men. At various stages of the journey similar scenes were witnessed. But the end was soon reached. In the churchyard of Rathronan, county Limerick, they laid him to rest. The green grass grows freshly around the vault in which he sleeps, and has long filled up the footprints of the multitude who broke the silence of that lonely spot by their sobs on the day he was buried; the winter gales will come and go, and, touched by the breath of spring, the wild flowers will blossom there through succeeding years, but never again will a purer spirit, a nobler mind, a patriot more brave, more chivalrous, or more true, give his heart to the cause of Ireland, than the silvered-haired, care-burdened gentleman whom they bore from Cahirmoyle to his grave on the 24th day of June, 1864.

THOMAS FRANCIS MEAGHER.

EARLY in 1846, when the Repeal Association was still powerful and great, and ere yet the country had ceased to throb to the magic of O'Connell's voice, there rose one day, from amongst those who crowded the platform of Conciliation Hall, a well-featured, gracefully-built, dark-eyed young gentleman, towards whom the faces of the assembly turned in curiosity, and whose accents, when he spoke, were those of a stranger to the audience. Few of them had heard of his name; not one of them—if the chairman, William Smith O'Brien, be excepted—had the faintest idea of the talents and capacities he possessed, and which were one day to enrapture and electrify his countrymen. He addressed the meeting on one of the passing topics of the day; something in his manner savoring of affectation, something in the semi-Saxon lisp that struggled through his low-toned utterances, something in the total lack of suitable gesture, gave his listeners at the outset an unfavorable impression of the young speaker. He was boyish, and, some did not scruple to hint, conceited; he had too much of the fine gentleman about his appearance, and too little of the native brogue and stirring declamation to which his listeners had been accustomed. The new man is a failure, was the first idea that suggested itself to the audience—but he was not; and when he resumed his seat, he had conquered all prejudices, and wrung the cheers of admiration from the meeting. Warming with his subject, and casting off the restraints that hampered his utterances at first, he poured forth a strain of genuine eloquence, vivified by the happiest allusions, and enriched by imagery and quotations as beautiful as they were appropriate, which startled the meeting from its indifference, and won for the young speaker the enthusiastic applause of his audience. O'Brien complimented him warmly on his success, and thus it was that the orator of young Ireland made his *début* on the political platform.

Meagher was not quite twenty-three years of age when his voice was first heard in Conciliation Hall. He was born in Waterford of an old Catholic family, which, through good and ill, had adhered to the national faith and the national cause; his school-boy days were passed partly at Clongowes-wood College, and partly under the superintendence of the Jesuit Fathers at Stoneyhurst in Lancashire. His early years gave few indications of the splendid wealth of genius that slumbered within his breast. He took little interest in his classical or mathematical studies; but he was an ardent student of English literature, and his compositions in poetry and prose invariably carried away the prize. He found his father fiillng the civic chair in Waterford, when he returned from Stoneyhurst to his native city. O'Connell was in the plenitude of his power; and from end to end of the land, the people were shaken by mighty thoughts and grand aspirations: with buoyant and unfaltering tread the nation seemed advancing towards the goal of freedom, and the manhood of Ireland seemed kindling at the flame which glowed before the altar of Liberty. Into the national movement young Meagher threw himself with the warmth and enthusiasm of his nature. At the early age of twenty we find him presiding over a meeting of Repealers in his native city, called to express sympathy with the state prisoners of '43 and he thenceforward became a diligent student of contemporary politics. He became known as an occasional speaker at local gatherings; but it was not until the event we have described that Meagher was fairly launched in the troubled tide of politics, and that his lot was cast for good or evil with the leaders of the national party.

Up to the date of secession Meagher was a frequent speaker at the meetings of the Repeal Association. Day by day his reputation as a speaker extended, until at length he grew to be recognized as the orator of the party, and the knowledge that he was expected to speak was sufficient to crowd Conciliation Hall to overflowing. When the influence of the *Nation* party began to be felt, and signs of disunion appeared on the horizon, O'Connell made a vigorous effort to detach Meagher from the side of Mitchel, Duffy, and O'Brien. "These Young Irelanders," he said, "will lead you into danger." "They may lead me into danger," replied Meagher, "but certainly not into dishonor."

Against the trafficking with the Whigs, which subsequently laid the Repeal Association in the dust, and shipwrecked a movement which might have ended in the disenthralment of Ireland, Meagher protested in words of prophetic warning. "The suspicion is abroad," he said, "that the national cause will be sacrificed to Whig supremacy, and that the people, who are now striding on to freedom, will be purchased back into factious vassalage. The Whigs calculate upon your apostasy, the Conservatives predict it." The place-beggars, who looked to the Whigs for position and wealth, murmured as they heard their treachery laid bare and their designs dissected in the impassioned appeals by which Meagher sought to recall them to the path of patriotism and duty. It was necessary for their ends that the bold denouncer of corruption, and the men who acted with him, should be driven from the Association; and to effect that object, O'Connell was hounded on to the step which ended in the secession. The "peace resolutions" were introduced, and Meagher found himself called on to subscribe to a doctrine which his soul abhorred—that the use of arms was at all times unjustifiable and immoral. The Lord Mayor was in the chair, and O'Brien, John O'Connell, Denis Reilly, Tom Steele, and John Mitchel had spoken, when Meagher rose to address the assembly. The speech he delivered on that occasion, for brilliancy and lyrical grandeur has never been surpassed. It won for him a reception far transcending that of Shiel or O'Connell as an orator; and it gave to him the title by which he was afterwards so often referred to—"Meagher of the sword."

He commenced by expressing his sense of gratitude, and his attachment to O'Connell. He said :—

"My lord, I am not ungrateful to the man who struck the fetters off my limbs while I was yet a child, and by whose influence my father, the first Catholic that did so for two hundred years, sat for the last two years in the civic chair of my native city. But, my lord," he continued, "the same God who gave to that great man the power to strike down one odious ascendancy in this country, and who enabled him to institute in this land the laws of religious equality— the same God gave to me a mind that is my own, a mind that has not been mortgaged to the opinion of any man or set of men; a mind that I was to use and not surrender."

Having thus vindicated freedom of opinion, the speaker went on to disclaim for himself the opinion that the Association ought to deviate from the strict path of legality. But he refused to accept the resolutions; because, he said, "there are times when arms alone will suffice, and when political ameliorations call for 'a drop of blood,' and for many thousand drops of blood." Then breaking forth into a strain of impassioned and dazzling oratory, he proceeded :—

"The soldier is proof against an argument—but he is not proof against a bullet. The man that will listen to reason—let him be reasoned with. But it is the weaponed arm of the patriot that can alone prevail against battalioned despotism.

"Then, my lord, I do not condemn the use of arms as immoral, nor do I conceive it profane to say that the King of Heaven—the Lord of Hosts! the God of Battles!—bestows his benediction upon those who unsheathe the sword in the hour of a nation's peril. From that evening on which, in the valley of Bethulia, he nerved the arm of the Jewish girl to smite the drunken tyrant in his tent, down to this our day, in which he has blessed the insurgent chivalry of the Belgian priest, His Almighty hand hath ever been stretched forth from His throne of light to consecrate the flag of freedom—to bless the patriot's sword! Be it in the defence or be it in the assertion of a people's liberty, I hail the sword as a sacred weapon; and if, my lord, it had sometimes taken the shape of the serpent, and reddened the shroud of the oppressor with too deep a dye, like the anointed rod of the High Priest, it has at other times, and as often, blossomed into celestial flowers to deck the freeman's brow.

"Abhor the sword—stigmatize the sword? No, my lord, for in the passes of the Tyrol it cut to pieces the banner of the Bavarian, and, through those cragged passes, struck a path to fame for the peasant insurrectionists of Inspruck! Abhor the sword—stigmatize the sword? No, my lord, for at its blow a giant nation started from the waters of the Atlantic, and by its redeeming magic, and in the quivering of its crimsoned light, the crippled colony sprang into the attitude of a proud Republic—prosperous, limitless, and invincible! Abhor the sword—stigmatize. the sword? No, my lord, for it swept the Dutch marauders out of the fine old towns of Belgium—scourged them back to their own phlegmatic swamps— and knocked their flag and sceptre, their laws and bayonets, into the sluggish waters of the Scheldt.

"My lord, I learned that it was the right of a nation to govern itself, not in this hall, but on the ramparts of Antwerp; I learned the first article of a nation's creed upon those ramparts, where freedom was justly estimated, and where the possession of the precious gift was purchased by the effusion of generous blood. My lord, I honor the Belgians for their courage and their daring, and I will not stigmatize the means by which they obtained a citizen-king, a chamber of deputies."

It was all he was permitted to say. With flushed face and excited gesture John O'Connell rose and declared he could not sit and listen to the expression of such sentiments. Either Mr. Meagher or he should leave the Association. O'Brien interceded to obtain a hearing for his young friend, and protested against Mr. O'Connell's attempts to silence him. But the appeal was wasted. O'Brien left the hall in disgust, and with him, Meagher, Duffy, Reilly, and Mitchel quitted it forever.

Meagher's subsequent career in Ireland is soon told. He was a regular attendant at the meetings of the Confederation, of which he was one of the founders; and the fame of his eloquence, his manly appearance, and the charms of his youthful frankness contributed immensely towards the growth of the new organization. He always acted with O'Brien, whom he loved in his inmost soul, but he was respected and admired by every section of nationalists, the Mitchelites, the Duffyites, and we might even say the O'Connellites. When the country began to feel the influence of the whirlwind of revolution which swept over the continent, overturning thrones and wrecking constitutions as if they were built of cardboard, Meagher shared the wild impulse of the hour, and played boldly for insurrection and separation. He was one of the three gentlemen appointed to present the address

from Ireland to the French Republican government in
1848; and in the speech delivered by him at the crowded
meeting in the Dublin Music Hall before his departure,
he counselled his countrymen to send a deputation to the
Queen, asking her to convene the Irish parliament in the
Irish capital. "If the claim be rejected," said Meagher,
"if the throne stand as a barrier between the Irish people
and the supreme right—then loyalty will be a crime, and
obedience to the executive will be treason to the country.
Depute your worthiest citizens to approach the throne,
and before that throne let the will of the Irish people
be uttered with dignity and decision. If nothing comes
of this," he added; "if the constitution opens to us no
path to freedom; if the Union be maintained in spite of
the will of the Irish people; if the government of Ireland insist on being a government of dragoons and bombardiers, of detectives and light infantry, then," he exclaimed in the midst of tumultuous cheering, "up with
the barricades, and invoke the God of Battles!"

While the republican spirit was in full glow in Ireland, Meagher astonished his friends by rushing down to
Waterford and offering himself as a candidate for the post
left vacant in parliament by the resignation of O'Connell.
By this time the Confederates had begun to despair of a
parliamentary policy, and they marvelled much to see
their young orator rush to the hustings, and throw himself into the confusion and turmoil of an election contest.
Que le diable allait il faire dans cette galere, muttered his
Dublin friends. Was not the time for hustings, orations,
and parliamentary agitation over now? Meagher, however, conceived, and perhaps wisely, that he could still
do some good for his country in the House of Commons.
He issued a noble address to the electors of his native
city, in which he asked for their support on the most
patriotic grounds. "I shall not meddle," he said, "with
English affairs. I shall take no part in the strife of parties—all factions are alike to me. I shall go to the
House of Commons to insist on the rights of this country
to be held, governed, and defended by its own citizens,
and by them alone. Whilst I live I shall never rest

satisfied until the kingdom of Ireland has won a parliament, an army, and a navy of her own." Mitchel strongly disapproved of his conduct. "If Mr. Meagher were in parliament," said the *United Irishman*, "men's eyes would be attracted thither once more; some hope of 'justice' might again revive in this too easily deluded people." The proper men to send to parliament were, according to Mitchel, "old placemen, pensioners, five pound Conciliation Hall Repealers." "We have no wish to dictate," concluded Mitchel in an article on the subject, full of the lurking satire and the quiet humor that leavened his writings; "but if the electors of Waterford have any confidence in us, we shall only say that we are for Costello!"

"Costello" was defeated, however, but so was Meagher. The Young Ireland champion was stigmatized as a Tory by the Whigs, and as a rebel by the Tories; if *the people*, as Mitchel remarks, had any power, he would have been elected by an overwhelming majority, but the people had no votes, and Sir Henry Winston Barron was returned. Meagher went back to Dublin almost a convert to Mitchel's views, leaving Whig, Tory, and West Briton to exult over his discomfiture.

We have already seen what Meagher did when the gauge of battle was thrown down, and when "the day all hearts to weigh" was imagined to have arrived, we have seen how he accompanied O'Brien in his expedition from Wexford to Kilkenny, and thence to Tipperary; and how, on the morning of July 29th, 1848, he left O'Brien at Ballingarry, little dreaming of the tragedy which was to make that day memorable, and expecting to be able to bring reinforcements to his leader from other quarters before the crisis came. He failed, however, in his effort to spread the flames of insurrection. The chilling news of O'Brien's defeat—distorted and exaggerated by hostile tongues—was before him everywhere, and even the most resolute of his sympathizers had sense enough to see that their opportunity, if it existed at all, had passed away. On the 12th day of August, 1848, Meagher was arrested on the roads between Clonoulty and Holycross, in Tip-

perary. He was walking along in company with Patrick
O'Donoghue and Maurice R. Leyne, two of his intimate
friends and fellow-outlaws, when a party of police passed
them by. Neither of the three was disguised, but Meagher
and Leyne wore frieze overcoats, which somewhat altered
their usual appearance. After a short time the police
returned; Meagher and his companions gave their real
names on being interrogated, and they were at once arrested and taken in triumph to Thurles. The three
friends bore their ill-fortune with what their captors must
have considered provoking nonchalance. Meagher smoked
a cigar on the way to the station, and the trio chatted as
gaily as if they were walking in safety on the free soil of
America, instead of being helpless prisoners on their way
to captivity and exile.

Meagher stood in the dock at Clonmel a week after
O'Brien had quitted it a convict. He was defended by
Mr. Whiteside and Isaac Butt, whose magnificent speech
in his defence was perhaps the most brilliant display of
forensic eloquence ever heard within the court in which
he stood. Of course the jury was packed (only eighteen
Catholics were named on a jury-panel of 300), and of course
the Crown carried its point. On the close of the sixth day
of the trial, the jury returned into court with a verdict of
"guilty," recommending the prisoner to mercy on the
ground of his youth.

Two days later he was brought back to the dock to
receive sentence. He was dressed in his usual style, appeared in excellent health, and bore himself—we are
told—throughout the trying ordeal, with fortitude and
manly dignity. He spoke as follows :—

"My lords, it is my intention to say a few words only. I desire
that the last act of a proceeding which has occupied so much of the
public time, should be of short duration. Nor have I the indelicate
wish to close the dreary ceremony of a state prosecution with a
vain display of words. Did I fear that hereafter, when I shall be
no more, the country I tried to serve would speak ill of me, I
might, indeed, avail myself of this solemn moment to vindicate my
sentiments and my conduct. But I have no such fear. The
country will judge of those sentiments and that conduct in a light
far different from that in which the jury by whom I have been con-

victed have viewed them ; and by the country the sentence which you, my lords, are about to pronounce, will be remembered only as the severe and solemn attestation of my rectitude and truth. Whatever be the language in which that sentence be spoken, I know that my fate will meet with sympathy, and that my memory will be honored. In speaking thus, accuse me not, my lords, of an indecorous presumption in the efforts I have made in a just and noble cause. I ascribe no main importance, nor do I claim for those efforts any high reward. But it so happens, and it will ever happen so, that they who have lived to serve their country—no matter how weak their efforts may have been—are sure to receive the thanks and blessings of its people. With my countrymen I leave my memory, my sentiments, my acts, proudly feeling that they require no vindication from me this day. A jury of my countrymen, it is true, have found me guilty of the crime of which I stood indicted. For this I entertain not the slightest feeling of resentment towards them. Influenced as they must have been by the charge of the Lord Chief Justice, they could perhaps have found no other verdict. What of that charge? Any strong observations on it I feel sincerely would ill-befit the solemnity of this scene; but I would earnestly beseech of you, my lord—you who preside on that bench—when the passions and the prejudices of this hour have passed away, to appeal to your own conscience, and ask of it was your charge what it ought to have been, impartial and indifferent between the subject and the Crown? My lords, you may deem this language unbecoming in me, and perhaps it may seal my fate; but I am here to speak the truth, whatever it may cost—I am here to regret nothing I have ever done, to regret nothing I have ever said—I am here to crave with no lying lip the life I consecrate to the liberty of my country. Far from it. Even here—here, where the thief, the libertine, the murderer, have left their footprints in the dust—here, on this spot, where the shadows of death surround me, and from which I see my early grave in an unanointed soil open to receive me—even here, encircled by these terrors, that hope which first beckoned me to the perilous sea on which I have been wrecked, still consoles, animates, and enraptures me. No; I do not despair of my poor old country—her peace, her liberty, her glory. For that country I can do no more than bid her hope. To lift this island up—to make her a benefactor to humanity, instead of being, as she is now, the meanest beggar in the world—to restore to her her native powers and her ancient constitution—this has been my ambition, and this ambition has been my crime. Judged by the law of England, I know this crime entails upon me the penalty of death; but the history of Ireland explains that crime and justifies it. Judged by that history, I am no criminal, you (addressing Mr. MacManus) are no criminal, you (addressing Mr. O'Donoghue) are no criminal, and we deserve no punishment; judged by that history, the treason of which I stand convicted loses all its guilt, has been sanctified as a duty, and will be ennobled as a sacrifice. With these sentiments

I await the sentence of the court. I have done what I felt to be my duty. I have spoken now, as I did on every other occasion during my short life, what I felt to be the truth. I now bid farewell to the country of my birth—of my passions—of my death; a country whose misfortunes have invoked my sympathies—whose factions I sought to quell—whose intelligence I prompted to a lofty aim—whose freedom has been my fatal dream. To that country I now offer as a pledge of the love I bore her, and of the sincerity with which I thought and spoke and struggled for her freedom, the life of a young heart; and with that life, the hopes, the honors, the endearments of a happy, a prosperous, and an honorable home. Proceed, then, my lords, with that sentence which the law directs—I am prepared to hear it—I trust I am prepared to meet its execution. I shall go, I think, with a light heart before a higher tribunal—a tribunal where a Judge of infinite goodness, as well as of infinite justice, will preside, and where, my lords, many, many of the judgments of this world will be reversed."

There is little more for us to add. Meagher arrived with O'Brien, O'Donoghue, and MacManus in Van Diemen's Land in October, 1849, and escaped to America in 1852. He started the *Irish News* in New York, which he enriched by personal recollections of the stirring scenes in which he participated; but his career as a journalist closed abruptly with the outbreak of the war of Secession, when he raised a zouave company to join Corcoran's 69th Regiment, with which he fought gallantly at Bull's Run. Every one remembers how the gallantry of the Irish regiment in which Meagher served, saved the Federal forces from annihilation on that field of disaster. Subsequently he raised and commanded the Irish Brigade, which won imperishable laurels throughout the hard-fought campaigns that ended with the capture of Richmond. When Mr. Johnson became President of the United States, he appointed Meagher to the position of Governor of Montana Territory, in the far West, a post which he held until his death.

His end was sad and sudden. One dark, wild night in July, 1867, a gentleman suddenly disappeared from the deck of the steamer on which he was standing, and fell into the great Missouri, where it winds its course by the hills of Montana. The accident was too sudden for availing assistance. A sudden slip, a splash, a faint cry, a brief struggle, and all was over; the hungry waters closed over him, and the rapid-rolling current swept away his lifeless corse. The finished scholar, the genial friend, the matchless orator, the ardent patriot, was no more. Thomas Francis Meagher was dead.

KEVIN IZOD O'DOHERTY.

ANOTHER bold, clever, and resolute opponent of British rule in Ireland was torn from the ranks of the popular leaders on the day that Kevin Izod O'Doherty was arrested. Amongst the cluster of talented and able men who led the Young Ireland phalanx, he was distinguished for his spirit and mental accomplishments; amongst the organizers of the party his ready words, manly address, and ceaseless activity gave him a prominent position; amongst its journalists he was conspicuous for fearlessness, frankness, and ability. Over the surging waves of the excitement and agitation that convulsed the country during the period which ended with the affray at Ballingarry, and through the haze which time has cast over the attempted revolution of '48, his figure looms up in bold proportions, suggestive of mental capacity, fortitude of soul, and tenacity of purpose. For him, as for many of his brilliant associates, the paths of patriotism led down to proscription and pain; but O'Doherty, fulminating the thunderbolts of the *Tribune*, or sowing the seeds of patriotism amongst the students of Dublin, was not one whit more self-possessed or undaunted than when, standing a convict in the Green-street dock, he awaited the sentence of the court.

Kevin Izod O'Doherty was born of respectable Catholic parents in Dublin, in June, 1824. He received a liberal education, by which he profited extensively, showing, even in his school-days, strong evidence of natural ability, and talents of more than average degree. He directed his attention to the medical profession on completing his education, and was in the full tide of lectures and hospital attendance when the development of the national sentiment that pervaded the year '48 drew him into the vortex of public life. He became a hard-working and enthusiastic member of the Young Ireland party,

KEVIN I. O'DOHERTY.
THOMAS F. MEAGHER.   TERENCE B. M'MANUS.

and was one of the founders of the Students' and Polytechnic Clubs, which were regarded by the leaders in Dublin as the *elite* of the national force in the capital. When Mitchel was struck down and his paper suppressed, O'Doherty was one of those who resolved that the political guidance which the *United Irishman* was meant to afford, should not be wanting to the people. In conjunction with Richard Dalton Williams—"Shamrock" of the *Nation*—he established the *Irish Tribune*, the first number of which saw the light on the 10th of June, 1848. There could be no mistake about the objects of the *Tribune*, or the motives of its founders in establishing it. The British government could ill afford to endure the attacks on their exactions and usurpations thundered forth weekly in its articles. Its career was cut short by the mailed hand of authority at its fifth number, and on the 10th of July, '48, Kevin Izod O'Doherty was an inmate of Newgate prison.

On the 10th of August he was placed at the bar of Green-street court-house, and arraigned on a charge of treason-felony, and a vigorous effort was made by the Crown to convict him. The attempt, however, was a failure; the jury-panel had not been juggled as effectively as usual, and a disagreement of the jury was the consequence. The Crown, however, had no idea of relaxing its grasp of its victim; after John Martin's conviction O'Doherty was put forward again, and a new jury selected to try him. Again were the government defeated; the second jury, like the first, refused to agree to a verdict of guilty, and were discharged without convicting the prisoner. A third time was O'Doherty arraigned, and this time the relentless hatred of his persecutors was gratified by a verdict of guilty. The speech delivered by Mr. O'Doherty after conviction was as follows:—

"My lords:—I did hope, I confess, that, upon being placed in this dock for the third time, after two juries of my fellow-citizens had refused to find a verdict against me, that while my prosecutors would have been scrupulous in their care in attempting to uphold their law, they would not have violated the very spirit of justice."

Judge Crampton :—"I have a great difficulty in preventing you from making any observations that may occur to you to be of service; but if you mean to cast imputations or obloquy upon the law officers of the Crown, the court cannot permit that."

Mr. O'Doherty :—" I only wish to mention a matter of fact. The Attorney-General stated that there were only three Roman Catholics set aside on my jury."

Judge Crampton again interposed, and requested the prisoner not to pursue this line of observation.

Mr. O'Doherty :—" I would feel much obliged if your lordship would permit me to mention a few more words with reference to my motives throughout this affair.

" I had but one object and purpose in view. I did feel deeply for the sufferings and privations endured by my fellow-countrymen. I did wish, by all means consistent with a manly and honorable resistance, to assist in putting an end to that suffering. It is very true, and I will confess it, that I desired an open resistance of the people to that government, which, in my opinion, entailed these sufferings upon them. I have used the words 'open and honorable resistance,' in order that I might refer to one of the articles brought in evidence against me, in which the writer suggests such things as flinging burning hoops on the soldiery. My lords, these are no sentiments of mine. I did not write that article. I did not see it or know of it until I read it when published in the paper. But I did not bring the writer of it here on the table. Why? I knew that, if I were to do so, it would only be handing him over at the court-house doors to what one of the witnesses has very properly called the fangs of the Attorney-General. With respect to myself, I have no fears. I trust I will be enabled to bear my sentence with all the forbearance due to what I believe to be the opinion of twelve conscientious enemies to me, and I will bear with due patience the wrath of the government whose mouthpiece they were; but I will never cease to deplore the destiny that gave me birth in this unhappy country, and compelled me, as an Irishman, to receive at your hands a felon's doom, for discharging what I conceived, and what I still conceive, to be my duty. I shall only add, that the fact is, that, instead of three Roman Catholic jurors being set aside by the Attorney-General, there were thirteen ; I hold in my hand a list of their names, and out of the twelve jurors he permitted to be sworn, there was not one Roman Catholic."

Mr. O'Doherty was sentenced to transportation for ten years. He sailed for Van Diemen's Land in the same ship that bore John Martin into exile. In the course of time he, like Martin and O'Brien, was set at liberty on condition of his residing anywhere out of "the United Kingdom." He came on to Paris, and there resumed his medical studies. He paid, however, one secret and hurried visit to Ireland. He came to wed and bear away with him, to share his fortune in other lands, a woman in every way worthy of him—one whose genius and talents, like his own, had been freely given to the cause of Ireland, and whose heart had long been his in the bonds of a most tender attachment. "Eva," one of the fair poetesses of the *Nation*, was the plighted wife of O'Doherty. Terrible must have been the shock to her gentle nature when her patriot lover was borne off a convict, and shipped for England's penal settlements in the far Southern seas. She believed, however, they would meet again, and she knew that neither time nor distance could chill the ardor of their mutual affection. The volumes of the *Nation* published during his captivity contain many exquisite lyrics from her pen mourning for the absent one, with others expressive of unchanging affection, and the most intense faith in the truth of her distant lover. "The course of true love" in this case ended happily. O'Doherty, as we have stated, managed to slip across from Paris to Ireland, and returned with "Eva" his bride. In 1856 the pardons granted to the exiles above named were made unconditional, and in the following year O'Doherty returned to Ireland, where he took out his degrees with great *eclat;* he then commenced the practice of medicine and surgery in Dublin, and soon came to be ranked amongst the most distinguished and successful members of his profession. After remaining some years in Ireland, Mr. O'Doherty sailed far away seawards once again, and took up his abode under the light of the Southern Cross. He settled in a rising colony of Australia, where he still lives, surrounded by troops of friends, and enjoying the position to which his talents and his high character entitle him.

TERENCE BELLEW MacMANUS.

THE excitement caused by the startling events of which this country was the scene in the summer of 1848, extended far beyond the shores of Ireland. Away beyond the Atlantic, the news from Ireland was watched for with glistening eyes by the exiles who dwelt by the shores of Manhattan, or in the backwoods of Canada. Amongst the Irish colony in England the agitation was still greater. Dwelling in the hearts of the monster towns of England, the glow of the furnace lighting up their swarthy faces; toiling on the canals, on the railways, in the steamboats; filling the factories, plying their brawny hands where the hardest work was to be done; hewers of wood, and drawers of water; living in the midst of the English, yet separated from them by all the marks of a distinctive nationality, by antagonistic feelings, by clashing interests, by jarring creeds,—such was the position of the men who carried the faith, the traditions, the politics, and the purpose of Ireland into the heart of the enemy's country. With their countrymen at home they were united by the warmest ties of sympathy and affection. In London, in Manchester, in Birmingham, in Leeds, Confederate Clubs were established, and actives measures taken for cooperating with the Young Ireland leaders in whatever course they might think proper to adopt. In Liverpool those clubs were organized on the most extensive scale; thousands of Irishmen attended their weekly meetings, and speeches, rivalling those delivered at the Rotundo and at the Music Hall in fervor and earnestness, were spoken from their platforms. Amongst the Irishmen who figured prominently at these gatherings there was one to whom the Irish in Liverpool looked up with peculiar confidence and pride. He was young, he was accomplished, he was wealthy, he filled a highly respectable position in society; his name was connected by every one with probity and honor; and, above all, he was a nationalist, unselfish, enthusiastic, and ardent. The Irishmen of Liverpool will not need to be told that we speak of Terence Bellew MacManus. The agitation of 1848 found MacManus in good business as a shipping agent, his income being estimated by his Liverpool friends at ten or twelve hundred a year. His patriotism was of too genuine a nature to be merged in his commercial success, and MacManus readily abandoned his prospects and his position when his country seemed to require the sacrifice. Instantly on discovering that the government were about to suspend the *Habeas Corpus* Act in Ireland, he took the steamer for Dublin, bringing with him the green and gold uniform which he owned in virtue of being a general of the '82 Club. In the same steamer came two detectives sent specially to secure his arrest in Dublin. MacManus drove from the quay, where he landed, to the *Felon* Office. He discovered that all the Confederate leaders out of prison had gone southwards, on hostile thoughts intent; and MacManus resolved on joining them without a moment's hesitation. Having managed to give the detectives the slip, he journeyed southwards to Tipperary, and joined O'Brien's party at Killenaule. He shared the fortunes of the insurgent leaders until the dispersion at Ballingarry, where he fought with conspicuous bravery and determination. He was the first to arrive before the house in which the police took refuge, and the last to leave it. The Rev. Mr. Fitzgerald, P. P., an eye-witness, gives an interesting account of MacManus' conduct during the attack on the Widow M'Cormick's house. He says:—

"With about a dozen men more determined than the rest, was MacManus, who indeed, throughout the whole day, showed more courage and resolution than any one else. With a musket in his hand, and in the face of the enemy, he reconnoitered the place, and observed every accessible approach to the house, and with a few colliers, under cover of a cart-load of hay, which they pushed on before them, came up to the postern-door of the kitchen. Here with his own hand he fired several pistol-shots to make it ignite, but from the state of the weather, which was damp and heavy, and from the constant down-pour of rain on the previous day, this attempt proved quite unsuccessful. With men so expert at the use of the pickaxe, and so large a supply of blasting-powder at the collieries, he could have quickly undermined the house, or blown it up ; but the circumstance of so many children being shut in with the police, and the certainty that, if they persevered, all would be involved in the same ruin, compelled him and his associates to desist from their purpose."

When it became useless to offer further resistance, MacManus retired with the peasantry to the hills, and dwelt with them several days. Having shaved off his whiskers, and made some other changes in his appearance, he succeeded in running the gauntlet through the host of spies and detectives on his trail, and he was actually on board a large vessel on the point of sailing for America from Cork harbor, when arrested by the police. His discovery was purely accidental; the police boarded the vessel in chase of an absconding defaulter, but, while prosecuting the search, one of the constables who had seen MacManus occasionally in Liverpool, recognized him. At first he gave his name as O'Donnell, said he was an Irish-American returning westward, after visiting his friends in the old land. His answers, however, were not sufficiently consistent to dissipate the constable's suspicion. He was brought ashore and taken handcuffed before a magistrate, whereupon he avowed his name, and boldly added that he did not regret any act he had done, and would cheerfully go through it again.

On the 10th of October, 1848, he was brought to trial for high treason in Clonmel. He viewed the whole proceedings with calm indifference, and, when the verdict of guilty was brought in, he heard the announcement with unaltered mien. A fortnight later he was brought up to receive sentence ; Meagher and O'Donoghue had been convicted in the interim, and the three Confederates stood side by side in the dock to hear the doom of the traitor pronounced against them. MacManus was the first to speak in reply to the usual formality, and his address was as follows:—

"My lords :—I trust I am enough of a Christian and enough of a man to understand the awful responsibility of the question which has been put to me. Standing upon my native soil—standing in an Irish court of justice, and before the Irish nation—I have much to say why the sentence of death, or the sentence of the law, should not be passed upon me. But upon entering into this court I placed my life—and what is of more importance to me, my honor—in the hands of two advocates; and if I had ten thousand lives and ten thousand honors, I should be content to place them all in the watchful and glorious genius of the one, and the patient zeal and talent of the other. I am, therefore, content, and with regard to that I have nothing to say. But I have a word to say, which no advocate, however anxious and devoted he may be, can utter for me. I say, whatever part I may have taken in the struggle for my country's independence, whatever part I may have acted in my short career, I stand before you, my lords, with a free heart and a light conscience, to abide the issue of your sentence. And now, my lords, this is perhaps the fittest time to put a sentence upon record, which is this—that, standing in this dock, and called to ascend the scaffold—it may be to-morrow—it may be now—it may be never—whatever the result may be, I wish to put this on record, that in the part I have taken I was not actuated by enmity towards Englishmen—for among them I have passed some of the happiest days of my life, and the most prosperous; and in no part which I have taken was I actuated by enmity towards Englishmen individually, whatever I may have felt of the injustice of English rule in this island; I therefore say, that it is not because I loved England less, but because I loved Ireland more, that I now stand before you."

In 1851, MacManus escaped from captivity in Van Diemen's Land, and he soon after settled in California, where he died. His funeral was the greatest ever witnessed upon earth. From the shores of the Pacific thousands of miles away, across continents and oceans, they brought him, and laid his ashes to rest in the land of his birth. On the 10th day of November, 1861, that wonderful funeral passed through the streets of Dublin to Glasnevin; and those who saw the gathering that followed his coffin to the grave, the thousands of stalwart men that marched in solemn order behind his bier, will never forget the sight. A silent slab unlettered and unmarked shows the spot where his remains were interred; no storied urn or animated bust, no marble column or commemorative tablet, has been consecrated to his memory, but the history of his life is graven in the hearts of his countrymen, and he enjoys, in their affectionate remembrance, a monument more enduring than human hands could build him.

THOMAS CLARKE LUBY.

LOOKING along the course of Irish history, it is easy to point out certain periods in which England could have found an opportunity for making terms with the Irish nation, healing some of the old wounds, and mitigating in some degree the burning sense of wrong and the desire of vengeance that rankled in the hearts of the Irish race. There were lulls in the struggle, intervals of gloomy calm, occasions when the heart of Ireland might have been touched by generous deeds, and when the offer of the olive branch, or even a few of its leaves, would have had a blessed effect. But England never availed of them—never for an instant sought to turn them to good account. She preferred, when Ireland was defeated, prostrate, and forlorn, to taunt her with her failure, scoff at her sufferings, and add to her afflictions. Such was her conduct during the mournful time that followed on the attempted insurrection of 1848.

It was an appalling time, in whose death-laden atmosphere political action was impossible. The famine had made of the country one huge graveyard. A silence fell upon the land, lately so clamorous for her rights, so hopeful, and so defiant. The Repeal organization spoke no more; the tramp of the Confederate clubs was no longer heard in the streets; O'Connell was dead; the Young Ireland leaders were fugitives or prisoners; and the people were almost bewildered by a sense of their great calamity. Then, if England had stooped to raise her fallen foe, offered her some kindly treatment, and spoken some gracious words, the bitterness of the old quarrel might have been in some degree assuaged, even though its cause should not be entirely obliterated. But England did not choose to take that politic and Christian course. She found it much pleasanter to chuckle over the discomfiture of the Irish patriots, to ridicule the failure of their peaceable agitation, to sneer at their poor effort in arms, to nickname and misrepresent and libel the brave-hearted gentleman who led that unlucky endeavor; and, above all, to felicitate herself on the reduction that had taken place in the Irish population. That—from her point of view—was the glorious part of the whole affair. The Irish were "gone with a vengeance!"—not all of them, but a goodly proportion, and others were going off every day. Emigrant ships clustered in the chief ports, and many sought their living freights in those capacious harbors along the Atlantic coast which nature seemed to have shaped for the accommodation of a great commerce, but where the visit of any craft larger than a fishing smack was a rare event. The flaming placards of the various shipping lines were posted in every town in Ireland,—on the chapel-gates, and the shutters of closed shops, and the doors of tenantless houses; and there appeared to be in progress a regular breaking up of the Irish nation. This, to the English mind, was positively delightful. For, here was the Irish question being settled, at last, by the simple process of the transference of the Irish people to the bottom of the deep sea, or else to the continent of America—nearly the same thing as far as England was concerned; for, in neither place—as it seemed to her—could they ever more trouble her peace, or have any claim on those fruits of the Irish soil which were needed for the stomachs of Englishmen. There they could no longer pester her with petitions for Tenant Right, or demands for a Repeal of the Union. English farmers, and drovers, and laborers, loyal to the English government, and yielding no sort of allegiance to the Pope, would cross the Channel and take possession of the deserted island, which would thenceforth be England's in such a sense as it never was before. O magnificent consummation! O most brilliant prospects, in the eyes of English statesmen! · They saw their way clear, they understood their game; it was: to lighten in no degree the pressure which they maintained upon the lives of the Irish people, to do nothing that could tend to render existence tolerable to them in

Ireland, or check the rush of emigration. Acting in conformity with this shallow and false estimate of the situation, they allowed to drift away unused the time which wise statesmen would have employed in the effectuation of conciliatory and tranquilizing measures, and applied themselves simply to the crushing out from the Irish mind of every hope of improved legislation, and the defeat of every effort to obtain it. Thus when the people—waking up from the stupefaction that followed on the most tragic period of the famine—began to breathe the breath of political life again, and, perceiving the danger that menaced the existence of the peasant classes, set on foot an agitation to procure a reform of the land-laws, the government resolutely opposed the project; defeated the bills which the friends of the tenantry brought into parliament, and took steps, which proved only too successful, for the break up of the organization by which the movement was conducted. And then, when Frederick Lucas was dead, and Mr. Duffy had gone into exile, and the patriot priests were debarred from taking part in politics, and Messrs. John Sadlier and William Keogh were bought over by bribes of place and pay, the government appeared to think that Irish patriotism had fought in its last ditch, and received its final defeat.

But they were mistaken. The old cause that had survived so many disasters was not dead yet. While the efforts of the Tenant Righters in Ireland were being foiled, and their party was being scattered, a couple of Irishmen, temporarily resident in Paris, fugitive because of their connection with the events of '48, were laying the foundations of a movement more profoundly dangerous to England than any of those with which she had grappled since the days of Wolfe Tone and Lord Edward Fitzgerald. Those men were John O'Mahony and James Stephens.

Since then their names have been much heard of, and the organization of which they were the originators has played an important part in Irish history. But at the period of which we are now writing, the general public knew nothing of O'Mahony or of Stephens beyond the fact that they were alleged to have taken some part in the recent insurrectionary demonstrations. Stephens, who was then a very young lad, had been present at the Ballingarry attack, and had been severely wounded by the fire of the police. He managed to crawl away from the spot to a ditch-side, where he was lost sight of. A report of his death was put into circulation, and a loyal journal published in Kilkenny—the native town of the young rebel, who in this instance played his first trick on the government—referred to his supposed decease in terms which showed that the rule *de mortuis nil nisi bonum* found acceptance with the editor. The following are the words of the obituary notice which appeared in the *Kilkenny Moderator* on or about the 19th of August, 1848:—

"Poor James Stephens, who followed Smith O'Brien to the field, has died of the wound which he received at Ballingarry, whilst acting as aide-de-camp to the insurgent leader. Mr. Stephens was a very amiable, and, apart from politics, most inoffensive young man, possessed of a great deal of talent, and we believe he was a most excellent son and brother. His untimely and melancholy fate will be much regretted by a numerous circle of friends."

It is said that his family very prudently fostered this delusion by going into mourning for the loss of young James—the suggestion of which clever *ruse* probably came from the dear boy himself. A short time afterwards he managed to escape, disguised as a lady's maid, to France. As one may gather from the paragraph above quoted, the family were much respected in the locality. Mr. Stephens, father of the future C. O. I. R., was clerk in the establishment of a respectable auctioneer and bookseller in Kilkenny. He gave his children a good education, and sent young James to a Catholic seminary, with a view to his being taught and trained for the priesthood. But circumstances prevented the realization of this design, and before any line of business could be marked out for young Stephens, the political events above referred to took place and shaped his future career.

John O'Mahony was a different stamp of man. He

belonged to the class known as gentlemen-farmers, and of that class he was one of the most respected. His family owned a considerable tract of land in the southern part of the county of Tipperary, of which they had been occupants for many generations. He was well educated, of studious habits, and thoroughly imbued with patriotic feeling, which came to him as a hereditary possession. When the Young Ireland leaders were electrifying the country by their spirited appeals to the patriotism and bravery of the Irish race, and the population in all the chief centres of intelligence were crystallizing into semi-military organizations, O'Mahony was not apathetic or inactive. One of the strongest of the Confederate clubs —which were thick sown in the contiguous districts of the counties of Cork, Waterford, and Tipperary—was under his presidency; and when in July, 1848, the leaders of the movement scattered themselves over the country for the purpose of ascertaining the degree of support they would receive if they should decide on unfurling the green banner, his report of the state of affairs in his district was one of their most cheering encouragements.

A few days afterwards, the outbreak under O'Brien occurred at Ballingarry. The failure of that attempt, and the irresolute manner in which it was conducted, had disheartened the country, but the idea of allowing the struggle to rest at that point was not universally entertained by the leaders of the clubs; and John O'Mahony was one of those who resolved that another attempt should be made to rally the people to the insurrectionary standard. He acted up to his resolution. On the night of the 12th of September there were signal-fires on the slopes of Slievenamon and the Comeragh mountains, and the district between Carrick-on-Suir and Callan was in a state of perturbation. Next day the alarm was spread in all directions. The gentry of the disturbed districts rushed into the nearest towns for protection; police from the outlying barracks were called in to reinforce the threatened stations, and troops were hastily summoned from Dublin and the neighboring garrisons.

Meanwhile parties of the insurgents began to move about. One proceeded to the police station at the Slate-quarries, and finding it deserted—the policemen having retired on Piltown—burned it to the ground. Another attempted the destruction of Grany bridge, to delay the advance of the soldiery. A third proceeded to attack the Glenbower station. The defenders of the barracks were in a rather critical position when another party of police, on their way from the Nine-Mile-House station to Carrick, came upon the spot, and the combined force speedily put their half-armed assailants to flight, with a loss to the latter of one man severely wounded and one killed. An attack was made on the barrack at Portlaw, but with a like result; two men were stricken dead by the bullets of the police. The people soon afterwards scattered to their homes, and the soldiery and police had nothing to do but hunt up for the leaders and other parties implicated in the movement. John O'Mahony narrowly escaped capture on three or four occasions. He lingered in the country, however, until after the conviction of the state prisoners at Clonmel, when it became clear to him that the cause was lost for a time; and he then took his way to Paris, whither several of his fellow outlaws, for whose arrest the government had offered large rewards, had gone before him.

In that famous centre of intellect and intrigue, the focus of political thought, the fountain-head of great ideas, John O'Mahony and James Stephens pondered long over the defeat that had come upon the Irish cause, and in their ponderings bethought them that the reason of the failure which they deplored was to be found in the want of that quiet, earnest, secret preparation, by means of which the Continental revolutionists were able to produce from time to time such volcanic effects in European politics, and cause the most firmly-rooted dynasties to tremble for their positions. The system of secret conspiracy—that ancient system, "old as the universe, yet not outworn"—a system not unknown in Ireland from the days of the Attacots to those of the Whiteboys—the system of Sir Phelim O'Neill and of Theobald Wolfe

Tone—that system, as developed, refined and elaborated by the most subtle intellects of modern times, those two men proposed to propagate among the Irish race at home and abroad. They divided the labor between them. O'Mahony took the United States of America for his field of action, and Stephens took the Old Country.

It was in the year 1858 that the first symptoms indicative of the work to which James Stephens had set himself, made their appearance in the extreme south-west of Ireland. Whispers went about that some of the young men of Kenmare, Bantry, and Skibbereen were enrolled in a secret sworn organization, and were in the habit of meeting for the purpose of training and drilling. Indeed the members of the new society took little pains to conceal its existence; they seemed rather to find a pride in the knowledge which their neighbors had of the fact, and relied for their legal safety on certain precautions adopted in the manner of their initiation as members. When informed firstly by well-known nationalists in a private manner, and subsequently by public remonstrances addressed to them by Catholic clergymen and the national journals, that the government were on their track, they refused to believe it; but ere long they suffered grievously for their incredulity and want of prudence. In the early days of December, 1858, the swoop of the government was made on the members of the "Phœnix Society" in Cork and Kerry, and arrests followed shortly after, in other parts of the country. The trials in the south commenced at Tralee in March, 1859, when a conviction was obtained against a man named Daniel O'Sullivan, and he was sentenced to penal servitude for ten years. The remaining cases were adjourned to the next assizes, and when they came on in July, 1859, the prisoners put in a plea of guilty, and were set at liberty on the understanding that, if their future conduct should not be satisfactory to the authorities, they would be called up for sentence. Amongst the Cork prisoners who took this course was Jeremiah O'Donovan (Rossa), whose name has since been made familiar to the public.

Those events were generally supposed to have extinguished the Phœnix conspiracy. And many of Ireland's most sincere friends hoped that such was the case. Recognizing fully the peculiar powers which a secret society can bring to bear against the government, they still felt a profound conviction that the risks, or rather the certain cost of liberty and life involved in such a mode of procedure, formed more than a counterpoise for the advantages which it presented. They were consequently earnest and emphatic in their endeavors to dissuade their countrymen from treading in the dangerous paths in which their steps were dogged by the spy and the informer. The Catholic clergy were especially zealous in their condemnation of secret revolutionary societies, urged thereto by a sense of their duty as priests and patriots. But there were men connected with the movement, both in America and Ireland, who were resolved to persevere in their design of extending the organization among the Irish people, despite of any amount of opposition from any quarter whatsoever. In pursuit of that object they were not overscrupulous as to the means they employed; they did not hesitate to violate many an honorable principle, and to wrong many an honest man, nor did they exhibit a fair share of common prudence in dealing with the difficulties of their position; but unexpected circumstances arose to favor their propagandism, and it went ahead despite of all their mistakes and of every obstacle. One of those circumstances was the outbreak of the civil war in America, which took place in April, 1861. That event seemed to the leaders of the Irish revolutionary organization, now known as the Fenian Brotherhood, to be one of the most fortunate for their purposes that could have happened. It inspired the whole population of America with military ardor; it opened up a splendid school in which the Irish section of the people could acquire a knowledge of the art of war, which was exactly what was needed to give real efficacy to their endeavors for the overthrow of British dominion in Ireland. Besides, there appeared to be a strong probability that the line of action in favor of the Southern States which England, notwithstanding her proclamation of neutrality, had adopted from an early stage of the conflict, would speedily involve her in a war with the Federal government. These things constituted a prospect dazzling to the eyes of the Irishmen who had "gone with a vengeance." Their hearts bounded with joy at the opportunities that appeared to be opening on them. At last the time was near, they believed, when the accumulated hate of seven centuries would burst upon the power of England, not in the shape of an undisciplined peasantry armed with pikes, and scythes, and pitchforks, as in 1798—not in the shape of a half-famished and empty-handed crowd, led to battle by orators and poets, as in 1848, but in the shape of an army, bristling with sharp steel, and flanked with thunderous cannon—an army skilled in the modern science of war, directed by true military genius, and inspired by that burning valor which in all times was one of the qualities of the Irish race. Influenced by such hopes and feelings, the Irish of the Northern States poured by thousands into the Federal ranks, and formed themselves into regiments that were at the same time so many Fenian circles. In the Southern army, too, there were many Irishmen who were not less determined to give to their native land the benefit of their military experience, as soon as the troubles of their adopted country should be brought to an end. Fenianism, with that glow of light upon it, spread like a prairie-fire through the States. The ranks of the organization swelled rapidly, and money contributions poured like a tide into its treasury. The impulse was felt also by the society in Ireland. It received a rapid development, and soon began to put on a bold front towards the government, and a still more belligerent one towards all Irishmen who, while claiming the character of patriots, declined to take part in the Fenian movement or recommend it to their countrymen. In November, 1863, the Brotherhood started the *Irish People* newspaper in Dublin, for the double purpose of propagating their doctrines and increasing the revenues of the society. James Stephens was the author of this most unfortunate project. The men whom he selected for working it out were

Thomas Clarke Luby, John O'Leary, and Charles Joseph Kickham.

From the date of its establishment up to the month of September, 1865—a period of nearly two years—the *Irish People* occupied itself in preaching what its editors regarded as the cardinal doctrines of the society, which were:—That constitutional agitation for the redress of Ireland's grievances was worse than useless; that every man taking part in such agitation was either a fool or a knave; that in political affairs clergymen should be held of no more account than laymen; and that the only hope for Ireland lay in an armed uprising of the people. These doctrines were not quite new; not one of them was absolutely true; but they were undoubtedly held by many thousands of Irishmen, and the Fenian society took care to secure for the journal in which they were advocated a large circulation. The office of the *Irish People* soon came to be regarded as, what it really was, the headquarters of the Fenian organization in Ireland. To it the choice spirits of the party resorted for counsel and direction; thither the provincial organizers directed their steps whenever they visited Dublin; into it poured weekly from all parts of the country an immense mass of correspondence, which the editors, instead of destroying after it had passed through their hands, foolishly allowed to accumulate upon their shelves, though every word of it was fraught with peril to the lives and liberties of their friends. In their private residences also they were incautious enough to keep numerous documents of a most compromising character. There is but one way of accounting for their conduct in this matter. They may have supposed that the legal proceedings against them, which they knew were certain to take place at one time or another, would be conducted in the semi-constitutional fashion which was adopted towards the national journals in 1848. If the staff of the *Irish People* had received a single day's notice that they were about to be made amenable to the law, it is possible that they would have their houses and their office immediately cleared of those documents which afterwards consigned so many of their countrymen to the horrors of penal servitude. But they saw no reason to suppose that the swoop was about to be made on them. On the fifteenth day of September, 1865, there were no perceptible indications that the authorities were any more on the alert in reference to Fenian affairs than they had been during the past twelve months. It was Friday; the *Irish People* had been printed for the next day's sale, large batches of the paper had been sent off to the agents in town and country, the editors and publishing clerks had gone home to rest after their week's labors—when suddenly, at about half-past nine o'clock in the evening, a strong force of police broke into the office, seized the books, manuscripts, papers and forms of type, and bore them off to the Castle yard. At the same time arrests of the chief Fenian leaders were being made in various parts of the city. The news created intense excitement in all circles of society, and more especially amongst the Fenians themselves, who had never dreamed of a government *coup* so sudden, so lawless, and so effective. The government had now thrown off the mask of apathy and impassiveness which it had worn so long, and it commenced to lay its strong hand upon its foes. Amongst the men who filled the prison cells on that miserable autumn evening were John O'Leary, Thomas Clarke Luby, and Jeremiah O'Donovan (Rossa). Before the Crown was ready to proceed with their trial, the third editor of the paper, Charles J. Kickham, was added to their company, having been arrested with James Stephens, Edward Duffy, and Hugh Brophy, on the 11th November, at Fairfield House, near Dublin.

On Monday, November 27th, 1865, the state trials commenced before a Special Commission in the courthouse, Green-street—the scene of so many a previous grapple between British law and the spirit of Irish patriotism. Mr. Justice Keogh and Mr. Justice Fitzgerald were the presiding judges. There was a long list of prisoners to be tried. James Stephens might have been honored with the first place amongst them, were it not that, two days previously, to the unspeakable horror and surprise of the government and all its friends, he had effected his escape, or rather, we might say, obtained, by the aid of friendly hands, his release from Richmond prison. In his regretted absence, the crown commenced their proceedings, by placing Thomas Clarke Luby in the dock to answer to a charge of treason-felony.

He stood up to the bar, between the jailors that clustered about him, a quiet-faced, pale, and somewhat sad-looking man, apparently of about forty years of age. A glance around the court-house showed him but few friendly faces—for, owing to the terrors felt by the judges, the crown prosecutors and other officials of the law, who dreaded the desperate resolves of armed conspirators, few were admitted into the building except policemen, detectives, and servants of the Crown in one capacity or another. In one of the galleries, however, he recognized his wife—daughter of J. De Jean Fraser, one of the sweetest poets of the '48 period—with the wife of his fellow-prisoner, O'Donovan Rossa, and the sister of John O'Leary. A brief smile of greeting passed between the party, and then all thoughts were concentrated on the stern business of the day.

There was no chance of escape for Thomas Clarke Luby or for his associates. The Crown had a plethora of evidence against them, acquired during the months and years when they appeared to be all but totally ignorant of the existence of the conspiracy. They had the evidence of the approver, Nagle, who had been an employé of the *Irish People* office and a confidential agent of James Stephens up to the night of the arrests, but who, during the previous eighteen months, had been betraying every secret of theirs to the government. They had the evidence of a whole army of detectives; but more crushing and fatal than all, they had that which was supplied by the immense store of documents captured at the *Irish People* office and the houses of some of the chief members of the conspiracy. Of all those papers, the most important was one found at the residence of Mr. Luby, in which James Stephens, being at the time about to visit America, delegated his powers over the organization

in Ireland, England, and Scotland, to Thomas Clarke
Luby, John O'Leary, and Charles J. Kickham. This,
which was referred to during the trials as the "executive
document," was worded as follows:—

"I hereby empower Thomas Clarke Luby, John O'Leary and
Charles J. Kickham a committee of organization, or executive,
with the same supreme control over the home organization, England, Ireland, and Scotland, as that exercised by myself. I further
empower them to appoint a committee of military inspection, and
a committee of appeal and judgment, the functions of which committee will be made known to every member of them. Trusting
to the patriotism and abilities of the executive, I fully endorse
their actions beforehand. I call on every man in our ranks to support and be guided by them in all that concerns the military
brotherhood.

"J. STEPHENS."

Not all the legal ingenuity and forensic eloquence of
their talented counsel, Mr. Butt, could avail to save the
men who, by the preservation of such documents as the
foregoing, had fastened the fetters on their own limbs.
The trial of Mr. Luby concluded on the fourth day of
the proceedings—Friday, December 1st, 1865—with a
verdict of guilty. The prisoner heard the announcement
with composure, and then, in response to the question
usual in such cases, addressed the court as follows:—

"Well, my lords and gentlemen, I don't think any person present here is surprised at the verdict found against me. I have been
prepared for this verdict ever since I was arrested, although I
thought it my duty to fight the British government inch by inch.
I felt I was sure to be found guilty, since the advisers of the
Crown took what the Attorney-General was pleased the other day
to call the 'merciful course.' I thought I might have a fair chance
of escaping, so long as the capital charge was impending over me ;
but when they resolved on trying me under the Treason-Felony
Act, I felt that I had not the smallest chance. I am somewhat
embarrassed at the present moment as to what I should say under
the circumstances. There are a great many things that I would
wish to say ; but knowing that there are other persons in the same
situation with myself, and that I might allow myself to say
something injudicious, which would peril their cases, I feel that
my tongue is to a great degree tied. Notwithstanding, there are
two or three points upon which I would say a few words. I have
nothing to say to Judge Keogh's charge to the jury. He did not
take up any of the topics that had been introduced to prejudice

the case against me; for instance, he did not take this accusation of an intention to assassinate, attributed to my fellow-prisoners and myself. The Solicitor-General, in his reply to Mr. Butt, referred to those topics. Mr. Barry was the first person who advanced those charges. I thought they were partially given up by the Attorney-General in his opening statement, at least they were put forward to you in a very modified form; but the learned Solicitor-General, in his very virulent speech, put forward those charges in a most aggravated manner. He sought even to exaggerate upon Mr. Barry's original statement. Now, with respect to those charges—in justice to my character—I must say that in this court there is not a man more incapable of anything like massacre or assassination than I am. I really believe that the gentlemen who have shown so much ability in persecuting me, in the bottom of their hearts believe me incapable of an act of assassination or massacre. I don't see that there is the smallest amount of evidence to show that I ever entertained the notion of a massacre of landlords and priests. I forget whether the advisers of the crown said I intended the massacre of the Protestant clergymen. Some of the writers of our enlightened press said that I did. Now, with respect to the charge of assassinating the landlords, the only thing that gives even the shadow of a color to that charge is the letter signed—alleged to be signed—by Mr. O'Keefe. Now, assuming— but by no means admitting, of course—that the letter was written by Mr. O'Keefe, let me make a statement about it. I know the facts that I am about to state are of no practical utility to me now, at least with respect to the judges. I know it is of no practical utility to me, because I cannot give evidence on my own behalf, but it may be of practical utility to others with whom I wish to stand well. I believe my words will carry conviction—and carry much more conviction than any words of the legal advisers of the Crown can—to more than 300,000 of the Irish race in Ireland, England, and America. Well, I deny absolutely that I ever entertained any idea of assassinating the landlords, and the letter of Mr. O'Keefe—assuming it to be his letter—is the only evidence on the subject. My acquaintance with Mr. O'Keefe was of the slightest nature. I did not even know of his existence when the *Irish People* was started. He came, after that paper was established a few months, to the office, and offered some articles— some were rejected, some were inserted, and I call the attention of the legal advisers of the Crown to this fact, that, amongst the papers which they got, those that were Mr. O'Keefe's articles had many paragraphs scored out; in fact we put in no article of his without a great deal of what is technically called 'cutting down.' Now, that letter of his to me was simply a private document. It contained the mere private views of the writer; and I pledge this to the court as a man of honor—and I believe in spite of the position in which I stand, amongst my countrymen I am believed to be a man of honor, and that, if my life depended on it, I would not speak falsely about the thing—when I read that letter, and the first to whom I gave it was my wife—I remember we read it with fits of laughter at its ridiculous ideas. My wife at the moment said—'Had I not better burn the letter?' 'Oh, no,' I said, looking upon it as a most ridiculous thing, and never dreaming for a moment that such a document would ever turn up against me, and produce the unpleasant consequences it has produced— I mean the imputation of assassination and massacre, which has given me a great deal more trouble than anything else in this case. That disposes—as far as I· can at present dispose of it—of the charge of wishing to assassinate the landlords. As to the charge of desiring to assassinate the priests, I deny it as being the most monstrous thing in the world. Why, surely, every one who read the articles in the paper would see that the plain doctrine laid down there was—to reverence the priests so long as they confined themselves to their sacerdotal functions; but when the priest descended to the arena of politics, he became no more than any other man, and would just be regarded as any other man. If he was a man of ability and honesty, of course he would get the respect that such men get in politics; if he was not a man of ability, there would be no more thought of him than of a shoemaker or any one else. This is the teaching of the *Irish People* with regard to the priests. I believe the *Irish People* has done a great deal of good, even amongst those who do not believe in its revolutionary doctrines. I believe the revolutionary doctrines of the *Irish People* are good. I believe nothing can ever save Ireland except independence; and I believe that all other attempts to ameliorate the condition of Ireland are mere temporary expedients and makeshifts——"

Mr. Justice Keogh :—" I am very reluctant to interrupt you, Mr. Luby."

Mr. Luby :—" Very well, my lord, I will leave that. I believe in this way the *Irish People* has done an immensity of good. It taught the people not to give up their right of private judgment in temporal matters to the clergy ; that, while they reverenced the clergy upon the altar, they should not give up their consciences in secular matters to the clergy. I believe that is good. Others may differ from me. No set of men, I believe, ever set themselves earnestly to any work, but they did good in some shape or form."

Judge Keogh :—" I am most reluctant, Mr. Luby, to interrupt you, but do you think you should pursue this ?"

Mr. Luby :—" Very well, I will not. I think that disposes of those things. I don't care to say much about myself. It would be rather beneath me. Perhaps some persons who know me would say I should not have touched upon the assassination charge at all— that, in fact, I have rather shown weakness in attaching so much importance to it. But, with regard to the entire course of my life— and whether it be a mistaken course or not will be for every man's individual judgment to decide—this I know, that no man ever loved Ireland more than I have done—no man has ever given up his whole being to Ireland to the extent I have done. From the time

I came to what has been called the years of discretion, my entire thought has been devoted to Ireland. I believed the course I pursued was right; others may take a different view. I believe the majority of my countrymen this minute, if, instead of my being tried before a petty jury, who, I suppose, are bound to find according to British law—if my guilt or innocence was to be tried by the higher standard of eternal right, and the case was put to all my countrymen—I believe this moment the majority of my countrymen would pronounce that I am not a criminal, but that I have deserved well of my country. When the proceedings of this trial go forth into the world, peop'e will say the cause of Ireland is not to be despaired of, that Ireland is not yet a lost country—that, as long as there are men in any country prepared to expose themselves to every difficulty and danger in its service, prepared to brave captivity, even death itself, if need be, that country cannot be lost. With these words I conclude."

On the conclusion of this address, Judge Keogh proceeded to pass sentence on the prisoner. The prisoner's speech, he said, was in every way creditable to him; but the bench could not avoid coming to the conclusion that, with the exception of James Stephens, he was the person most deeply implicated in the conspiracy. The sentence of the court was, that he be kept in penal servitude for a term of twenty years. Mr. Luby heard the words without any apparent emotion—gave one sad farewell glance to his wife and friends, and stepping down the little stairs from the dock, made way for the next prisoner.

JOHN O'LEARY.

WHILE the jury in the case of Thomas Clarke Luby were absent from the court deliberating on and framing their verdict, John O'Leary was put forward to the bar.

He stepped boldly to the front, with a flash of fire in his dark eyes, and a scowl on his features, looking hatred and defiance on judges, lawyers, jurymen, and all the rest of them. All eyes were fixed on him, for he was one of those persons whose exterior attracts attention, and indicates a character above the common. He was tall, slightly built, and of gentlemanly deportment; every feature of his thin, angular face gave token of great intellectual energy and determination, and its pallid hue was rendered almost deathlike by contrast with his long black hair and flowing moustache and beard. Easy it was to see that, when the government placed John O'Leary in the dock, they had caged a proud spirit, and an able and resolute enemy. He had come of a patriot stock, and from a part of Ireland where rebels to English rule were never either few or faint-hearted. He was born in the town of Tipperary, of parents whose circumstances were comfortable, and who, at the time of their decease, left him in possession of property worth a couple of hundred pounds per annum. He was educated for the medical profession in the Queen's College, Cork, spent some time in France, and subsequently visited America, where he made the acquaintance of the chief organizers of the Fenian movement, by whom he was regarded as a most valuable acquisition to the ranks of the Brotherhood. After his return to Ireland he continued to render the Fenian cause such services as lay in his power; and when James Stephens, who knew his courage and ability, invited him to take the post of chief editor of the Fenian organ which he was about to establish in Dublin, O'Leary readily obeyed the call, and accepted the dangerous position. In the columns of the *Irish People* he labored hard to defend and extend the principles of the Fenian organization until the date of his arrest and the suppression of the paper. The trial lasted from Friday, the 1st, up to Wednesday, the 6th of December, when it was closed with a verdict of guilty and a sentence of twenty years' penal servitude —Mr. Justice Fitzgerald remarking that no distinction in the degree of criminality could be discovered between the case of the prisoner and that of the previous convict. The following is the address delivered by O'Leary, who appeared to labor under much excitement, when asked in the usual terms if he had any reason to show why sentence should not be passed upon him :—

"I was not wholly unprepared for this verdict, because I felt that the government which could so safely pack the bench could not fail to make sure of its verdict."

Mr. Justice Fitzgerald :—"We are willing to hear anything in reason from you, but we cannot allow language of that kind to be used."

Mr. O'Leary :—"My friend, Mr. Luby, did not wish to touch on this matter from a natural fear lest he should do any harm to the other political prisoners ; but there can be but little fear of that now, for a jury has been found to convict me of this conspiracy upon the evidence. Mr. Luby admitted that he was technically guilty according to British law ; but I say that it is only by the most torturing interpretation that these men could make out their case against me. With reference to this conspiracy there has been much misapprehension in Ireland, and serious misapprehension. Mr. Justice Keogh said, in his charge against Mr. Luby, that men would be always found ready for money, or for some other motive, to place themselves at the disposal of the government; but I think the men who have been generally bought in this way, and who certainly made the best of the bargain, were agitators and not rebels. I have to say one word in reference to the foul charge upon which that miserable man, Barry, has made me responsible."

Mr. Justice Fitzgerald :—"We cannot allow that tone of observation."

Mr. O'Leary continued :—"That man has charged me—I need not defend myself or my friends from the charge. I shall merely denounce the moral assassin. Mr. Justice Keogh the other day spoke of revolutions, and administered a lecture to Mr. Luby. He spoke of cattle being driven away, and of houses being burned down, that men would be killed, and so on. I would like to know if all that does not apply to war as well as to revolution? One word more, and I shall have done. I have been found guilty of treason or treason-felony. Treason is a foul crime. The poet Dante consigned traitors to, I believe, the ninth circle of hell; but what kind of traitors? Traitors against king, against country, against friends and benefactors. England is not my country ; I have betrayed no friend, no benefactor. Sidney and Emmet were legal traitors, Jeffreys was a loyal man, and so was Norbury. I leave the matter there."

One hour after the utterance of these words John O'Leary, dressed in convict garb, his hair clipped, and his beard shaved off, was the occupant of a cell in Mountjoy prison, commencing his long term of suffering in expiation of the crime of having sought to obtain self-government for his native land.

JEREMIAH O'DONOVAN (ROSSA).

IN one of the preceding pages we have mentioned the fact that at the Cork Summer Assizes of 1859, a conviction was recorded against Jeremiah O'Donovan (Rossa) for his complicity in the Phœnix conspiracy, and he was then released on the understanding that, if he should be found engaging in similar practices, the Crown would bring him up for judgment. It is characteristic of the man that, with this conviction hanging like a millstone about his neck, he did not hesitate to take an active and an open part with the promoters of the Fenian movement. He travelled through various parts of Ireland in furtherance of the objects of the society; he visited America on the same mission, and, when the *Irish People* was started, he took the position of business manager in that fore-doomed establishment.

He was brought into the dock immediately after John O'Leary had been taken from it; but on representing that certain documents which he had not then at hand were necessary for his defence, he obtained a postponement of his trial for a few days. When he was again brought up for trial, he intimated to the court that he meant to conduct his own defence. And he entered upon it immediately. He cross-examined the informers in fierce fashion, he badgered the detectives, he questioned the police, he debated with the crown-lawyers, he argued with the judges, he fought with the crown side all round. But it was when the last of the witnesses had gone off the table that he set to work in good earnest. He took up the various publications that had been put in evidence against him, and claimed his legal right to read them all through. One of them was the file of the *Irish People* for the whole term of its existence! Horror sat upon the faces of judges, jurymen, sheriffs, lawyers, turnkeys, and all, when the prisoner gravely informed them that, as a compromise, he would not insist upon reading the advertisements! The bench were unable to deny that the prisoner was entitled to read, if not the entire, at any rate a great portion of the volume, and O'Donovan then applied himself to the task, selecting his readings more especially from those articles in which the political career of Mr. Justice Keogh was made the subject of animadversion. Right on he read, his lordship striving to look as composed and indifferent as possible, while every word of the bitter satire and fierce invective written against him by Luby and O'Leary was being launched at his heart. When articles of that class were exhausted, the prisoner turned to the most treasonable and seditious documents he could find, and commenced the reading of them, but the judges interposed; he claimed to be allowed to read a certain article—Judge Keogh objected—he proposed to read another—that was objected to also—he commenced to read another—he was stopped—he tried another—again Judge Keogh was down on him—then another—and he fared no better. So the fight went on throughout the livelong day, till the usual hour of adjournment had come and gone, and the prisoner himself was feeling parched, and weary, and exhausted. Observing that the lights were being now renewed, and that their lordships appeared satisfied to sit out the night, he anxiously inquired if the proceedings were not to be adjourned till morning. "Proceed, sir," was the stern reply of the judge, who knew that the physical powers of the prisoner could not hold out much longer. "A regular Norbury," gasped O'Donovan. "It's like a '98 trial." "You had better proceed, sir, with propriety," exclaimed the judge. "When do you propose stopping, my lord?" again inquired the prisoner. "Proceed, sir," was the reiterated reply. O'Donovan could stand it no longer, He had been reading and speaking for eight hours and a half. With one final protest against the arrangement by which Judge Keogh was sent to try the cases of men who had written and published such articles against him, he sat down, exclaiming that "English law might now take its course."

Next day the jury handed down their verdict of guilty. The Attorney-General then addressed the court, and referred to the previous conviction against the prisoner. O'Donovan was asked what he had to say in reference to that part of the case; and his reply was, that "the government might add as much as they pleased to the term of his sentence on that account, if it was any satisfaction to them." And when the like question was put to him regarding the present charge, he said :—

"With the fact that the government seized papers connected with my defence and examined them—with the fact that they packed the jury—with the fact that the government stated they would convict—with the fact that they sent Judge Keogh, a second Norbury, to try me—with these facts before me, it would be useless to say anything."

Judge Keogh proceeded to pass sentence. "The prisoner," he said, "had entertained those criminal designs since the year 1859 ;" whereupon O'Donovan broke in with the remark that he was "an Irishman since he was born." The judge said, "he would not waste words by trying to bring him to a sense of his guilt ; " O'Donovan's reply was—" It would be useless for you to try it." The judge told him his sentence was, that he be kept in penal servitude for the term of his natural life. "All right, my lord," exclaimed the unconquerable rebel, and with a smile to the sympathizing group around him, he walked with a light step from the dock.

The court was then adjourned to the 5th of January, 1866; and next day the judges set off for Cork city, to dispose of the Fenian prisoners there awaiting trial.

BRYAN DILLON, JOHN LYNCH, AND OTHERS.

On Wednesday, December 16th, the trial of O'Donovan (Rossa) was brought to a conclusion in Dublin. Next morning, away went judges, crown lawyers, spies, detectives, and informers, for the good city of Cork, where another batch of men accused of conspiring against British rule in Ireland—"the old crime of their race"—were awaiting the pronouncement of British law upon their several cases. Cork city in those days was known to be one of the *foci* of disaffection; perhaps it was its chief stronghold. The metropolis may have given an absolutely larger number of members to the Fenian organization, but, in proportion to the number of its population, the southern city was far more deeply involved in the movement. In Dublin, the seat of British rule in Ireland, many influences, which are but faintly represented in other parts of the country, are present and active to repress the national ardor of the people. Those influences are scarcely felt in the city of Saint Finbar. Not in Ireland is there a town in which the national sentiment is stronger or more widely diffused than in Cork. The citizens are a warm-hearted, quick-witted and high-spirited race, gifted with fine moral qualities, and profoundly attached to the national faith in religion and politics. Merchants, traders, professional men, shopkeepers, artisans, and all, are comparatively free from the spells of Dublin Castle, and the result is visible in their conduct. The Crown looks dubiously and anxiously upon a Cork jury; the patriot, when any work for Ireland is in hand, looks hopefully to the Cork people. The leaders of the Fenian movement thoroughly understood these facts, and devoted much of their time and attention to the propagation of their society among men so well inclined to welcome it. Their labors, if labors they could be called, were rewarded with a great measure of success. The young men of Cork turned into the organization by hundreds. There was no denying the fact; every one knew it; evidences of it were to be seen on all sides. The hope that was filling their hearts revealed itself in a thousand ways: in their marchings, their meetings, their songs, their music. The loyal party in the neighborhood grew alarmed, and the government shared their apprehensions. At the time of which we write, the opinion of the local magistracy, and that of the authorities at Dublin Castle, was, that Cork was a full-charged mine of "treason."

Thither was the Commission now sped, to carry terror, if the "strong arm of the law" could do it, into the hearts of those conspirators "against the royal name, style, and dignity" of her Majesty, Queen Victoria. As no one in the Castle could say to what desperate expedients those people might have recourse, it was thought advisable to take extraordinary precautions to insure the safety of the train which carried those important personages, her Majesty's judges, lawyers, witnesses, and informers, through the Munster counties, and on to the city by the Lee. "Never before," writes the special correspondent of the *Nation*, "had such a sight been witnessed on an Irish railway as that presented on Thursday along the line between Dublin and Cork. Armed sentries paced each mile of the railway; the platforms of the various stations through which the trains passed were lined with bodies of constabulary, and the bridges and viaducts on the way were guarded by a force of military, whose crimson coats and bright accoutrements stood out in bold relief from the dark ground on which they were stationed, against the grey December sky. As a further measure of precaution, a pilot engine steamed in advance of the train in which their lordships sat, one carriage of which was filled with armed police. And so, in some such manner as Grant or Sheridan might have journeyed along the Petersburg and Lynchburg railway while the flag of the Confederacy floated in Richmond, the two judges travelled down in safety to the headquarters of Fenianism in Munster."

Immediately on their arrival in Cork, the judges proceeded to the court-house and formally opened the business of the Commission. Next day Charles Underwood O'Connell and John M'Afferty were placed in the dock. These two men belonged to a class which formed the hope of the Fenian organization, and which the government regarded as one of the most dangerous elements of the conspiracy. They were Irish-American soldiers, trained to war, and inured to the hardships of campaigning in the great struggle which had but recently closed in America. They were a sample of the thousands of Irishmen who had acquired in that practical school the military knowledge which they knew was needed for the efficient direction of an insurrectionary movement in Ireland, and who were now burning for the time and opportunity to turn that knowledge to account. It was known that many of these men were, as quietly and secretly as might be, dropping into Queenstown as steamer after steamer arrived from the Land of the West, and were moving about through the southern counties, inspiriting the hearts of the Brotherhood by their presence and their promises, and imparting to them as much military instruction as was possible under the circumstances. To hunt down these "foreign emissaries," as the crown lawyers and the loyal prints were pleased to call them, and to deter others from following in their footsteps, was naturally a great object with the government; and when they placed Charles Underwood O'Connell and John M'Afferty in the dock, they felt they had made a good beginning. And these were representative men in their way. "It was a strange fate," says the writer from whom we have already quoted, "which had brought these men together in a felon's dock. They had been born in different lands—they had been reared thousands of miles apart—and they had fought and won distinction under different flags, and on opposing sides, in the American war. M'Afferty, born of Irish parents in Ohio, won his spurs in the Confederate army. O'Connell, who emigrated from Cork little more than two years ago, after the ruin of his family by a cruel act of confiscation and eviction, fought under the Stars and Stripes, and, like M'Afferty, obtained a captain's commission as the reward of his services. Had they crossed each other's path two years ago, they would probably have fought *a la mort;* but the old traditions, which linger in spite of every circumstance in the hearts of Irishmen, were strong in both, and the cause of Ireland united them, only, alas! that they might each of them pay the cost of their honest, if imprudent, enthusiasm, by sharing the same prison in Ireland, and falling within the grasp of the government which they looked on as the oppressor of their fatherland."

M'Afferty, however, was not fated to suffer on that occasion. Proof of his foreign birth having been adduced, the court held that his arrest on board the steamer in Queenstown harbor, when he had committed no overt act evidencing a treasonable intent, was illegal, and his trial was abandoned. The trial of Underwood O'Connell was then postponed for a few days, and two men, reputed to be "Centres" of the organization in Cork, were brought to the bar.

They were Bryan Dillon and John Lynch. Physically, they presented a contrast to the firm-built and wiry soldiers who had just quitted the dock. Dillon was afflicted with curvature of the spine, the result of an accident in early life; and his companion was far gone in that blighting and fatal disease, consumption. But, though they were not men for the toils of campaigning, for the mountain march, and the bivouac, and the thundering charge of battle, they had hearts full of enthusiasm for the cause in which they were engaged, and heads that could think, and plot, and plan, for its advancement.

We need not here go through the sad details of their trials. Our purpose is to bring before our readers the courage and the constancy of the martyrs to the cause of Irish nationality, and to record the words in which they gave expression to the patriotic sentiments that inspired them. It is, however, to be recollected that many of the accused at these commissions—men as earnest, as honest, and as devoted to the cause of their country as any that ever lived—made no such addresses from the dock as we can include in this volume. All men are not orators; and it will often occur that one who has been tried for life and liberty in a British court of law, on the evidence of spies and informers, will have much to press upon his mind, and many things more directly relevant to the trial than any profession of political faith would be, to say, when called upon, to show reason why sentence should not be passed upon him. The evidence adduced in these cases is usually a compound of truth and falsehood. Some of the untruths sworn to are simply blunders, resulting from the confused impressions and the defective memory of the witnesses; others are deliberate inventions, made, sworn to, backed up, and persevered in, for the purpose of insuring a successful result for the prosecution. Naturally the first impulse of the accused, when he is allowed to speak for himself, is to refer to these murderous falsehoods; and, in the excitement and trouble of those critical moments, it is all that some men can venture to do. Such criticisms of the prosecution are often valuable to the prisoner from a moral point of view, but rarely have they any influence upon the result of the trial. All things considered, it must be allowed that they act best who do not forget to speak the words of patriotism, according to the measure of their abilities, before the judge's fiat has sealed their lips, and the hand of British law has swept them away to the dungeon or the scaffold.

"Guilty" was the verdict returned by the jury against Bryan Dillon and John Lynch. The evidence against them, indeed, was strong, but its chief strength lay in the swearing of an approver named Warner, a callous and unscrupulous wretch, from whose mind the idea of conscience seemed to have perished utterly. If there was any check upon the testimony of this depraved creature, it existed only in some prudential instinct, suggesting to him that, even in such cases as these, a witness might possibly overdo his work; and perhaps in a caution or two given him in a private and confidential manner by some of the managers of the prosecution. Warner's evidence in this case was conclusive to the minds of all who chose to believe it; and therefore it was that those prisoners had not long been occupants of the dock when the question was put to them what they had to say why sentence should not be passed on them. In reply, Bryan Dillon said:—

"My lords, I never was for one minute in Warner's company. What Warner swore about me was totally untrue. I never was at a meeting at Geary's house. The existence of the Fenian organization has been proved sufficiently to your lordships. I was a Centre in that organization; but it does not follow that I had to take the chair at any meeting, as it was a military organization. I do not want to conceal anything. Warner had no connection with me whatever. With respect to the observation of the Attorney-General, which pained me very much, that it was intended to seize property, it does not follow because of my social station that I intended to seize the property of others. My belief in the ultimate independence of Ireland is as fixed as my religious belief——."

At this point he was interrupted by Judge Keogh, who declared he could not listen to words that were, in fact, a repetition of the prisoner's offence. But it was only words of this kind that Bryan Dillon cared to say at the time; and as the privilege of offering some remarks in defence of his political opinions—a privilege accorded to all prisoners in trials for treason and treason-felony up to that time—had been denied to him, he chose to say no more. And then the judge pronounced the penalty of his offending, which was, penal servitude for a term of ten years.

John Lynch's turn to speak came next. Interrogated in the usual form, he stood forward, raised his feeble frame to its full height, and with a proud, grave smile upon his pallid features, he thus addressed the court:—

"I will say a very few words, my lords. I know it would be only a waste of public time if I entered into anye xplanations of my political opinions—opinions which I know are shared by the vast majority of my fellow-countrymen. Standing here as I do will be to them the surest proof of my sincerity and honesty. With reference to the statement of Warner, all I have to say is, and I say it honestly and solemnly, that I never attended a meeting at Geary's, that I never exercised with a rifle there, that I never learned the use of the rifle, nor did any of the other things he swore to. With respect to my opinions on British rule in this country—"

Mr. Justice Keogh:—" We can't hear that."

The Prisoner:—" All I have to say is, that I was not at Geary's house for four or five months before my arrest, so that Warner's statement is untrue. If, having served my country honestly and sincerely be treason, I am not ashamed of it. I am now prepared to receive any punishment British law can inflict on me."

The punishment decreed to this pure-minded and brave-spirited patriot was ten years of penal servitude. But to him it was practically a sentence of death. The rigors and horrors of prison life were more than his failing constitution could long endure ; and but a few months from the date of his conviction elapsed when his countrymen were pained by the intelligence that the faithful-hearted John Lynch filled a nameless grave in an English prison-yard. He died in the hospital of Woking prison on the 2d day of June, 1866.

When Bryan Dillon and John Lynch were removed from the dock (Tuesday, December 19th), two men named Jeremiah Donovan and John Duggan were put forward, the former charged with having been a Centre in the Fenian organization, and the latter with having sworn some soldiers into the society. Both were found guilty. Donovan made no remarks when called upon for what he had to say. Duggan contradicted the evidence of the witnesses on several points, and said :—

"I do not state those things in order to change the sentence I am about to receive. I know your lordships' minds are made up on that. I state this merely to show what kind of tools the British government employ to procure those convictions. I have only to say, and I appeal to any intelligent man for his opinion, that the manner in which the jury list was made out for these trials clearly shows that in this country political trials are a mere mockery."

At this point the judge cut short the prisoner's address, and the two men were sentenced, Donovan to five years and Duggan to ten years of penal servitude.

The trial of Underwood O'Connell was then proceeded with. It concluded on December 21st, with a verdict of guilty. In response to the question which was then addressed to him, he spoke at considerable length, detailing the manner of his arrest, complaining of the horrible indignities to which he had been subjected in prison, and asserting that he had not received a fair and impartial trial. He spoke amidst a running fire of interruptions from the court, and, when he came to refer to his political opinions, his discourse was peremptorily suppressed. "The sentiments and hopes that animate me," he said, "are well known." "Really we will not bear those observations," interposed Mr. Justice Keogh. "It has been brought forward here," said the prisoner, "that I held a commission in the 99th regiment—in Colonel O'Mahony's regiment. Proud as I am of having held a commission in the United States service, I am equally proud of holding command under a man——" Here his speech was stopped by the judges, and Mr. Justice Keogh proceeded to pass sentence. In the course of his address his lordship made the following observations:—

"You, it appears, went to America; you entered yourself in the American army, thus violating, to a certain extent, your allegiance as a British subject. But that is not the offence you are charged with here to day. You say you swore allegiance to the American Republic, but no man, by so doing, can relieve himself from his allegiance to the British Crown. From the moment a man is born in this country he owes allegiance, he is a subject."

Hearing these words, and remembering the great outcry that was being made by the friends of the government against the Irish-American Fenians on the ground that they were "foreigners," the prisoner interposed the apt remark on his lordship's legal theory:—

"If that is so, why am I charged with bringing over foreigners? John O'Mahony is no foreigner."

To that remark Judge Keogh did not choose to make any reply. It overturned him completely. Nothing could better exhibit the absurdity of railing against those Irishmen as "foreigners" in one breath, and in the next declaring their allegiance to the British Crown perpetual and inalienable. His lordship may have winced as the point was so quickly and neatly brought home to him; but at all events he went on with his address, and informed the prisoner that his punishment was to be ten years of penal servitude. Upon which, the comment of the prisoner as he quitted the dock was, that he hoped there would be an exchange of prisoners before that time.

In quick succession four men named Casey, Regan, Hayes, and Barry, were tried, convicted, and sentenced. Each in turn impugned the evidence of the informer Warner, protested against the constitution of the juries, and attempted to say a few words declaratory of their devotion to the cause of Ireland. But the judges were quick to suppress every attempt of this kind, and only a few fragments of sentences are on record to indicate the thoughts to which these soldiers of liberty would have given expression if the opportunity had not been denied to them.

John Kennealy was the next occupant of the dock. He was a young man of high personal character, and of great intelligence, and was a most useful member of the organization; his calling—that of commercial traveller— enabling him to act as agent and missionary of the society without attracting to himself the suspicion which would be aroused by the movements of other men. In his case, also, the verdict was given in the one fatal word. And when asked what he had to say for himself, his reply was in these few forcible and dignified sentences :—

"My lord, it is scarcely necessary for me to say anything. I am sure, from the charge of your lordship, the jury could find no other verdict than has been found. The verdict against me has been found by the means by which political convictions have always been found in this country. As to the informer Warner, I have only to say that, directly or indirectly, I never was in the same room with him, nor had he any means of knowing my political opinions. As to my connection with Mr. Luby, I am proud of that connection. I neither regret it, nor anything else I have done, politically or otherwise."

On the conclusion of this trial, on Saturday, January 2d, 1866, two other cases were postponed without option of bail; some other persons were allowed to stand out on sureties, and we read that " John M'Afferty and

William Mackay, being aliens, were admitted to bail on their own recognizance, and Judge Keogh said that, if they left the country, they would not be required up for trial when called." We read, also, in the newspapers of that time, that "the prisoners, M'Afferty and Mackay, when leaving the courts, were followed by large crowds, who cheered them loudly through the streets."

The Cork Commission was then formally closed, and next day the judges set off to resume in Dublin the work of trying Irish conspirators against the rule of England over their native land.

CHARLES JOSEPH KICKHAM.

In the year 1825, in the village of Mullinahone, county Tipperary, Charles J. Kickham first saw the light. His father, John Kickham, was proprietor of the chief drapery establishment in that place, and was held in high esteem, by the whole country round about, for his integrity, intelligence, and patriotic spirit. During the boyhood of young Kickham the Repeal agitation was at its height, and he soon became thoroughly versed in its arguments, and inspired by its principles, which he often heard discussed in his father's shop and by his hearth, and amongst all his friends and acquaintances. Like all the young people of the time, and a great many of the old ones, his sympathies went with the Young Ireland party at the time of their withdrawal from the Repeal ranks. In 1848 he was the leading spirit of the Confederation Club at Mullinahone, which he was mainly instrumental in founding; and after the *fiasco* at Ballingarry he was obliged to conceal himself for some time, in consequence of the part he had taken in rousing the people of his native village to action. When the excitement of that period had subsided, he again appeared in his father's house, resumed his accustomed sports of fishing and fowling, and devoted much of his time to literary pursuits, for which he had great natural capacity, and towards which he was all the more inclined because of the blight put upon his social powers by an unfortunate accident which occurred to him when about the age of thirteen years. He had brought a flask of powder near the fire, and was engaged either in the operation of drying it or casting some grains into the coals for amusement, when the whole quantity exploded. The shock, and the injuries he sustained, nearly proved fatal to him; when he recovered, it was with his hearing nearly quite destroyed, and his sight permanently impaired. But Kickham had the poet's soul within him, and it was his compensation for the losses he had sustained. He could still hold communion with nature and with his own mind, and could give to the national cause the service of a bold heart and a finely-cultivated intellect. Subsequent to the decadence of the '48 movement he wrote a good deal in prose and verse, and contributed gratuitously to various national publications. His intimate acquaintance with the character and habits of the peasantry gave a great charm to his stories and sketches of rural life; and his poems were always marked by grace, simplicity, and tenderness. Many of them have attained a large degree of popularity amongst his countrymen in Ireland and elsewhere, and taken a permanent place in the poetic literature of the Irish race. Amongst these, his ballads entitled "Patrick Sheehan," "Rory of the Hill," and "The Irish Peasant Girl," are deserving of special mention. To these remarks it remains to be added that, as regards personal character, Charles J. Kickham was one of the most amiable of men. He was generous and kindly by nature, and was a pious member of the Catholic Church, to which his family had given priests and nuns.

Such was the man whom the myrmidons of the law placed in the dock of Green-street court-house, when, on January 5th, 1866, after the return of the judges from Cork, the Commission was reopened in Dublin. His appearance was somewhat peculiar. He was a tall, strong, rough-bearded man, with that strained expression of face which is often worn by people of dim sight. Around his neck he wore an india-rubber tube, or ear trumpet, through which any words that were necessary to be addressed to him were shouted into his ear by some of his friends, or by his solicitor. His trial did not occupy much time, for, on the refusal of the crown lawyers and judges to produce the convict, Thomas Clarke Luby, whom he conceived to be a material witness for his defence, he directed his lawyers to abandon the case, and contented himself with reading to the court some remarks on the evidence which had been offered against him. The chief feature in this address was his denial of all knowledge of the "executive document." He had never seen or heard of it until it turned up in connection with those trials. Referring to one of the articles with the authorship of which he was charged, he said he wondered how any Irishman, taking into consideration what had occurred in Ireland during the last eighty-four years, could hesitate to say to the enemy—"Give us our country to ourselves, and let us see what we can do with it." Alluding to a report that the government contemplated making some concession to the claims of the Catholic bishops, he remarked that concessions to Ireland had always been a result of Fenianism in one shape or another, and that he believed the present manifestation of the national spirit would have weight, as former ones had, with the rulers of the country. As regards the landed class in Ireland, the *Irish People*, he contended, had said nothing more than was said by Thomas Davis, whose works every one admired. That eminent Irishman, afflicted and stung to the heart by witnessing the system of depopulation which was going on throughout the country, had written these words:—

> "God of Justice, I sighed, send your Spirit down
> On those lords so cruel and proud,
> And soften their hearts, and relax their frown,
> Or else, I cried aloud,
> Vouchsafe Thy strength to the peasant's hand
> To drive them at length from out the land."

He had not gone farther than the writer of these lines, and now, he said, they might send him to a felon's doom if they liked.

And they did send him to it. Judge Keogh, before passing sentence, asked him if he had any further remarks to make in reference to his case. Mr. Kickham briefly replied:—

"I believe, my lords, I have said enough already. I will only add that I am convicted for doing nothing but my duty. I have endeavored to serve Ireland, and now I am prepared to suffer for Ireland."

Then the judge, with many expressions of sympathy for the prisoner, and many compliments in reference to his intellectual attainments, sentenced him to be kept in penal servitude for fourteen years. His solicitor, Mr. John Lawless, announced the fact to him through his ear trumpet. Charles J. Kickham bowed to the judges, and with an expression of perfect tranquillity on his features, went into captivity.

GENERAL THOMAS F. BURKE

THE year of grace, 1867, dawned upon a cloudy and troublous period in Irish politics. There was danger brewing throughout the land ; under the crust of society the long-confined lava of Fenianism effervesced and glowed. There were strange rumors in the air; strange sounds were heard at the death of night on the hillsides and in the meadows ; and through the dim moonlight masses of men were seen in secluded spots moving in regular bodies, and practising military evolutions. From castle and mansion and country-seat the spectre of alarm glided to and fro, whispering with bloodless lips of coming convulsions and slaughter, of the opening of the crater of revolution, and of a war against property and class. Symptoms of danger were everywhere seen and felt ; the spirit of disaffection had not been crushed ; it rode on the night-wind and glistened against the rising sun ; it filled rath and fort and crumbling ruin with mysterious sounds; it was seen in the brightening eyes and the bold demeanor of the peasantry ; in the signals passing amongst the people ; in their secret gatherings and closely guarded conclaves. For years and years Fenianism had been threatening, boasting, and promising, and now the fury of the storm, long pent-up, was about to burst forth over the land—the hour for action was at hand.

Between the conviction of Luby, O'Leary, and Kickham, and the period at which we are now arrived, many changes of importance had taken place in the Fenian organization. In America the society had been revolutionized—it had found new leaders, new principles, new plans of action ; it had passed through the ordeal of war, and held its ground amidst flashing swords and the smoke of battle ; it had survived the shocks of division, disappointment, and failure ; treachery, incapacity and

GENERAL THOMAS F. BURKE.

open hostility had failed to shatter it; and it grew apace in strength, influence, and resources. At home Fenianism, while losing little in numerical strength, had declined in effectiveness, in prestige, in discipline, and in organization. Its leaders had been swept into the prisons, and though men perhaps as resolute stepped forward to fill the vacant places, there was a loss in point of capacity and intelligence; and to the keen observer it became apparent that the Fenian Society in Ireland had attained to the zenith of its power on the day that the *Irish People* office was sacked by the police. Never again did the prospects of Fenianism, whatever they might then have been, look equally bright; and when the Brotherhood at length sprang to action, they fought with a sword already broken to the hilt, and under circumstances the most ominous and inauspicious.

The recent history of the Fenian movement is so thoroughly understood that anything like a detailed account of its changes and progress is, in these pages, unnecessary. We shall only say that, when James Stephens arrived in America in May, 1866, after escaping from Richmond prison, he found the society in the States split up into two opposing parties between whom a violent quarrel was raging. John O'Mahony had been deposed from his position of "Head Centre" by an all but unanimous vote of the Senate, or governing body of the association, who charged him and his officials with a reckless and corrupt expenditure of the society's funds; and these, in turn, charged the Senate party with the crime of breaking up the organization for mere personal and party purposes. A large section of the society still adhered to O'Mahony, in consideration of his past services in their cause; but the greater portion of it, and nearly all its oldest, best-known and most trusted leaders gave their allegiance to the Senate and to its elected President, William R. Roberts, an Irish merchant of large means, of talent and energy, of high character and unquestionable devotion to the cause of his country. Many friends of the Brotherhood hoped that James Stephens would seek to heal the breach between these parties, but the course he took was not calculated to effect that purpose. He denounced the "senators" in the most extravagant terms, and invited both branches of the organization to unite under himself as supreme and irresponsible leader and governor of the entire movement. The O'Mahony section did not answer very heartily to this invitation; the Senate party indignantly rejected it, and commenced to occupy themselves with preparations for an immediate grapple with British power in Canada. Those men were thoroughly in earnest; and the fact became plain to every intelligence, when, in the latter part of May, 1866, the Fenian contingents from the various States of the Union began to concentrate on the Canadian border. On the morning of the 1st June some hundreds of them crossed the Niagara river, and took possession of the village of Fort Erie on the Canadian side. They were soon confronted with detachments of the volunteer force which had been collected to resist the invasion, and at Limestone Ridge they were met by the "Queen's Own" regiment of volunteers from Toronto, under the command of Colonel Booker. A smart battle ensued, the result of which was that the "Queen's Own" were utterly routed by the Irish under Colonel John O'Neill, and forced to run in wild confusion for a town some miles distant, Colonel Booker on his charger leading the way and distancing all competitors. Had the Irish been allowed to follow up this victory, it is not unlikely that they would have swept Canada clear of the British forces, and then, according to their programme, made that country their base of operations against British power in Ireland. But the American government interfered and put an effectual stopper on their progress; they seized the arms of the Irish soldiers on the frontier, they sent up large parties of the States soldiery to prevent the crossing of hostile parties into British territory, and stationed war-vessels in the river for the same purpose. Reinforcements being thus cut off from them, the victors of Limestone Ridge found themselves under the necessity of recrossing the river to the American shore, which they did on the night of the 2d of June, bringing with them the flags and other trophies which they had captured from the royal troops. The first brush between the Fenian forces and the Queen's troops inspired the former with high hopes, and with great confidence in their capacity to humble "the English red below the Irish green," if only they could start on anything like fair terms. But now that the American government had forbidden the fight in Canada, what was to be done? James Stephens answered that question. He would have a fight in Ireland—the right place, he contended, in which to fight *for* Ireland. The home organization was subject to his control, and would spring to arms at his bidding. He would not only bid them fight, but would lead them to battle, and that at no distant day. The few remaining months of 1866 would not pass away without witnessing the commencement of the struggle. So he said, and so he swore, in the most solemn manner, at various public meetings which he had called for the purpose of obtaining funds wherewith to carry on the conflict. The prudence of thus publishing the date which he had fixed for the outbreak of the insurrection was very generally questioned; but, however great might be his error in this respect, many believed that he would endeavor to make good his words. The British government believed it, and prepared for the threatened rising by hurrying troops and munitions of war across to Ireland, and putting the various forts and barracks in a state of thorough defence. As the last days and nights of 1866 wore away, both the government and the people expected every moment to hear the first crash of the struggle. But it came not. The year 1867 came in, and still all was quiet. What had become of James Stephens? The astonished and irate Fenians of New York investigated the matter, and found that he was peacefully and very privately living at lodgings in some part of that city, afraid to face the wrath of the men whom he had so egregiously deceived. We need not describe the outburst of rage and indignation which followed on the discovery; suffice it to say that the once popular and powerful Fenian leader soon found it prudent to quit the United States, and take up his abode in a part of the world where there were no Fenian circles, and no settlements of the swarming Irish race.

Amongst the men who had rallied round James Stephens in America there were many whose honesty was untainted, and who had responded to his call with the full intention of committing themselves, without regard to consequences, to the struggle which he promised to initiate. They believed his representations respecting the prospects of an insurrection in Ireland, and they pledged themselves to fight by his side and perish, if necessary, in the good old cause, in defence of which their fathers had bled. They scorned to violate their engagements; they spurned the idea of shrinking from the difficulty they had pledged themselves to face, and resolved that, come what may, the reproach of cowardice and bad faith should never be uttered against them. Accordingly, in January, '67, they began to land in scattered parties at Queenstown, and spread themselves through the country, taking every precaution to escape the suspicion of the police. They set to work diligently and energetically to organize an insurrectionary outbreak; they found innumerable difficulties in their path; they found the people almost wholly unarmed; they found the wisest of the Fenian leaders opposed to an immediate outbreak, but still they persevered. How ably they performed their work, there is plenty of evidence to show; and if the Irish outbreak of '67 was short-lived and easily suppressed, it was far from contemptible in the preconcert and organization which it evidenced.

One hitch did occur in the accomplishment of their designs. On Wednesday, February 13th, the exciting news was flashed throughout the land that the Fenians had broken into insurrection at Kerry. The news was true. The night of the 12th of February had been fixed for a simultaneous rising of the Fenians in Ireland; but the outbreak had been subsequently postponed, and emissaries were despached to all parts of the country with the intelligence of the change of date. The change of date was everywhere learned in time to prevent premature action except at Cahirciveen, in the west of Kerry, where the members of the Brotherhood, acting upon the orders received, unearthed their arms, and gaily proceeded towards Killarney to form a junction with the insurgents, who, they imagined, had converged from various parts of the county in that town. Before many hours had elapsed they discovered their mistake: they heard, before arriving at Killarney, that they were the only representatives of the Irish Republic that had appeared in the field, and, turning to the mountains, they broke up and disappeared.

Short-lived as was their escapade, it filled the heart of England with alarm. In hot haste the *Habeas Corpus* Suspension Act, which had been permitted to lapse a month before, was reënacted; the arrests and police raids were renewed, and from the Giant's Causeway to Cape Clear the gaols were filled with political prisoners. Still the Irish-Americans worked on; some of them were swept off to prison, but the greater number of them managed to escape detection, and in spite of the vigilance of the authorities, and the extraordinary power possessed by the government and its officials, they managed to carry on the business of the organization, to mature their plans, and to perfect their arrangements for the fray.

We do not propose to write here a detailed account of the last of the outbreaks which, since the Anglo-Norman invasion, have periodically convulsed our country. The time is not yet come when the whole history of that extraordinary movement can be revealed, and such of its facts as are now available for publication, are fresh in the minds of our readers. On the night of the 5th of March, the Fenian bands took the field in Dublin, Louth, Tipperary, Cork, Waterford, Limerick and Clare. They were, in all cases, wretchedly armed, their plans had been betrayed by unprincipled associates, and ruin tracked their venture from the outset. They were everywhere confronted by well-armed, disciplined men, and their reckless courage could not pluck success for the maze of adverse circumstances that surrounded them. The elements, too, befriended England as they had often done before. Hardly had the insurgents left their homes when the clear March weather gave place to the hail and snow of mid-winter. The howling storm, edged by the frost and hail, swept over mountain and valley, rendering life in the open air all but impossible to man. The weather in itself would have been sufficient to dispose of the Fenian insurgents. Jaded and exhausted they returned to their homes, and twenty-four hours after the flag of revolt had been unfurled, the Fenian insurrection was at an end.

Amongst the Irish officers who left America to share in the expected battle for Irish rights, a conspicuous place must be assigned Thomas F. Burke. He was born at Fethard, county Tipperary, on the 10th of December, 1840, and twelve years later sailed away towards the setting sun, his parents having resolved on seeking a home in the far West. In New York, young Burke attended the seminary established by the late Archbishop Hughes, where he received an excellent education, after which he was brought up to his father's trade—that of house-painter. For many years he worked steadily at his trade, contributing largely to the support of his family. The outbreak of the war, however, acted in the same manner on Burke's temperament as on thousands of his fellow-countrymen. He threw aside his peaceful avocation, and joined the Confederate army. He served under General Patrick Cleburne, who died in his arms, and he fought side by side with the son of another distinguished exile, John Mitchel. When the war had closed, he returned a Brevet-General, northwards, with a shattered limb and an impaired constitution. In June, 1865, he joined the Wolfe Tone Circle of the Fenian Brotherhood in New York, and was appointed soon afterwards to act as organizer in the Brotherhood for the district of Manhattan. He filled this post with great satisfaction to his associates, and continued to labor energetically in this capacity until his departure for Ireland, at the close of 1866.

Tipperary was assigned to Burke as the scene of his revolutionary labors in Ireland. He arrived in Clonmel early in February, where he was arrested on suspicion, but was immediately discharged—his worn appearance and physical infirmity giving strong corroboration of his assertion, that he had come to Ireland for the benefit of his health. On the night of the insurrection he placed himself at the head of the Fenian party that assembled in the neighborhood of Tipperary, but he quickly saw the folly of attempting a revolution with the scanty band of unarmed men that rallied round him. On the evening of the 6th his followers were attacked by a detachment of soldiers at Ballyhurst Fort, about three miles from Tipperary; Burke saw the uselessness of resistance, and advised his followers to disperse—an injunction which they appear to have obeyed. Burke himself was thrown from his horse and captured. He was conveyed to the jail of Tipperary, and was brought to trial in the Green-street court-house, in Dublin, on the 24th of April following. He was convicted of high treason, and sentenced to death in the usual form. The following speech delivered by him after conviction is well worthy of a place in the Irish heart:—

"My lords:—It is not my intention to occupy much of your time in answering the question—what I have to say why sentence should not be passed upon me? But I may, with your permission, review a little of the evidence that has been brought against me. The first evidence that I would speak of is that of Sub-inspector Kelly, who had a conversation with me in Clonmel. He states that he asked me, either how was my friend, or what about my friend, Mr. Stephens, and that I made answer and said that he was the most idolized man that ever had been, or that ever would be, in America. Here, standing on the brink of my grave, and in the presence of the Almighty and ever-living God, I brand that as being the foulest perjury that ever man gave utterance to. In any conversation that occurred, the name of Stephens was not mentioned. I shall pass from that, and then touch on the evidence of Brett. He states that I assisted in distributing the bread to the parties in the fort, and that I stood with him in the wagon or cart. This is also false. I was not in the fort at the time; I was not there when the bread was distributed. I came in afterwards. Both of these assertions have been made and submitted to the men in whose hands my life rested, as evidence made on oath by these men—made solely and purely for the purpose of giving my body to an untimely grave. There are many points, my lords, that have been sworn to here, to prove my complicity in a great many acts it has been alleged I took part in. It is not my desire now, my lords, to give utterance to one word against the verdict which has been pronounced upon me. But fully conscious of my honor as a man, which has never been impugned; fully conscious that I can go into my grave with a name and character unsullied, I can only say that these parties, actuated by a desire either of their own aggrandizement, or to save their paltry, miserable lives, have pandered to the appetite, if I may so speak, of justice, and my life shall pay the forfeit. Fully convinced and satisfied of the righteousness of my every act in connection with the late revolutionary movement in Ireland, I have nothing to recall—nothing that I would not do again, nothing for which I should feel the blush of shame mantling my brow ; my conduct and career, both here as a private citizen, and in America— if you like—as a soldier, are before you ; and even in this, my hour of trial, I feel the consciousness of having lived an honest man, and I will die proudly, believing that, if I have given my life to give freedom and liberty to the land of my birth, I have done only that which every Irishman, and every man whose soul throbs with a feeling of liberty, should do. I, my lords, shall scarcely—I feel I should not at all—mention the name of Massey. I feel I should not pollute my lips with the name of that traitor, whose illegitimacy has been proved here—a man whose name even is not known, and who, I deny point-blank, ever wore the star of a colonel in the Confederate army. Him I shall let rest. I shall pass him, wishing him, in the words of the poet :—

'May the grass wither from his feet ;
The woods deny him shelter ; earth a home ;
The dust a grave ; the sun his light ;
And heaven its God !'

"Let Massey remember from this day forth that he carries with him, as my able and eloquent counsel (Mr. Dowse) has stated, a serpent that will gnaw his conscience—will carry about him in his breast a living hell from which he can never be separated. I, my lords, have no desire for the name of a martyr ; I seek not the death of a martyr ; but if it is the will of the Almighty and Omnipotent God that my devotion for the land of my birth shall be tested on the scaffold, I am willing there to die in defence of the right of men to free governmen—the right of an oppressed people to throw off the yoke of thraldom. I am an Irishman by birth, an American by adoption ; by nature a lover of freedom—an enemy to the power that holds my native land in the bonds of tyranny. It has so often been admitted that the oppressed have a right to throw off the yoke of oppression, even by English statesmen, that I do not deem it necessary to advert to the fact in a British court of justice. Ireland's children are not, never were, and never will be, willing or submissive slaves ; and as long as England's flag covers one inch of Irish soil, just so long will they believe it to be a divine right to conspire, imagine, and devise means to hurl it from power, and to erect in its stend the godlike structure of self-government. I shall now, my lords, before I go any further, perform one important duty to my learned, talented, and eloquent counsel. I offer them that which is poor enough, the thanks, the sincere and heartfelt thanks of an honest man. I offer them, too, in the name of America, the thanks of the Irish people. I know that I am here without a relative—without a friend—in fact, 3,000 miles away from my family. But I know that I am not forgotten there. The great and generous Irish heart of America to-day feels for me—to-day sympathizes with and does not forget the man who is willing to tread the scaffold—aye, defiantly, proudly, conscious of no wrong—in defence of American principles—in defence of liberty. To Messrs. Butt, Dowse, O'Loghlen, and all the counsel for the prisoners, for some of whom I believe Mr. Curran will appear, and my very able solicitor, Mr. Lawless, I return, individually and collectively, my sincere and heartfelt thanks.

" I shall now, my lords, as no doubt you will suggest to me, think of the propriety of turning my attention to the world beyond the grave. I shall now look only to that home where sorrows are at an end, where joy is eternal. I shall hope and pray that freedom may yet dawn on this poor down-trodden country. It is my hope, it is my prayer, and the last words that I shall utter will be a prayer to God for forgiveness, and a prayer for poor old Ireland. Now, my lords, in relation to the other man, Corridon, I will make a few remarks. Perhaps before I go to Corridon, I should say much has been spoken on that table of Colonel Kelly, and of the meetings held at his lodgings in London. I desire to state I never knew where Colonel Kelly's lodgings were. I never knew where he lived in London, till I heard the informer Massey announce it on the table. I never attended a meeting at Colonel Kelly's; and the hundred other statements that have been made about him, I now solemnly declare on my honor as a man, as a dying man,—these statements have been totally unfounded and false from beginning to end. In relation to the small paper that was introduced here and brought against me as evidence, as having been found on my person in connection with that oath, I desire to say that that paper was not found on my person. I knew no person whose name was on that paper. O'Beirne, of Dublin, or those other delegates you heard of, I never saw or met. That paper has been put in there for some purpose. I can swear positively it is not in my handwriting. I can also swear I never saw it; yet it is used as evidence against me. Is this justice? Is this right? Is this manly? I am willing, if I have transgressed the laws, to suffer the penalty, but I object to this system of trumping up a case to take away the life of a human being. True, I ask for no mercy. I feel that, with my present emaciated frame and somewhat shattered constitution, it is better that my life should be brought to an end than that I should drag out a miserable existence in the prison dens of Portland. Thus it is, my lords, I accept the verdict. Of course

my acceptance of it is unnecessary, but I am satisfied with it.
And now I shall close. True it is there are many feelings that actuate me at this moment. In fact, these few disconnected remarks can give no idea of what I desire to state to the court. I have ties to bind me to my life and society as strong as any man in this court can have. I have a family I love as much as any man in this court loves his family. But I can remember the blessing I received from an aged mother's lips as I left her the last time. She, speaking as the Spartan mother did. said—'Go, my boy, return either with your shield or upon it.' This reconciles me—this gives me heart. I submit to my doom ; and I hope that God will forgive me my past sins. I hope, also, that, inasmuch as He has for seven hundred years preserved Ireland, notwithstanding all the tyranny to which she has been subjected, as a separate and distinct nationality, He will also assist her to retrieve her fallen fortunes— to rise in her beauty and majesty, the Sister of Columbia, the peer of any nation in the world."

General Burke, as our readers are well aware, was not executed. The government shrank from carrying out the barbarous sentence of the law, and his punishment was changed to the still more painful, if less appalling, fate, of penal servitude for life. Of General Burke's private character we have said little ; but our readers will be able to understand it from the subjoined brief extracts from two of his letters. On the very night previous to his trial he wrote to his mother from Kilmainham prison :—

" * * * On last Easter Sunday I partook of holy communion at a late Mass. I calculated the difference of time between this longitude and yours, for I knew that you and my dear sisters were partaking of the sacrament at early Mass on that day, as was your wont, and I felt that our souls were in communion together."

We conclude with the following letter from General Burke, which has never before been published, and which we are sure will be of deep interest to our readers. It is addressed to the reverend gentleman who had been his father confessor in Clonmel :—

"KILMAINHAM GAOL,
4th, Month of Mary.

"DEAR REV. FATHER:

" * * * I am perfectly calm and resigned, with my thoughts firmly centred with hope in the goodness and mercy of that kind Redeemer, whose precious blood was shed for my salvation ; as also in the meditation and intercession of His Blessed Mother, who is my Star of Hope and Consolation. I know, dear father, I need not ask you to be remembered in your prayers, for I feel that in your supplication to the Throne of Mercy I have not been forgotten. * * * I have only one thought which causes me much sorrow, and that is that my good and loving mother will break down under the weight of her affliction, and, O God! I who loved her more than the life which animates the hand that writes, to be the cause of it! This thought unmans and prostrates me. I wrote to her at the commencement of my trial, and told her how I thought it would terminate, and spoke a long and last farewell. I have not written since—it would break my heart to attempt it; but I would ask you as an especial favor that you would write to her and tell her I am happy and reconciled to the will of God, who has given me this opportunity of saving my immortal soul. I hope to hear from you before I leave this world.

"Good-by, father, and that God may bless you in your ministry is the prayer of an obedient child of the Church.

"THOMAS F. BURKE."

CAPTAIN JOHN M'AFFERTY.

IT is not Irish-born men alone whose souls are filled with a chivalrous love for Ireland, and a stern hatred of her oppressor. There are, amongst the ranks of her patriots, none more generous, more resolute, or more active in her cause than the children born of Irish parents in various parts of the world. In London, Liverpool, Manchester, Birmingham, Glasgow, and all the large towns of Great Britain, throughout the United States, and in the British colonies, many of the best known and most thorough-going "Irishmen" are men whose place of birth was not beneath the Irish skies, and amongst them are some who never saw the shores of the Green Isle. One of these men was Captain John M'Afferty. He was born of Irish parents in the State of Ohio, in the year 1838, and at their knees he heard of the rights and wrongs of Ireland, learned to sympathize with the sufferings of that country, and to regard the achievement of its freedom as a task in which he was bound to bear a part. He grew up to be a man of adventurous and daring habits, better fitted for the camp than for the ordinary ways of peaceful life; and when the civil war broke out he soon found his place in one of those regiments of the Confederacy, whose special duty lay in the accomplishment of the most hazardous enterprises. He belonged to the celebrated troop of Morgan's guerillas, whose dashing feats of valor so often filled the Federal forces with astonishment and alarm. In the latter part of 1865 he crossed over to this country to assist in leading the insurrection which was then being prepared by the Fenian organization. He was arrested, as already stated in these pages, on board the steamer at Queenstown, before he had set foot on Irish soil; when brought to trial at Cork, in the month of December, the lawyers discovered that being an alien, and having committed no overt act of treason within the Queen's dominions, there was no case against him, and he was consequently discharged. He then went back to America, took an active part in some Fenian meetings, made a speech at one of them which was held at Jones's Wood, and when the report of the proceedings appeared in print, he, with a sense of grim humor, posted a copy containing his oration to the governor of Mountjoy prison, Dublin. In the latter part of 1866, when James Stephens was promising to bring off immediately the long-threatened insurrection, M'Afferty again crossed the ocean, and landed in England. There he was mainly instrumental in planning and organizing that extraordinary movement, the raid on Chester, which took place on Monday, 11th of February, 1867. It is now confessed, even by the British authorities themselves, that, but for the timely intimation of the design given by the informer Corridon, M'Afferty and his party would probably have succeeded in capturing the old Castle, and seizing the large store of arms therein contained. Finding their movements anticipated, the Fenian party left Chester as quietly as they had come, and the next that was heard of M'Afferty was his arrest, and that of his friend and companion, John Flood, on the 23d of February, in the harbor of Dublin, after they had got into a small boat from out of the collier *New Draper*, which had just arrived from Whitehaven. M'Afferty was placed in the dock of Green-street court-house for trial on Wednesday, May 1st, while the jury were absent considering their verdict in the case of Burke and Doran. On Monday, May the 6th, he was declared guilty by the jury. On that day week a Court of Appeal, consisting of ten of the Irish judges, sat to consider some legal points raised by Mr. Butt in the course of the trial, the most important of which was the question whether the prisoner, who had been in custody since February 23d, could be held legally responsible for the events of the Fenian rising which occurred on the night of the 5th of March. Their lordships gave an almost unanimous judgment against the prisoner on Saturday, May 18th, and on the

Monday following he was brought up for sentence, on which occasion, in response to the usual question, he spoke as follows:—

"My lords:—I have nothing to say that can, at this advanced stage of the trial, ward off that sentence of death, for I might as well hurl my complaint (if I had one) at the orange-trees of the sunny South, or the tall pine-trees of the bleak North, as now to speak to the question why sentence of death should not be passed upon me according to the law of the land; but I do protest loudly against the injustice of that sentence. I have been brought to trial upon a charge of high treason against the government of Great Britain, and guilt has been brought home to me upon the evidence of one witness, and that witness a perjured informer. I deny distinctly that there have been two witnesses to prove the overt act of treason against me. I deny distinctly that you have brought two independent witnesses to two overt acts. There is but one witness to prove the overt act of treason against me. I grant that there has been a cloud of circumstantial evidence to show my connection (if I may please to use that word) with the Irish people in their attempt for Irish independence; and I claim that, as an American and as an alien, I have a reason and a right to sympathize with the Irish people, or any other people who may please to revolt against that form of government by which they believe they are governed tyrannically. England sympathized with America. She not only sympathized, but she gave her support to both parties; but who ever heard of an Englishman having been arrested by the United States government for having given his support to the Confederate States of America, and placed on his trial for high treason against the government? No such case ever has been. I do not deny that I have sympathized with the Irish people—I love Ireland—I love the Irish people. And, if I were free to-morrow, and the Irish people were to take the field for independence, my sympathy would be with them; I would join them if they had any prospect whatever of independence, but I would not give my sanction to the useless effusion of blood, however done; and I state distinctly that I had nothing whatever to do, directly or indirectly, with the movement that took place in the county of Dublin. I make that statement on the brink of my grave. Again, I claim that I have a right to be discharged of the charge against me by the language of the law by which I have been tried. That law states that you must have two independent witnesses to prove the overt act against the prisoner. That is the only complaint I have to make, and I make that aloud. I find no fault with the jury, no complaint against the judges. I have been tried and found guilty. I am perfectly satisfied that I will go to my grave. I will go to my grave like a gentleman and a Christian, although I regret that I should be cut off at this stage of my life—still many a noble Irishman fell in defence of the rights of my southern clime. I do not wish to make any flowery speech to win sympathy in the court of justice. Without any further remarks I will now accept the sentence of the court."

Mr. Justice Fitzgerald then, in the "solemn tone of voice" adopted on such occasions, proceeded to pass sentence in the usual form, fixing the 12th day of June as the date on which the execution should take place.

The prisoners heard the sentence without giving the slightest symptoms of emotion, and then spoke the follows:—

"I will accept my sentence as becomes a gentleman and a Christian. I have but one request to ask of the tribunal, and that is, that after the execution of the sentence my remains shall be turned over to Mr. Lawless to be by him interred in consecrated ground as quietly as he possibly can. I have now, previous to leaving the dock, once more to return my grateful and sincere thanks to Mr. Butt, the star of the Irish bar, for his able and devoted defence on behalf of me and my friends. Mr. Butt, I thank you. I also return the same token of esteem to Mr. Dowse, for the kind and feeling manner in which he alluded to the scenes in my former life. Those kind allusions recall to my mind many moments—some bright, beautiful, and glorious—and yet some sad recollections arise of generous hopes that floated o'er me, and now sink beyond the grave. Mr. Butt, please convey to Mr. Dowse my grateful and sincere thanks. Mr. Lawless, I also return you my thanks for your many acts of kindness —I cant do no more."

He was not executed, however. The commutation of Burk's sentence necessitated the like course in all the other capital cases, and M'Afferty's doom was changed to penal servitude for life.

EDWARD DUFFY.

On the day following that on which M'Afferty's sentence was pronounced, the trial of three men, named John Flood, Edward Duffy, and John Cody, was brought to a conclusion. When they were asked what they had to say why sentence should not to be passed on them, Cody denied, with all possible earnestness, the charge of being president of an assassination committee, which had been brought against him. Flood—a young man of remarkably handsome exterior—declared that the evidence adduced against himself was untrue in many particulars. He alluded to the Attorney-General's having spoken of him as "that wretched man, Flood." "My lords," said he, " if to love my country more than my life makes me a wretched man, then I am a very wretched man indeed." Edward Duffy, it might be supposed by any one looking at his emaciated frame, wasted by consumption, and with the seal of death plainly set on his brow, would not be able to offer any remarks to the court; but he roused himself to the effort. The noble-hearted young fellow had been previously in the clutches of the government for the same offence. He was arrested with James Stephens and others at Fairfield House, in November 1865, but after a brief imprisonment was released in consideration of the state of his health, which seemed such as would not leave him many days to live. But, few or many, Duffy could not do otherwise than devote them to the cause he had at heart. He was rearrested at Boyle on the 11th of March, and this time the government took care they would not quit their hold of him. The following is the speech which, by a great physical effort, he delivered from the dock, his dark eyes brightening, and his pallid features lighting up with the glow of an earnest and lofty enthusiasm while he spoke:—

"The Attorney-General has made a wanton attack on me, but I leave my countrymen to judge between us. There is no political act of mine that I in the least regret. I have labored earnestly and sincerely in my country's cause, and I have been actuated throughout by a strong sense of duty. I believe that a man's duty to his country is part of his duty to God, for it is He who implants the feeling of patiotism in the human breast. He, the great searcher of hearts, knows that I have been actuated by no mean or paltry ambition—that I have never worked for any selfish end. For the late outbreak I am not responsible; I did all in my power to prevent it, for I knew that, circumstanced as we then were, it would be a failure. It has been stated in the course of those trials that Stephens was for peace. This is a mistake. It may be well that it should not go uncontradicted. It is but too well known in Ireland that he sent numbers of men over here to fight, promising to be with them when the time would come. The time did come, but not Mr. Stephens. He remained in France to visit the Paris Exhibition. It may be a very pleasant sight, but I would not be in his place now. He is a lost man—lost to honor, lost to country. There are a few things I would wish to say relative to the evidence given against me at my trial, but I would ask your lordships to give me permission to say them after sentence. I have a reason for asking to be allowed to say them after sentence has been passed."

The Chief Justice :—"That is not the usual practice. Not being tried for life, it is doubtful to me whether you have a right to speak at all. What you are asked to say is why sentence should not be passed upon you, and whatever you have to say you must say now."

"Then, if I must say it now, I declare it before my God that what Kelly swore against me on the table is not true. I saw him in Ennisgroven; but that I ever spoke to him on any political subject, I declare to heaven I never did. I knew him from a child in that little town, herding with the lowest and vilest. Is it to be supposed I'd put my liberty into the hands of such a character? I never did it. The next witness is Corridon. He swore that, at the meeting he referred to, I gave him directions to go to Kerry to find O'Connor, and put himself in communication with him. I declare to my God every word of that is false. Whether O'Connor was in the country or whether he had made his escape, I know just as little as your lordships; and I never heard of the Kerry rising until I saw it in the public papers. As to my giving the American officers money that night, before my God, on the verge of my grave, where my sentence will send me, I say that also is false. As to the writing that the policeman swore to in that book, and which is not a prayer-book, but the 'Imitation of Christ,' given to me by a lady to whom I served my time, what was written in that book was written by another young man in her employment. That is his writing, not mine. It is the writing of a young man in the house, and I never wrote a line of it."

The Lord Chief Justice:—"It was not sworn to be in your handwriting."

"Yes, my lord, it was. The policeman swore it was in my handwriting."

The Lord Chief Justice:—"That is a mistake. It was said to be like yours."

"The dream of my life has been that I might die fighting for Ireland. The jury have doomed me to a more painful, but not less glorious death. I now bid farewell to my friends and all who are dear to me.

'There is a world where souls are free,
Where tyrants taint not nature's bliss;
If death that bright world's opening be,
Oh, who would live a slave in this?'

"I am proud to be thought worthy of suffering for my country; when I am lying in my lonely cell I will not forget Ireland, and my last prayer will be that the God of liberty may give her strength to shake off her chains."

John Flood and Edward Duffy were then sentenced each to fifteen years of penal servitude, and Cody to penal servitude for life.

Edward Duffy's term of suffering did not last long. A merciful Providence gave his noble spirit release from its earthly tenement before one year from the date of his sentence had passed away. On the 21st of May, 1867, his trial concluded; on the 17th of January, 1868, the patriot lay dead in his cell in Millbank prison, London. The government permitted his friends to remove his remains to Ireland for interment; and they now rest in Glasnevin Cemetery, Dublin, where friendly hands oft renew the flowers on his grave, and many a heartfelt prayer is uttered that God would give the patriot's soul eternal rest, and "let perpetual light shine unto him."

STEPHEN JOSEPH MEANY.

THE connection of Stephen Joseph Meany with Irish politics dates back to 1848, when he underwent an imprisonment of some months in Carrickfergus Castle, under the provisions of the *Habeas Corpus* Suspension Act. He had been a writer on one of the national newspapers of that period, and was previously a reporter for a Dublin daily paper. He joined the Fenian movement in America, and was one of the "Senators" in O'Mahony's organization. In December, 1866, he crossed over to England, and in the following month he was arrested in London, and was brought in custody across to Ireland. His trial took place in Dublin on the 16th of February, 1867, when the legality of the mode of his arrest was denied by his counsel, and, as it was a very doubtful question, the point was reserved to be considered by a Court of Appeal. The tribunal sat on May the 13th, 1867, and on May the 18th, their decision, confirming the conviction, was pronounced. It was not until the 21st of the following month, at the Commission of Oyer and Terminer, that he was brought up for sentence. He then delivered the following able address to show "why sentence should not be passed on him:"—

"My lords :—There are many reasons I could offer why sentence should not—could not—be pronounced upon me according to law, if seven months of absolute solitary imprisonment, and the almost total disuse of speech during that period, had left me energy enough, or even language sufficient to address the court. But yielding obedience to a suggestion coming from a quarter which I am bound to respect, as well indeed as in accordance with my own feelings, I avoid everything like speech-making for outside effect. Besides, the learned counsel who so ably represented me in the Court of Appeal, and the eminent judges who in that court gave judgment for me, have exhausted all that could be said on the law of the case. Of their arguments and opinions your lordships have judicial knowledge. I need not say that both in interest as in conviction I am in agreement with the constitutional principles laid down by the minority of the judges in that court; and I have sufficient respect for the dignity of the court—sufficient regard to what is due to myself—to concede fully and frankly to the majority a conscientious view of a novel and, it may be, a difficult question.

"But I do not ask too much in asking that, before your lordships proceed to pass any sentence, you will consider the manner in which the court was divided on that question—to bear in mind that the minority declaring against the legality and the validity of the conviction was composed of some of the ablest and most experienced judges of the Irish bench or any bench—to bear in mind that one of these learned judges who had presided at the Commission Court was one of the most emphatic in the Court of Criminal Appeal in declaring against my liability to be tried; and moreover—and he ought to know—that there was not a particle of evidence to sustain the cause set up at the last moment, and relied upon by the Crown, that I was an 'accessory before the fact' to that famous Dublin overt act, for which, as an after-thought of the Crown, I was in fact tried. And I ask you further to bear in mind that the affirmance of that conviction was not had on fixed principles of the law—for the question was unprecedented—but on a speculative view of a suppositious case, and I must say a strained application of an already over-strained and dangerous doctrine—the doctrine of constructive criminality—the doctrine of making a man at a distance of three thousand miles, or more, legally responsible for the words and acts of others whom he had never seen, and of whom he had never heard, under the fiction or the 'supposition' that he was a co-conspirator. The word 'supposition' is not mine, my lords; it is the word put forward descriptive of the point by the learned judges presiding at my trial; for I find in the case prepared by these judges for the Court of Criminal Appeal the following paragraph:—

"'Sufficient evidence was given on the part of the Crown of acts of members of the said association in Ireland, not named in the indictment, in the promotion of several objects aforesaid, and done within the county of the city of Dublin, to sustain some of the overt acts charged in the indictment, supposing them to be the acts of the defendant himself.'

"Fortified by such facts—with a court so divided, and with opinions so expressed—I submit that, neither according to act of parliament, nor in conformity with the practice of common law, nor in any way in pursuance of the principles of that apocryphal abstraction, that magnificent myth—the British constitution—am I amenable to the sentence of this court—or any court in this country. True, I am in the toils, and it may be vain to discuss how I was brought into them. True, my long and dreary imprisonment—shut away from all converse or association with humanity, in a cell twelve feet by six—the humiliation of prison discipline—the hardships of prison fare—the handcuffs and the heartburnings—this court and its surroundings of power and authority—all these are 'hard practical facts,' which no amount of indignant protests can negative—no denunciation of the wrong refine away; and it may be, as I have said, worse than useless—vain and absurd—to question the right where might is predominant. But the invitation just extended to me by the officer of the court means, if it mean anything—if it be not like the rest, a solemn mockery—that there is still left to me the poor privilege of complaint. And I do complain. I complain that law and justice have been violated in my regard; I complain that the much belauded attribute, 'British fair play,' has been for me a nullity; I complain that the pleasant fiction described in the books as 'personal freedom' has had a most unpleasant illustration in my person; and I furthermore and particularly complain that, by the design and contrivance of what are called 'the authorities,' I have been brought to this country, not for trial, but for condemnation—not for justice, but for judgment.

"I will not tire the patience of the court, or exhaust my own strength, by going over the history of this painful case—the kidnapping in London on the mere belief of a police-constable that I was a Fenian in New York—the illegal transportation to Ireland—the committal for trial on a specific charge, whilst a special messenger was despatched to New York to hunt up informers to justify the illegality and the outrage, and to get a foundation for any charge. I will not dwell on the 'conspicuous absence' of fair play in the Crown at the trial having closed their cases without any reference to the Dublin transaction, but, as an afterthought, suggested by their discovered failure, giving in evidence the facts and circumstances of that case, and thus succeeding in making the jury convict me for an offence with which, up to that moment, the Crown did not intend to charge me. I will not say what I think of the mockery of putting me on trial in the Commission Court in Dublin for alleged words and acts in New York, and though the evidence was without notice, and the alleged overt acts without date, taunting me with not proving an *alibi*, and sending that important ingredient to a jury already ripe for a conviction. Prove an *alibi* to-day in respect of meetings held in Clinton Hall, New York, the allegations relating to which only came to my knowledge yesterday! I will not refer with any bitter feeling to the fact that, whilst the validity of the conviction so obtained was still pending in the Court of Criminal Appeal, the Right Hon. and Noble the Chief Secretary for Ireland declared in the House of Commons that 'that conviction was the most important one at the Commission'—thus prejudicing my case, I will not say willingly; but the observation was, at least, inopportune, and for me unfortunate.

"I will not speak my feeling on the fact that, in the arguments in the case in the Court for Reserved Cases, the Right Hon. the Attorney-General appealed to the passions—if such can exist in judges—and not to the judgment of the court; for I gather from the judgment of Mr. Justice O'Hagan that the right hon. gentleman made an earnest appeal 'that such crimes' as mine 'should not be allowed to go unpunished'—forgetful, I will not say designedly forgetful, that he was addressing the judges of the land, in the highest court of the land, on matters of law, and not speaking to a pliant Dublin jury on a treason trial in the court-house of Green-street.

"Before I proceed further, my lords, there is a matter which, as simply personal to myself, I should not mind, but which, as involving high interests to the community, and serious consequences to individuals, demands a special notice. I allude to the system of manufacturing informers. I want to know, if the court can inform me, by what right a responsible officer of the Crown entered my solitary cell at Kilmainham prison on Monday last—unbidden and unexpected—uninvited and undesired. I want to know what justification there was for his coming to insult me in my solitude and in my sorrow—ostensibly informing me that I was to be brought up for sentence on Thursday, but in the same breath adroitly putting to me the question if I knew any of the men recently arrested near Dungarvan, and now in the prison of Kilmainham. Coming thus, with a detective dexterity, carrying in one hand a threat of sentence and punishment, in the other, as a counterpoise and, I suppose, an alternative, a temptation to treachery,—did he suppose that seven months of imprisonment had so broken my spirit, as well as my health, that I would be an easy prey to his blandishments? Did he dream that the prospect of liberty which newspaper rumor and semi-offical information held out to me, was too dear to be forfeited for a trifling forfeiture of honor? Did he believe that by an act of secret turpitude I would open my prison doors only to close them the faster on others who may or may not have been my friends—or did he imagine he had found in me a Massey to be moulded and manipulated into the service of the Crown, or a Corridon to have cowardice and cupidity made the incentives to his baseness? I only wonder how the interview ended as it did; but I knew I was a prisoner, and self-respect preserved my patience and secured his safety. Great, my lords, as has been my humiliation in prison, hard and heart-breaking as have been the ordeals through which I have passed since the 1st of December last, there was no incident or event of that period fraught with more pain on the one hand, or more suggestiveness on the other, than this sly and secret attempt at improvising an informer. I can forget the pain in view of the suggestiveness; and unpleasant as is my position here to day, I am almost glad of the opportunity which may end in putting some check to the spy system in prisons. How many men have been won from honor and honesty by the stealthy visit to the cell, is more of course than I can say; how many have had their weakness acted upon, or their weakness fanned into flame by which means, I have no opportunity of knowing; in how many frailty and folly may have blossomed into falsehood, it is for those concerned to estimate. There is one thing, however, certain—operating in this way is more degrading to the tempter than to the tempted; and the government owes it to itself to put an end to a course of tactics pursued in its name, which in the results can only bring its humiliation: the public are bound in self-protection to protect the prisoner from the prowling visits of a too zealous official.

"I pass over all these things, my lords, and I ask your attention to the character of the evidence on which alone my conviction was obtained: the evidence of a special, subsidized spy, and of an infamous and ingrate informer.

"In all ages, and amongst all peoples, the spy has been held in marked abhorrence. In the amnesties of war there is for him alone no quarter; in the estimate of social life, no toleration; his self-abasement excites contempt, not compassion; his patrons despise while they encourage; and they who stoop to enlist his services, shrink with disgust from the moral leprosy covering the servitor. Of such was the witness put forward to corroborate the informer, and still not corroborating him. Of such was that phenomenon, a police spy, who declared himself an unwilling witness for the Crown! There was no reason why in my regard he should be unwilling—he knew me not previously. I have no desire to speak harshly of Inspector Doyle; he said in presence of the Crown Solicitor, and was not contradicted, that he was compelled by threats to ascend the witness table. He may have had cogent reasons for his reluctance in his own conscience. God will judge him.

"But how shall I speak of the informer, Mr. John Devany? What language should be employed in describing the character of one who adds to the guilt of perfidy to his associates the crime of perjury to his God?—the man who, eating of your bread, sharing your confidence, and holding, as it were, your very purse-strings, all the time meditates your overthrow, and pursues it to its accomplishment? How paint the wretch who, under pretence of agreement in your opinions, worms himself into your secrets only to betray them; and who, upon the same altar with you, pledges his faith and fealty to the same principles, and then sells faith, and fealty, and principles, and you alike, for the unhallowed Judas guerdon? Of such, on his own confession, was that distinguished upholder of the British Crown and government, Mr. Devany. With an effrontery that did not falter, and knew not how to blush, he detailed his own participation in the acts for which he was prosecuting me as a participator. And is the evidence of a man like that—a conviction obtained upon such evidence—any warrant for a sentence depriving me of all that makes life desirable or enjoyable?

"He was, first, spy for the crown—in the pay of the Crown, under the control of the Crown, and think you he had any other object than to do the behests of the Crown?

"He was next the traitor spy, who had taken that one fatal step, from which in this life there is no retrogression—that one plunge in infamy from which there is no receding—that one treachery for which there is no earthly forgiveness; and, think you, he hesitated about a perjury more or less to secure present pay and future patronage? Here was one to whom existence offers now no prospect save in making his perfidy a profession, and think you he was deterred by conscience from recommending himself to his patrons? Think you that when, at a distance of three thousand miles from the scenes he professed to describe, he could lie with impunity and invent without detection, he was particular to a shade in doing his part of a most filthy bargain? It is needless to describe a wretch of that kind—his own actions speak his character. It were superfluous to curse him: his whole existence will be a living, a continuing curse. No necessity to use the burning words of the poet and say:—

'May life's unblessed cup for him
Be drugged with treacheries to the brim.'

"Every sentiment in his regard of the country he has dishonored, and the people he has humbled, will be one of horror and hate. Every sigh sent up from the hearts he has crushed, and the homes he has made desolate, will be mingled with execrations on the name of the informer. Every heart-throb in the prison cells of this land where his victims count time by corroding his thought—every grief that finds utterance from these victims in the quarries of Portland, will go up to heaven freighted with curses on the Nagles, the Devanys, the Masseys, the Gillespies, the Corridons, and the whole host of mercenary miscreants, who, faithless to their friends and recreant to their professions, have, paraphrasing the words of Moore, taken their perfidy to heaven, seeking to make an accomplice of their God—wretches who have embalmed their memories in imperishable infamy, and given their accursed names to an inglorious immortality. Nor will I speculate on their career in the future. We have it on the best existing authority that a distinguished informer of antiquity, seized with remorse, threw away his blood-money, 'went forth and hanged himself.' We know that in times within the memory of living men a government actually set the edifying and praiseworthy example of hanging an informer when they had no further use of his valuable services—thus *dropping* his acquaintance with effect. I have no wish for such a fate to any of the informers who have cropped out so luxuriantly in these latter days—a long life and a troubled conscience would, perhaps, be their correct punishment—though certainly there would be a consistent compensation—a poetic justice—in a termination so exalted to a career so brilliant.

"I leave these fellows and turn for a moment to their victims. And I would here, without any reference to my own case, earnestly implore that sympathy with political sufferers should not be merely telescopic in its character, 'distance lending enchantment to the view;' and that when your statesmen sentimentalize upon, and your journalists denounce, far-away tyrannies—the horrors of Neapolitan dungeons—the abridgment of personal freedom in continental countries—the exercise of arbitrary power by irresponsible authority in other lands—they would turn their eyes homeward, and examine the treatment and the sufferings of their own political prisoners. I would, in all sincerity, suggest that humane and well-meaning men, who exert themselves for the remission of the death-penalty as a mercy, would rather implore that the doors of solitary and silent captivity should be remitted to the more merciful doom of an immediate relief from suffering by immediate execution—the opportunity of an immediate appeal from man's cruelty to God's justice. I speak strongly on this point, because I feel it deeply. I speak not without example. At the Commission at which I was tried, there was tried also and sentenced a young man named Stowell. I well remember that raw and dreary morning, the 12th March, when, handcuffed to Stowell, I was sent from Kilmainham prison to the county gaol of Kildare. I well remember our traversing, so handcuffed, from the town of Sallins to the town of Naas, ancle-deep in snow and mud, and I recall now with pain our sad foreboding of that morning. These in part have been fulfilled. Sunday after Sunday I saw poor Stowell at chapel in Naas gaol, drooping and dying. One such Sunday—the 12th May —passed, and I saw him no more. On Wednesday, the 15th, he was, as they say, *mercifully* released from prison, but the fiat of mercy had previously gone forth from a higher power—the political convict simply reached his own home to die, with loving eyes watching by his death-bed. On Sunday, the 19th May, he was consigned to another prison home in Glasnevin Cemetery. May God have mercy on his soul—may God forgive his persecutors— may God give peace and patience to those who are doomed to follow!

"Pardon this digression, my lords, I could not avoid it. Returning to the question, why sentence should not be pronounced upon me, I would ask your lordships' attention to the fact showing, even in the estimate of the Crown, the case is not one for sentence.

"On the morning of my trial, and before the trial, terms were offered to me by the Crown. The direct proposition was made through my solicitor, through the learned counsel who so ably defended me, through the Governor of Kilmainham prison—by all three—that, if I pleaded guilty to the indictment, I should get off with six months' imprisonment. Knowing the pliancy of Dublin juries in political cases, the offer was, doubtless, a tempting one. Valuing liberty, it was almost resistless—in view of a possible penal servitude—but, having regard to principle, I spurned the compromise. I then gave unhesitatingly, as I would now give, the answer, that not for a reduction of the punishment to six hours would I surrender faith—that I need never look, and could never look, wife or children, friends or family, in the face, if capable of such a selfish cowardice. I could not, to save myself, imperil the safety of others —I could not plead guilty to an indictment in which six others were distinctly charged by name as co-conspirators with me—one of those six since tried, convicted, and sentenced to death—I could not consent to obtain my own pardon at their expense—furnish the Crown with a case in point for future convictions, and become, even though indirectly, worthy to rank with that brazen battalion of venal vagabonds who have made the Holy Gospel of God the medium of barter for their unholy gain, and obtained access to the inmost heart of their selected victim only to coin its throbbing into the traitor's gold, and traffic on its very life-blood.

"Had I been charged simply with my own words and deeds, I would have no hesitation in making acknowledgment. I have nothing to repent and nothing to conceal—nothing to retract and nothing to countermand; but, in the language of the learned Lord Chief Baron in this case, I could not admit 'the preposterous idea of thinking by deputy' any more than I could plead guilty to an indictment which charges others with crime. Further, my lords, I could not acknowledge culpability for the acts and words of others at a distance of three thousand miles—others whom I had never seen, of whom I had never heard, and with whom I never had had communication. I could not admit that the demoniac atrocities, described as Fenian principles by the constabulary-spy, Talbot, ever had my sanction or approval, or the sanction or approval of any man in America.

"If, my lords, six months' imprisonment was the admeasurement of the law officers of the Crown as an adequate punishment for my alleged offence—assuming that the court had jurisdiction to try and punish—then, am I now entitled to my discharge, independent of all other grounds of discharge, for I have gone through seven months of an imprisonment which could not be excelled by demon ingenuity in horror and in hardship—in solitude, in silence and in suspense. Your lordships will not only render further litigation necessary by passing sentence for the perhaps high crime—but still the untried crime—of refusing to yield obedience to the Crown's proposition for my self-abasement. You will not, I am sure, visit upon my rejection of Mr. Anderson's delicate overture—you will not surely permit the events occurring, unhappily occurring, since my trial, to influence your judgments. And do not, I implore you, accept as a truth, influencing that judgment, Talbot's definition of the objects of Fenianism. Hear what Devany, the American informer, describes them to be. 'The members,' he says, 'were *pledged by word of honor* to promote love and harmony amongst all classes of Irishmen, and to labor for the independence of Ireland.' Talbot says that in Ireland 'the members are *bound by oath* to seize the property of the country and murder all opposed to them.' Can any two principles be more distinct from each other? Could there be a conspiracy for a common object by such antagonistic means? To murder all opposed to your principles may be an effectual way of producing unanimity, but the quality of love and harmony engendered by such a patent process would be extremely equivocal. Mr. Talbot, for the purposes of his evidence, must have borrowed a leaf from the History of the French Revolution, and adopted, as singularly telling and appropriate for effect, the saying attributed to Robespierre: 'Let us cut everybody's throat but our own, and then we are sure to be masters.'

" No one in America, I venture to affirm, ever heard of such designs in connecion with the Fenian Brotherhood. No one in America would countenance such designs. Revolutionists are not ruffians or rapparees. A judge from the bench at Cork, and a noble lord in his place in parliament, bore testimony to that fact, in reference to the late movement; I and I ask you, my lords—I would ask the country from this court—for the sake of the character of your countrymen—to believe Devany's interpretation of Fenianism—tainted traitor though he be—rather than believe that the kindly instincts of Irishmen at home and abroad—their generous impulses—their tender sensibilities—all their human affections, in a word—could degenerate into the attributes of the assassin, as stated by that hog-in-armor, that crime-creating Constable Talbot.

"Taking other ground, my lords, I object to any sentence upon me. I stand at this bar a declared citizen of the United States of America, entitled to the protection of such citizenship; and I protest against the right to pass any sentence in any British court for acts done, or words spoken, or alleged to be done or spoken, on American soil, within the shades of the American flag, and under the sanction of American institutions. I protest against the assumption that would in this country limit the right of thought, or control the liberty of speech in an assemblage of American citizens in an American city. The United States will, doubtless, respect and protect her neutrality laws and observe the comity of nations, whatever they may mean in practice, but I protest against the monstrous fiction—the transparent fraud—that would seek, in ninety years after the evacuation of New York by the British, to bring the people of New York within the vision and venue of a British jury—that, in ninety years after the last British bayonet had glistened in an American sunlight, after the last keel of the last of the English fleet ploughed its last furrow in the Hudson or the Delaware—after ninety years of republican independence—would seek to restore that city of New York and its institutions to the dominion of the Crown and government of Great Britain. This is the meaning of it, and, disguise it as you may, so will it be interpreted beyond the Atlantic. Not that the people of America care one jot whether S. J. Meany were hanged, drawn, and quartered to-morrow, but that there is a great principle involved. Personally, I am of no consequence; politically, I represent in this court the adopted citizen of America—for, as the *New York Herald*, referring to this case, observed, if the acts done in my regard are justifiable, there is nothing to prevent the extension of the same justice to any other adopted citizen of the States visiting Great Britain. It is, therefore, in the injustice of the case the influence lies, and not in the importance of the individual.

"Law is called 'the perfection of reason.' Is there not danger of its being regarded as the very climax of absurdity, if fictions of this kind can be turned into realities on the mere caprice of power? As a distinguished English journalist has suggested in reference to the case, 'Though the law may doubtless be satisfied by the majority in the Court of Appeal, yet common sense and common law would be widely antagonistic if sentence were to follow a judgment so obtained.'

"On all grounds, then, I submit, in conclusion, this is not a case for sentence. Waiving for the purpose the international objection, and appealing to British practice itself, I say it is not a fair case for sentence. The professed policy of that practice has ever been, to give the benefit of doubt to the prisoner. Judges in their charges to juries have ever theorized on this principle, and surely judges themselves will not refuse to give practical effect to the theory. If ever there was a case which more than another was suggestive of doubt, it is surely one in which so many judges have pronounced against the legality of the trial and the validity of the conviction on which you are about to pass sentence. Each of these judges, be it remembered, held competent in his individuality to administer the criminal law of the country—each of whom, in fact, in his individuality, does so administer it, unchallenged and unquestioned.

"A sentence under such circumstances, be it for a long period or a short, would be wanting in the element of moral effect—the effect of example—which could alone give it value, and which is professedly the aim of all legal punishment. A sentence under such circumstances would be far from reassuring to the public mind as to the 'certainties' of the law, and would fail to commend the approval or win the respect of any man 'within the realm or without.' While to the prisoner, to the sufferer-in-chief, it would only bring the bitter, and certainly not the repentant feeling that he suffered in the wrong—that he was a victim of an injustice based on an inference which not even the tyrant's plea of necessity can sustain—namely, that at a particular time he was at a distance of three thousand miles from the place where he then actually stood in bodily presence, and that at that distance he actually thought the thoughts and acted the acts of men unknown to him even by name. It will bring to the prisoner, I repeat, the feeling—the bitter feeling—that he was condemned on an unindicted charge pressed suddenly into the service, and for a constructive crime which some of the best authorities in the law have declared not to be a crime cognizable in any of your courts.

"Let the Crown put forward any supposition they please—indulge in what special pleadings they will—sugar over the bitter pill of constructive conspiracy as they can—to this complexion must come the triangular injustice of this case—the illegal and unconstitutional kidnapping in England—the unfair and invalid trial and conviction in Ireland for the alleged offence in another hemisphere and under another sovereignty. My lords, I have done."

CAPTAIN JOHN M'CLURE.

CAPTAIN JOHN M'CLURE, like Captain M'Afferty, was an American born, but of Irish parentage. He was born at Dobb's Ferry, twenty-two miles from New York, on July 17th, 1846, and he was therefore a mere youth when, serving with distinguished gallantry in the Federal ranks, he attained the rank of captain. He took part in the Fenian rising of the 5th March, and was prominently concerned in the attack and capture of Knockadoon coast-guard station. He and his companion, Edward Kelly, were captured by a military party at Kilclooney Wood, on March 31st, after a smart skirmish, in which their compatriot, the heroic and saintly Peter Crowley, lost his life. His trial took place before the Special Commission at Cork, on May 22d and 23d, 1867. The following are the spirited and eloquent terms in which he addressed the court, previous to sentence being pronounced on him :—

"My lords :—In answer to the question as to why the sentence of the court should not now be passed upon me, I would desire to make a few remarks in relation to my late exertions in behalf of the suffering people of this country, in aiding them in their earnest endeavors to attain the independence of their native land. Although not born upon the soil of Ireland, my parents were, and from history, and tradition, and fireside relations, I became conversant with the country's history from my earliest childhood ; and as the human race will ever possess these godlike qualities which inspire mankind with sympathy for the suffering, a desire to aid poor Ireland to rise from her moral degradation took possession of me. I do not now wish to say to what I assign the failure of that enterprise with which are associated my well-meant acts for this persecuted land. I feel fully satisfied of the righteousness of my every act in connection with the late revolutionary movement in this country, being actuated by a holy desire to assist in the emancipation of an enslaved and generous people. I derive more pleasure from having done the act than from any other event that has occurred to me during my eventful but youthful life. I wish it to be distinctly understood here, standing as I do, perhaps, on the brink of an early grave, that I am no filibuster or freebooter, and that I had no personal object or inclination to gain anything in coming to this country. I came solely through love of Ireland and sympathy for her people. If I have forfeited my life, I am ready to abide the issue. If my exertions on behalf of a distressed people be a crime, I am willing to pay the penalty, knowing, as I do, that what I have done was in behalf of a people whose cause is just—a people who will appreciate and honor a man, although he may not be a countryman of their own—still a man who is willing to suffer in defence of that divine, that American principle—the right of self-government. I would wish to tender to my learned and eloquent counsel, Mr. Heron and Mr. Waters, and to my solicitor, Mr. Collins, my sincere and heartfelt thanks for the able manner in which they have conducted my defence. And now, my lords, I trust I will meet in a becoming manner the penalty which it is now the duty of your lordships to pronounce upon me. I have nothing more to say."

EDWARD KELLY.

ON the same occasion the prisoner, Edward Kelly, delivered the following soul-stirring address:—

"My lords:—The novelty of my situation will plead for any want of fluency on my part; and I beg your lordships' indulgence if I am unnecessarily tedious. I have to thank the gentlemen of the jury for their recommendation, which I know was well meant; but knowing, as I do, what that mercy will be, I heartily wish that recommendation will not be received. Why should I feel regret? What is death? The act of passing from this life into the next. I trust that God will pardon me my sins, and that I will have no cause to fear entering into the presence of the ever-living and most merciful Father. I don't recollect in my life of ever having done anything with a deliberately bad intention. In my late conduct I do not see anything for regret. Why then, I say, should I feel regret? I leave the dread of death to such wretches as Corridon and Massey—Corridon, a name once so suggestive of sweetness and peace, now the representative of a loathsome monster. If there be anything that can sink that man Corridon lower in the scales of degradation, it is—"

The Chief Justice:—"We cannot listen to any imputation on persons who were examined as witnesses. Strictly speaking, you are only to say why sentence of death should not be passed upon you: at the same time we are very unwilling to hold a very strict hand, but we cannot allow imputations to be made on third persons, witnesses or others, who have come forward in this trial."

Prisoner:—"Well, my lord, I will answer as well as I can the question put to me. The Irish people, through every generation, ever since England has obtained a footing in Ireland, have protested against the occupation of our native soil by the English. Surely that is answer enough why sentence of death should not be passed upon me. In the part I have taken in the late insurrection, I feel conscious that I was doing right. Next to serving his Creator, I believe it is a man's solemn duty to serve his country. [Here the prisoner paused to suppress his emotion, which rendered his utterance very feeble, and continued.] My lords, I have nothing more to say except to quote the words of the sacred Psalmist, in which you will understand that I speak of my country as he speaks of his:—'If I forget thee, O Jerusalem! let my right hand be forgotten. Let my tongue cleave to my jaws if I do not remember thee: if I make not Jerusalem the beginning of my joy. Remember, O Lord! the children of Edom in the day of Jerusalem' who say, raze, raze it, even to the foundation thereof. O daughter of Babylon, miserable! blessed be he who shall repay thee thy payment which thou hast paid us.' In conclusion, my lords, I wish to give my thanks to my attorney, Mr. Collins, for his untiring exertions, and also to my counsel, Mr. Heron, for his able defence, and to Mr. Waters."

CAPTAIN WILLIAM MACKAY.

IN the evidence adduced at the Cork Summer Assizes of 1867, on the trials of persons charged with participation in the Fenian rising of March 5th, the name of Captain Mackay frequently turned up. The captain, it would appear, was a person of influence and importance in the insurrectionary army. He had taken part in many councils of the Fenian leaders, he was trusted implicitly by his political friends, and much deference was paid to his opinion. But more than all this, he had taken the field on the night of the rising, led his men gallantly to the attack of Ballyknockane police-barrack, and, to the great horror of all loyal subjects, committed the enormous offence of capturing it. This, and the similar successes achieved by Lennon at Stepaside and Glencullen, county Wicklow, were some of the incidents of the attempted rebellion which most annoyed the government, who well knew the influence which such events, occurring at the outset of a revolutionary movement, are apt to exercise on the popular mind. Captain Mackay, therefore, was badly "wanted" by the authorities after the Fenian rising; there was any money to be given for information concerning the whereabouts of Captain Mackay, but it came not. Every loyal-minded policeman in Cork county, and in all the other Irish counties, and every detective, and every spy, and every traitor in the pay of the government, kept a sharp look out for the audacious Captain Mackay, who had compelled the garrison of one of her Majesty's police barracks to surrender to him, and hand him up their arms in the quietest and most polite manner imaginable; but they saw him not, or, if they saw, they did not recognize him.

So month after month rolled on, and no trace of Captain Mackay could be had. The vigilant guardians and servants of English law in Ireland then began to think he must have managed to get clear out of the country, and rather expected that the next thing they would hear of him would be that he was organizing and lecturing amongst the Irish enemies of England in the United States. There, however, they were quite mistaken, as they soon found out to their very great vexation and alarm.

On the 27th day of December, 1867, there was strange news in Cork, and strange news all over the country, for the telegraph wires spread it in every direction. The news was, that on the previous evening a party of Fenians had entered the Martello tower at Foaty, on the north side of the Cork river, made prisoners of the gunners who were in charge, and had then taken possession of and borne away all the arms and ammunition they could find in the place! Startling news this was undoubtedly. Loyal men stopped each other in the streets, and asked if anything like it had ever been heard of. They wanted to know if things were not coming to a pretty pass, and did not hesitate to say they would feel greatly obliged to any one who could answer for them the question, "What next?" For this sack of the Martello tower was not the first successful raid for arms which the Fenians had made in that neighborhood. About a month before—on the night of November 28th—they had contrived to get into the shop of Mr. Richardson, gunmaker, Patrick-street, and abstract from the premises no fewer than 120 revolvers and eight Snider rifles, accomplishing the feat so skilfully that no trace either of the weapons or the depredators had since been discovered. This was what might be called a smart stroke of work, but it shrunk into insignificance compared with the audacious act of plundering one of her Majesty's fortified stations.

The details of the affair, which were soon known, were received by the public with mingled feelings of amusement and amazement. The Fenian party, it was learned, had got into the tower by the usual means of entrance— a step-ladder, reaching to the door, which is situated at some height from the ground. One party of the invaders remained in the apartment just inside the entrance door, while another, numbering five persons, proceeded to an inner room where they found two of the gunners, with their families, just in the act of sitting down to tea. In an instant revolvers were placed at the heads of the men, who were told not to stir on peril of their lives. At the same time assurances were given to them and to the affrighted women that, if they only kept quiet and complied with the demands of the party, no harm whatever should befall them. The garrison saw that resistance was useless, and promptly acceded to those terms. The invaders then asked for and got the keys of the magazine, which they handed out to their friends, who forthwith set to work to remove the ammunition which they found stored in the vaults. They seized about 300lbs. of gunpowder, made up in 8lb. cartridges, a quantity of fuses, and other military stores, and then proceeded to search the entire building for arms. Of these, however, they found very little—nothing more than the rifles and sword bayonets of the two or three men who constituted the garrison—a circumstance which seemed to occasion them much disappointment. They were particularly earnest and pressing in their inquiries for hand-grenades, a species of missile which they had supposed was always kept "in stock" in such places. They could scarcely believe that there were none to be had. Some charges of grape-shot which they laid hands on might be, they thought, the sort of weapon they were in quest of, and they proceeded to dissect and analyze one of them. Grape-shot, we may explain to the unlearned in these matters, is "an assemblage, in the form of a cylindrical column, of nine balls resting on a circular plate, through which passes a pin serving as an axis. The balls are contained in a strong canvas bag, and are bound together on the exterior of the latter by a cord disposed about the column in the manner of a net." This was not the sort of thing the Fenian party wanted; grape-shot could be of no use to them, for the Fenian organization, to its great sorrow, was possessed of no artillery; they resolved, therefore, to leave those ingeniously-constructed packages behind them, and to retire with the more serviceable spoils they had gathered. While the search was proceeding, the Fenian sentries, with revolvers ready in their hands, stood guard over the gunners, and prevented any one— young or old—from quitting the room. They spoke kindly to all, however, chatted with the women, and won the affectionate regards of the youngsters by distributing money among them. One of these strange visitors became so familiar as to tell one of the women that if she wished to know who he was, his name was Captain Mac—a piece of information which did not strike her at the time as being of any peculiar value. When the party had got their booty safely removed from the building, this chivalrous captain and his four assistant sentries prepared to leave; they cautioned the gunners, of whom there were three at this time in the building—one having entered while the search was proceeding—against quitting the fort till morning, stating that men would be on the watch outside to shoot them if they should attempt it. So much being said and done, they bade a polite good evening to her Majesty's gunners and their interesting families, and withdrew.

The heroic garrison did not venture out immediately after they had been relieved of the presence of the Fenian party; but finding that a few charges of powder were still stowed away in a corner of the fort, they hurried with them to the top of the building, and commenced to blaze away from the big gun which was there *in situ*. This performance they meant as a signal of distress; but, though the sounds were heard and the flashes seen far and wide, no one divined the object of what appeared to be nothing more than an oddly-timed bit of artillery practice. Next morning the whole story was in every one's mouth. Vast was the amusement which it afforded to the Corkonians generally, and many were the encomiums which they passed on the dashing Irish-Americans and smart youths of Cork's own town who had accomplished so daring and clever a feat. Proportionally great was the irritation felt by the sprinkling of loyalists and by the paid servants of the Crown in that quarter. One hope, at all events, the latter party had, that the leader in the adventure would soon be "in the hands of justice;" and one comforting assurance, that never again would the Fenians be able to replenish their armory in so easy and so unlawful a manner.

Four days afterwards there was another "sensation" in Cork. The Fenian collectors of arms had made another haul! And this time their mode of action surpassed all their previous performances in coolness and daring. At nine o'clock in the morning, on the 30th of December, eight men, who had assumed no disguise, suddenly entered the shop of Mr. Henry Allport, gunmaker, of Patrick-street, and producing revolvers from their pockets, covered him and his two assistants, telling them at the same time that, if they ventured to stir, or raise any outcry, they were dead men. While the shopmen remained thus bound to silence, five of the party proceeded to collect all the rifles and revolvers in the establishment, and place them in a canvas sack which had been brought for the purpose. This sack, into which a few guns and seventy-two splendid revolvers of the newest construction had been put, was then carried off by two men, who, having transferred the contents to the safe-keeping of some confederate, returned with it very quickly to receive and bear away a large quantity of revolver cartridges which had been found in the shop. This second "loot" having been effected, the guards who stood over Mr. Allport and his men, lowered their weapons, and after cautioning all three not to dare to follow them, quitted the shop in a leisurely manner, and disappeared down one of the by-streets. As soon as he was able to collect his scattered wits, Mr. Allport rushed to the nearest police station, and gave information of what had occurred. The police hastened to the scene of this daring exploit, but of course the "birds were flown," and no one could say whither.

Needless to say how this occurrence intensified the perplexity and the rage of the government party in all parts of the country. There was surely some fierce swearing in Dublin Castle on the day that news arrived; and perhaps many a passionate query blurted out as to whether police, detectives, magistrates, and all in that southern district, were not secretly in league with the rebels. In fact, a surmise actually got into the papers that the proprietors of the gunshops knew more about the disappearance of the arms, and were less aggrieved by the "seizure," than they cared to acknowledge. However this might be, the popular party enjoyed the whole thing immensely, laughed over it heartily, and expressed in strong terms their admiration of the skill and daring displayed by the operators. The following squib, which appeared in the *Nation* at the time, over the initials "T. D. S.," affords an indication of the feelings excited among Irish nationalists by those extraordinary occurrences:—

THE CORK MEN AND NEW YORK MEN.

" Oh, the gallant Cork men,
Mixed with New York men,
I'm sure their equals they can't be found;
For persevering
In deeds of daring,
They set men staring the world around.
No spies can match them,
No sentries watch them,
No specials catch them or mar their play,
While the clever Cork men
And 'cute New York men
Work new surprises by night and day.

"Sedate and steady,
Calm, quick, and ready,
They boldly enter, and make no din,
Where'er such trifles
As Snider rifles
And bright six-shooters are stored within.
The Queen's round towers
Can't baulk their powers,
Off go the weapons by sea and shore,
To where the Cork men
And smart New York men
Are daily piling their precious store.

"John Bull, in wonder,
With voice like thunder,
Declares such plunder he must dislike,
They next may rowl in
And sack Haulbowline,
Or on a sudden run off with Spike.
His peace is vanished,
His joys are banished,
And gay or happy no more he'll be,
Until those Cork men
And wild New York men
Are sunk together beneath the sea.

"O bold New York men
And daring Cork men!
We own your pleasures should all grow dim,
On thus discerning
And plainly learning
That your amusement gives pain to *him*.
Yet, from the nation,
This salutation
Leaps forth, and echoes with thunderous sound—
'Here's to all Cork men,
Likewise New York men,
Who stand for Ireland, the world around!'"

But Captain Mackay, skilful and "lucky" as he was, was trapped at last.

On the evening of the 7th of February, 1868, he walked into the grocery and spirit shop of Mr. Cronin in Market-street—not to drink whiskey or anything of that sort, for he was a man of strictly temperate habits, and he well knew that, of all men, those who are engaged in the dangerous game of conspiracy and revolution can least afford to partake of drinks that may unloose their tongues and let their wits run wild. He called for a glass of lemonade, and recognizing some persons who were in the shop at the time, he commenced a conversation with them.

Only a few minutes from the time of his entrance had elapsed when a party of police, wearing a disguise over their uniforms, rushed into the shop, and commanded the door to be shut.

The men inside attempted to separate and escape, but they were instantly grappled by the police. One of the force seized Captain Mackay by the collar, and a vigorous struggle between them at once commenced. The policeman was much the larger man of the two, but the Fenian captain was wiry and muscular, and proved quite a match for him. They fell and rose, and fell and rose again, the policeman undermost sometimes, and at other times the Fenian captain. They struggled for nearly twenty minutes.

"Dead or alive, I'll take you," said the policeman, as he drew his revolver from his pocket.

"I have but one life to lose, and if it goes, so be it," replied Mackay, drawing a weapon of the same kind.

In another instant there was a clash as of striking steel, and a discharge of one of the weapons.

"Good God! I'm shot!" exclaimed Constable Casey from the end of the room, and he fell upon the floor.

Captain Mackay's revolver had gone off in the struggle, and the ball had struck the constable in the leg, inflicting on him a serious wound.

By this time several parties of police had arrived in the street and stationed themselves so as to prevent the formation of a crowd, and deter the people from any attempt at rescue. A reinforcement having turned into the house in which the struggle was going on, Captain Mackay, and others who had been in his company, were made prisoners, and marched off in custody.

Some days afterwards, the wounded constable, who had refused to submit to amputation of the wounded limb, died in hospital.

On the 10th of March, 1868, at the Cork Assizes, Judge O'Hagan presiding, Captain Mackay was put on his trial for murder. The evidence established a probability that the discharge of the prisoner's revolver was not intended or effected by him, but was a consequence of its having been struck by the revolver of the policeman who was struggling with him. The verdict of the jury, therefore, was one of acquittal.

But then came the other charge against him, the charge of treason-felony, for his connection with the Fenian Brotherhood, and his part in the recent "rising." For this he was put on trial on the 20th day of March. He was ably defended by Mr. Heron, Q. C., but the evidence against him was conclusive. To say nothing of the testimony of the informers, which should never for a moment be regarded as trustworthy, there was the evidence and the identification supplied by the gunners of the Martello tower and their wives, and the policemen of Ballyknockane station and the wife of one of them. This evidence, while establishing the fact that the prisoner had been concerned in the levying of war against the Crown, established also the fact that he was a man as chivalrous and gentle as he was valorous and daring. Some of the incidents proved to have occurred during the attack which was made, under his leadership, on the police barrack, are worthy of special mention in any sketch, however brief, of the life and adventures of this remarkable man. After he, at the head of his party, had demanded the surrender of the barrack in the name of the Irish Republic, the police fired, and the fire was returned. Then the insurgents broke in the door, and set fire to the lower part of the barrack. Still the police held out. "Surrender!" cried the insurgents. "*You want to commit suicide, but we don't want to commit murder.*" One of the policemen cried out that a little girl, his daughter, was inside, and asked if the attacking party would allow her to be passed out? Of course they would, gladly; and the little girl was taken out of the window with all tenderness, and given up to her mother who had chanced to be outside the barrack when the attack commenced. At this time a Catholic clergyman, the Rev. Mr. Neville, came on the spot. He asked the insurgent leader whether, if the police surrendered, any harm would be done to them? "Here is my revolver," said Captain Mackay "let the contents of it be put through me if one of them should be injured." Well did Mr. Heron, in his able speech referring to these facts, say: "Though they were rebels who acted that heroic part, who could say their hearts were not animated with the courage of Leonidas, and the chivalry of Bayard?"

On the second day of the trial the jury brought in

their verdict, declaring the prisoner guilty, but at the same time recommending him to the merciful consideration of the court, because of the humanity which he had displayed towards the men whom he had in his power. The finding took no one by surprise, and did not seem to trouble the prisoner in the faintest degree. During the former trial some shades of anxiety might have been detected on his features; the charge of "murder" was grievous to him, but when that was happily disposed of, the world seemed to brighten before him, and he took his treason-felony trial cheerily. He knew what the verdict on the evidence would be, and he was conscious that the penalty to be imposed on him would be no trivial one; he felt that it was hard to part from faithful comrades and dear friends, and, above all, from the young wife whom he had married only a few short months before; but then it was in Ireland's cause he was about to suffer, and for that he could endure all.

And yet, Ireland was not his native land. He was born in Cincinnati, Ohio, in the year 1841. But his parents, who were natives of Castle-Lyons, near Fermoy, in the county Cork, were true children of Erin, and they taught their son to love, even as they did themselves, that green isle far away, from which a hard fate had compelled them to roam. Patriotism, indeed, was hereditary in the family The great-grandfather of our hero suffered death for his fidelity to the cause of Ireland in the memorable year 1798; and a still more remarkable fact is, that Captain Mackay—or William Francis Lomasney, to call him by his real name—in leaving America for Ireland, in 1865, to take part in the contemplated rising, merely took the place which his father wished and intended to occupy. The young man induced him to remain at home, and claimed for himself the post of danger. Well may that patriotic father be proud of such a son.

When called upon for such remarks as he might have to offer on his own behalf, Captain Mackay, without any of the airs of a practised speaker, but yet with a manner that somehow touched every heart, and visibly affected the humane and upright judge who sat on the bench, delivered the following address:—

"My lord:—What I said last evening I think calls for a little explanation. I then said I was fully satisfied with the verdict—that it was a fair and just one. I say so still; but I wish to state that I consider it only so in accordance with British law, and that it is not in accordance with my ideas of right and justice. I feel that, with the strong evidence there was against me, according to British law, the jury could not, as conscientious men, do otherwise. I feel that. I thank them again for their recommendation to mercy, which, I have no doubt, was prompted by a good intention towards me, and a desire to mitigate what they considered would be a long and painful imprisonment. Still, I will say, with all respect, that I feel the utmost indifference to it. I do so for this reason—I am now in that position that I must rely entirely upon the goodness of God, and I feel confident that He will so dispose events that I will not remain a prisoner so long as your lordship may be pleased to decree. The jury having now found me guilty, it only remains for your lordship to give effect to their verdict. The eloquence, the ability, the clear reasoning, and the really splendid arguments of my council, failed, as I knew they would, to affect the jury. I feel, therefore, that with my poor talents it would be utterly vain and useless for me to attempt to stay the sentence which it now becomes your lordship's duty to pronounce. I believe, my lord, from what I have seen of your lordship, and what I have heard of you, it will be to you a painful duty to inflict that sentence upon me. To one clinging so much to the world and its joys—to its fond ties and pleasant associations, as I naturally do, retirement into banishment is seldom—very seldom—welcome. Of that, however, I do not complain. But to any man whose heart glows with the warmest impulses and the most intense love of freedom; strongly attached to kind friends, affectionate parents, loving brother and sisters, and a devotedly fond and loving wife, the contemplation of a long period of imprisonment must appear most terrible and appalling. To me, however, viewing it from a purely personal point of view, and considering the cause for which I am about to suffer, far from being dismayed—far from its discouraging me—it proves to me rather a source of joy and comfort. True, it is a position not to be sought—not to be looked for; it is one which, for many, very many reasons there is no occasion for me now to explain, may be thought to involve disgrace or discredit. But so far from viewing it in that light, I do not shrink from it, but accept it readily, feeling proud and glad that it affords me an opportunity of proving the sincerity of those soul-elevating principles of freedom which a good old patriotic father instilled into my mind from my earliest years, and which I still entertain with a strong love, whose fervor and intensity are second only to the sacred homage which we owe to God. If, having lost that freedom, I am to be deprived of all those blessings—those glad and joyous years I should have spent amongst loving friends—I shall not complain, I shall not murmur, but, with calm resignation and cheerful expectation, I shall joyfully submit to God's blessed will, feeling confident that He will open the strongly locked and barred doors of British prisons. Till that glad time arrives, it is consolation and reward enough for me to know that I have the fervent prayers, the sympathy and loving blessings of Ireland's truly noble and generous people, and far easier, more soothing and more comforting to me will it be to go back to my cheerless cell, than it would be to live in slavish ease and luxury—a witness to the cruel sufferings and terrible miseries of this down-trodden people. Condemn me, then, my lord—condemn me to a felon's doom. To-night I will sleep in a prison cell, to-morrow I will wear a convict's dress, but to me it will be a far nobler garb than the richest dress of slavery. Coward slaves they be who think the countless sufferings and degradation of prison life disgrace a man. I feel otherwise. It is as impossible to subdue the soul animated with freedom as it will be for England to crush the resolute will of this nation, determined as it is to be free, or perish in the attempt. According to British law, those acts proved against me—fairly proved against me, I acknowledge—may be crimes, but morally, in the eyes of freemen and the sight of God, they are more ennobling than disgraceful. Shame is only a connection with guilt. It is surely not a crime to obey God's law, or to assist our fellow-men to acquire those God-given rights which no men—no nation—can justly deprive them of. If love of freedom and a desire to extend its unspeakable blessings to all God's creatures irrespective of race, creed, or color, be a crime—if devotion to Ireland, and love of its faithful, its honest, its kindly people be a crime, then I say I proudly and gladly acknowledge my guilt. If it is a disgrace, all I can say is, I glory in such shame and dishonor; and, with all respect for the court, I hold in thorough and utmost contempt the worst punishment that can be inflicted upon me, so far as it is intended to deprive me of this feeling, and degrade me in the eyes of my fellow-men. Oh! no, it is impossible, my lord; the freeman's soul can never be dismayed. England will most miserably fail if she expects by force and oppression to crush out—to stamp out, as the *Times* exclaimed—this glorious longing for national life and independence which now fills the breasts of millions of Irishmen, and which only requires a little patience and the opportunity to effect its purpose. Much has been said, on these trials, on the objects and intentions of Fenianism. I feel confidently, my lord, as to my own motives. I shall not be guilty of the egotism to say whether they are pure or otherwise. I shall leave that to others to judge. I am not qualified to judge that myself; but I know in my soul that the motives which prompted me were pure, patriotic, and unselfish. I know the motives that actuate the most active members of the Fenian organization; and I know that very few persons, except such contemptible wretches as Corridon, have profited by their connection with Fenianism. My best friends lost all they ever possessed by it. Talbot and Corridon, I believe, have sworn on previous trials that it was the intention of the Fenians to have divided the lands of Ireland amongst themselves in the event of success. Though an humble member of the organization, I have the honor and satisfaction of being acquainted with the great majority of the leaders of Fenianism on both sides of the Atlantic; and I never knew one of them to have exhibited a desire other than to have the proud satisfaction of freeing Ireland, which was the only reward they ever yearned for—the only object that ever animated them. As to myself, I can truly say that I entered into this movement without any idea of personal aggrandizement. When, in 1865, I bade my loving friends and parents good-by in America, and came to Ireland, I was fully satisfied with the thought that I was coming to assist in the liberation of an enslaved nation; and I knew that the greatest sacrifices must be endured on our parts before the country could be raised to that proud position which is so beautifully described by the national poet as:—

'Great, glorious, and free,
First flower of the earth, first gem of the sea.'

Well, it was with that only wish and that only desire I came to Ireland, feeling that to realize it were to an honest man a greater reward than all the honors and riches and power this world could bestow. I cannot boast of learning, my lord; I have not had much opportunity of cultivating those talents with which Providence may have blessed me. Still I have read sufficient of the world's history to know that no people ever acquired their liberty without enormous sacrifices—without losing, always, I may say, some of the purest, bravest, and best of their children. Liberty, if worth possessing, is surely worth struggling and fighting for; and in this struggle—of which, although the crown lawyers and the government of England think they have seen the end, but of which I tell them they have not yet seen the commencement—I feel that enormous sacrifices must be made. Therefore, my lord, looking straight before me now, I say I was determined and was quite ready to sacrifice my life, if necessary, to acquire that liberty; and I am not now going to be so mean-spirited, so cowardly, or so contemptible, as to shrink from my portion of the general suffering. I am ready, then, for the sentence of the court, satisfied that I have acted right, confident that I have committed no wrong, outrage, or crime whatever, and that I have cast no disgrace upon my parents, my friends, upon my devoted wife, or upon myself. I am, with God's assistance, ready to meet my fate. I rest in the calm resignation of a man whose only ambition through life has been to benefit and free, not to injure, his fellow-men; and whose only desire this moment is to obtain their prayers and blessings. With the approval of my own conscience, above all hoping for the forgiveness of God for anything I may have done to displease Him, and relying upon His self-sustaining grace to enable me to bear any punishment, no matter how severe, so long as it is for glorious old Ireland. I had intended, my lord, to refer to my notes which I took at

the trial ; but I feel that was so ably done by my counsel, it would
be a mere waste of time for me to do so, but I just wish to make an
explanation. Sir C. O'Loghlen made a statement—unintentionally
I am sure it was on his part—which may or may not affect me. He
said I sent a memorial to the Lord Lieutenant praying to be released from custody. I wish to say I sent no such thing. The
facts of the matter are these:—I was liberated in this court because
in reality the Crown could not make out a case against me at the
time ; and as I could, at the same time, be kept in prison until the
next assizes, I, on consultation with my friends and with my fellow-
captive, Captain M'Afferty, consented, as soon as I should receive
a remittance from my friends in America, to return there. On
these conditions I was set at liberty, understanding, at the same
time, that, if found in the country by the next assizes, I would be
brought up for trial. I did not want to give annoyance, and I
said I would go to America. I honestly intended to do so then—
not, however, as giving up my principles. but because I saw there
was no hope of an immediate rising in Ireland. While agreeing
to those conditions, I went to Dublin, and there met M'Afferty, and
it was on that occasion I made the acquaintance of Corridon. I
met him purely accidentally. He afterwards stated that he saw me
in Liverpool, but he did not see me there. I went over with an object, and while there I was arrested by anticipation, before the
Habeas Corpus Act was really suspended. I defy the government
to prove I had any connection with Fenianism from the time I was
released from Cork jail until February, 1867. I was afterwards
removed to Mountjoy prison, and, while there, Mr. West came to
me and said he understood I was an American citizen, and asked
why I did not make that known. I said I had a double reason—
first, because I expected the Crown would see they had broken their
pledge with me in having been so soon arrested : and also that I
expected my government would make a general demand for all its
citizens. By Mr. West's desire I put that statement in writing;
and I do not think that there is a word in it that can be construed
into a memorial to the Lord Lieutenant. One of the directors of
the prison came to me and asked me was I content to comply with
the former conditions, and I said I was. I was liberated upon
those conditions, and complied with them ; but there was no condition whatever named that I was never to return to Ireland, nor to
fight for Irish independence. At that time I would sooner have
remained in prison than enter into any such compact. Now. with
reference to Corridon's information. He states he met me in
Liverpool after the rising, and I stated to him that somebody ' sold
the pass' upon us—to use the Irish phrase. Now, it is a strange
thing, my lord, that he got some information that was true, and I
really was in Liverpool, but not with the informer. The fact is,
the month previous to that I knew, and so did M'Afferty, that
Corridon had sold us. We left instructions at Liverpool to have
him watched, but owing to circumstances it is needless now to
refer to, that was not attended to, and he came afterwards to Ireland

and passed as a Fenian, and the parties here, not knowing he had betrayed them, still believed in him. But I knew very well that Corridon had betrayed that Chester affair, and so did Captain M'Afferty ; and if I had met him at that time in Liverpool, I don't think it would be he I would inform of our plans. I only want to show, my lord, how easily an informer can concoct a scene. I never in my life attended that meeting that Corridon swore to. All his depositions with respect to me are false. I did meet him twice in Dublin, but not on the occasions he states. I wish to show how an informer can concoct a story that it will be entirely out of the power of the prisoner to contradict. With reference to the witness Curtin, whom I asked to have produced—and the Crown did produce all the witnesses I asked for—your lordship seemed to be under the impression that I did not produce him because he might not be able to say I was not in his house that night. Now, the fact is that, as my attorney learned the moment Mr. Curtin was brought to town, he knew nothing whatever about the circumstance, as he was not in his own tavern that night at all. That was why I did not produce the evidence. But I solemnly declare I never was in Curtin's public-house in my life till last summer, when I went in with a friend on two or three occasions, and then for the first time. That must have been in June or July, after the trials were over in Dublin. So that everything Corridon said in connection with my being there that night was absolutely false. I solemnly declare I was never there till some time last summer, when I went in under the circumstances I have stated. In conclusion, my lord, though it may not be exactly in accordance with the rules of the court, I wish to return your lordship my most sincere thanks for your fair and impartial conduct during this trial. If there was anything that was not impartial in it at all, I consider it was only in my favor, and not in favor of the Crown. This I consider is the duty of a judge, and what every judge should do—because the prisoner is always on the weak side, and cannot say many things he would wish ; while the Crown, on the other hand, have all the power and influence that the law and a full exchequer can give them. I must also return my sincere and heartfelt thanks to my able and distinguished counsel, who spoke so eloquently in my favor. As for Mr. Collins, I feel I can never sufficiently thank him. He served me on my trial at a great sacrifice of time and money, with noble zeal and devotion, such as might be more readily expected from a friend than a solicitor. There are many more I would like to thank individually, but, as this may not be the proper time and place to do so, I can only thank all my friends from the bottom of my heart. I may mention the name at least of Mr. Joyce, who, in the jail, showed a great deal of kind feeling and attention. And now, my lord, as I have already stated, I am ready for my sentence. I feel rather out of place in this dock (the prisoner here smiled gently). It is a place a man is very seldom placed in, and even if he is a good speaker, he might be put out by the circumstance of having to utter his remarks from this place. But speaking at all is not my *forte;* and there are such emotions filling my breast at this moment that I may be pardoned for not saying all I would wish. My heart is filled with thoughts of kind friends—near at hand and far away—of father and mother, brothers and sisters, and my dear wife. Thoughts of these fill my breast at this moment, and check my utterance. But I will say to them that I am firmly convinced I will yet live to see, and that God will be graciously pleased in His own good time to order, the prosperity and freedom of this glorious country. I would only repeat the powerful, touching, and simple words of Michael Larkin, the martyr of Manchester, who, in parting from his friends, said, 'God be with you, Irishmen and Irishwomen;' and the burning words of my old friend, Edward O'Mara Condon, which are now known throughout Ireland and the world, 'God save Ireland!' And I, too, would say, 'God be with you, Irish men and women; God save you; God bless Ireland; and God grant me strength to bear my task for Ireland as becomes a man. Farewell!' (A sound of some females sobbing was here heard in the gallery. Several ladies in court, too, visibly yielded to emotion at this point. Perceiving this, the prisoner continued:—) My lord, if I display any emotion at this moment, I trust it will not be construed into anything resembling a feeling of despair, for no such feeling animates me. I feel, as I have already said, confidence in God. I feel that I will not be long in imprisonment; therefore I am just as ready to meet my fate now as I was six weeks ago, or as I was six months ago. I feel confident that there is a glorious future in store for Ireland, and that, with a little patience, a little organization, and a full trust in God on the part of the Irish people, they will be enabled to obtain it at no distant date."

During the concluding passages of this address many persons sobbed and wept in various parts of the court. At its close the learned judge, in language that was really gentle, considerate, and even complimentary towards the prisoner, and in a voice shaken by sincere emotion, declared the sentence which he felt it to be his duty to impose. It was penal servitude for a term of twelve years.

THE "ERIN'S HOPE" SALUTING THE GREEN FLAG.

"GOD SAVE IRELAND."

THE

DOCK AND THE SCAFFOLD:

THE MANCHESTER TRAGEDY:

AND

THE CRUISE OF THE JACKMEL.

"Far dearer the grave and the prison
Illumed by one patriot's name,
Than the trophies of all who have risen,
On liberty's ruins, to fame."
—MOORE.

THE DOCK AND THE SCAFFOLD.

THE 23d day of November, 1867, witnessed a strange and memorable scene in the great English city of Manchester. Long ere the grey winter's morning struggled in through the crisp, frosty air—long ere the first gleam of the coming day dulled the glare of the flaming gas jets, the streets of the Lancashire capital were all astir with bustling crowds, and the silence of the night was broken by the ceaseless footfalls and the voices of hurrying throngs. Through the long, dim streets, and past tall rows of silent houses, the full tide of life eddied and poured in rapid current; stout burghers, closely muffled and staff in hand; children grown prematurely old, with the hard marks of vice already branded on their features; young girls with flaunting ribbons and bold, flushed faces; pale operatives, and strong men whose brawny limbs told of the Titanic labors of the foundry; the clerk from his desk; the shopkeeper from his store; the withered crone, and the careless navvy, swayed and struggled through the living mass; and with them trooped the legions of want, and vice, and ignorance, that burrow and fester in the fetid lanes and purlieus of the large British cities; from the dark alleys where misery and degradation forever dwell, and from reeking cellars and nameless haunts, where the twin demons of alcohol and crime rule supreme; from the gin-palace, and the beer-shop, and the midnight haunts of the tramp and the burglar, they came in all their repulsiveness and debasement, with the rags of wretchedness upon their backs, and the cries of profanity and obscenity upon their lips. Forward they rushed in a surging flood through many a street and by-way, until where the narrowing thoroughfares open into the space surrounding the New Bailey Prison, in that suburb of the great city known as the Borough of Salford, they found their further progress arrested. Between them and the massive prison walls rose piles of heavy barricading, and the intervening space was black with a dense body of men, all of whom faced the gloomy building beyond, and each of whom carried a special constable's baton in his hand. The long railway bridge running close by was occupied by a detachment of infantry, and from the parapet of the frowning walls the muzzle of cannon, trained on the space below, might be dimly discerned in the darkness. But the crowd paid little attention to these extraordinary appearances; their eyes were riveted on the black projection which jutted from the prison wall, and which, shrouded in dark drapery, loomed with ghastly significance through the haze. Rising above the scaffold, which replaced a portion of the prison wall, the outlines of a gibbet were descried; and from the cross-beam there hung three ropes, terminating in nooses, just perceptible above the upper edge of the curtain which extended thence to the ground. The grim excrescence seemed to possess a horrible fascination for the multitude. Those in position to see it best stirred not from their post, but faced the fatal cross-tree, the motionless ropes, the empty platform, with an untiring, an insatiable gaze, that seemed pregnant with some terrible meaning, while the mob behind them struggled, and pushed, and raved, and fought; and the haggard hundreds of gaunt, diseased, stricken wretches, that vainly contested with the stronger types of ruffianism for a place, loaded the air with their blasphemies and imprecations. The day broke slowly and doubtfully upon the scene; a dense, yellow, murky fog floated round the spot, wrapping in its opaque folds the hideous gallows and the frowning mass of masonry behind. An hour passed, and then a hoarse murmur swelled upwards from the glistening rows of upturned faces. The platform was no longer empty; three pinioned men, with white caps drawn closely over their faces, were standing upon the drop. For a moment the crowd was awed into stillness; for a moment the responses, " Christ have mercy on us," " Christ have mercy on us," were heard from the lips of the doomed men, towards whom the sea of faces was turned. Then came a dull

crash, and the mob swayed backwards for an instant.
The drop had fallen, and the victims were struggling in
the throes of a horrible death. The ropes jerked and
swayed with the convulsive movements of the dying men.
A minute later, and the vibrations ceased—the end had
come, the swaying limbs fell rigid and stark, and the souls
of the strangled men had floated upwards from the cursed
spot—up from the hateful crowds and the sin-laden atmosphere—to the throne of the God who made them.

So perished, in the bloom of manhood, and the flower
of their strength, three gallant sons of Ireland—so passed
away the last of the martyred band whose blood has sanctified the cause of Irish freedom. Far from the friends
whom they loved, far from the land for which they suffered,
with the scarlet-clad hirelings of England around them,
and watched by the wolfish eyes of a brutal mob, who
thirsted to see them die, the dauntless patriots, who, in
our own day, have rivalled the heroism and shared the
fate of Tone, Emmet, and Fitzgerald, looked their last
upon the world. No prayer was breathed for their parting
souls—no eye was moistened with regret amongst the
multitude that stretched away in compact bodies from the
foot of the gallows; the ribald laugh and the blasphemous
oath united with their dying breath; and callously as the
Roman mob from the blood-stained amphitheatre, the
English masses turned homewards from the fatal spot.
But they did not fall unhonored or unwept. In the
churches of the faithful in that same city the sobs of
mournful lamentation were mingled with the solemn
prayers for their eternal rest; and from thousands of wailing women and stricken-hearted men, the prayers for
mercy, peace, and pardon, for the souls of MICHAEL
O'BRIEN, WILLIAM PHILIP ALLEN, and MICHAEL
LARKIN, rose upwards to the avenging God. Still less
were they forgotten at home. Throughout the Irish land,
from Antrim's rocky coast to the foam-beaten headlands
of Cork, the hearts of their countrymen were convulsed
with passionate grief and indignation; and, blended with
the sharp cry of agony that broke from the nation's lips,
came the murmurs of defiant hatred, and the pledges of a

bitter vengeance. Never, for generations, had the minds of the Irish people been more profoundly agitated—never had they writhed in such bitterness and agony of soul. With knittted brows and burning cheeks, the tidings of the bloody deed were listened to. The names of the martyred men were upon every lip, and the story of their heroism and tragic death was read with throbbing pulse and kindling eyes by every fireside in the land. It is to assist in perpetuating that story, and in recording for future generations the narrative which tells of how Allen, O'Brien, and Larkin died, that this narrative is written; and few outside the nation whose hands are red with their blood, will deny that at least so much recognition is due to their courage, their patriotism, and their fidelity. In Ireland we know it will be welcomed; amongst a people by whom chivalry and patriotism are honored, a story so touching and ennobling will not be despised; and the race which guards with reverence and devotion the memories of Tone, and Emmet, and the Sheareses, will not soon surrender to oblivion the memory of the three true-hearted patriots, who, heedless of the scowling mob, unawed by the hangman's grasp, died bravely, that Saturday morning, at Manchester, for the good old cause of Ireland.

Early before daybreak, on the morning of November 11th, 1867, the policemen on duty in Oak-street, Manchester, noticed four broad-shouldered, muscular men, loitering in a suspicious manner about the shop of a clothes-dealer in the neighborhood. Some remarks dropped by one of the party reaching the ears of the policemen, strengthened their impression that an illegal enterprise was on foot, and the arrest of the supposed burglars was resolved on. A struggle ensued, during which two of the suspects succeeded in escaping, but the remaining pair, after offering a determined resistance, were overpowered and carried off to the police station. The prisoners, who, on being searched, were found to possess loaded revolvers on their persons, gave their names as Martin Williams and John Whyte, and were charged under the Vagrancy Act before one of the city magistrates. They declared themselves American citizens, and claimed their discharge. Williams said he was a bookbinder out of work; Whyte described himself as a hatter, living on the means brought with him from America. The magistrate was about disposing summarily of the case, by sentencing the men to a few days' imprisonment, when a detective officer applied for a remand, on the ground that he had reason to believe the prisoners were connected with the Fenian conspiracy. The application was granted, and, before many hours had elapsed, it was ascertained that Martin Williams was no other than Colonel Thomas J. Kelly, one of the most prominent of the (O'Mahony-Stephens) Fenian leaders, and that John Whyte was a brother officer and conspirator, known to the circles of the Fenian Brotherhood as Captain Deasey.

Of the men who had thus fallen into the clutches of the British government the public had already heard much, and one of them was widely known for the persistency with which he labored as an organizer of Fenianism, and the daring and skill which he exhibited in the pursuit of his dangerous undertaking. Long before the escape of James Stephens from Richmond Bridewell startled the government from its visions of security, and swelled the breasts of their disaffected subjects in Ireland with rekindled hopes, Colonel Kelly was known in the Fenian ranks as an intimate associate of the revolutionary chief. When the arrest at Fairfield House deprived the organization of its crafty leader, Kelly was elected to the vacant post, and he threw himself into the work with all the reckless energy of his nature. If he could not be said to possess the mental ability or administrative capacity essential to the office, he was at least gifted with a variety of other qualifications well calculated to recommend him to popularity amongst the desperate men with whom he was associated. Nor did he prove altogether unworthy of the confidence reposed in him. It is now pretty well known that the successful plot for the liberation of James Stephens was executed under the personal supervision of Colonel Kelly, and that he was one of the group of friends who grasped the hand of the Head Centre within the gates of Richmond Prison on that night in November,

'65, when the doors of his dungeon were thrown open. Kelly fled with Stephens to Paris, and thence to America, where he remained attached to the section of the Brotherhood which recognized the authority and obeyed the mandates of the " C. O. I. R." But the time came when even Colonel Kelly and his party lost confidence in the leadership of James Stephens. The chief whom they had so long trusted, but who had disappointed them by the non-fulfilment of his engagement to fight on Irish soil before January, '67, was deposed by the last section of his adherents, and Colonel Kelly was elected " Deputy Central Organizer of the Irish Republic," on the distinct understanding that he was to follow out the policy which Stephens had shrunk from pursuing. Kelly accepted the post, and devoted himself earnestly to the work. In America he met with comparatively little coöperation; the bulk of Irish Nationalists in that country had long ranged themselves under the leadership of Colonel W. R. Roberts, an Irish gentleman of character and integrity, who became the President of the reconstituted organization ; and the plans and promises of the " Chatham-street wing," as the branch of the Brotherhood which ratified Colonel Kelly's election was termed, were regarded, for the most part, with suspicion and disfavor. But from Ireland there came evidences of a different state of feeling. Breathless envoys arrived almost weekly in New York, declaring that the Fenian Brotherhood in Ireland were burning for the fray—that they awaited the landing of Colonel Kelly with feverish impatience—that it would be impossible to restrain them much longer from fighting—and that the arrival of the military leaders, whom America was expected to supply, would be the signal for a general uprising. Encouraged by representations like these, Colonel Kelly and a chosen body of Irish-American officers departed for Ireland in January, and set themselves, on their arrival in the old country, to arrange the plans of the impending outbreak. How their labors eventuated, and how the Fenian insurrection of March, '67, resulted, it is unnecessary to explain; it is enough for our purpose to state that for several months after that ill-starred movement was crushed, Colonel Kelly continued to reside in Dublin, moving about with an absence of disguise and a disregard for concealment which astonished his confederates, but which, perhaps, contributed in no slight degree to the success with which he eluded the efforts directed towards his capture. At length the Fenian organization in Ireland began to pass through the same changes that had given it new leaders and fresh vitality in America. The members of the organization at home began to long for union with the Irish Nationalists, who formed the branch of the Confederacy regenerated under Colonel Roberts; and Kelly, who, for various reasons, was unwilling to accept the new *régime*, saw his adherents dwindle away, until at length he found himself all but discarded by the Fenian circles in Dublin. Then he crossed over to Manchester, where he arrived but a few weeks previous to the date of his accidental arrest in Oak-street.

The arrest of Colonel Kelly and his aide-de-camp, as the English papers soon learned to describe Deasey, was hailed by the government with the deepest satisfaction. For years they had seen their hosts of spies, detectives, and informers, foiled and outwitted by this daring conspirator, whose position in the Fenian ranks they perfectly understood; they had seen their traps evaded, their bribes spurned, and their plans defeated at every turn; they knew, too, that Kelly's success in escaping capture was filling his associates with pride and exultation; and now at last they found the man, whose apprehension they so anxiously desired, a captive in their grasp. On the other hand, the arrests in Oak-street were felt to be a crushing blow to a failing cause by the Fenian circles in Manchester. They saw that Kelly's capture would dishearten every section of the organization; they knew that the broad meaning of the occurrence was, that another Irish rebel had fallen into the clutches of the British government, and was about to be added to the long list of their political victims. It was felt by the Irish in Manchester, to abandon the prisoners helplessly to their fate would be regarded as an act of submission to the laws which rendered patriotism a crime, and as an acceptance of the policy which left Ireland trampled, bleeding, and impoverished. There were hot spirits amongst the Irish colony that dwelt in the great industrial capital, which revolted from such a conclusion; and there were warm, impulsive hearts which swelled with a firm resolution to change the triumph of their British adversaries into disappointment and consternation. The time has not yet come when anything like a description of the midnight meetings and secret councils which followed the arrest of Colonel Kelly in Manchester can be written; enough may be gathered, however, from the result, to show that the plans of the conspirators were cleverly conceived and ably digested.

On Wednesday, September 18th, Colonel Kelly and his companion were a second time placed in the dock of the Manchester police office. There is reason to believe that means had previously been found of acquainting them with the plans of their friends outside; but this hypothesis is not necessary to explain the coolness and *sang froid* with which they listened to the proceedings before the magistrate. Hardly had the prisoners been put forward, when the Chief Inspector of the Manchester Detective Force interposed. They are both, he said, connected with the Fenian rising, and warrants were out against them for treason-felony. "Williams," he added, with a triumphant air, "is Colonel Kelly, and Whyte, his confederate, is Captain Deasey." He asked that they might again be remanded,—an application which was immediately granted. The prisoners, who imperturbably bowed to the detective, as he identified them, smilingly quitted the dock, and were given in charge to Police Sergeant Charles Brett, whose duty it was to convey them to the borough gaol.

The van used for the conveyance of prisoners between the police office and the gaol was one of the ordinary long black boxes on wheels, dimly lit by a grating in the door and a couple of ventilators in the roof. It was divided interiorly into a row of small cells at either side, and a passage running the length of the van between; and the practice was, to lock each prisoner into a separate cell, Brett sitting in charge on a seat in the passage, near the door. The van was driven by a policeman; another usually sat beside the driver on the box—the whole escort thus consisting of three men, carrying no other arms than their staves; but it was felt that on the present occasion a stronger escort might be necessary. The magistrates well knew that Kelly and Deasey had numerous sympathizers amongst the Irish residents in Manchester, and their apprehensions were quickened by the receipt of a telegram from Dublin Castle, and another from the Home Office in London, warning them that a plot was on foot for the liberation of the prisoners. The magistrates doubted the truth of the information, but they took precautions, nevertheless, for the frustration of any such enterprise. Kelly and Deasey were both handcuffed, and locked in separate compartments of the van; and, instead of three policemen, not less than twelve were intrusted with its defence. Of this body, five sat on the box-seat, two were stationed on the step behind, four followed the van in a cab, and one (Sergeant Brett) sat within the van, the keys of which were handed into him through the grating after the door had been locked by one of the policemen outside. There were, in all, six persons in the van; one of these was a boy, aged twelve, who was being conveyed to a reformatory; three were women convicted of misdemeanors, and the two Irish-Americans completed the number. Only the last-mentioned pair were handcuffed, and they were the only persons whom the constables thought necessary to lock up, the compartments in which the other persons sat being left open.

At half-past three o'clock the van drove off, closely followed by the cab containing the balance of the escort. Its route lay through some of the principal streets, then through the suburbs on the south side, into the borough of Salford, where the county jail is situated. In all about two miles had to be traversed, and of this distance the first half was accomplished without anything calculated to excite suspicion being observed; but there was mischief brewing, for all that, and the crisis was close at hand.

Just as the van passed under the railway arch that spans the Hyde-road at Bellevue, a point midway between the city police office and the Salford Gaol, the driver was suddenly startled by the apparition of a man standing in the middle of the road with a pistol aimed at his head, and immediately the astonished policeman heard himself called upon, in a loud, sharp voice, to "pull up." At the spot where this unwelcome interruption occurred there are but few houses; brick-fields and clay-pits stretch away at either side, and the neighborhood is thinly inhabited. But its comparative quiet now gave way to a scene of bustle and excitement so strange, that it seems to have almost paralyzed the spectators with amazement. The peremptory command levelled at the driver of the van was hardly uttered, when a body of men, numbering about thirty, swarmed over the wall which lined the road, and, surrounding the van, began to take effectual measures for stopping it. The majority of them were well-dressed men, of powerful appearance; a few carried pistols or revolvers in their hands—all seemed to act in accordance with a preconcerted plan. The first impulse of the policemen in front appears to have been to drive through the crowd, but a shot, aimed in the direction of his head, brought the driver tumbling from his seat, terror-stricken, but unhurt; and almost at the same time, the further progress of the van was effectually prevented by shooting one of the horses through the neck. A scene of indescribable panic and confusion ensued; the policemen scrambled hastily to the ground, and betook themselves to flight almost without a thought of resistance. Those in the cab behind got out, not to resist the attack, but to help the running away; and in a few minutes the strangers, whose object had by this time become perfectly apparent, were undisputed masters of the situation. Pickaxes, hatchets, hammers, and crowbars were instantly produced, and the van was besieged by a score stout pairs of arms, under the blows from which its sides groaned, and the door cracked and splintered. Some clambered upon the roof, and attempted to smash it in with heavy stones; others tried to force an opening through the side; while the door was sturdily belabored by another division of the band. Seeing the Fenians, as they at once considered them, thus busily engaged, the policemen, who had in the first instance retreated to a safe distance, and who were now reinforced by a large mob attracted to the spot by the report of firearms, advanced towards the van, with the intention of offering some resistance; but the storming party immediately met them with a counter-movement. Whilst the attempt to smash through the van was continued without pause, a ring was formed round the men thus engaged, by their confederates, who, pointing their pistols at the advancing crowd, warned them, as they valued their lives, to keep off. Gaining courage from their rapidly swelling numbers, the mob, however, continued to close in round the van, whereupon several shots were discharged by the Fenians, which had the effect of making the Englishmen again fall back in confusion. It is certain that these shots were discharged for no other purpose than that of frightening the crowd; one of them did take effect in the heel of a bystander, but in every other case the shots were fired high over the heads of the crowd. While this had been passing around the van, a more tragic scene was passing inside it. From the moment the report of the first shot reached him, Sergeant Brett seems to have divined the nature and object of the attack. "My God! it's these Fenians," he exclaimed. The noise of the blows showered on the roof and sides of the van was increased by the shrieks of the female prisoners, who rushed frantically into the passage, and made the van resound with their wailings. In the midst of the tumult a face appeared at the grating, and Brett heard himself summoned to give up the keys. The assailants had discovered where they were kept, and resolved on obtaining them as the speediest way of effecting their purpose. "Give up the keys, or they will shoot you," exclaimed the women; but Brett refused. The next instant he fell heavily backwards, with the hot blood welling from a bullet-wound in the head. A shot fired into the keyhole, for the purpose of blowing the lock to pieces, had taken effect in his temple: the terror-stricken women lifted him up, screaming,

"He's killed." As they did so, the voice which had been heard before called out to them through the ventilator to give up the keys. One of the women then took them from the pocket of the dying policeman, and handed them out through the trap. The door was at once unlocked, the terrified women rushed out, and Brett, weltering in blood, rolled out heavily upon the road. Then a pale-faced young man, wearing a light overcoat, a blue tie, and a tall brown hat, who had been noticed taking a prominent part in the affray, entered the van, and unlocked the compartment in which Kelly and Deasey were confined. A hasty greeting passed between them, and then the trio hurriedly joined the band outside. "I told you, Kelly, I would die before I parted with you," cried the young man who unlocked the doors; then seizing Kelly by the arm, he helped him across the road, and over the wall, into the brick-fields beyond. Here he was taken charge of by others of the party, who hurried with him across the country, while a similar office was performed for Deasey, who, like Colonel Kelly, found himself hampered to some extent by the handcuffs on his wrists. The main body of those who had shared in the assault occupied themselves with preventing the fugitives from being pursued; and not until Kelly, Deasey, and their conductors had passed far out of sight, did they think of consulting their own safety. At length, when further resistance to the mob seemed useless and impossible, they broke and fled, some of them occasionally checking the pursuit by turning around and presenting pistols at those who followed. Many of the fugitives escaped, but several others were surrounded and overtaken by the mob. And now the " chivalry " of the English nature came out in its real colors. No sooner did the cowardly set, whom the sight of a revolver kept at bay while Kelly was being liberated, find themselves with some of the Irish party in their power, than they set themselves to beat them with savage ferocity. The young fellow who had opened the van door, and who had been overtaken by the mob, was knocked down by a blow of a brick, and then brutally kicked and stoned; the only Englishman who ventured to cry out " shame " being himself assaulted for his display of humanity. Several others were similarly ill-treated; and not until the blood spouted out from the bruised and mangled bodies of the prostrate men, did the valiant Englishmen consider they had sufficiently tortured their helpless prisoners. Meanwhile, large reinforcements appeared on the spot; police and military were despatched in eager haste in pursuit of the fugitives; the telegraph was called into requisition, and a description of the liberated Fenians flashed through the neighboring towns; the whole detective force of Manchester was placed on their trail, and in the course of a few hours thirty-two Irishmen were in custody, charged with having assisted in the attack on the van. But of Kelly or Deasey no trace was ever discovered; they were seen to enter a cottage not far from the Hyde-road, and leave it with their hands unfettered, but all attempts to trace their movements beyond this utterly failed. While the authorities in Manchester were excitedly discussing the means to be adopted in view of the extraordinary event, Brett lay expiring in the hospital to which he had been conveyed. He never recovered consciousness after receiving the wound, and he died in less than two hours after the fatal shot had been fired.

Darkness had closed in around Manchester before the startling occurrence that had taken place in their midst became known to the majority of its inhabitants. Swiftly the tidings flew throughout the city, till the whisper in which the rumor was first breathed swelled into a roar of astonishment and rage. Leaving their houses and leaving their work, the people rushed into the streets and trooped towards the newspaper offices for information. The rescue of Colonel Kelly and the death of Sergeant Brett were described in thousands of conflicting narratives, until the facts almost disappeared beneath the mass of inventions and exaggerations, the creations of excitement and panic, with which they were overloaded. Meanwhile the police, maddened by resentment and agitation, struck out wildly and blindly at the Irish. They might not be able to recapture the escaped Fenian leaders, but they could load the gaols with their countrymen and co-religionists;

they might not be able to apprehend the liberators of
Colonel Kelly and Captain Deasey, but they could
glut their fury on members of the same nationality : and
this they did most effectually. The whole night long the
raid upon the Irish quarter in Manchester was continued ;
houses were broken into, and their occupants dragged off
to prison, and flung into cells, chained as though they
were raging beasts. Mere Irish were set upon in the
streets, in the shops, in their homes, and hurried off to
prison, as if the very existence of the empire depended on
their being subjected to every kind of brutal violence and
indignity. The yell for vengeance filled the air ; the cry
for Irish blood arose upon the night-air like a demoniacal
chorus ; and before morning broke their fury was somewhat
appeased by the knowledge that sixty of the
proscribed race—sixty of the hated Irish—were lying
chained within the prison cells of Manchester.

Fifteen minutes was the time occupied in setting Kelly
free—only fifteen minutes ; but during that short space of
time an act was accomplished which shook the whole
British Empire to its foundation. From the conspiracy to
which this daring deed was traceable, the English people
had already received many startling surprises. The liberation
of James Stephens and the short-lived insurrection
that filled the snow-capped hills with hardy fugitives, six
months before, had both occasioned deep excitement in
England; but nothing that Fenianism had yet accomplished
acted in the same bewildering manner on the
English mind. In the heart of one of their largest cities,
in the broad daylight, openly and undisguisedly, a band
of Irishmen had appeared in arms against the Queen's
authority, and set the power and resources of the law at
defiance. They had rescued a co-conspirator from the
grasp of the government, and slain an officer of the law in
pursuit of their object. Within a few minutes' walk of
barracks and military depots—in sight of the royal ensign
that waved over hundreds of her Majesty's defenders, a
prison van had been stopped and broken open, and its
defenders shot and put to flight. Never had the English
people heard of so audacious a proceeding—never did they

feel more insulted. From every corner of the land the cry swelled up for vengeance fierce and prompt. Victims there would be; blood—Irish blood—the people *would* have; nor were they willing to wait long for it. It might be that, falling in hot haste, the sword of justice might strike the innocent, and not the guilty; it might be that, in the thirst for vengeance, the restraints of humanity would be forgotten; but the English nature, now thoroughly aroused, cared little for such considerations. It was Irishmen who had defied and trampled on their power; the whole Irish people approved of the act; and it mattered little who the objects of their fury might be, provided they belonged to the detested race. The prisoners, huddled together in the Manchester prisons with chains round their limbs, might not be the liberators of Colonel Kelly—the slayers of Brett might not be amongst them; but they were Irishmen, at any rate, and so they would answer the purpose. Short shrift was the cry. The ordinary forms of law, the maxims of the constitution, the rules of judicial procedure, the proprieties of social order and civilization, might be outraged and discarded, but speedy vengeance should, at all hazards, be obtained. The hangman could not wait for his fee, nor the people for their carnival of blood; and so it was settled that, instead of being tried at the ordinary Commission, in December, a special Commission should be issued on the spot for the trial of the accused.

On Thursday, the 25th of October, the prisoners were brought up for committal, before Mr. Fowler, R. M., and a bench of brother magistrates. Some of the Irishmen arrested in the first instance had been discharged—not that no one could be found to swear against them (a difficulty which never seems to have arisen in these cases), but that the number of witnesses who could swear to their innocence was so great, that an attempt to press for conviction in their cases would be certain to jeopardize the whole proceedings. The following is a list of the prisoners put forward, the names being, as afterwards appeared, in many cases fictitious :—

William O'Mara Allen, Edward Shore, Henry Wilson, William

Gould, Michael Larkin, Patrick Kelly, Charles Moorhouse, John Brennan, John Bacon, William Martin, John F. Nugent, James Sherry, Robert M'Williams, Michael Maguire, Thomas Maguire, Michael Morris, Michael Bryan, Michael Corcoran, Thomas Ryan, John Carroll, John Gleason, Michael Kennedy, John Morris, Patrick Kelly, Hugh Foley, Patrick Coffey, Thomas Kelly, and Thomas Scally.

It forms no part of our purpose to follow out the history of the proceedings in the Manchester court on the 25th of September and the following days; but there are some circumstances in connection with that investigation which it would be impossible to pass over without comment. It was on this occasion that the extraordinary sight of men being tried in chains was witnessed, and that the representatives of the English Crown came to sit in judgment on men still innocent in the eyes of the law, yet manacled like convicted felons. With the blistering irons clasped tight round their wrists, the Irish prisoners stood forward, that justice—such justice as tortures men first and tries them afterwards—might be administered to them. "The police considered the precaution necessary," urged the magistrate, in reply to the scathing denunciation of the unprecedented outrage which fell from the lips of Mr. Ernest Jones, one of the prisoners' counsel. The police considered it necessary, though within the court-house no friend of the accused could dare to show his face—though the whole building bristled with military and with policemen with their revolvers ostentatiously displayed; necessary, though every soldier in the whole city was standing to arms—necessary there, in the heart of an English city, with a dense population thirsting for the blood of the accused, and when the danger seemed to be, not that they might escape from custody—a flight to the moon might be equally practicable—but that they might be butchered in cold blood by the angry English mob that scowled on them from the galleries of the court-house, and howled round the building in which they stood. In vain did Mr. Jones protest, in scornful words, against the brutal indignity—in vain did he appeal to the spirit of British justice, to ancient precedent and modern practice—in vain did he inveigh against a proceeding which forbade the intercourse necessary between him and his clients—and in vain did he point out that the prisoners in the dock were guiltless and innocent men according to the theory of the law. No arguments, no expostulations would change the magistrate's decision. Amidst the applause of the cowardly set that represented the British public within the court-house, he insisted that the handcuffs should remain on; and then Mr. Jones, taking the only course left to a man of spirit under the circumstances, threw down his brief and indignantly quitted the desecrated justice-hall. Fearing the consequences of leaving the prisoners utterly undefended, Mr. Cottingham, the junior counsel for the defence, refrained from following Mr. Jones's example, but he, too, protested loudly, boldly, and indignantly against the cowardly outrage, worthy of the worst days of the French monarchy, which his clients were being subjected to. The whole investigation was in keeping with the spirit evinced by the bench. The witnesses seemed to come for the special purpose of swearing point-blank against the hapless men in the dock, no matter at what cost to truth, and to take a fiendish pleasure in assisting in securing their condemnation. One of the witnesses was sure "the whole lot of them wanted to murder every one who had any property;" another assured his interrogator in the dock that "he would go to see him hanged;" and a third had no hesitation in acknowledging the attractions which the reward offered by the government possessed for his mind. Men and women, young and old, all seemed to be possessed of but the one idea—to secure as much of the blood-money as possible, and to do their best to bring the hated Irish to the gallows. Of course, an investigation, under these circumstances, could have but one ending, and no one was surprised to learn, at its conclusion, that the whole of the resolute body of stern-faced men, who, manacled and suffering, confronted their malignant accusers, had been committed to stand their trial in hot haste for the crime of "wilful murder."

Of the men thus dealt with, there were four with whose fate this narrative is closely connected, and whose names are destined to be long remembered in Ireland. They have won for themselves, by their courage, constancy, and patriotism, a fame that will never die; and through all future time they will rank beside the dauntless spirits that in days of darkness and disaster perished for the sacred cause of Ireland. Great men, learned men, prominent men, they were not—they were poor, they were humble, they were unknown; they had no claim to the reputation of the warrior, the scholar, or the statesman; but they labored, as they believed, for the redemption of their country from bondage; they risked their lives in a chivalrous attempt to rescue from captivity two men whom they regarded as innocent patriots, and, when the forfeit was claimed, they bore themselves with the unwavering courage and single-heartedness of Christian heroes. Their short and simple annals are easily written; but their names are graven on the Irish heart, and their names and actions will be cherished in Ireland when the monumental piles that mark the resting-places of the wealthy and the proud have returned, like the bodies laid beneath them, to dust.

William Philip Allen was born near the town of Tipperary, in April, 1848. Before he was quite three years old his parents removed to Bandon, county Cork, where the father, who professed the Protestant religion, received the appointment of bridewell-keeper. As young Allen grew up, he evinced a remarkable aptitude for the acquirement of knowledge, and his studious habits were well known to his playmates and companions. He was a regular attendant at the local training-school for the education of teachers for the Protestant schools of the parish, but he also received instruction at the morning and evening schools conducted under Catholic auspices, in the same town. He was not a wild boy, but he was quick and impulsive—ready to resent a wrong, but equally ready to forgive one; and his natural independence of spirit and manly disposition rendered him a favorite with all his acquaintances. The influence and example of his father did not prevent him from casting a wistful eye towards the ancient faith. His mother, a good, pious Catholic, whose warmest aspiration was to see her children in the fold of the true Church, encouraged this disposition by all the means in her power; and the result of her pious care shortly became apparent. A mission, opened in the town by some Catholic order of priests, completed the good work, which the prayers and the example of an affectionate mother had commenced; and young Allen, after regularly attending the religious services and exercises of the mission, became so much impressed with the truth of the lectures and sermons he had listened to, that he formally renounced the alien religion, and was received by the respected parish priest of the town into the bosom of the Catholic Church. His only sister followed his example, while his brothers, four in number, remained in the Protestant communion. The subject of our sketch was apprenticed to a respectable master carpenter and timber merchant in Bandon; but circumstances, highly creditable to the young convert, induced the severance of the connection before his period of apprenticeship was expired, and we next find him working at his trade in Cork, where he remained for some six months, after which he returned to Bandon. He next crossed over to Manchester, at the request of some near relatives living there. Subsequently he spent a few weeks in Dublin, where he worked as builder's clerk; and finally he revisited Manchester, where he had made himself numerous friends. It was in the summer of '67 that Allen last journeyed to Manchester. He was then little more than nineteen years old, but there is reason to believe that he had long before become connected with the Fenian conspiracy. In his ardent temperament the seeds of patriotism took deep and firm root; and the dangers of the enterprise to which the Fenians were committed, served only to give it a fresh claim upon his enthusiastic nature. When Colonel Kelly quitted Dublin and took up his quarters in Manchester, Allen was one of his most trusted and intimate associates; and when the prison door grated behind the Fenian leader, it was Allen who roused his countrymen to the task of effecting his liberation. Allen had by this time grown into a comely young man of prepossessing appearance; he was a little over the middle height, well shaped, without presenting the appearance of unusual strength, and was always seen neatly and respectably dressed. His face was pale and wore a thoughtful expression, his features, when in repose, wearing an appearance of pensiveness approaching to melancholy. His eyes were small, the eyelids slightly marked; a mass of dark hair clustered gracefully over a broad pale forehead, while the absence of any beard gave him a peculiarly boyish appearance. Gentle and docile in his calmer moments, when roused to action he was all fire and energy. We have seen how he bore himself during the attack on the prison van, for he it was whom so many witnesses identified as the pale-faced young fellow who led the attack, and whose prophetic assurance that he would die for him greeted Colonel Kelly on regaining his freedom. During the magisterial investigation he bore himself firmly, proudly, and, as the English papers would have it, defiantly. His glance never quailed during the trying ordeal. The marks of the brutality of his cowardly captors were still upon him, and the galling irons that bound his hands cut into his wrists; but Allen never winced for a moment, and he listened to the evidence of the sordid crew, who came to barter away his young life, with resolute mien. The triumph was with him. Out of the jaws of death he had rescued the leader whose freedom he considered essential to the success of a patriotic undertaking, and he was satisfied to pay the cost of the venture. He had set his foot upon the ploughshare, and would not shrink from the ordeal which he had challenged.

Amongst the crowd of manacled men committed for trial by the Manchester magistrates, not one presented a finer or more impressive exterior than Michael O'Brien, set down in the list above given as Michael Gould. Standing in the dock, he seemed the impersonation of vigorous manhood. Frank, fearless, and resolute, with courage and truth imprinted on every feature, he presented to the eye a perfect type of the brave soldier. He was tall and well proportioned, and his broad shoulders and well-developed limbs told of physical strength in keeping with the firmness reflected in his face. His gaze, when it rested on the unfriendly countenances before him, was firm and undrooping; but a kindly light lit his hazel eyes, and his features relaxed into a sympathizing and encouraging expression as often as he glanced at Allen, who stood behind him, or bent his gaze upon any of his other fellow-prisoners. O'Brien was born near Ballymacoda, county Cork, the birthplace of the ill-fated and heroic Peter Crowley. His father rented a large farm in the same parish, but the blight of the bad laws which are the curse of Ireland fell upon him, and in the year 1856, the O'Briens were flung upon the world, dispossessed of lands and home, though they owed no man a penny at the time. Michael O'Brien was apprenticed to a draper in Youghal, and earned, during the period of his apprenticeship, the respect and esteem of all who knew him. He was quiet and gentlemanly in manners, and his character for morality and good conduct was irreproachable. Having served out his time in Youghal, he went to Cork, and he spent some time as an assistant in one of the leading drapery establishments of that city. He afterwards emigrated to America, where some of his relatives were comfortably settled. Like many of the bravest of his fellow-countrymen, the outbreak of the civil war kindled a military ardor within his bosom, and O'Brien found himself unable to resist the attractions which the soldier's career possessed for him. His record throughout the war was highly honorable; his bravery and good conduct won him speedy promotion, and long before the termination of the conflict he had risen to the rank of lieutenant. When his regiment was disbanded he recrossed the Atlantic, and returned to Cork, where he again obtained employment as assistant in one of the large commercial establishments. Here he remained until the night before the Fenian rising, when he suddenly disappeared, and all further trace was lost of him, until arrested for participation in the attack upon the prison van in Manchester.

Close by his side in the dock stood Michael Larkin, an intelligent-looking man, older-looking than most of his fellow-prisoners. The following are a few facts relating to his humble history:—

"He was," writes a correspondent who knew him, "a native of the parish of Lusmagh, in the south-western corner of the King's county, where for many generations his ancestors have been residents on the Cloghan Castle estate (then in possession of the O'Moore family), and where several of his relatives still reside; and was grandson to James Quirke, a well-to-do farmer, who was flogged and transported in '98 for complicity in the rebellion of that time, and whose name, in this part of the country, is remembered with pleasure and affection for his indomitable courage and perseverance in resisting the repeated allurements held out by the corrupt minions of the Crown to induce him to become a traitor to his companions and his country. But all their importunities were vain; Quirke steadily persevered in the principles of his gallant leader, Robert Emmet. Larkin's father was a respectable tradesman, carrying on his business for many years in his native parish; he removed to Parsonstown, where he contrived to impart to his son Michael a good English education, and then taught him his own profession. When Michael had attained a thorough knowledge of his business, he was employed till '58, at Parsonstown; he then went to England, to improve his condition, and after some time he married, and continued to work on industriously at his business till May, '67, when he visited his native country, to receive the last benediction of his dying father. He again returned to England with his wife and family, to resume his employment. After some time he was arrested for assisting to release two of his fellow-countrymen from bondage. I cannot attempt to enumerate the many good qualities of the deceased patriot: the paternal affection, exhibited from the earliest age; the mildness and affability of manner, good temper, affectionate and inoffensive disposition; his sobriety and good moral conduct—endeared him to all who had the pleasure and honor of his acquaintance. Throughout his whole life he was remarkable for his 'love of country,' and expressions of sincere regret for the miserable condition of many of his countrymen were ever on his lips. He was, in the true sense of the idea, a good son, an affectionate husband and father, and a sincere friend."

On Monday, October 28th, the three Irishmen, whose lives we have glanced at, were placed at the bar of the

Manchester Assize Court, and formally placed on their trial for wilful murder. With them were arraigned Thomas Maguire, a private belonging to the Royal Marines, who was on furlough in Liverpool at the time of Kelly's liberation, and who was arrested merely because he happened to be an Irishman, and who, though perfectly innocent of the whole transaction, had been sworn against by numerous witnesses as a ringleader in the attack; and Edward O'Meagher Condon (*alias* Shore), a fine-looking Irish-American, a citizen of the State of Ohio, against whom, like his four companions, true bills had been found by the Grand Jury. It would take long to describe the paroxysms of excitement, panic, and agitation that raged in the English mind from the period that intervened between the committal of the prisoners and the date at which we are now arrived. Nothing was heard of but the Fenians; nothing was talked of but the diabolical plots and murderous designs they were said to be preparing. The Queen was to be shot at; Balmoral was to be burned down; the armories had been attacked; the barracks were undermined; the gas works were to be exploded, the bank blown up, the water poisoned. Nothing was too infernal or too wicked for the Fenians, and every hour brought some addition to the monstrous stock of *canards*. North and south, east and west, the English people were in a ferment of anxious alarm; and everywhere Fenianism was cursed as an unholy thing to be cut from society as an ulcerous sore—to be banned and loathed as a pestilence—a foul creation with murder in its glare, and the torch of the incendiary burning in its gory hand. Under these circumstances, there was little chance that an unprejudiced jury could be empanelled for the trial of the Irish prisoners; and their counsel, seeing the danger, sought to avert it by a motion for the postponement of the trials. The Home Secretary was memorialed on the subject, and the application was renewed before the judges in court, but the efforts to obtain justice were fruitless. The blood of the British lion was up; with bloodshot eyes and bristling mane he stood awaiting his prey, and there was danger in trifling with his rage. Even Special Commissions were voted slow, and a cry arose for martial law, Lynch law, or any law that would give the blood of the victims without hindrance or delay. So the appeal for time was spurned; the government was deaf to all remonstrance; British bloodthirstiness carried the day, and the trials proceeded without interruption.

We have not patience to rehearse calmly the story of these trials, which will long remain the reproach of British lawyers. We shall not probe the motives which led to the appointment of two such men as Justice Mellor and Justice Blackburne as judges of the Commission, but history will be at no loss to connect the selection with their peculiar character on the bench. Nor shall we analyze the speeches of the Attorney-General and his colleagues, in which the passions and prejudices of the jury were so dexterously appealed to. The character of the evidence demands more study. The witnesses consisted of the policemen present at the attack, the prisoners who were locked with Kelly and Deasey in the van, and the by-standers who saw the affray, or assisted in stoning the prisoners before and after they were captured. They swore with the utmost composure against the four prisoners. Allen was identified as one of the leaders, and he it was whom most of the witnesses declared to have fired through the door. On this point, indeed, as on many others, there was confusion and contradiction in the evidence: some of the witnesses were sure it was O'Brien fired through the door; others were inclined to assign the leading part to Condon; but before the trial had gone far, it seemed to be understood that Allen was the man to whom the death of Brett was to be attributed, and that the business of the witnesses was to connect the other prisoners as closely as possible with his act. On one point nearly all of the witnesses were agreed—whoever there might be any doubt about, there could be none concerning Maguire. Seven witnesses swore positively to having seen him assisting in breaking open the van, and some of them even repeated the words which they said he addressed to them while thus engaged. On the evening of Friday, November 1st, the trials terminated. It was past five o'clock when Judge Mellor concluded his charge. The court was densely crowded, and every eye was strained to mark the effect of the judge's words on the countenances of the prisoners; but they, poor fellows, quailed not as they heard the words which they knew would shortly be followed by a verdict consigning them to the scaffold. Throughout the long trial their courage had never flagged, their spirits had never failed them for an instant. Maguire, who had no real connection with the other four, and who knew that the charge against him was a baseless concoction, did, indeed, betray traces of anxiety and bewilderment as the trial progressed; but Allen, O'Brien, Larkin, and Condon went through the frightful ordeal with a heroic display of courage to which even the most malignant of their enemies have paid tribute.

The judge has done, and now the jury turned from the box "to consider the verdict." An hour and twenty minutes they remained absent; then their returning tread was heard. The prisoners turned their eyes upwards; Maguire looked towards them, half hopefully, half appealingly; from Allen's glance nothing but defiance could be read; Larkin fixed his gaze on the foreman, who held the fatal record in his hand, with calm resolution; while a quiet smile played round O'Brien's lips, as he turned to hear the expected words.

"Guilty!" The word is snatched up from the lips of the foreman of the jury, and whispered through the court. They were all "guilty." So said the jury; and a murmur of applause came rolling back in response to the verdict. "Guilty!" A few there were in that court upon whom the fatal words fell with the bitterness of death, but the Englishmen who filled the crowded gallery and passages exulted at the sound : the vengeance which they longed for was at hand.

The murmur died away; the sobs that rose from the dark recesses where a few stricken-hearted women had been permitted to stand, were stifled; and then, amidst breathless silence, the voice of the Crown Clerk was heard demanding "if the prisoners had anything to say why sentence of death should not be pronounced on them."

The first to respond was Allen. A slight flush reddened

his cheeks, and his eyes lit up with the fire of enthusiasm and determination, as, advancing to the front of the dock, he confronted the court, and spoke in resolute tones as follows:—

"My Lords and Gentlemen:—It is not my intention to occupy much of your time in answering your question. Your question is one that can be easily asked, but requires an answer which I am ignorant of. Abler and more eloquent men could not answer it. Where were the men who have stood in the dock—Burke, Emmet, and others, who have stood in the dock in defence of their country ? When the question was put, what was their answer ? Their answer was null and void. Now, with your permission, I will review a portion of the evidence that has been brought against me."

Here Mr. Justice Blackburne interrupted. " It was too late," he said, " to criticize the evidence, and the court had neither the right nor the power to alter or review it. If," he added, " you have any reason to give why, either upon technical or moral grounds, the sentence should not be passed upon you, we will hear it, but it is too late for you to review the evidence to show that it was wrong."

" Cannot that be done in the morning, sir?" asked Allen, who felt in his heart how easily the evidence on which he had been convicted might be torn to shreds. But the Judge said not. " No one," he said, " could alter or review the evidence in any way after the verdict had been passed by the jury. We can only," he said in conclusion, " take the verdict as right; and the only question for you is, why judgment should not follow."

Thus restricted in the scope of his observations, the young felon proceeded to deliver the following patriotic and spirited address:—

"No man in this court regrets the death of Sergeant Brett more than I do, and I positively say, in the presence of the Almighty and ever-living God, that I am innocent, aye, as innocent as any man in this court. I don't say this for the sake of mercy : I want no mercy—I'll have no mercy. I'll die, as many thousands have died, for the sake of their beloved land, and in defence of it. I will die proudly and triumphantly in defence of republican principles and the liberty of an oppressed and enslaved people.—Is it possible we are asked why sentence should not be passed upon us, on the evidence of prostitutes off the streets of Manchester, fellows out of work, convicted felons—aye, an Irishman sentenced to be hung when an English dog would have got off? I say positively and defiantly, justice has not been done me since I was arrested. If justice had been done me, I would not have been handcuffed at the preliminary investigation in Bridge-street; and in this court justice has not been done me in any shape or form. I was brought up here, and all the prisoners by my side were allowed to wear overcoats, and I was told to take mine off. What is the principle of that? There was something in that principle, and I say positively, that justice has not been done me. As for the other prisoners, they can speak for themselves with regard to that matter. And now with regard to the way that I have been identified. I have to say that my clothes were kept for four hours by the policemen in Fairfield-station, and shown to parties to identify me as being one of the perpetrators of this outrage on Hyde-road. Also in Albert-station, there was a handkerchief kept on my head the whole night, so that I could be identified the next morning in the corridor by the witnesses. I was ordered to leave on the handkerchief for the purpose that the witnesses could more plainly see I was one of the parties who committed the outrage. As for myself, I feel the righteousness of my every act with regard to what I have done in defence of my country. I fear not. I am fearless—fearless of the punishment that can be inflicted on me; and with that, my lords, I have done. (After a moment's pause)—I beg to be excused. One remark more. I return Mr. Seymour and Mr. Jones my sincere and heartfelt thanks for their able eloquence and advocacy on my part in this affray. I wish also to return to Mr. Roberts the very same. My name, sir, might be wished to be known. It is not William O'Meara Allen. My name is William Philip Allen. I was born and reared in Bandon, in the county of Cork. and from that place I take my name; and I am proud of my country, and proud of my parentage. My lords, I have done."

A sigh of mingled applause and admiration rose faintly on the air, as the gallant young Irishman, inclining his head slightly to the court, retired to make way at the front of the bar for one of his companions in misfortune. But his chivalrous bearing and noble words woke no response within the prejudice-hardened hearts of the majority of his auditors; they felt that the fearless words of the fearless youth would overbear all that his accusers had uttered, and the world would read in them the condemnation of the government and of the people whose power he so bravely defied.

Michael Larkin spoke next. He looked a shade paler than on the first day of the trial, but no want of resolution was expressed in his firm set face. He gazed with an

unquailing glance round the faces eagerly bent forward
to catch his words, and then spoke in distinct tones as
follows:—

"I have only got a word or two to say concerning Sergeant Brett.
As my friend here said, no one could regret the man's death as much
as I do. With regard to the charge of pistols and revolvers, and
my using them, I call my God as a witness that I neither used
pistols, revolvers, nor any instrument on that day that would deprive
a child of life, let alone a man. Nor did I go there on purpose
to take life away. Certainly, my lords, I do not want to deny that
I did go to give aid and assistance to those two noble heroes that
were confined in that van—Kelly and Deasey. I did go to do
as much as lay in my power to extricate them out of their bondage,
but I did not go to take life, nor, my lord, did any one else. It is a
misfortune there was life taken; but if it was taken, it was not
done intentionally, and the man who has taken life, we have not got
him. I was at the scene of action, when there were over, I dare
say, one hundred and fifty people standing by there when I was. I
am very sorry I have to say, my lord, but I thought I had some
respectable people to come up as witnesses against me; but I am
sorry to say as my friend said. I will make no more remarks concerning that. All I have to say, my lords and gentlemen, is, that so
far as my trial went, and the way it was conducted, I believe I have
got a fair trial. So far as my noble council went, they did their
utmost in the protection of my life; likewise, my worthy solicitor,
Mr. Roberts, has done his best; but I believe as the old saying is a
true one, what is decreed a man in the page of life, he has to fulfil, either
on the gallows, drowning, a fair death in bed, or on the battlefield.
So I look to the mercy of God. May God forgive all who have
sworn my life away. As I am a dying man, I forgive them from
the bottom of my heart. God forgive them."

As Larkin ceased speaking, O'Brien, who stood to the
right of him, moved slightly in advance, and intimated
by a slight inclination to the court his intention of addressing them. His stalwart form seemed to dilate with
proud defiance and scorn as he faced the ermine-clad
dignitaries who were about to consign him to the gibbet.
He spoke with emphasis, and in tones which seemed to
borrow a something of the fire and spirit of his words.
He said:—

"I shall commence by saying that every witness who has sworn
anything against me has sworn falsely. I have not had a stone in
my possession since I was a boy. I had no pistol in my possession

on the day when it is alleged this outrage was committed. You call it an outrage; I don't. I say further, my name is Michael O'Brien. I was born in the county of Cork, and have the honor to be a fellow-parishioner of Peter O'Neal Crowley, who was fighting against the British troops at Mitchelstown last March, and who fell fighting against British tyranny in Ireland. I am a citizen of the United States of America, and if Charles Francis Adams had done his duty towards me, as he ought to do in this country, I would not be in this dock answering your questions now. Mr. Adams did not come, though I wrote to him. He did not come to see if I could not find evidence to disprove the charge, which I positively could, if he had taken the trouble of sending or coming to see what I could do. I hope the American people will notice that part of the business. [The prisoner here commenced reading from a paper he held in his hand.] The right of man is freedom. The great God has endowed him with affections that he may use, not smother them, and a world that may be enjoyed. Once a man is satisfied he is doing right, and attempts to do anything with that conviction, he must be willing to face all the consequences. Ireland, with its beautiful scenery, its delightful climate, its rich and productive lands, is capable of supporting more than treble its population in ease and comfort. Yet no man, except a paid official of the British government, can say there is a shadow of liberty, that there is a spark of glad life amongst its plundered and persecuted inhabitants. It is to be hoped that its imbecile and tyrannical rulers will be forever driven from her soil, amidst the execration of the world. How beautifully the aristocrats of England moralize on the despotism of the rulers of Italy and Dahomey—in the case of Naples with what indignation did they speak of the ruin of families by the detention of its head or some loved member in a prison! Who has not heard their condemnations of the tyranny that would compel honorable and good men to spend their useful lives in hopeless banishment?"

The taunt went home to the hearts of his accusers, and, writhing under the lash thus boldly applied, Judge Blackburne hastened to intervene. Unable to stay, on *legal grounds*, the torrent of scathing invective by which O'Brien was driving the blood from the cheeks of his British listeners, the judge resorted to a device which Mr. Justice Keogh had practised very adroitly, and with much success, at various of the State trials in Ireland. He appealed to the prisoner, " entirely for his own sake," to cease his remarks. "The only possible effect of your observations," he said, "must be to tell against you with those who have to consider the sentence. I advise you to say nothing more of that sort. I do so entirely for your own sake."

But O'Brien was not the man to be cowed into submission by this artful representation. Possibly he discerned the motive of the interruption, and estimated at its true value the disinterestedness of Judge Blackburne's "advice." Mr. Ernest Jones in vain used his influence to accomplish the Judge's object. O'Brien spurned the treacherous bait, and resolutely proceeded:—

"They cannot find words to express their horror of the cruelties of the King of Dahomey because he sacrificed 2,000 human beings yearly, but why don't those persons who pretend such virtuous indignation at the misgovernment of other countries look at home, and see if greater crimes than those they charge against other governments are not committed by themselves or by their sanction? Let them look at London, and see the thousands that want bread there, while those aristocrats are rioting in luxuries and crimes. Look to Ireland; see the hundreds of thousands of its people in misery and want. See the virtuous, beautiful, and industrious women, who only a few years ago—aye, and yet—are obliged to look at their children dying for want of food. Look at what is called the majesty of the law on one side, and the long, deep misery of a noble people on the other. Which are the young men of Ireland to respect—the law that murders or banishes their people, or the means to resist relentless tyranny and ending their miseries forever under a home government? I need not answer that question here. I trust the Irish people will answer it to their satisfaction soon. I am not astonished at my conviction. The government of this country have the power of convicting any person. They appoint the judge; they choose the jury; and by means of what they call patronage (which is the means of corruption) they have the power of making the laws to suit their purposes. I am confident that my blood will rise a hundred-fold against the tyrants who think proper to commit such an outrage. In the first place, I say I was identified improperly, by having chains on my hands and feet at the time of identification; and thus the witnesses who have sworn to my throwing stones and firing a pistol have sworn to what is false, for I was, as those ladies said, at the gaol gates. I thank my council for their able defence, and also Mr. Roberts, for his attention to my case."

Edward Maguire spoke next. He might well have felt bewildered at the situation in which he found himself, but he spoke earnestly and collectedly, nevertheless. He had had an experience of British law, which, if not without precedent, was still extraordinary enough to create amazement. He knew that he had never been a Fenian;

he knew that he never saw Colonel Kelly—never heard of him until arrested for assisting in his liberation; he knew that, while the van was being attacked at Bellevue, he was sitting in his own home, miles away; and he knew that he had never in his life placed his foot in the scene of the rescue; yet there he found himself convicted, by regular process of law, of the murder of Constable Brett. He had seen witness after witness enter the box, and deliberately swear they saw him take a prominent part in the rescue. He saw policemen and civilians coolly identify him as a ringleader in the affair; he had heard the crown lawyers weave around him the subtle meshes of their logic; and now he found himself pronounced guilty by the jury, in the teeth of the overwhelming array of unimpeachable evidence brought forward in his defence. What "the safeguards of the Constitution" mean—what "the bulwark of English freedom" and "the Palladium of British freedom" are worth, when Englishmen fill the jury-box and an Irishman stands in the dock, Maguire had had a fair opportunity of judging. Had he been reflectively inclined, he might, too, have found himself compelled to adopt a rather low estimate of the credibility of English witnesses, when they get an opportunity of swearing away an Irishman's life. An impetuous man might have been goaded by the circumstances into cursing the atrocious system under which "justice" had been administered to him, and calling down the vengeance of Heaven on the whole nation from which the perjured wretches who swore away his life had been drawn. But Maguire acted more discreetly; he began, indeed, by declaring that all the witnesses who swore against him were perjurers—by vehemently protesting that the case, as regarded him, was one of mistaken identity; but he shortly took surer ground, by referring to his services in the navy, and talking of his unfailing loyalty to "his Queen and his country." He went through the record of his services as a marine; appealed to the character he had obtained from his commanding officers, in confirmation of his words; and concluded by solemnly protesting his perfect innocence of the charge on which he had been convicted.

While Maguire's impressive words were still ringing in the ears of his conscience-stricken accusers, Edward O'Meagher Condon commenced to speak. He was evidently more of an orator than either of those who had preceded him, and he spoke with remarkable fluency, grace, and vigor. The subjoined is a correct report of his spirited and able address:—

"My Lords:—This has come upon me somewhat by surprise. It appeared to me rather strange that upon any amount of evidence, which of course was false, a man could have been convicted of wilfully murdering others he never saw or heard of before he was put in prison. I do not care to detain your lordships, but I cannot help remarking that Mr. Shaw, who has come now to gloat up a his victims, after having sworn away their lives—that man has sworn what is altogether false; and there are contradictions in the depositions which have not been brought before your lordships' notice. I suppose, the depositions being imperfect, there was no necessity for it. As to Mr. Batty, he swore at his first examination before the magistrates that a large stone fell on me, a stone which Mr. Roberts said at the time would have killed an elephant. But not the slightest mark was found on my head; and if I was to go round the country, and him with me, as exhibiting the stone having fallen on me, and him as the man who would swear to it, I do not know which would be looked for with the most earnestness. However, it has been accepted by the jury. Now he says he only thinks so. There is another matter to consider. I have been sworn to, I believe, by some of the witnesses who have also sworn to others, though some of them can prove they were in another city altogether— in Liverpool. Others have an overwhelming *alibi*, and I should by right have been tried with them; but I suppose your lordships cannot help that. We have, for instance, Thomas the policeman, who swore to another prisoner. He identified him on a certain day, and the prisoner was not arrested for two days afterwards. As for Thomas, I do not presume that any jury could have believed him. He had heard of the blood money, and of course was prepared to bid pretty high for it. My *alibi* has not been strong, and unfortunately I was not strong in pocket, and was not able to produce more testimony to prove where I was at exactly that time. With regard to the unfortunate man who has lost his life, I sympathize with him and his family as deeply as your lordships or the jury, or any one in the court. I deeply regret the unfortunate occurrence, but I am as perfectly innocent of his blood as any man. I never had the slightest intention of taking life. I have done nothing at all in connection with that man, and I do not desire to be accused of a murder which I have not committed. With regard to another matter, my learned counsel has, no doubt for the best, expressed some opinions on these matters and the misgovernment to which my country has been subjected. I am firmly convinced there is prejudice in the minds of the people, and it has been increased and excited by the newspapers, or by some of them, and to a certain extent has influenced the minds of the jury to convict the men standing in this dock, on a charge of which—a learned gentleman remarked a few nights since—they would be acquitted if they had been charged with murdering an old woman for the sake of the money in her pocket, but a political offence of this kind they could not. Now, sir, with regard to the opinions I hold on national matters—with regard to those men who have been released from that van, in which, unfortunately, life was lost, I am of opinion that certainly to some extent there was an excuse. Perhaps it was unthought; but if those men had been in other countries, occupying other positions—if Jefferson Davis had been released in a northern city, there would have been a cry of applause throughout all England. If Garibaldi, who, I saw before I was shut out from the world, had been arrested, was released, or something of that kind had taken place, they would have applauded the bravery of the act. If the captives of King Theodore had been released, that, too, would have been applauded. But, as it happened to be in England, of course it is an awful thing, while yet in Ireland murders are perpetrated on unoffending men, as in the case of the riots in Waterford, where an unoffending man was murdered, and no one was punished for it. I do not desire to detain your lordships. I can only say that I leave this world without a stain on my conscience that I have been wilfully guilty of anything in connection with the death of Sergeant Brett. I am totally guiltless. I leave this world without malice to any one. I do not accuse the jury, but I believe they were prejudiced. I don't accuse them of wilfully wishing to convict, but prejudice has induced them to convict when they otherwise would not have done. With reference to the witnesses, every one of them has sworn falsely. I never threw a stone or fired a pistol; I was never at the place as they have said; it is all totally false. But as I have to go before my God, I forgive them. They will be able to meet me, some day, before that God who is to judge us all, and then they and the people in this court, and every one, will know who tells the truth. Had I committed anything against the Crown of England, I would have scorned myself had I attempted to deny it; but with regard to those men, they have sworn what is altogether false. Had I been an Englishman, and arrested near the scene of that disturbance, I would have been brought as a witness to identify them; but, being an Irishman, it was supposed my sympathy was with them, and on suspicion of that sympathy I was arrested; and in consequence of the arrest, and the rewards which were offered, I was identified. It could not be otherwise. As I said before, my opinions on national matters do not at all relate to the case before your lordships. We have been found guilty, and, as a matter of course, we accept our death as gracefully as possible. We are not afraid to die—at least I am not."

"Nor I," "Nor I," "Nor I," swelled up from the lips of his companions; and then, with a proud smile, Condon continued :—

"I have no sin or stain upon me; and I leave this world at peace with all. With regard to the other prisoners who are to be tried afterwards, I hope our blood at least will satisfy the craving for it. I hope our blood will be enough, and that those men who, I honestly believe, are guiltless of the blood of that man—that the other batches will get a fair, free, and a more impartial trial. We view matters in a different light from what the jury do. We have been imprisoned, and have not had the advantage of understanding exactly to what this excitement has led. I can only hope and pray that this prejudice will disappear—that my poor country will right herself some day, and that her people, so far from being looked upon with scorn and aversion, will receive what they are entitled to, the respect not only of the civilized world, but of Englishmen. I, too, am an American Citizen, and on English territory I have committed no crime which makes me amenable to the Crown of England. I have done nothing ; and, as a matter of course, I did expect protection—as this gentleman (pointing to Allen) has said, the protection of the ambassador of my government. I am a citizen of the State of Ohio ; but I am sorry to say my name is not Shore. My name is Edward O'Meagher Condon. I belong to Ohio, and there are loving hearts there that will be sorry for this. I have nothing but my best wishes to send them, and my best feelings, and assure them I can die as a Christian and an Irishman ; and that I am not ashamed or afraid of anything I have done, or the consequences, before God or man. They would be ashamed of me if I was in the slightest degree a coward, or concealed my opinions. The unfortunate divisions of our countrymen in America have, to a certain extent, neutralized the efforts that we have made either in one direction or another for the liberation of our country. All these things have been thwarted, and, as a matter of course, we must only submit to our fate. I only trust again, that those who are to be tried after us will have a fair trial, and that our blood will satisfy the cravings which I understand exist. You will soon send us before God, and I am perfectly prepared to go. I have nothing to regret, or to retract, or to take back. I can only say, GOD SAVE IRELAND."

Again were the voices of his companions raised in unison. "God save Ireland!" they cried defiantly, in chorus. "God save Ireland!" The cry rung through the packed justice-hall, and fell on the ears of its bloodthirsty occupants like the voice of an accusing angel. "God save Ireland!" they said; and then the brave-hearted fellows gazed fiercely around the hostile gathering, as if daring them to interfere with the prayer. "God save Ireland!"—from the few broken-hearted relatives who listened to the patriots' prayer the responsive "Amen" was breathed back, and the dauntless young Irishman continued:

"I wish to add a word or two. There is nothing in the close of my political career which I regret. I don't know of one act which could bring the blush of shame to my face, or make me afraid to meet my God or fellow-man. I would be most happy, and nothing would give me greater pleasure than to die on the field for my country in defence of her liberty. As it is, I cannot die on the field, but I can die on the scaffold, I hope, as a soldier, a man, and a Christian."

And now the last was spoken. As true Irishmen and as true patriots they had borne themselves. No trace of flinching did they give for their enemies to gloat over—no sign of weakness which could take from the effect of their deathless words. With bold front and steady mien they stood forward to listen to the fatal decree their judges were ready to pronounce. The judges produced the black caps, with which they had come provided, and then Justice Mellor proceeded to pass sentence. No person, he said, who had witnessed the proceedings could doubt the propriety of the verdict, which he insisted was the result of "a full, patient, and impartial investigation." He made no distinction. "I am perfectly convinced," he said, "that all of you had resolved, at any risk, and by any amount of dangerous violence and outrage, to accomplish your object; and that, in fact, Charles Brett was murdered because it was essential to the completion of your common design that he should be." The stereotyped words of exhortation to repentance followed, and then the judge concluded:—

"The sentence is that you, and each of you, be taken hence to the place whence you came, and thence to a place of execution, and that you be there hanged by the neck until you shall be dead, and that your bodies be afterwards buried within the precincts of the prison wherein you were last confined after your respective convictions; and may God, in His infinite mercy, have mercy upon you."

With quiet composure the doomed men heard the words. They warmly shook hands with their counsel, thanked them for their exertions, and then, looking towards the spot where their weeping friends were seated, they turned to leave the dock. "God be with you, Irishmen and Irishwomen!" they cried, and, as they disappeared from the court, their final adieu was heard in the same prayer that had swelled upwards to Heaven from them before—

"GOD SAVE IRELAND!"

Scarcely had the Manchester court-house ceased to echo those voices from the dock, when the glaring falseness of the verdict became the theme of comment amongst even the most thoroughgoing Englishmen who had been present throughout the trial.

Without more ado down sate some thirty or forty reporters, who, as representatives of the English metropolitan and provincial press, had attended the Commission, and addressed a memorial to the Home Secretary, stating that they had been long accustomed to attend at trials on capital charges; that they had extensive experience of such cases, from personal observation of prisoners in the dock and witnesses on the table; and that they were solemnly convinced, the swearing of the witnesses and the verdict of the jury to the contrary notwithstanding, that the man Maguire had neither hand, act, nor part in the crime for which he had been sentenced to death. The following is the petition referred to:—

"We, the undersigned, members of the metropolitan and provincial press, having had long experience in courts of justice, and full opportunity of observing the demeanor of prisoners and witnesses in cases of criminal procedure, beg humbly to submit that, having heard the evidence adduced before the Special Commission, on the capital charge preferred against Thomas Maguire, private in the Royal Marines, we conscientiously believe that the said Thomas Maguire is innocent of the crime of which he has been convicted, and that his conviction has resulted from mistaken identity. We, therefore, pray that you will be pleased to advise her Majesty to grant her most gracious pardon to the said Thomas Maguire."

"GOD SAVE IRELAND!"

This was a startling event; it was a proceeding utterly without precedent. Nothing but the most extraordinary circumstances could have called it forth. The blunder of the jury must have been open, glaring, painfully notorious, indeed, when such an astonishing course was adopted by the whole staff of the English press.

It was most embarrassing. For what had those newspaper reporters seen or heard that the jurors had not seen and heard?—and yet the jurors said Maguire was guilty. What had those reporters seen or heard that the judges had not seen and heard?—and yet the judges said they "fully concurred in the verdict of the jury." The reporters were not sworn on the Evangelists of God to give a true deliverance—but the jurors were. The reporters were not sworn to administer justice—were not dressed in ermine—were not bound to be men of legal ability, judicial calmness, wisdom, and impartiality—but the judges were. Yet the unsworn reporters told the government Maguire was an innocent man; while judge and jury told the government—*swore* to it—that he was a guilty murderer!

What was the government to do? Was it to act on the verdict of newspaper reporters who had happened to be present at this trial, and not on the verdict of the jury who had been solemnly sworn in the case? Behind the reporters' verdict lay the huge sustaining power of almost universal conviction, mysteriously felt and owned, though as yet nowhere expressed. Every one who had calmly and dispassionately weighed the evidence arrived at conclusions identical with those of the press jury, and utterly opposed to those of the sworn jury. The ministers themselves—it was a terribly embarrassing truth to own— felt that the reporters were as surely right as the jurors were surely wrong. But what were they to do? What a frightful imputation would the public admission of that fact cast upon the twelve sworn jurors—upon the judges! What a damning imputation on their judgment or their impartiality! Was it to be admitted that newspaper reporters could be right in a case so awful, where twelve sworn jurors and two judges were wrong?

And then, look at the consequences. The five men were

convicted in the one verdict. There were not five separate verdicts, but one indivisible verdict. If the (jurors') verdict were publicly vitiated—if the government confessed or admitted that verdict to be false—it was not one man, but five men, who were affected by it. To be sure, the reporters' jury, in *their* verdict, did not include Allen, O'Brien, Larkin and Shore; but was it to be conveyed by implication that omission from the reporters' verdict of acquittal was more fatal to a man than inclusion in the verdict of guilty by a sworn jury? Might not twenty, or thirty, or forty men, quite as intelligent as the reporters, be soon forthcoming to testify as forcibly of Allen, O'Brien, Larkin and Shore, as the press-men had testified of Maguire? Was it only *reporters* whose judgment could set aside the verdict of sworn jurors, endorsed by ermined judges? But, in any event, the five men were convicted by the one verdict. To cut that, loosed all—not necessarily in law, perhaps, but inevitably as regarded public conscience and universal judgment; for there was not in all the records of English jurisprudence a precedent for executing men on a verdict acknowledged to have been one of blunder or perjury. Clearly, if the jurors were to be told by the government that, in a case where life and death hung on the issue, they had been so blinded by excitement, passion, or prejudice, that they declared to be a guilty murderer a man whose innocence was patent even to unofficial lookers-on in court, the moral value of such a verdict was gone—ruined forever; and to hang *any one* on such a verdict—*on that identical verdict, thus blasted and abandoned*—would, it was pointed out, be murder, for all its technical legality; neither more nor less, morally, than cool, deliberate, cold-blooded murder.

Everybody saw this; but every one in England saw also the awkward difficulty of the case. For, to let Allen, O'Brien, Larkin, and Shore go free of death, in the face of their admitted complicity in the rescue, would balk the national demand for vengeance. It was necessary that some one should be executed. Here were men, though they almost certainly had no hand in causing, even accidentally, the death of Brett, dared boast of their participation in the affray in the course of which that lamentable event unhappily occurred—that rescue which had so painfully wounded and humiliated English national pride. If these men were saved from execution, owing to any foolish scruples about hanging a possibly—nay, probably —innocent man along with them, a shout of rage would ascend from that virtuous nation amongst whom Charlotte Winsor, the professional infant-murderess, walks a free woman, notwithstanding a jury's verdict of wilful murder and a judge's sentence of death.

So, for a time it seemed that, notwithstanding the verdict of the reporters, the government would act upon the verdict of the jury, and assume it to be correct. No doubt Maguire might be innocent, but it was his misfortune to be included in an indivisible verdict with other men, who, though perhaps as guiltless as he of wilful murder, were surely guilty of riot and rescue, aggravated by the utterance of the most bitter reflections on the British Constitution, which all men know to be the "envy of surrounding nations." If they were not guilty of the crime laid against them on the trial, they were guilty of something else—they had outraged British pride. It was necessary they should die; and as Maguire's was not separate from theirs, he must die too, rather than that they should escape

But after a while the idea gained ground in England that this would be rather *too* monstrous a proceeding. Maguire's utter innocence of any participation whatsoever in the rescue was too notorious. The character of the witnesses on whose evidence he was convicted became known: some were thieves, pickpockets, or gaol-birds of some other denomination; others were persons palpably confused by panic, excitement, passion, or prejudice. True, these same witnesses were those who likewise swore against Allen, Larkin, O'Brien, and Shore. Indeed, a greater number swore against Maguire than against some of the others. Nevertheless, the overwhelming notoriety of the jury's blunder or perjury, in his case at least, became daily more and more an obstacle to his execution; and eventually, on the 21st of November, it was announced that his conviction had been cancelled, by the only means existing under the perfect laws of Great Britain—namely, a "free *pardon*" for a crime never committed. The prison doors were opened for Maguire; the sworn jurors were plainly told in effect that their blunder or perjury had well-nigh done the murder of at least one innocent man. The judges were in like manner told that shorthand writers had been more clear-headed or dispassionate to weigh evidence and judge guilt than they. The indivisible verdict had been openly proclaimed worthless.

The news was received with a sense of relief in Ireland, where the wholesale recklessness of the swearing, and the transparent falseness of the verdict, had, from the first, created intense indignation and resentment. Every one knew and saw that, whatever might have been the participation of those men in the rescue of Col. Kelly, they had not had a fair trial; nay, that their so-called trial was an outrage on all law and justice; that witnesses, jurors, and judges were in the full fierce heat of excitement, panic, and passion,—much more ready to swear evidence, to find verdicts, and to pass sentences against innocent men than they themselves were, perhaps, conscious of, while laboring under such influences. The public and official recognition of the falseness and injustice of the Manchester verdict was therefore hailed with intense satisfaction.

Maguire was at once liberated; Allen, Larkin, Shore, and O'Brien were still detained in custody. It was universally concluded that, notwithstanding the abandonment by the Crown of the verdict on which they had been sentenced, they, because of their admitted complicity in the rescue, would be held to imprisonment—probably penal servitude—for a term of years. Considerable astonishment was excited, some days subsequently to Maguire's pardon, by a statement that, in the case of the other prisoners included in the verdict, "the law should take its course." No one credited this declaration for an instant, and most persons felt that the Crown officials were indulging in an indecent piece of mockery. Amidst this universal incredulity, however—this disdainful and indignant disbelief—the prisoners' solicitor, Mr. Roberts, vigilant and untiring to the last, took the necessary steps to pray arrest of execution pending decision of the serious law points raised on the trial. Some of the most eminent counsel in England certified solemnly that these points were of the gravest nature, and would, in their opinion, be fully established on argument before the judges; in which event the conviction would be legally quashed, independently of the substantial abandonment of it as false and untenable by the Crown in Maguire's case.

The first idea of the merest possibility—the faintest chance—of the remaining four men being executed on the vitiated verdict, arose when it became known that the judges, or some of them, had informally declared to the government, (without waiting to hear any argument on the subject) that the points raised by the prisoners' counsel were not tenable, or were not of force. Mr. Roberts was officially informed that the sentence would infallibly be carried out. By this time barely a few days remained of the interval previous to the date fixed for the execution, and the strangest sensations swayed the public mind in Ireland. Even still, no one would seriously credit that men would be put to death on a verdict notoriously false. Some persons who proposed memorials to the Queen were met on all hands with the answer that it was all "acting" on the part of the government; that, even though it should be at the foot of the scaffold, the men would be reprieved; that the government would not—*dare not*—take away human life on a verdict already vitiated and abandoned as a perjury or blunder.

The day of doom approached; and now, as it came nearer and nearer, a painful and sickening alternation of incredulity and horror surged through every Irish heart. Meanwhile, the press of England, on both sides of the Channel, kept up a ceaseless cry for blood. The government were told that to let these men off, innocent or guilty, would be "weakness." They were called upon to be "firm"—that is, to hang first, and reflect afterwards. As the 23d of November drew near, the opinion began to gain ground, even in England, that things had been too hastily done—that the whole trial bore all the traces of panic—and that, if a few weeks were given for alarm and passion to calm down, not a voice would approve the Manchester verdict. Perceiving this—perceiving that time or opportunity for reflection, or for the subsidence of panic, would almost certainly snatch its prey from vengeance—a deafening yell arose from the raving creatures of blood-hunger, demanding that not a day, not an hour, not a second, should be granted to the condemned.

Still the Irish people would not credit that, far towards the close of the nineteenth century, an act so dreadful durst be done.

During all this time the condemned lay in Salford gaol, tortured by the suspense inevitably created by Maguire's reprieve. Although every effort was made by their friends to keep them from grasping at or indulging in hope, the all-significant fact of that release seemed to imperatively forbid the idea of their being executed on a verdict whose falseness was thus confessed. The moment, however, that the singular conduct of the judges in London defeated the application of Mr. Roberts, they, one and all, resigned themselves to the worst; and while their fellow-countrymen at home were still utterly and scornfully incredulous on the subject, devoted their remaining hours exclusively to spiritual preparation for death upon the scaffold.

It was now that each character "rushed to its index." It was now—within the very shadow of death—in the most awful crisis that can test the soul—that these men rose into the grandeur and sublimity of true heroism. They looked death in the face with serene and cheerful composure. So far from requiring consolation, it was they who strove most earnestly to console the grieving friends they were leaving behind; imploring them to exhibit resignation to the will of God, and assuring them that, ignominious as was death upon the gallows, and terrible as was the idea of suffering such a fate unjustly, it was "not hard to die" with a clear and tranquil conscience, as they were dying, for the cause of native land.

It may be questioned whether the martyrology of any nation in history can exhibit anything more noble, more edifying, more elevating and inspiring, than the last hours of these doomed Irishmen. Their every thought, their every utterance, was full of tenderness and holiness —full of firmness and cheerful acceptance of God's will. The farewell letters addressed by them to their relatives and friends—from which we take a few—amply illustrate the truth of the foregoing observations. Here is O'Brien's last letter to his brother :—

NEW BAILEY PRISON, SALFORD,
Nov. 14th, 1867.

MY DEAR BROTHER :—I have been intending to write to you for some time, but having seen a letter from a Mr. Moore, addressed to the governor of this prison, and knowing from that that you must be in a disagreeable state of suspense, I may therefore let you know how I am at once. With reference to the trial and all connected with it, it was unfair from beginning to end ; and if I should die in consequence, it will injure my murderers more than it will injure me. Why should I fear to die, innocent as I am of the charge which a prejudiced jury, assisted by perjured witnesses, found me guilty of? I will do judge and jury the justice of saying they believed me guilty of being—a citizen of the United States, a friend to liberty, a hater of relentless cruelty, and therefore no friend to the British government, as it exists in our beautiful island. I must say, though much I would like to live, that I cannot regret dying in the cause of liberty and Ireland. It has been made dear to me by the sufferings of its people, by the martyrdom and exile of its best and noblest sons. The priest, the scholar, the soldier, the saint, have suffered and died proudly, nobly ; and why should I shrink from death in a cause made holy and glorious by the numbers of its martyrs and the heroism of its supporters, as well as by its justice. You don't, and never shall, forget that Peter O'Neill Crowley died only a short time since in this cause.

"Far dearer the grave or the prison,
  Illum'd by one patriot name,
Than the trophies of all who have risen,
  On liberty's ruins, to fame."

I should feel ashamed of my manhood if I thought myself capable of doing anything mean to save my life, to get out of here, or for any other selfish purpose. Let no man think a cause is lost because some suffer for it. It is only a proof that those who suffer are in earnest, and should be an incentive to others to be equally so—to do their duty with firmness, justice, and disinterestedness. *I feel confident of the ultimate success of the Irish cause, as I do of my own existence.* God, in His great mercy and goodness, will strengthen the arm of the patriot, and give him wisdom to free his country. Let us hope that

He, in His wisdom, is only trying our patience. The greater its sufferings, the more glorious will He make the future of our unfortunate country and its people.
The shriek of the famine-stricken mother and the helpless infant, as well as the centuries of misery, calls to heaven for vegeance. God is slow, but just! The blood of Tone, Fitzgerald, Emmet, and others, has been shed—how much good has it done the tyrant and the robber? None. Smith O'Brien, M'Manus, and Mitchel suffered for Ireland, yet not their sufferings, nor those of O'Donovan (Rossa) and his companions, deterred Burke, M'Afferty, and their friends from doing their duty. Neither shall the sufferings of my companions, nor mine, hinder my countrymen from taking their part in the inevitable struggle, but rather nerve their arms to strike. I would write on this subject at greater length, but I hope that I have written enough to show you that, if a man dies for liberty, his memory lives in the breasts of the good and virtuous. You will also see that there is no necessity for my father, mother, sisters or relations fretting about me. When I leave this world it will be (with God's help) to go to a better, to join the angels and saints of God, and sing His praises for all eternity. I leave a world of suffering for one of eternal joy and happiness. I have been to holy communion, and, please God, intend going shortly again. I am sorry we cannot hear Mass—the good priest is not allowed to say it in this prison.

Give my love to my father and mother, to Mary, Ellen, John Philips, Tim, Catharine, uncles, aunts, and cousins.

Farewell.

From your affectionate brother,

MICHAEL O'BRIEN (*alias* William Gould).

The following is one of Allen's letters to his relatives, written the day before his execution:—

SALFORD, NEW BAILEY PRISON, Nov. 23d, 1867.

TO YOU, MY LOVING AND SINCERE DEAR UNCLE AND AUNT HOGAN.

I suppose this is my last letter to you at this side of the grave. Oh! dear uncle and aunt, if you reflect on it, it is nothing. I am dying an honorable death: I am dying *for Ireland*—dying for the land that gave me birth—dying for the Island of Saints—and dying for liberty. Every generation of our countrymen has suffered; and where is the Irish heart could stand by unmoved? I should like to know what trouble, what passion, what mischief could separate the true Irish heart from its own native isle. Dear uncle and aunt, it is sad to be parting from you all, at my early age; but we must all die some day or another. A few hours more and I will breathe my last, and on English soil. Oh, that I could be buried in Ireland! What a happiness it would be to all my friends and to myself—where my countrymen could kneel on my grave! I cannot express what joy it afforded me, when I found Aunt Sarah and you were admitted. Dear uncle, I am sure it was not a very pleasant place I had to receive you and my aunt; but we must put up with all trials until we depart this life. I am sure it will grieve you very much to leave me in such a place, on the evidence of such characters as the witnesses were that swore my life away. But I forgive them, and may God forgive them. I am dying, thank God! an Irishman and a Christian. Give my love to all friends; same from your ever affectionate nephew,

W. P. ALLEN.

Pray for us. Good by, and remember me. Good by, and may Heaven protect ye, is the last wish of your dying nephew,

W. P. ALLEN.

Larkin was the only one of the condemned four who was married. There were to weep his fall, besides his aged parents, a devoted wife and three little children—all young; and it redounds rather to his honor, that, though flinching in nowise, lacking nought in courageous firmness, home ties were painfully strong around his heart. With him it was anguish indeed to part forever from the faithful wife and little ones who used to nestle in his bosom. Ah! he was never more to feel these little arms twining round his neck—never more to see those infant faces gazing into his own—never more to part the flaxen curls over each unfurrowed brow! Henceforth they would look for his coming and hearken for his footfall in vain! They would call upon him, and be answered only by the convulsive sobs of their widowed mother. And who would now fill his place for them, even as a bread-winner? Mayhap, when he lay in the grave, these cherished little ones, for whom he would draw the life-blood from his heart, would feel the hunger-pangs of orphanage in squalid misery and obscurity! But no. If such a thought approached Larkin's heart, it was at once repelled. Assuredly, he had more faith in his countrymen—more faith in the fidelity and generosity of his race—than to believe they would suffer one of those orphans to want loving, helping, guiding hands. As he himself said, he was not, after all, leaving them fatherless: he was bequeathing them to Ireland and to God.

And the Father of the fatherless, even on the instant, raised up a friend for them—sent an angel missioner of blessed comfort to give poor Larkin, even on the brink of the grave, assurance that no pang of poverty should ever wound those little ones thus awfully bereaved. One day the confessor met the prisoners with beaming face, holding in his hand a letter. It was from the Dowager Marchioness of Queensberry to the condemned Irishmen in Salford gaol, and ran as follows:—

MY DEAR FRIENDS:—

It may be that these few lines may minister some consolation to you on your approaching departure from this world. I send you by the hands of a faithful messenger some help for your wife, or wives, and children, in their approaching irreparable loss, and with the assurance that, so long as I live, they shall be cared for to the utmost of my power.

Mr. M'Donnell, the bearer of this for me, will bring me their address, and the address of the priest who attends you.

It will also be a comfort for your precious souls to know that we remember you here at the altar of God, where the daily remembrance of that all-glorious sacrifice on Calvary, for you all, is not neglected.

We have daily Mass for you here; and if it be so that it please the good God to permit you thus to be called to Himself on Saturday morning, the precious body and blood of Our Lord and Saviour and our Friend will be presented for you before God, at eight o'clock, on that day—that blood so precious, that cleanses from all sin. May your last words and thoughts be Jesus. Rest on Him, who is faithful, and willing and all-powerful to save. Rest on Him, and on His sacrifice on that Cross for you, instead of you, and hear Him say, "*To-day thou shalt be with me in Paradise.*" Yet will we remember your souls constantly at the altar of God, after your departure, as well as those whom you leave in life.

Farewell! and may Jesus Christ, the Saviour of sinners, save us all, and give you His last blessing upon earth, and an eternal continuance of it in heaven.

CAROLINE QUEENSBERRY.

This letter enclosed £100. On hearing it read, poor Larkin burst into tears; the other prisoners were also deeply affected. Surely, never was act more noble! Never was woman's sex more exalted—never was woman's mission more beautifully exemplified, than by this glorious act of bravery, tenderness, and generosity.

Two days before the fatal 23d, the calm resignation which the condemned by this time enjoyed was once more cruelly disturbed, and almost destroyed. Once again the government came to fill their hearts with the torturing hope, if not, indeed, the strong conviction, that after all, even though it should be at the foot of the gallows, they would one and all be reprieved. *Another man of the five included in the vitiated verdict was reprieved*—Shore was to have his sentence commuted.

This second reprieve was the most refined and subtle torture to men who had made up their minds for the worst, and who, by God's strengthening grace, had already become, as it were, dead to the world. It rendered the execution of the remaining men almost an impossibility. Maguire notoriously was innocent even of complicity in the rescue—the verdict of the sworn jury, concurred in by the "learned judge," to the contrary notwithstanding. But *Shore* was *avowedly a full participator in the rescue:* he was no more, no less, guilty than Allen, Larkin, O'Brien. In the dock he proudly gloried in the fact. What wonder if the hapless three, as yet unrespited, found the wild hope of life surging irresistibly through heart and brain!

To the eternal honor of the artisans of London be it told, they signalized themselves in this crisis by a humanity, a generosity, that will not soon be forgotten by Irishmen. At several crowded meetings they adopted memorials to the government, praying for the respite of the condemned Irishmen—or rather, protesting against their contemplated execution. These memorials were pressed with a devoted zeal that showed how deeply the honest hearts of English workingmen were stirred; but the newspaper press—the "high-class" press especially—the enlightened "public instructors"—howled at, reviled, and decried these demonstrations of humanity. The Queen's officials treated the petitions and petitioners with corresponding contempt; and an endeavor to approach the Sovereign herself, then at Windsor, resulted in the contumelious rejection from the palace gate of the petitioners, who were mobbed and hooted by the tradesmen and flunkeys of the royal household!

In Ireland, however, as might be supposed, the respite of Shore was accepted as settling the question: there would be no execution. On the 21st of November men heard, indeed, that troops were being poured into Manchester, that the streets were being barricaded, that the public buildings were strongly guarded, and that special constables were being sworn in by thousands. All this was laughed at as absurd parade. Ready as were Irishmen to credit England with revengeful severity, there was, in their opinion, nevertheless, a limit even to that. To hang Allen, O'Brien, and Larkin now, on the broken-down verdict, would, it was judged, be a measure of outrage which even the fiercest hater of England would frankly declare too great for her.

A few there were, however, who did not view the situation thus. They read, in the respite of Shore, *fear;* and they gloomily reflected that justice or magnanimity towards the weak seldom characterizes those who exhibit cowardice towards the strong. *Shore was an American.* By this simple sentence a flood of light is thrown on the fact of respiting him alone amongst the four men admittedly concerned in the rescue. Shore was an American. He had a country to avenge him, if legally slaughtered on a vitiated verdict. To hang *him* was dangerous; but as for Allen, Larkin, and O'Brien, *they had no country* (in the same sense) to avenge them. America was strong, but Ireland was weak. If it was deemed dangerous to sport with the life of the American, it was deemed safe to be brutal and merciless towards the Irishmen. On these the full arrear of British vengeance might be glutted.

But there were not many to discern, in the first flush of its proclamation, this sinister aspect of Shore's respite. The news reached Ireland on Friday, 22d November, and was, as we have already said, generally deemed conclusive evidence that the next day would bring like news in reference to Allen, Larkin, and O'Brien.

Early next morning—Saturday, 23d November, 1867—men poured into the cities and towns of Ireland reached by telegraphic communication, to lean "the news from Manchester." Language literally fails to convey an idea of the horror—the stupefaction—that ensued when that news was read:—

"*This morning, at eight o'clock, the three condemned Fenians, Allen, Larkin, and O'Brien, were executed in front of Salford Gaol.*"

Men gasped in awe-struck horror—speech seemed denied them. Could it be a dream, or was this a reality? Had men lived to see the day when such a deed could be done? For the reason that incredulity had been so strong before, wild, haggard horror now sat on every countenance, and froze the life-blood in every heart. Irishmen had lain quiescent, persuaded that in this seventh decade of the nineteenth century, some humanizing influences would be found to sway that power that in the past, at least, had ever been so merciless to Irish victims. But now! Alas!——

In that dreadful hour the gulf between the two nations seemed widened and deepened, until it gaped and yawned wide, deep, and dark as hell itself. There was a scowl on every brow. Men went about—sullen, moody, silent, morose—with clenched teeth and darkened faces, terrible passions raging in their bosoms. For all knew that the sacrifice of those Irish patriots was a cold-blooded and cowardly act of English policy, more than a judicial proceeding—an act of English panic, cowardice, hate, and terror. All knew that Allen, Larkin, and O'Brien would never have been hanged on the evidence of those forsworn witnesses, and on the verdict of that jury, whose perjury or blunder was openly confessed and proclaimed, but for the political aspirations and designs of which the rescue was judged to be an illustration. Had their offence been non-political, they would not have been held a day on such a verdict. They were put to death for their political opinions. They were put to death for political reasons. Their execution was meant to strike terror into Irishmen daring to mutter of liberty. Had they been Americans, like Shore, they would have been respited; but, as they were Irishmen, they were immolated.

The full story of how those patriots met their fate at the

last reached Ireland two days afterwards, and intensified a thousand-fold the national emotions. Men were alternately melted into tears or maddened into passion, as they read that sad chapter of Irish martrydom.

Even before the respite of Shore, the government had commenced the most formidable military preparations in view of the bloody act of state policy designed for the 23d. Troops were hurried by rail to all the English cities and towns where an "Irish element" existed; and Manchester itself resembled a city besieged. The authorities called for "special constables," and partly attracted by the plenteous supply of drink and free feeding,* and partly impelled by their savage fury against the "Hirish" or the "Fenians"—suddenly become convertible terms with English writers and speakers—a motley mass of several thousands, mainly belonging to the most degraded of the population, were enrolled. All the streets in the neighborhood of the prison were closed against public traffic, were occupied by police or "specials," and were crossed at close intervals by ponderous wooden barriers. Positions commanding the space in front of the scaffold were strategetically scanned, "strengthened," and occupied by military. The scaffold was erected in a space or gap made in the upper part of the outer or boundary wall of the prison in New Bailey-street. The masonry was removed to the width necessary for the scaffold, which was then projected over the street, at the outer side of the wall. It was approached or ascended from the prison yard below, by a long wooden stair or stepladder, close alongside the wall on the inside. Against the wall on the inner side, on either hand of the scaffold, were erected platforms within about four feet below the wall coping. These platforms were filled with soldiers, "crouching down," as the reporters described, "with the muzzles of their rifles just resting on the top of the wall." The space in the street immediately beneath the scaffold was railed off by a

---

* The Manchester papers inform us that the specials were plentifully fed with hot pork pies, and beer *ad libitum*, which seemed to have a powerful effect in bringing in volunteers from the lower classes.

strong wooden barrier, and outside this barrier were massed the thousands of police, special constables, and volunteers.

On Friday the doomed men took leave for the last time of the few relatives allowed to see them. The parting of Larkin and his family is described as one of the most agonizing scenes ever witnessed. Poor Allen, although not quite twenty years of age, was engaged to a young girl whom he loved, and who loved him most devotedly. She was sternly refused the sad consolation of bidding him farewell. In the evening the prisoners occupied themselves for some time in writing letters, and each of them drew up a "declaration," which they committed to the chaplain. They then gave not another thought to this world. From that moment until all was over, their whole thoughts were centred in the solemn occupation of preparing to meet their Creator. In these last hours Father Gadd, the prison chaplain, was assisted by the Very Rev. Canon Cantwell and the Rev Father Quick, whose attentions were unremitting to the end. From the first the prisoners exhibited a deep, fervid, religious spirit, which could scarcely have been surpassed among the earliest Christian martyrs. They received holy communion every alternate morning, and spent the greater part of their time in spiritual devotion. On Friday evening they were locked up for the night at the usual hour—about half-past six o'clock. In their cells they spent a long interval in prayer and meditation—disturbed ever and anon, alas! by the shouts of brutal laughter and boisterous choruses of the mob already assembled outside the prison walls. At length the fated three sought their dungeon pallets for the last time. "Strange as it may appear," says one of the Manchester papers chronicling the execution, "those three men, standing on the brink of the grave, and about to suffer an ignominious death, *slept as soundly* as had been their wont." Very "strange," no doubt, it appeared to those accustomed to see *criminals* die; but no marvel to those who know how innocent men, at peace with God and man, can mount the scaffold, and offer their lives a sacrifice for the cause of liberty.

Far differently that night was spent by the thronging

countrymen of Broadhead, who came as to a holiday to see the "Fenians die." Early on the preceding evening crowds had taken up their places wherever the occupying bodies of the military, police, or specials did not prevent; and the pictures drawn of their conduct by the newspaper reporters, one and all, are inexpressibly revolting. It was the usual English crowd assembled to enjoy an execution. They made the air resound with laughter at obscene jokes, shouts, cries and repartees; and chorused in thousands (beneath the gallows!) snatches of "comic" ballads and pot-house songs, varied by verses of " Rule Britannia" and " God Save the Queen," by way of exultation over the Irish. Once or twice, in the early part of the night, the police had to remove the mob from the portion of the prison nearest the condemned cells, as the shouts and songs were painfully disturbing the hapless men engaged at that moment preparing for eternity.

Saturday, the 23d November, dawned misty, murky, dull, and cold over Salford. During the first hours after the past midnight the weather had been clear and frosty, and a heavy hoar covered the ground; but as daylight approached, a thick mist or fog crept like a pallid pall over the waking city.

The condemned were roused from sound and tranquil slumbers about a quarter to five o'clock. Having dressed, they attended Mass, Rev. Canon Cantwell, Rev. Mr. Gadd, and Rev. Mr. Quick officiating. They heard this, their last Mass, with a fervor and solemnity which no words could describe. The Holy Sacrifice having been offered, the condemned and the three priests remained in prayer and spiritual exercises until seven o'clock, when the prisoners partook of breakfast. "The last preparations," says an English eye-witness, "were then begun." At twelve minutes to eight o'clock the executioner, Calcraft, and his assistant, were introduced into the cell in which the prisoners were placed, and the process of pinioning their arms was gone through. The priests stood by the side of the unhappy men, administering the consolations of religion, and exhorting them to firmness to meet the last dreadful ordeal. " The convicts at this time," continues the English reporter, "manifested a remarkable fortitude. Not one of them flinched in the least."

The same eye-witness describes as follows the last act of the tragedy, with a brief general sketch of which we commenced this narrative:—

"At a quarter to eight o'clock the interior court of the gaol presented a strange and striking spectacle. Behind the wall in New Bailey-street was erected the long staircase leading to the scaffold, and by its side were platforms for the use of the military. The fog was so dense, that objects could be but faintly distinguished at a distance of thirty yards. Suddenly the words of military command were heard, and a company of the 72d Highlanders marched round the Roundhouse, and took up a position in line at the foot of the staircase. Simultaneously, small detachments of the same regiment ascended to the platform, and crouched there, with their loaded rifles slightly projecting over the prison wall. At almost the same moment the heads of a line of soldiers arose above the parapet of the railway viaduct. A line of warders was formed in the gaol court. The sentries on duty ceased their walk; magistrates and reporters stood aside, and a dead silence prevailed for a few moments, as a signal was given from the corner of the Roundhouse. At three minutes past eight o'clock the solemn voice of a minister repeating the litany of the Catholic Church was heard, and the head of the procession became visible through a thick fog, about thirty yards from the foot of the staircase. The Rev. Canon Cantwell walked first by the side of Allen. The convict was deadly pale; his eyes wandered alternately from the priests to the individuals standing round, and then he uplifted his gaze, in a vain endeavor to pierce the dense canopy which hung above him. He walked with a tolerably steady step, and uttered the response, 'Lord, have mercy upon us,' in a firm voice."

Next to him came Larkin, in whose appearance confinement and anxiety of mind had wrought a striking change. His physical strength seemed shaken, and he required to be assisted by one of the warders in ascending the long wooden stair that led to the scaffold. Last of all came O'Brien, whose noble, firm, and dignified bearing won the approbation of every one who beheld him. A partition running in the line of the wall divided the scaffold into an outer and an inner platform, a small door opening between them. Allen and O'Brien, and their attendants, having reached the top of the stair, waited on the inner platform until Larkin and the rest of the attendant warders and officials came up. Then, all being ready, the door was flung open, and the boy-martyr was first led out upon the drop. His face, which was deathly pale, appeared working with the effects of strong mental agony. The high-priest of English rule over Irishmen, Calcraft, came forward, placed the treacherous noose around Allen's neck, pulled a thin white cap over his ashen face, and then stooped, and securely tied his feet together. The pinioning of the arms, which had been done in the cell, allowed his hands, from the elbows downward, sufficient freedom to clasp on his breast a crucifix, which ever and anon, as he spoke aloud the response of the litany, the poor young fellow seemed to press closer and closer to his heart.

Next O'Brien was led forth. On his fine, manly face the closest scrutiny could not detect a trace of weakness. He looked calmly and sadly around; then, stepping up to where Allen stood capped and pinioned, he clasped him by the hand, and kissed him affectionately on the cheek, speaking to him a word or two not overheard. Then O'Brien himself was placed by Calcraft on the drop, the rope was fixed upon his neck, the cap was drawn on his face, and his feet were securely bound.

Larkin was now brought out, and led directly to his place on the left hand of O'Brien, who was in the middle. The sight of his two brother-martyrs capped and pinioned, and with the fatal cord around each neck, seemed to unman the poor fellow utterly. He stumbled on touching an uneven plank on the scaffold, so that many thought he had fainted; but it was not so, though he unquestionably was laboring under intense agony of mind. O'Brien, firm and unshrinking to the last, turned and looked at him encouragingly, and to him also spoke a few words in a low tone.

Calcraft now disappeared from view, and the three men stood for a moment before the multitude, their voices ringing out clearly in the still morning air, "Lord Jesus, have mercy on us." Suddenly the click of the bolts was heard; the three bodies sunk through the traps; England's three halters strained and tugged and twitched convulsively for a few moments, and the deed was done—her vengance was accomplished.

That afternoon her functionaries bore to three gravepits in the prison-yard three lumps of lifeless clay, that a few short hours before had been three of God's noblest creatures. Like carrion, they were flung into those unconsecrated pits, and strewed with quicklime. For this was British law. The wolf and the tiger leave some vestiges of their victims; but a special ordinance of English law required even the corpses of those martyred Irishmen to be calcined.

They had purposed addressing the crowd from the scaffold, but were prevented from so doing by order of the government! They had each one, however, committed to writing, as already mentioned, a last solemn message to the world. These declarations of the dying men were intrusted to the care of their confessor, who eventually gave them up for publication. They created the most intense and painful sensation in Ireland. They made more and more clear the dreadful fact that the hapless men had been cruelly sacrificed. Standing, as it might be said, in the presence of their God and Judge, they one and all protested their innocence, and declared the falseness of the evidence on which they had been convicted. But not in querulous repining or denunciation were these truths proclaimed, but in language and with sentiments worthy of men who professed the faith preached by the Crucified on Calvary. Every line breathed the purest humility, the most perfect resignation, and the most intense devotion to God, mingled with the most fervent love of country. Those men were all of humble circumstances in life, and, with the exception of O'Brien, had but slight literary advantages; yet the simple pathos, beauty, and eloquence of their dying messages moved every heart.

Poor Larkin was, of all three, the least endowed with education, yet his letter has been aptly described as "a perfect *poem* in prose." We here append those memorable documents:—

DECLARATION OF WILLIAM PHILIP ALLEN.

I wish to say a few words relative to the charge for which I am to die. In a few hours more I will be going before my God. I state, in the presence of that great God, that I am not the man who shot Sergeant Brett. If that man's wife is alive, never let her think that I am the person who deprived her of her husband; and if his family is alive, let them never think I am the man who deprived them of their father.

I confess I have committed other sins against my God, and I hope He will accept of my death as a homage and adoration which I owe His Divine Majesty, and in atonement for my past transgressions against Him.

There is not much use in dwelling on this subject much longer; for by this time I am sure it is plain that I am not the man that took away the life of Sergeant Brett.

I state this to put juries on their guard for the future, and to have them inquire into the characters of witnesses before they take away the lives of innocent men. But, then, I ought not to complain. Was not our Saviour sold for money, and His life sworn away by false witnesses? With the help of the great God, I am only dying to a world of sorrow to rise to a world of joy. Before the judgment-seat of God there will be no false witnesses tolerated; every one must render an account for himself.

I forgive all the enemies I ever may have had in this world. May God forgive them. Forgive them, sweet Jesus, forgive them! I also ask pardon of all whom I have injured in any way.

In reference to the attack on the van, I confess I nobly aided in the rescue of the gallant Colonel Kelly and Captain Deasey. It is well known to the whole world what my poor country has to suffer, and how her sons are exiles the world over; then tell me where is the Irishman who could look on unmoved, and see his countrymen taken prisoners, and treated like murderers and robbers in British dungeons?

May the Lord have mercy on our souls, and deliver Ireland from her sufferings. God save Ireland!

WILLIAM PHILIP ALLEN.

DECLARATION OF MICHAEL LARKIN.

Men of the world—I, as a dying man, going before my God, solemnly declare I have never fired a shot in all my life, much less the day the attack was made on the van, nor did I ever put a hand to the van. The world will remember the widow's son's life that was sworn away, by which he leaves a wife and four children to mourn a loss. I am not dying for shooting Brett, but for mentioning Colonel Kelly's and Deasey's names in the court. I am dying a patriot for my God and my country, and Larkin will be remembered in time to come by the sons and daughters of Erin.

Farewell, dear Ireland, for I must leave you, and die a martyr for your sake. Farewell, dear mother, wife, and children, for I must leave you all for poor Ireland's sake. Farewell, uncles, aunts, and cousins, likewise sons and daughters of Erin. I hope in heaven we will meet another day. God be with you. Father in heaven, forgive those that have sworn my life away. I forgive them and the world. God bless Ireland!

MICHAEL LARKIN.

DECLARATION OF MICHAEL O'BRIEN.

I have only to make these few remarks: I did not use a revolver or any other firearm, or throw stones, on the day that Colonel Kelly and Captain Deasey were so gallantly rescued. I was not present, too, when the van was attacked. I say this, not by way of reproach, or to give annoyance to any person; but I say it in the hope that witnesses may be more particular when identifying, and that juries may look more closely to the character of witnesses, and to their evidence, before they convict a person to send him before his God. I trust that those who swore to seeing me with a revolver, or throwing stones, were nothing more than mistaken. I forgive them from my heart, and likewise I forgive all who have ever done me or intended to do me any injury. I know I have been guilty of many sins against my God; in satisfaction for those sins I have tried to do what little penance I could, and having received the sacraments of the Church, I have humbly begged that He would accept my sufferings and death, to be united to the sufferings and death of His innocent Son, through whom my sufferings can be rendered acceptable.

My Redeemer died a more shameful death, as far as man could make it, that I might receive pardon from Him and enjoy His glory in heaven. God grant it may be so. I earnestly beg my countrymen in America to heal their differences, to unite in God's name for the sake of Ireland and liberty. I cannot see any reason, even the slightest, why John Savage should not have the entire confidence of all his countrymen. With reference to Colonel Kelly, I believe him to be a good, honorable man, unselfish, and entirely devoted to the cause of Irish freedom.

MICHAEL O'BRIEN.

So ends the story of the memorable events which gave three new names to the list of Ireland's martyrs; so closes the sad and thrilling record which tells how Allen, Larkin, and O'Brien died. Over the neglected plot in which their calcined remains are lying, no stone stands inscribed with their names—no emblem to symbolize their religion or their nationality. But to that gloomy spot the hearts of the Irish people will ever turn with affectionate remembrance; and the day will never come when, in this the land that bore them, the brave men whose ashes repose within it will be forgotten.

THE CRUISE OF THE JACKMEL.

THERE was wild commotion among the Irish people in America, when on the 6th of March, 1867, the Atlantic cable flashed across to them the news that on the previous night the Fenian circles, from Louth to Kerry, had turned out in arms, and commenced the long-promised rebellion. It was news to send a thrill of excitement through every Irish heart—to fire the blood of the zealous men who for years had been working to bring the Irish question to this issue; and news to cause a profound and anxious thought to that large class of Irishmen who, deeply occupied with commercial and professional pursuits, are less energetic than the members of the Fenian Brotherhood in their political action, but who scarcely differ from them in principle. It was, for all who had Irish blood in their veins and Irish sympathies in their hearts, a serious consideration that once again the banner of insurrection against English rule had been unfurled in Ireland, and that on many a spot of Irish earth the organized forces of England were in conflict with hastily-collected, ill-supplied, and almost unarmed levies of Irish patriotism.

The question, whether the cause of Ireland would be advantaged or injured by the struggle and its inevitable results, was differently answered by different minds. Some saw in the conflict nothing but defeat and suffering for the country—more, gyves and chains—more, sorrow and humiliation for her sons, and a fresh triumph for the proud and boastful power of England. Others, while only too well convinced that the suppression of the insurrectionary movement was sure to be speedily accomplished, viewed the position with a certain fierce and stern satisfaction, and discerned therein the germ of high hopes for the future.

But to certain of the Fenian leaders and Fenian circles in America, the news came with a pressing and peculiar interest. They were largely responsible for the outbreak;

the war was, in a manner, their war. Their late Head
Centre, James Stephens, was chargeable with it only in a
certain degree. He had promised to initiate the struggle
before the 1st of January of that year. Conscious that
his veracity was regarded in somewhat of a dubious light
by many of his followers, he reiterated the declaration with
all possible passion and vehemence, and even went the
length of swearing to it by invocations of the Most High,
before public assemblies of his countrymen. When the
time came for the fulfilment of his pledges he failed to
keep them, and was immediately deposed from his position by the disappointed and enraged circles which had
hitherto trusted him. But in the meantime, relying on his
engagement to lead off an insurrection in Ireland, those
circles had made certain preparations for the event, and a
number of their members, brave Irishmen who had had
actual experience of war in the armies of America, had
crossed the Atlantic, and landed in England and Ireland,
to give the movement the benefit of their services. To
these men the break-down of James Stephens was a
stunning blow, an event full of shame and horror; they
felt their honor compromised by his conduct; they considered that they could not return to America with their
mission unattempted, and they resolved to establish
their own honesty and sincerity at all events, as well as
the courage and earnestness of the Fenian Brotherhood in
Ireland, by taking the desperate course of engaging
forthwith in open insurrection. It was in conformity
with their arrangements, and in obedience to their directions, that the rising took place on the night of the 5th of
March, 1867.

The ill-success which attended the attempted insurrection was reported in America almost as soon as it was
known in Ireland, by the agency of the Atlantic telegraph.
But, whoever believed the statements of its speedy and
utter collapse, which were forwarded through the cable,
the Fenian circles certainly did not. They felt certain
that the truth was being withheld from them; that the
cable, which was an instrument in the hands of the
British government, was being employed to mislead them;

and that, when it reported all quiet in Ireland, and no movement afoot save that of the British troops employed in "scouring" the mountains of Cork and Tipperary, there was, in reality, a guerilla warfare being waged over a great extent of the country, and many a tough fight was being fought in pass, and glen, and wood, amidst the picturesque scenery of the Munster counties. Their incredulity was but natural. They had no reason whatever to rely on the truthfulness of the cable messages. If there had been Fenian successes to report, it is very likely that no fair account of them would have been allowed to pass by that route. Still, as day after day went by, and brought no news of battles lost or won by any party, the conviction began to force itself on the minds of the American Fenians that the movement in Ireland was hanging fire, and that it was going hard with the brave men who had committed themselves to it at the outset. It was necessary that something should be done, if those men were to be sustained, and the outbreak developed into a struggle worthy of the cause, and of the long years of preparation, the bold threats and the glowing promises of the Fenian Brotherhood, the risks they had incurred, and the sacrifices they had made.

What was to be done? What was needed to give force and power to the insurrectionary uprising in Ireland? They knew the answer. Arms and officers were wanted. To supply them, at least in some measure, was, therefore, the great object that now presented itself to their minds. How they sought to accomplish it is known to the public —if the Attorney-General and his witnesses, at the opening of the Commission in Dublin, in November, 1867, told a true story.

Any references we shall here make to that particular subject, that is to the alleged voyage of a Fenian cruiser conveying men and arms from New York to Ireland, shall be derived entirely from the statements made in open court on that occasion, with an extract or two from a document otherwise published. We shall add nothing to them, neither shall we vouch for the authenticity of all or any of them, for, at the time of our writing, "the Crown," as the government lawyers call themselves, are not yet done with some of the cases arising out of this alleged expedition. But, taking the narrative as we find it in the newspaper reports of the trials of Colonel John Warner and Augustine E. Costello, and in the lecture delivered in America, under the auspices of the Fenian Brotherhood, by Colonel S. R. Tresilian, John Savage, Esq., C. E. F. B., in the chair, reported in the *Irish People*, New York, and in other journals, we summarize briefly, as follows, its chief particulars.

It appears, then, that at the time to which we have referred, when the necessity of transmitting a quantity of arms, and sending a number of military leaders to Ireland for the sustainment of the insurrectionary movement, had impressed itself on the minds of the Fenian leaders in America, they resolved on an attempt to supply, to some extent, those requirements. Two ways were open to them of setting about this difficult and hazardous undertaking. One was to avail of the ordinary mail steamers and trading ships between the two countries, send the men across as ordinary passengers, and ship the arms as goods of different kinds. Much had been done in that way during the previous three or four years, but it was plainly too slow and uncertain a process to adopt on the present occasion. The other course was to procure a vessel for this special purpose, freight her with the men and arms, place her under the command of a skilful and experienced captain, and trust to his skill and luck for landing the entire in safety somewhere on the west coast of Ireland.

This was the course adopted. How it was carried out, the Attorney-General, with whatever degree of authority may attach to his words in such a case, has thus described:—

On the 12th of April, 1867, a party of forty or fifty men, almost all of whom had been officers or privates in the service of the American government, went down from New York to Sandyhook, in a steamer, a distance of about eighteen miles. There they found a brigantine of about 200 tons burden, which had been purchased for the expedition, and in that brigantine these men embarked, and sailed for Ireland. She was called the *Jackmel* and she sailed without papers or colors. For the purpose of keeping their movements as free from observation as possible, these men embarked without luggage—a rather extraordinary thing in men the great majority of whom had been officers in the American service. The commander of the expedition was named John F. Kavanagh, and he had filled the office of brigadier-general in the American army, and was at one time a member of the American Congress. These men had on board a very large quantity of arms, packed in pianocases, cases for sewing machines, and wine barrels, in order to conceal them effectually; and the parcels were consigned to a merchant firm in Cuba. The ship steered for one day towards the West Indies, in order to avoid suspicion, and then shaped her course towards Ireland. Vessels occasionally came in sight, and, when they did, English colors were hoisted. Nothing remarkable occurred until Easter Sunday, April 29th, nearly nine days after they had sailed from New York. The parties determined to celebrate that day as a festival, and they hoisted the green flag with a sunburst, fired a salute, and changed the name of the vessel, calling her *Erin's Hope.* Kavanagh then produced Fenian commissions and distributed them, and also produced sealed orders, from which it appeared that he was to sail to Sligo Bay, and there land his men and arms; and if he found it impracticable to land them there, he was to proceed to some other place in Ireland. Some days after this, they came in sight of the coast of the county of Limerick, and then they sailed towards Sligo; but they overshot the mark, and arrived off the coast of Donegal. They then turned back, and arrived at Sligo Bay on the 20th of May.

The learned gentleman then went on to describe certain occurrences alleged to have taken place on board the vessel while she remained in and about Sligo Bay. He said that on one evening a hooker came alongside, from which a man, who appeared to be a gentleman, got on board the brigantine. This person went down into the cabin, conversed with the officers, and told them the landing could not be effected at Sligo, after which he returned on board the hooker, and sailed for the shore. The Attorney-General said :—

About the 26th of May the ship left the Sligo coast. On the 1st of June she arrived at Dungarvan. During the voyage, councils were held on board. Provisions were running short, and they could not remain much longer at sea. These matters were made the subjects of discussion. Some were for going to America, and some for landing; and at last the conclusion was arrived at that the majority of the officers should be landed, and that the others should go either to America or to the Western Isles—the Hebrides. They hailed a large fishing boat, and offered the man on board £2 to put two men on shore. He went on board the brigantine, and when he did so, twenty-eight men, who were hitherto concealed, rushed on board his ship. He asked them if he should land them at Helwick Point, and they said no, because there was a coastguard station there. They were eventually landed about two miles from that point, and they were compelled to wade through water three-and-a-half feet deep to the shore.

So far the learned gentleman, her Majesty's Attorney-General for Ireland. His statement was supported by the informations and the evidence of an informer, Daniel J. Buckley, the Judas of the expedition. He, however, represented Kavanagh as the captain of the vessel, and General James E. Kerrigan as chief of the military expedition. As to the armament on board, they had, he said, "some Spencer's repeating rifles, seven-shooters, and some Enfield rifles, Austrian rifles, Sharp's and Burnside's breechloaders, and some revolvers. There were about 5,000 stands of arms on board, and three pieces of artillery, which would fire three-pound shot or shell. With these pieces the salute was fired on the occasion of hoisting the sunburst on Easter-Sunday. As regards ammunition, there were about a million and a half rounds on board."

Colonel S. R. Tresilian, in the lecture already alluded to, gave the following facetious account of the warlike stores which were on board the vessel:—

We found the cargo to consist of 5,000 rat-tail files of different sizes and descriptions. Then there were several smaller files that mechanics carry in their pockets; then again there was the flat file, in respectable numbers, that is used for cutting on either edge, and that is carried in a sheath, to prevent the mechanics from cutting their neighbors' fingers. These files were to be distributed to the paupers in Ireland, to enable them to sharpen their teeth, so that they could masticate animal food at the grand barbecue that was to be given on the landing of our vessel. Another portion of the cargo was 200,000 puffballs and sugar-plums, for gratuitous distribution among our English friends and brethren in Ireland.

It, surely, was a daring venture to run that craft, freighted as she was, across the ocean, and sail her for days along the coast of Ireland. The lecturer gave the following account of her voyagings:—

The craft made three landings in Ireland, and one in England, and they were very near being captured several times. At no time were they over twelve miles from a British man-of-war, a frigate, ram, or gun-boat, and were continually annoyed by pilots. They were at sea 107 days; 38 days from America to Ireland, in which they sailed 3,665 miles; 24 days around the coast of Ireland and England, 2,023 miles; 47 days from Ireland to America, 3,577 miles; making a grand total of 9,265 miles.

As regards the return voyage, the lecturer gave the following information :—

On the return trip they had, in starting from the coast of Ireland, one barrel of sound bread, one barrel of mouldy bread, one of rice, pork 6 lbs., one box of fish, one barrel of beef, one bushel of beans, two quarts of molasses, one half lb. of sugar, tea and coffee in sufficient quantities, and one-third rations of water. They ran out of everything except bread and water before reaching the Banks of Newfoundland, where they received assistance from a fishing-smack, and again, off Boston, from a vessel bound to San Francisco. They succeeded in landing the entire cargo safely in America, and it is now in the hands of the Fenian Brotherhood.

It is a strange story altogether. The voyage of the vessel to and fro, and along the well-watched coast of Ireland, unchallenged by a British ship, is a fact of no small significance, even if it be not quite conclusive as regards the argument of the lecturer, that the Fenian Brotherhood of America can, when they please, land large supplies, men and arms, in Ireland. Then the interest of the narrative is greatly enhanced by some of its romantic incidents, more especially by the remarkable scene stated to have occurred on Easter-Sunday morning.

News of the landing which had been effected near Dungarvan was quickly spread amongst the coastguards and the police, and a few hours afterwards some twenty-seven men were under arrest, charged with having come into the country under suspicious circumstances. Amongst them were two whose trials, for having formed part of an armed expedition destined to aid a rebellion in Ireland, have since been had at the Commission which opened in Dublin on the 28th of November, 1867, and whose spirited defence of themselves in the dock it is our purpose to record in these pages. They were Colonel John Warren, of the American army, and Augustine E. Costello.

The trial of the first-named of those gentlemen is likely, owing to the spirited and statesmanlike course which he adopted on the occasion, to become memorable for all time, and to have a prominent place in the history of two great nations—England and America. One of its results, now actually in progress, is an alteration, in the law of America, on a point of great importance to both countries; and this alteration will necessitate a corresponding change, if not in the law, at least the practice, of the English courts. From these changes will ensue consequences of the utmost gravity to England, but of unquestionable advantage to the Irish people, and the cause which they have at heart; for all which, the name of Colonel Warren will long be held in honor and in grateful remembrance among his countrymen.

Colonel Warren, who is a native of the town of Clonakilty in the county of Cork, and of respectable parentage, emigrated to the United States some twelve years ago, and, in due course of time, like most of his countrymen who transfer their domicile to that free and great country, he took out papers of naturalization, and became one of its adopted citizens. That act of naturalization is the declaration of a contract between the American government, on the one hand, and the new-made citizen on the other, whereby the latter formally and solemnly transfers his allegiance to that government, and withdraws it from any other which might previously have had a claim on it; and whereby the government, on its part, in exchange for that allegiance, engages to extend to him all the liberties and rights possessed by its native-born subjects—the benefit of its laws, the full scope of its franchises, the protection of its flag. In this way many hundreds of thousands of men, hunted by British law and British policy out of Ireland, who have during recent years been added to the number of brave and devoted citizens possessed by the United States. But yet, it seems, the law of England affords no recognition to this transfer of allegiance, expressly denies the legality of any such act, and claims as subjects of the British Crown, not only all persons born within British jurisdiction, but also their sons and grandsons, wherever their domicile and their place of birth may be. Between the

COLONEL WARREN.

British law on the subject of allegiance and the American system of naturalization, there is, therefore, an irreconcilable discrepancy; and the course taken by Colonel Warren, on his trial, was to bring this question of law between the two governments to a direct issue. He took his stand on his American citizenship; he claimed to be tried as an alien; and, the bench refusing to accede to his demand, he abandoned all legal defence, directed his counsel to withdraw from the case, and put it upon his government to maintain the honor and vindicate the laws of America, by affording him the protection to which he was entitled.

Other Irishmen, naturalized citizens of America, had previously been tried and sentenced for Fenian practices, including acts done and words spoken by them in America, which would not have come within the cognizance of the court had they been tried otherwise than as British subjects; and in their addresses to the court they had made reference, proudly and hopefully, to the fact that they were adopted sons of that great country; but none of them had struck upon a course so well calculated as that taken by Colonel Warren to raise the international question, and necessitate a distinct and speedy solution of it.

He had a good case to go before the jury, had he allowed himself to be legally defended, and he was perfectly aware of that fact; but he clearly perceived that, by taking the other course, whatever might be the consequences to himself, he would be able to render better service both to his adopted country and his native land.

He took that course, and it is, therefore, that he is to-day in a British convict prison, far away from his home and friends, from his wife and his children, subject to all the restraints and indignities imposed by England on the vilest and meanest of her criminals, and with a term of fifteen years of such treatment decreed to him. Let us be able to say, at least, that his countrymen are not unmindful of the sacrifice.

In the course of the trial, which was had before Chief Baron Pigot and Mr. Justice Keogh, in the Commission Court, Dublin, Colonel Warren offered some few remarks on the evidence, and put some questions to the witnesses, all of which showed considerable acumen on his part, and were thoroughly *ad rem*. He complained particularly of the manner in which his identification was obtained. Gallagher, who had piloted the *Erin's Hope* around the west coast of Ireland, swore to his identity as one of the party who were on board; but the prisoner contended that Gallagher's knowledge of him was acquired, not on board that vessel, but in Kilmainham gaol, where Gallagher had been his fellow-prisoner for some weeks, during which time he had abundant opportunities of learning his, Colonel Warren's, name, and the charge against him. But it was a vain thing, as far as the jury were concerned, to indulge in such criticisms of the evidence. There were times in Irish and in English history, when juries could rise above the panic of the hour, and refuse to minister to the passion of the government, but we have fallen upon other times, and, nowadays, to be accused of a political crime means to be convicted.

A verdict of "guilty" against Colonel Warren was returned as a matter of course. On Saturday, November the 16th, he, with two other prisoners, was brought up for sentence. On the usual interrogatory being put to him, the following proceedings took place:—

WARREN:—I claim the privilege established by precedent. I have had no opportunity of making any remarks on my case, and I would now wish to say a few words.

THE CHIEF BARON:—Just state what you have to say; we are ready to hear you.

WARREN:—I desire, in the first place, to explain, while ignoring the jurisdiction of this court to sentence me, and while assuming my original position, my reasons for interfering in this case at all. I can see, beyond my present position, the importance of this case, and I was desirous to instruct the jury, either directly or indirectly, of the importance of their decision, while never for a moment deviating from the position which I assumed. I submit that I effectually did that. They, incautiously, and foolishly for themselves and the country of which they claim to be subjects, have raised an issue which has to be settled by a higher tribunal than this court.

CHIEF BARON:—I cannot allow you to continue these observations.

PRISONER:—I propose to show that the verdict is contrary to evidence.

THE CHIEF BARON:—I must again tell you that you are not at liberty to do that.

PRISONER:—I propose to answer briefly the question why the sentence of the court should not be pronounced upon me. Do I understand you to refuse me that privilege?

THE CHIEF BARON:—Certainly not; but I am bound in point of law to refuse to hear you upon any matter respecting the verdict. We are bound by that verdict just as much as you are. That is the law.

PRISONER:—I have been indicted with a number of parties, one of whom had been identified in America. I have been tried and convicted. What position do I stand in now? Am I convicted on the evidence of Corydon, who swears that I belonged to the Fenian Brotherhood in 1863? Does that prove that I belonged to it in 1867?

The Chief Baron then explained that what he left to the jury was, that, if they believed upon the evidence that, on the 5th of March, the prisoner belonged to the Fenian confederacy, having for its object the deposition of the Queen, he would be answerable for the acts done by his confederates, whether he was present or absent at the time.

PRISONER:—You instructed the jury, at the same time, that the fact of my holding the position of a colonel in '63 was sufficient corroboration of the evidence that I belonged to it in 1867.

THE CHIEF BARON:—I told the jury that holding the rank of colonel was evidence for their consideration, upon which to determine whether you previously belonged to the Fenian confederacy. I told them they were at liberty to consider whether you would have got that rank if you then joined for the first time.

PRISONER:—Precisely the same thing, but in different phraseology. Am I to understand that I have not liberty to address the court as to why sentence should not be pronounced upon me?

THE CHIEF BARON:—You are not so to consider. You are at liberty to address the court, but you are not at liberty to comment upon the evidence to show that the verdict was wrong.

PRISONER:—What can I speak on? To what can I speak, if not to something connected with my case? I am not here to refer to a church matter or any political question.

THE CHIEF BARON:—I have informed you what we are bound to rule.

PRISONER:—Then I state, my lords, that, as an American citizen, I protest against the whole jurisdiction of this court, from the commencement of my arraignment down to the end of my trial. I protest against being brought here forcibly, and against my being convicted on the evidence of a man whom you yourselves designated a man of the most odious character. You instructed the jury pointedly on one occasion, and subsequently you said that no respectable jury could act on his evidence, and that it was a calamity for any government to have to resort to the evidence of such a man. I do not wish to say anything disrespectful to this court, but I think I may say that, if I stand here as a convicted felon, the privilege should be accorded to me that has been accorded to every other person who stood here before me in a similar position. There is a portion of the trial to which I particularly wish to refer. This is, in reference to the oath which it was stated the pilot was forced to take on board the vessel. Much importance was attached to the matter, and therefore I wish to ask you and others in this court to look and to inquire if there is any man here who could suppose that I am scoundrel enough and ignorant enough to take an ignorant man, put a pistol to his face, and force him to take an oath ? I ask you, in the first place, not to believe that I am such a scoundrel, and, in the second place, that I am not such an idiot. If I were at this moment going to my grave, I could say that I never saw that man Gallagher till I saw him in Kilmainham prison. These men, although they have been, day after day, studying lessons under able masters, contradicted each other on the trial and have been perjuring themselves. Gallagher, in his evidence, swore that his first and second informations were false, and that he knew them to be false. It is contrary to all precedent to convict a man on the evidence of a witness who admits that he swore what was false. In America, I have seen judges, hundreds of times, sentencing men who were taken off the table, put into the dock, and sent to prison. In this case this poor, ignorant man was brought into Kilmainham gaol on the 1st of July. He knew my name, heard it called several times, knew of the act of which I was suspected, and, on the 2d of August, he was taken away. On the 12th of October, he was brought back, and, out of a party of forty or fifty, he identifies only three. If that man came on board the vessel, he did so in his ordinary capacity as a pilot. He did his duty, got his pay, and left. His subsequent evidence was additions. With respect to the vessel, I submit that there was not a shadow of evidence to prove that there was any intention of a hostile landing, and that the evidence as to the identity of the vessel would not stand for a moment where either law or justice would be regarded. Now, as to the Flying Dutchman which, it is said, appeared on the coast of Sligo and on the coast of Dungarvan, in Gallagher's information, nothing is said about the dimensions of the vessel. Neither length, breadth, nor tonnage is given, but, in making his second information, he revised the first.

The prisoner then proceeded to argue that there was nothing to show that the vesssel which had appeared off Sligo harbor was the same as that which appeared off Dungarvan, except the testimony of the informer Buckley, of which there was no corroboration. He also denied the truth of Corydon's evidence, in several particulars, and then went on to say :—

As to the position in which I am now placed by British law, I have to repeat that I am an American citizen, and owe allegiance to the government of the United States. I am a soldier, and have belonged to the National Militia of America. Now, if war had broken out between the two countries, and that I had been taken prisoner, the English government, according to English law, would hold me guilty of high treason. I would not be treated as an ordinary prisoner of war, but would be liable to be strung up at the yard-arm. See then the position of England towards the United States. The Crown should not be in such haste to act thus. It was hardly a judicious policy. Andrew Johnson was the grandson of an Irishman ; Mr. Seward was the son of an Irishwoman ; General Jackson was the son of an Irishman ; General Washington and Benjamin Franklin lived and died British subjects, if this law be correct. There is another point to which I wish to refer—it is to the manner in which my government has acted in this matter—

THE CHIEF BARON :—We cannot allow you to enter into remarks on the conduct of any government. We have simply to sit here to administer the law which we are called upon to discharge.

THE PRISONER :—I wish simply to call your attention to one point. On the 3d of August I wrote to my government——

THE CHIEF BARON:—I cannot allow you to refer to that.

THE PRISONER :—The President of the United States, on a report submitted to him——

THE CHIEF BARON:—I cannot allow you to proceed with any reference to what has been done by any government. We have nothing to do with the conduct of any government. We are only here to administer the laws which we are sworn to administer.

THE PRISONER:—I was simply going to state that while the vile officials of your government——

THE CHIEF BARON :—We have nothing to do with the conduct of any government. We are here to dispense justice according to law, and whatever the officials of our government or the American government have done cannot have the slightest influence upon our judgment. It can neither affect us favorably or unfavorably to the prisoner or to the Crown. We stand indifferently between both.

THE PRISONER:—I beg simply to call your lordship's attention to the correspondence——

THE CHIEF BARON :—We cannot allow you to do so. We cannot allow you to refer to the correspondence between the officials of one government and the officials of another.

THE PRISONER:—If America does not resent England's conduct towards me, and protect that allegiance to her government which

I proudly own is the only allegiance I ever acknowledged, I shall call on thirteen millions of Irishmen——

THE CHIEF BARON:—I cannot allow you to use the position in which you stand there as the arena for those observations.

PRISONER:—I must then state, in conclusion, that, while I protest against the jurisdiction, I am confident that the position which I take will be sustained. I know that the verdict of the jury will be reversed, and, while returning you, my lord, thanks for your kindness during the trial, I must say you have taken from me the privilege I am entitled to get. I am sure that I shall live longer than the British Constitution.

AUGUSTINE E. COSTELLO.

AUGUSTINE E. COSTELLO.

AFTER the verdict had been returned against Colonel Warren, Augustine E. Costello was put on his trial charged with the same offence—that of having formed one of the invading party who landed from the *Erin's Hope* in the neighborhood of Dungarvan. He, too, was an adopted citizen of the United States, and he declared that he was anxious to follow the course that had been taken by his friend, Colonel Warren, in reference to his trial; but deferring to the strongly-expressed wish of his counsel, he would leave his case in their hands. An able defence was made for him by Messrs. Heron and Molloy, Q. C., instructed by Mr. Scallan, Solicitor; but it was all in vain. When he was called on to say why sentence should not be pronounced on him, he delivered the following address in a loud tone of voice, his fresh young face glowing with emotion as he spoke, and his manner showing deep excitement, but withal a fearless and noble spirit:—

In answer to the question put to me by the Clerk of the Court, I will speak a few words. I don't intend to say much, and I will trespass on forbidden ground but as little as possible. I am perfectly satisfied that there has not been one fact established or proved that would justify a conscientious and impartial jury in finding me guilty of treason-felony. There is an extreme paucity of evidence against me—that every one who has been here while this case has been proceeded with, will admit frankly and candidly. We need no stronger proof of this fact than that the first jury that was empanelled to try me had, after a long and patient hearing of the case, to be discharged without having found me guilty of treason-felony. Ah! there were a few honest men on that jury. They knew that Augustine E. Costello was not guilty of the crime trumped up against him. They knew I was not guilty. Mr. Anderson, sitting there, knows that I am not a felon, but that I am an honest man; that as such I stand here in this dock, where Robert Emmet stood, where Robert Emmet spoke from; and the actions and the words of that Emmet have immortalized him, and he now lies embalmed in the hearts of the world.

THE LORD CHIEF JUSTICE :—I cannot allow you to proceed in that strain.

COSTELLO :—I can say to those assembled here, and who are now listening to me, that I stand here, branded, as I am, a felon, but with a clear conscience. No one can point the finger of scorn against me, and say I have sold my brother and committed perjury. Can every man in this court-house lay his hand on his heart and say the same? Answer me, Mr. Anderson. Answer me, Governor Price.

THE LORD CHIEF BARON :—You are again transgressing. You had better stop for a moment or two; you seem to be excited.

COSTELLO :—My lord, as you truly remark, I have allowed my feelings to run away with my discretion; but it is hard for a man to stand here, satisfied as I am of innocence, knowing full well that I have committed no wrong; it is hard for a man in the bloom of youth, when the world looks fair and prosperous to him—when all he loves is in that world—it is hard that a man should be torn from it, and incarcerated in a living tomb. My lords, I am an humble individual; I claim no rights but the rights that emanated from a Godhead—the rights that were given to me at the hour of my birth. That right is my inalienable liberty, and that no government, no people, has a right to take from me. I am perfectly satisfied to stand before a British tribunal to answer for acts or words of mine, if I break any of the laws of the country; but, my lords, you must admit that I have transgressed no law. His lordship, Judge Keogh—I must now candidly admit that I have heard a great deal about that gentleman that was not at all complimentary to him— but I say for myself that his lordship, Judge Keogh, has dealt with me in the fairest manner he could have done. I have nothing to say against the administration of the law, as laid down by you; but I say a people who boast of their freedom—who hold up their magnanimous doings to the world for approval and praise—I say those people are the veriest slaves in existence to allow laws to exist for a moment which deprive a man of liberty.

THE LORD CHIEF BARON :—It is impossible for a court administering the law to allow you to speak in such terms against such law.

COSTELLO :—I speak under correction, my lord. You must, if you please, be assured that I do not attribute any wrong to your lordships—far be it from me; I acknowledge and again reiterate that, so far as the law is concerned, I have had a dose that has almost killed me; but if there was a little—a very little—justice mixed in that law, I would not now be addressing your lordships. Of the law I have had sufficient, but I have come to the conclusion that justice is not to be found inside a British court-house. My lords, I complain, and grievously, of what my friend, Colonel Warren, and my friend, General Halpin, complained—of being tried in this court as a British subject; and I think your lordships will not reprimand me much for that expression. I left the shores of my native land—Ireland is the land of my birth, and I am proud to own it. I am proud to say that I am an Irishman, but I am also proud and happy to state that I am an adopted citizen of the United States; and while true to the land of my birth, I can never be false to the land of my adoption. That is not an original phrase, but it expresses the idea which I mean to convey. Now, my lords, my learned and very able counsel, who have conducted my case with the greatest ability and zeal, and of whom I cannot speak in terms of sufficient praise, demanded for me a jury half alien. I was refused it. I was born in this country, and I was, while breath remained in my body, a British subject. In God's name—if I may mention His holy name without sufficient reasons—what affection should I have for England? You cannot stamp out the instincts that are in the breast of man—man will be man to the end of time—the very worm you tread upon will turn upon your feet. If I remained in this country till I descended to the grave, I would remain in obscurity and poverty. I left Ireland, not because I disliked the country—I love Ireland as I love myself—I left Ireland for the very good and cogent reason that I could not live in Ireland. But why could I not live here? I must not say; that would be trespassing. I must not mention why I was forced to leave Ireland—why I am now placed in this dock. Think you, my lords, that I would injure a living being—that I would, of my own free accord, willingly touch a hair upon the head of any man? No, my lords; far would it be from me; but the government which has left our people in misery—

THE LORD CHIEF BARON:—I cannot allow you to trespass on political grievances.

COSTELLO :—I am afraid I am occupying the time of the court too much, but really a man placed in such a position as I now occupy finds it necessary to make a few observations. I know it savors of a great deal that is bad and foul to be mixed up with Fenian rebels, assassins, and cutthroats. It is very bad ; it is not a very good recommendation for a young man. Even were that fact proved home to me—that I were a Fenian—no act of mine has ever thrown dishonor on the name. I know not what Fenian means. I am an Irishman, and that is all-sufficient.

The prisoner then proceeded to criticize the evidence against him at considerable length. He declared emphatically that one of the documents sworn to be in his handwriting was not written by him. He thus continued :—

Your lordships are well aware that there are many contradictions in the informers' testimony, and now here is a matter which I am going to mention for the first time. Corydon, in his first information at Kilmainham, swears that he never knew me until he saw me at a Fenian picnic, and this he modifies afterwards by the remark, that any one would be allowed into these picnics on the payment of a certain sum. I did not pay much attention to what the fellow was saying about me, as I thought it did not affect me in the least ; but this I can distinctly remember, that Mr. Anderson, Jun.—and he is there to say if I am saying anything false—said that the evidence of Corydon did not affect any one of. the prisoners put in this dock but another and myself. It is very strange if that was said by Mr. Anderson. He knew that there was nothing more to be got out of Corydon the informer—that he had told everything he knew in his information, but on pressure there was found to be a little left in the sponge. They refreshed his memory a little, and he comes to think that he saw Costello at a meeting in 814 Broadway, I think he gives it. And here is a singular occurrence—that Devany, who never swore an information against me, comes on the table and swears that he also saw me at 814 Broadway. Here is one informer striving to corroborate the other. It is a well-known fact that these informers speak to each other, go over the evidence, and what is more likely than that they should make their evidence agree—say, "I will corroborate your story, you corroborate mine"? By this means was it that the overt acts of the 5th of March, which took place at Stepaside, Glencullen, and Tallaght, were brought home to Costello—a man who was 4,000 miles away, and living—and I say it on the word of a man, a Christian man—peaceably, not belonging to that confederation. I did not belong to the Fenian Brotherhood for twelve months before I left America, if I did belong to it any other time, so help me God ! God witnesses what I say, and He records my words above. It is a painful position to be placed in. I know I am a little excited. Were I to speak of this matter under other circumstances, I would be more cool and collected. Were I conscious of guilt—did I know that I merited this punishment, I would not speak a word, but say that I deserved and well merited the punishment about to be inflicted upon me. But, my lords, there never was a man convicted in this court more innocent of the charges made against him than Costello. The overt acts committed in the county of Dublin, admitting that the law of England is as it was laid down by your lordship, that a man, a member of this confederacy, if he lived in China, was responsible for the acts of his confederates—admitting that to be law—I am still an innocent man. Admitting and conceding that England has a right to try me as a British subject, I still am an innocent man. Why do I make these assertions? I know full well they cannot have any effect in lessening the term of my sentence. Can I speak for the sake of having an audience here to listen to me? Do I speak for the satisfaction of hearing my own feeble voice? I am not actuated by such motives. I speak because I wish to let you know that I believe myself innocent; and he would be a hard-hearted man, indeed, who would grudge me those few sentences. Now, my lords, I have observed I did not belong to the Fenian confederacy in March of this present year. I did not belong to the Fenian confederacy anterior to the period that Corydon and Devany allege that they saw me act as centre and secretary to Fenian meetings; that, anterior to that period, I never took act or part in the Fenian conspiracy up to the period of my leaving America. Does it do me any good to make these statements? I ask favors, as Halpin said, from no man. I ask nothing but justice—stern justice—even-handed justice. If I am guilty—if I have striven to overthrow the government of this country, if I have striven to revolutionize this country, I consider myself enough of a soldier to bare my breast to the consequences, no matter whether those consequences may reach me on the battle-field or in the cells of Pentonville. I am not afraid of punishment. I have moral courage to bear all that can be heaped upon me in Pentonville, Portland, or Kilmainham, designated by one of us as the modern Bastile. I cannot be worse treated, no matter where you send me to. There never was a more infernal dungeon on God's earth than Kilmainham. It is not much to the point, my lord. I will not say another word about it. I believe I saw in some of the weekly papers that it would be well to appoint a commission to inquire——

THE LORD CHIEF BARON:—I cannot allow you to proceed with that subject.

COSTELLO:—I will not say another word. I will conclude now. There is much I could say, yet a man in my position cannot help speaking. There are a thousand and one points affecting me here, affecting my character as a man, affecting my life and well-being, and he would be a hard-hearted man who could blame me for speaking in strong terms. I feel that I have within me the seeds of a disease that will soon put me into an early grave, and I have within my breast the seeds of a disease which will never allow me to see the expiration of my imprisonment. It is, my lord, a disease, and I hope you will allow me to speak on this subject, which has resulted from the treatment I have been subjected to. I will pass over it as rapidly as I can, because it is a nasty subject—Kilmainham. But the treatment that I have received at Kilmainham—I will not particularize any man, or the conduct of any man—has been most severe, most harsh, not fit for a beast, much less a human being. I was brought to Kilmainham, so far as I know, without any warrant from the Lord Lieutenant. I was brought on a charge the most visionary and airy. No man knew what I was. No one could tell me or specify to me the charge on which I was detained. I asked the magistrates at Dungarvan to advise me of these charges. They would not tell me. At last I drove them into such a corner as I might call it, that one of them rose up and said, with much force, "You are a Fenian." Now, my lords, that is a very accommodating word. If a law man only breaks a window now, he is a Fenian. If I could bring, or if I had only the means of bringing witnesses from America, I would have established my innocence here without a probability of doubt. I would have brought a host of witnesses to prove that Costello was not the centre of a circle in 1866. I would have brought a host of witnesses to prove that he was not the secretary of a circle—never in all his life. My lords, I speak calmly, and weigh well, and understand every word that I say. If I speak wrong, time will bring the truth to the surface, and I would sooner have fifteen years added to my sentence than that any man might say I spoke from this dock, which I regard as a holy place, where stood those whom I revere as much as I do any of our saints——

THE LORD CHIEF BARON:—I cannot suffer you to proceed thus.

COSTELLO:—I would not speak one word from this dock which I knew to be other than truth. I admit there is a great deal of suspicion, but beyond that there are no facts proved to bring home the charge against me. What I have stated are facts, every one of them. Now, my lords, is it any wonder that I should speak at random and appear a little bit excited? I am not excited in the least. I would be excited in a degree were I expressing myself on any ordinary topic to any ordinary audience. It is my manner, your lordships will admit, and you have instructed the jury not to find me guilty, but to discharge me from the dock, if they were not positive that I was a Fenian on the 5th March. I believe these are the instructions that his lordship, Justice Keogh, gave to the jury—if I were not a Fenian on the 5th March, I was entitled to an acquittal. Well, I was not a Fenian at that time. I say so as I have to answer to God. Now, to conclude. I have not said much about being an American citizen. For why? I am not permitted to speak on that subject. Now, as Colonel Warren remarked, if I am an American citizen, I am not to be held responsible but to the American government. I did not press myself on that government. They extended to me those rights and those privileges; they said to me: "Come forward, young man; enroll yourself under our banner, under our flag; we extend to you our rights and privileges—we admit you to franchise." I came not before I was asked. The invitation was extended to me. I had no love then, and never will have, towards England, and I accepted the invitation. I did forswear allegiance to all foreign potentates, and more particularly I forswore all allegiance to the Crown of Great Britain. Your lordships say that the law of the land rules that I had no right to do anything of the kind. That is a question for the governments to settle. America is guilty of a great fraud if I am in the wrong.

THE LORD CHIEF BARON:—I cannot allow you to proceed in that line of argument.

COSTELLO:—I will take up no more of your time. If I am still a British subject, America is guilty.

THE LORD CHIEF BARON:—I cannot allow you to refer either to the American people or to the American government.

COSTELLO:—Would you allow me to state they enticed me from my allegiance to England? Therefore she (America) is guilty of high treason?

THE LORD CHIEF BARON:—We cannot allow you to speak on that subject.

COSTELLO:—I will conclude, then. I have nothing to say further than to thank your lordships for the latitude you have given me in these few remarks, and also to thank your lordships for your kindness during my trial. I know you have done me every justice; you did not strain the law against me; you did everything that was consistent with your duty to do, and I have nothing to complain of there. I must again thank my learned and able counsel for the able, zealous, and eloquent manner in which they defended me. I am at a loss for words to express the gratitude I owe to each and every one of those gentlemen who have so ably conducted my case. Now, my lords, I will receive that sentence which is impending. I am prepared for the worst. I am prepared to be torn from my friends, from my relations, from my home. I am prepared to spend the bloom of my youth in a tomb more dark and horrible than the tomb wherein the dead rest. But there is one consolation that I will bring into exile—if I may so call that house of misery—a clear conscience, a heart whose still, small voice tells me that I have done no wrong to upbraid myself with. This is the consolation that I have—that my conscience is clear. I know it appears somewhat egotistical for me to speak thus, but it is a source of consolation for me that I have nothing to upbraid myself with; and I will now say in conclusion, that, if my sufferings can ameliorate the wrongs or the sufferings of Ireland, I am willing to be offered up as a sacrifice for the good of old Erin.

GENERAL W. HALPIN.

AT the same Commission, before the same judges who had tried the cases of Colonel Warren and Augustine E. Costello, General William Halpin was put on his trial for treason-felony. It was alleged that he was one of the military officers of the Fenian organization, and had been appointed to take command, in the Dublin district, in the rising which had taken place on the 5th of March; and this it was sought to prove by the evidence of the informers, Massey, Corydon, Devany, and others.

General Halpin employed no counsel, and undertook the conduct of his case himself. The considerations that had induced him to take this course, he thus explained to the jury:—

> Two reasons operated on my mind, and induced me to forego the advantage I would derive from having some of the able and learned counsel that plead at this bar. The first reason is, that if you, gentlemen, are a jury selected by the Crown, as juries are known to be selected heretofore in political cases—if you are, in fact, a jury selected with the express purpose of finding a verdict for the Crown—then, gentlemen, all the talent and ability that I could employ would avail me nothing. If, on the other hand, by any chance the Attorney-General permitted honest men to find their way into the box, then, gentlemen, lawyers were equally unnecessary for me.

Not an inaccurate view of the case, perhaps; the experience of the Fenian trials, from first to last, certain'y goes to support it.

The general set about his work of defending himself, with infinite coolness and self-possession. He was supplied with a chair, a small table, and writing materials in the dock. When he had any notes to make, he sat down, cleaned and adjusted his spectacles, and wrote out what he wanted. When he wished to cross-examine a witness, he removed his glasses, came to the front of the dock, and put his questions steadily and quietly, without a trace of excitement in his manner, but always with a close application to the subject in hand. One could almost refuse to believe, while listening to him, that he had not been educated and trained for the bar; and undoubtedly many of those who wear wigs and gowns in her Majesty's courts are far from exhibiting the same degree of aptitude for the profession. But it was in his address to the jury that the remarkable talents of the man were most brilliantly revealed. It was an extraordinary piece of argument and eloquence, seasoned occasionally with much quiet humor, and enriched with many passages that showed a high and courageous spirit. His scathing denunciations of the system of brutality practised towards the political prisoners in Kilmainham gaol, and his picture of Mr. Governor Price as "the old gorilla," will long be remembered. One portion of his remarks ran as follows:—

> The whole conduct of the Crown since my arrest has been such as to warrant me in asserting that I have been treated more like a beast of prey than a human being. If I had been permitted to examine witnesses, I would have shown them how the case had been got up by the Crown. I would have shown them how the Crown Solicitor, the gaolers, the head gaoler, and the deputy gaolers of Kilmainham, and the Protestant chaplain of that institution, had gone in, day and night, to all the witnesses—to the cells of the prisoners—with a bribe in one hand and a halter in the other. I would have shown how political cases were got up by the Crown in Ireland. I would have shown how there existed, under the authority of the Castle, a triumvirate of the basest wretches that ever conspired to take away the lives and liberties of men. One of these represented the law, another the gibbet in front of the gaol, and another was supposed to represent the Church militant.

Here the Chief Baron interposed; but the prisoner soon after reverted to the subject, and said that every opportunity was taken in that gaol to wrong and torture the men incarcerated there on political charges. Every petty breach of discipline was availed of to punish them, by sending them down to work the crank, and reducing their scanty rations. For the crime of not saluting Mr. Governor Price, they were placed upon a dietary of seven ounces of what was called brown bread and a pint of Anna Liffey, in the twenty-four hours. Brown, indeed, the article was, but whether it deserved the name of bread, was quite another question. The turf-mould taken from the Bog of Allen was the nearest resemblance to it that he could think of. For his own part, he did not mean to complain of his rations—he could take either rough or smooth as well as most men—but what he would complain of was the system of petty insults and indignities offered by Mr. Price and his warders to men of finer feelings than their own, and whom they knew to be their superiors. He concluded his address in the following terms:—

I ask you if I have not thoroughly and sufficiently explained away the terror, if I may use the term, of these papers, which were taken from walls and other places, to be brought against me here? I ask you, gentlemen, as reasonable men, if there be a shadow of a case against me? I ask you if I have been connected by an untainted witness with any act, in America or Ireland, that would warrant you in deciding that I was guilty of the charge of which I stand accused? Is there one single overt act proved against me; or have I violated any law, for the violation of which I can be made amenable in this court? I ask you if, in these letters which have been brought up against me—one found in Thomas-street, another in the pocket of a fellow-prisoner—there is anything that can affect me? Recollect, gentlemen of the jury, that I speak to you now as men imbued with a spirit of justice. I speak to you, gentlemen, believing that you are honest, recognizing your intelligence, and confident that you will give a verdict in accordance with the dictates of your conscience. If you are the jury that the Attorney-General hopes you are, gentlemen of the jury, I am wasting time in speaking to you. If you are, gentlemen, that jury which the Attorney-General hopes to make the stepping-stone to the bench—for, gentlemen, I do not accuse the Attorney-General of wishing to prosecute me for the purpose of having me punished; I believe he is above any paltry consideration of that sort—but, gentlemen, all men are influenced by one motive or another, and the Attorney-General, though he is the first law officer of the Crown in Ireland, is human like ourselves; he is not above human frailty, but, like other men, doubtless likes office, and likes the emoluments which office brings. But, gentlemen of the jury, it will be your fault if you make your shoulders the stepping-stone for the Attorney-General to spring upon the bench. I say these words to you in sober, solemn earnestness. You are now trying a man who has lived all his lifetime in a country where freedom is venerated and adored. You may believe, gentlemen, that you have the speech of freedom here; but I claim, gentlemen, that the real spirit of freedom has fled these shores many a century ago—has sped across the Atlantic, and perched upon American soil—and, gentlemen, it ought to be your wish and desire—as I am sure it is, for I am unwilling to believe that you are the men the Attorney-General deems you to be—to do me justice, and prove that Dublin juries do not on all occasions bring in a verdict at the dictation of the Crown. Gentlemen, the principle of freedom is at stake. Every man that is born into this world has a right to freedom, unless he forfeits that right by his own misdemeanor. Perhaps you have read the Declaration of American Independence. In that declaration, drawn up by one Thomas Jefferson, it is stated that every man born into this world is born free and equal; that he has the right—the inalienable right—to live in liberty and the pursuit of happiness. These are the cardinal principles of liberty. I claim these rights, unless I have forfeited them by my own misconduct. I claim there is not one particle, one scintilla, of evidence to warrant you in finding a verdict for the Crown. I have not conspired with General Roberts or any of these other generals. There is no evidence to show you anything about any such conspiracy, as far as I am concerned. With these facts before you, I ask you, as reasonable men, is there one particle of evidence to show that I am guilty of the charges preferred against me? I shall simply conclude by repeating the words with which I commenced, that I leave it between your conscience and your God to find a verdict according to the evidence and the truth. I leave it to you in the name of that sacred justice which we all profess to venerate, and I ask you not to allow your passions or your prejudices to cloud your judgment; not to allow the country to say that the Dublin juries are in the breeches-pocket of the Attorney-General. Never let it be said that a prisoner, forced into your country, carried off from the steamer which was bearing him away from yours to his own, has been found guilty on the evidence of perjured witnesses. Never let the world say that a Dublin jury are not as honest as any other. Do not allow those acrimonious feelings which, unfortunately, in this country difference of sect engenders, to have anything to do with your verdict. As far as I am concerned, I ask no favor from you. I ask no favor from any man that lives in the world. I have always, gentlemen, adhered to my own principles, and will do so while I am able. If you consent to send me for my life to a penitentiary, you will not make the slightest impression on me. I am pleading for life and liberty—I am pleading in the cause of justice, and I leave it in your hands. I demand that you should exercise your best judgment to render a verdict before the Omnipotent Creator of the universe, who is looking into your hearts as well as mine; to render a verdict for which you will not be sorry; to render a verdict that your countrymen will cheer; to render a verdict that will make you venerated and admired in the land of your birth while you live on this earth.

The jury, however, found not for the prisoner, but for the Crown.

When General Halpin took his place in the dock with his fellow "convicts," Colonel Warren and Augustine E. Costello, to receive his sentence, he appeared calm and unimpassioned as ever. The question why sentence should not be passed on him having been put—

The prisoner said that, before he spoke to the question put him by the Clerk of the Crown, he wished to say a few words on another topic. The day before yesterday he was handed by the Governor of Kilmainham a letter which had come from America, and enclosed a draft. The draft the Governor refused to give up, and also refused to state what disposition he intended to make of it. The Deputy Governor had other moneys of his, and he requested that those, as well as the draft, should be restored to him.

The Attorney-General, in an undertone, having addressed some observations to the bench,

The Lord Chief Baron said that the prisoner, having been convicted of felony, his property was at the disposal of the authorities, and that any representation he had to make on the subject should be made to the government.

Halpin said that he wished that the money might be transferred to the governor of whatever jail he was to be imprisoned in, so that he might have the use of it to purchase necessaries should he require them.

LORD CHIEF BARON:—If you desire to make any representation, it must be through the government.

PRISONER:—I don't wish to make any representation to the government on the subject. I will permit the government to add robbery to perjury.

The prisoner, in reply to the question asked by the Clerk of the Crown, said that justice had not been dealt out to him as he thought it might have been. He had been prevented by the Crown from getting witnesses for his defence, and from seeing his witnesses, while the Crown had taken four months to get their witnesses properly trained, and to ransack all the Orange lodges of Dublin for jurors. He complained of the rules of the jail, and of the law that permitted them to be in force, and said :—

I deny the jurisdiction of this court in common with Colonel Warren. I owe no allegiance to this country, and, were I a free man to-morrow, I would sooner swear allegiance to the King of Abyssinia than give half-an-hour's allegiance to the government of this country—a government that has blasted the hopes of half the world and disgusted it all. I am not, I suppose, permitted to speak of the verdict given against me by the jury. It was entirely unnecessary for the Crown to produce one single witness against me. The jury had their lesson before they came to the box.

THE CHIEF BARON:—It is impossible for me to allow you to proceed with this line of observation.

HALPIN:—I wish to say simply, that the jury exhibited an extreme anxiety to find a verdict against me before I had even said a word to them. I saw their anxiety. I knew, from the moment they were put into the box, that a verdict of guilty would be returned against me. I knew it from looking at the conduct of the jury in the box; I knew it from the way the jury were empanelled, and I knew the Attorney-General relied upon the jury for a verdict when he set three citizens aside. I therefore conclude, and rightly, that all the eloquent talent that ever pleaded at this bar would be entirely useless to me whilst such a jury were in the box. The Crown, in order to give some color to the proceedings, thought proper to produce several witnesses against me. Eleven witnesses were examined, and out of these no less than nine committed absolute, diabolical, and egregious perjury.

THE CHIEF BARON:—You are transcending the limit within which the law confines you.

HALPIN:—I do not blame you for enforcing the law as it stands. By no means. I have to thank your lordship for your kindness during the progress of my trial. I do not blame you because the law stands as it does; but what I say is that the law is absurd in taking me and trying me as a British subject whilst I am a citizen of the United States, without a particle of evidence to show that I was born under the jurisdiction of the British Crown. I must say that I look to another place, another government, and another people, to see that justice shall be done me.

THE CHIEF BARON:—Here again you are transcending the limits which the law allows. We could not deal with any considerations connected with what any government will do.

HALPIN:—I am aware that it is not within your province to deal with the acts of another government, but I may be permitted to say this—that the outrages offered me and those gentlemen who claim, like me, to be citizens of the United States, will be gladly submitted to, if they only have the effect of making the sword of Brother Jonathan spring from its scabbard.

THE CHIEF BARON:—I cannot suffer you to proceed with this line of observation. I cannot suffer you to make this a place of appeal to persons in this country or in America.

HALPIN:—I am not making any appeal to any man. Although I was found guilty by a jury of this court, I deem my conduct above reproach. I know how I have been convicted, and will still assert that the first gun fired in anger between this country and America will be a knell of comfort to my ears.

THE CHIEF BARON:—I will be compelled to remove you from where you are now, if you proceed with this line of observation.

HALPIN:—Well, then, if I am not permitted to say that——
CHIEF BARON:—You are not permitted to make any observation upon what any government of any country may do.
HALPIN:—I think the reference has not anything to do with any government or any country. It refers to a fact that will come to pass; and when I shall hear the death-knell of this infamous government——
THE CHIEF BARON:—I will not allow you to proceed.
HALPIN:—Well, I cannot be prevented thinking it. Now, I will refer to a subject which I may be allowed to speak upon. You will recollect that I had addressed a letter to Mr. Price, asking him to furnish me, at my own expense, with two of the morning papers—the *Irish Times* and *Freeman's Journal*. I believe they are both loyal papers; at least they claim to be loyal, and I have no doubt they are of the admitted character of loyalty registered in the purlieus of Dublin Castle. The reason why I wanted these papers was, that I believed that the best reports of the trials since the opening of the Commission would be found in them. I said to Mr. Price that it was important that I should see all the evidence given by the informers who were to be produced against me, to enable me to make up my defence. I was denied, even at my own expense, to be furnished with these papers: and that I complain of as a wanton outrage. Perhaps Mr. Price was governed by some rule of Kilmainham, for it appears that the rules of Kilmainham are often as far outside the law of the country as I have been said to be by the Attorney-General. In fact, Mr. Price stated, when giving his testimony, that he was not governed by any law or rule, but that he was governed solely and entirely by his own imperial will.
CHIEF BARON:—That I cannot allow to be said without at once setting it right. Mr. Price said no such thing. He said that, with respect to one particular matter, namely, the reading of prisoners' correspondence, he was bound to exercise his own discretion as to what he would send out of the jail, and what he would hold. This is the only matter in which Mr. Price said he would exercise his own discretion.
PRISONER:—I think, my lord, you will allow your memory to go back to the cross-examination of Mr. Price, and you will find that, when I asked him by what authority he gave the letters he suppressed into the hands of the Crown to be produced here, he stated he had no other authority than his own will for so doing.
CHIEF BARON:—You are quite right with respect to the correspondence.
PRISONER:—I say he violated the law of the land in so doing, and I claim that he had no right to use those letters written by me in my private capacity to friends in America, asking for advice and assistance, and the very first letter that he read was a letter written to a man named Byrne. That, you may recollect, was put into the hands of the Attorney-General—kept by him for four months. That was the first intimation I had of its suppression

or of its production here by the Crown. Now, the letter was addressed to a friend in New York, asking him to look after my trunk, which had been taken away without my consent by the captain of the vessel in which I was arrested. Mr. Price never told me he suppressed that letter, and I was three months waiting for a reply, which, of course, I did not receive, as the letter never went. Mr. Price suppressed another letter yesterday. It was written to a friend of mine in Washington, in relation to my trial and conviction, and asking him to present my case to the President of the United States, detailing the case as it proceeded in this court. Mr. Price thought proper to suppress that letter, and I ask that he be compelled to produce it, so that, if your lordships think fit, it may be read in court.

THE CHIEF BARON:—I cannot do that. I cannot have a letter of that character read in open court.

HALPIN:—Am I entitled to get the letter to have it destroyed, or is Price to have it, to do with it as he pleases?

THE CHIEF BARON:—I can make no order in the matter.

HALPIN:—Then Price is something like Robinson Crusoe— "monarch of all he surveys," monarch of Kilmainham; and when I ask if he is to be controlled, I find there is no law to govern him.

THE CHIEF BARON:—You have now no property in these letters, being a convict.

THE PRISONER:—I will very soon be told I have no property in myself. I claim to have been arrested on the high seas, and there was then no case against me, and the Crown had to wait four months to pick up papers and get men from Stepaside, and arrange plans between Mr. Price and his warders to fill up any gap that might be wanted. I was arrested out of the *habeas corpus* jurisdiction, without authority, and detained four months in jail until the Crown could trump up a case against me. Have I not a right to complain that I should be consigned to a dungeon for life in consequence of a trumped-up case? I am satisfied that your lordships have stated the case as it stands, but I am not satisfied that I have been convicted under any law. I have been four months in durance vile, and vile durance it has been. The preachers tell us that hell is a very bad place, and the devil a very bad boy, but he could not hold a candle to old Price.

THE CHIEF BARON:—You are trespassing very much upon a very large indulgence. I must adopt a more decisive course if you persevere.

HALPIN (laughing):—Well, my lord, I will say no more about the old gorilla. The Crown officers have laid much stress upon the fact that I have travelled under different names, and therefore I was guilty of a great crime. I have precedent for it when I read in the papers that some continental monarchs travel under an assumed name, and I hear that the Prince of Wales does so, also, when he thinks proper to go to the London brothels.

At this point the Court cut short his address, and Chief

Baron Pigot proceeded to pass sentence on the three prisoners.

THE SENTENCES.

After some share of preliminary remarks, the Chief Baron announced the sentence of the court. It was for

John Warren, 15 years' penal servitude.
William Halpin, 15 years' penal servitude.
Augustine E. Costello, 12 years' penal servitude.

The prisoners heard the announcement without manifesting any emotion. General Halpin remarked that he would take fifteen years more any day for Ireland. Colonel Warren informed the court that he did not think a lease of the British Empire worth thirty-seven-and-a-half cents; and then all three, followed by a *posse* of warders, disappeared from the dock.

And thus were three men of education and ability added to the hundreds who are now rotting their lives away in British dungeons, because of the love they bore to their country, and their hatred of the misrule which makes her the most afflicted and miserable land on earth. It is hard for Ireland to see such men stricken down and torn from her upon such an accusation; yet, looking at the noble bearing of that long list of devoted men when confronted with the worst terrors to which their enemies could subject them, she has something which may well cause the light of pride to glisten in her eyes, even while the tears of love and pity are falling from them. And we should say to her, in the noble words of a French writer, one of the many generous-hearted foreigners, whose affectionate admiration has been won by her sufferings and her constancy, the Rev. Adolphe Perraud, Priest of the Oratory, Paris:—

"'Take heart! your trials will not last forever; the works of iniquity are passing and perishable: '*Vidi impium superexaltatum et elevatum sicut cedros Libani, et ecce non erat!*' (Ps. xxxvi.) Patience, then, even still! Do not imagine that you are forsaken: God forsakes not those that believe in Him. The day of retribution will come—

to teach men that no struggle against right is rightful, that probation is not abandonment; that God and conscience have unimagined resources against brutal spoliation and the triumphs of injustice; and that, if men are often immoral in their designs and actions, there are still, in the general course of history, a sovereign morality, and judgments, the forerunners of the infallible judgment of God."

THE

"WEARING OF THE GREEN,"

OR,

THE PROSECUTED FUNERAL PROCESSION.

> Let the echoes fall unbroken,
> Let our tears in silence flow;
> For each word thus nobly spoken,
> Let us yield a nation's woe;
> Yet, while weeping, sternly keeping
> Wary watch upon the foe."
> *Poem in the "* NATION.*"*

THE PROSECUTED FUNERAL PROCESSION.

The news of the Manchester executions on the morning of Saturday, 23d November, 1867, fell upon Ireland with sudden and dismal disillusion.

In time to come, when the generation now living shall have passed away, men will probably find it difficult to fully realize or understand the state of stupor and amazement which ensued in this country on the first tidings of that event; seeing, as it may be said, that the victims had lain for weeks under sentence of death, to be executed on this date. Yet surprise indubitably was the first and most overpowering emotion; for, in truth, no one up to that hour had really credited that England would take the lives of those three men on a verdict already publicly admitted and proclaimed to have been a blunder. Now, however, came the news that all was over—that the deed was done—and soon there was seen such an upheaving of national emotion as had not been witnessed in Ireland for a century. The public conscience, utterly shocked, revolted against the dreadful act perpetrated in the outraged name of justice. A great billow of grief rose and surged from end to end of the land. Political distinctions disappeared or were forgotten. The Manchester victims—the Manchester Martyrs, they were already called—belonged to the Fenian organization, a conspiracy which the wisest and truest patriots of Ireland had condemned and resisted; yet, the men who had been prominent in withstanding, on national grounds, that hopeless and disastrous scheme—priests and laymen —were now amongst the foremost and the boldest in denouncing at every peril the savage act of vengeance perpetrated at Manchester. The Catholic clergy were the first to give articulate expression to the national emotion. The executions took place on Saturday. Before night the telegraph had spread the news through the island; and on the next morning, Sunday, from a thousand altars the sad event was announced to the assembled worshippers, and prayers were publicly offered for the souls of the the victims. When the news was announced, a moan of sorrowful surprise burst from the congregation, followed by the wailing and sobbing of women; and, when the priest, his own voice broken with emotion, asked all to join with him in praying the merciful God to grant those young victims a place beside His throne, the assemblage with one voice responded, praying and weeping aloud!

The manner in which the national feeling was demonstrated on this occasion was one peculiarly characteristic of a nation in which the sentiments of religion and patriotism are so closely blended. No stormy "indignation meetings" were held; no tumult, no violence, no cries for vengeance arose. In all probability—nay, to a certainty—all this would have happened, and these ebullitions of popular passion would have been heard, had the victims not passed into eternity. But now, they were gone where prayer alone could follow; and, in the presence of this solemn fact, the religious sentiment overbore all others with the Irish people. Cries of anger, imprecations, and threats of vengeance, could not avail the dead; but happily religion gave a vent to the pent-up feelings of the living. By prayer and mourning they could, at once, most fitly and most successfully demonstrate their horror of the guilty deed, and their sympathy with the innocent victims.

Requiem Masses forthwith were announced and celebrated in several churches, and were attended by crowds everywhere too vast for the sacred edifices to contain. The churches in several instances were draped with black, and the ceremonies conducted with more than ordinary solemnity. In every case, however, the authorities of the Catholic church were careful to insure that the sacred functions were sought and attended for spiritual considerations, not used merely for illegitimate political purposes; and wherever it was apprehended that the holy rites were in danger of such use, the masses were said privately.

And soon public feeling found yet another vent—a mode of manifesting itself scarcely less edifying than the Requiem Masses, namely, funeral processions. The brutal vengeance of the law consigned the bodies of Allen, Larkin, and O'Brien to dishonored graves, and forbade the presence of sympathizing friend or sorrowing relative who might drop a tear above their mutilated remains. Their countrymen now, however, determined that ample atonement should be made to the memory of the dead for this denial of the decencies of sepulture. On Sunday, 1st December, in Cork, Manchester, Mitchelstown, Middleton, Limerick, and Skibbereen, funeral processions, at which thousands of persons attended, were held; that in Cork being admittedly the most imposing, not only in point of numbers, but in the character of the demonstration and the demeanor of the people.

For more than twenty years Cork city has held an advanced position in the Irish national struggle. In truth, it has been one of the great strongholds of the national cause since 1848. Nowhere else did the national spirit keep its hold so tenaciously and so extensively amidst the people. In 1848, Cork city contained probably the most formidable organization in the country; formidable, not merely in numbers, but in the superior intelligence, earnestness, and determination of the men; and even in the Fenian conspiracy, it is unquestionable that the southern capital contributed to that movement men—chiefly belonging to the mercantile and commercial classes—who, in personal worth and standing, as well as in courage, intelligence, and patriotism, were the flower of the organization. Finally, it must be said that it was Cork city, by its funeral demonstration of the 1st December, that struck the first great blow at the Manchester verdict, and set all Ireland in motion.*

---

* It may be truly said, set the Irish race all over the world in motion. There is probably no parallel in history for the singular circumstances of these funeral processions being held by the

Meanwhile the Irish capital had moved, and was organizing a demonstration destined to surpass all that had yet been witnessed. Early in the second week of December, a committee was formed for the purpose of organizing a funeral procession in Dublin, worthy of the national metropolis. Dublin would have come forward sooner, but the question of the *legality* of the processions that were announced to come off the previous week in Cork and other places, had been the subject of fierce discussion in the government press; and the national leaders were determined to avoid the slightest infringement of the law, or the least inroad on the public peace. It was only when, on the 3d of December, Lord Derby, the Prime Minister, replying in the House of Lords to Lord Dufferin, declared the opinion of the Crown that the projected processions were not illegal, that the national party in Dublin decided to form a committee and organize a procession. The following were Lord Derby's words:—

"He could assure the noble lord that the government would continue to carry out the law with firmness and impartiality. The Party Processions Act, however, did not meet the case of the funeral processions, the parties engaged in them having, by not displaying banners or other emblems, kept within the law as far as his information went."

Still more strong assurance was contained in the reply of the Irish Chief Secretary, Lord Mayo, to a question put by Sir P. O'Brien in the House of Commons. Lord Mayo publicly announced and promised that, if any new opinion as to the legality of the procession should be arrived at—

---

dispersed Irish in lands remote, apart, as pole from pole—in the old hemisphere and in the new—in Europe, in America, in Australia, prosecutions being set on foot by the English government to punish them at both ends of the world—in Ireland and in New Zealand! In Hokatika the Irish settlers—most patriotic of Ireland's exiles—organized a highly impressive funeral demonstration. The government seized and prosecuted its leaders, the Rev. Father Larkin, a Catholic clergyman, and Mr. Wm. Manning, editor of the *Hokatika Celt*. A jury, terrified by Fenian panic, brought them in "guilty," and the patriot priest and journalist were consigned to a dungeon for the crime of mourning for the dead and protesting against judicial murder.

that is, should the Crown see in them anything of illegality —*due and timely notice would be given* by proclamation, so that no one might offend through ignorance. Here are his words:—

"It is the wish of the government to act strictly in accordance with the law; *and of course ample notice will be given either by proclamation or otherwise.*"

The Dublin funeral committee thereupon at once issued the following announcement, by placard and advertisement:—

GOD SAVE IRELAND!

A PUBLIC FUNERAL PROCESSION
In honor of the Irish Patriots
Executed at Manchester, 23d November,
Will take place in Dublin
On Sunday next, the 8th inst.

The procession will assemble in Beresford-place, near the Custom House, and will start from thence at the hour of twelve o'clock noon.

No flags, banners, or party emblems will be allowed.

IRISHMEN,
Assemble in your thousands, and show, by your numbers and your orderly demeanor, your sympathy with the fate of the executed patriots.

IRISHWOMEN.
You are requested to lend the dignity of your presence to this important National Demonstration.
By Order of the Committee.

JOHN MARTIN, Chairman.
J. C. WATERS,
JAMES SCANLAN, } Hon. Secretaries.
J. J. LALOR,

DONAL SULLIVAN, Up. Buckingham-street,
Treasurer.

The appearance of the "funeral procession placards" all over the city on Thursday, 5th December, increased the public excitement. No other topic was discussed in any place of public resort, but the event forthcoming on Sunday. The first evidence of what it was about to be, was the appearance of the drapery establishments in the city on Saturday morning; the windows, exteriorly and interiorly, being one mass of crape and green ribbon—funeral knots, badges, scarfs, hatbands, neckties, etc., exposed for sale. Before noon most of the retail, and several of the wholesale houses had their entire stock of green ribbon and crape exhausted, it being computed that *nearly one hundred thousand yards* had been sold up to midnight of Saturday! Meantime the committee sat *en permanence*, zealously pushing their arrangements for the orderly and successful carrying out of their great undertaking—appointing stewards, marshals, etc,—in a word, completing the numerous details on the perfection of which it greatly depended whether Sunday was to witness a successful demonstration or a scene of disastrous disorder. On this, as upon every occasion when a national demonstration was to be organized, the trades of Dublin, Kingstown, and Dalkey, exhibited that spirit of patriotism for which they have been proverbial in our generation. From their ranks came the most efficient aids in every department of the preparations. On Saturday evening the carpenters, in a body, immediately after their day's work was over, instead of seeking home and rest, refreshment or recreation, after their week of toil, turned into the *Nation* office machine rooms, which they quickly improvised into a vast workshop, and there, as volunteers, labored away till near midnight, manufacturing "wands" for the stewards of next morning's procession.

Sunday, 8th December, 1867, dawned through watery skies. From shortly after daybreak, rain, or rather half-melted sleet, continued to fall; and many persons concluded that there would be no attempt to hold the procession under such inclement weather. This circumstance was, no doubt, a grievous discouragement, or rather a discomfort and an inconvenience; but, so far from preventing the procession, it was destined to add a hundred-fold to the significance and importance of the demonstration. Had the day been fine, tens of thousands of persons, who eventually only lined the streets, wearing the funeral emblems, would have marched in the procession, as they had originally intended; but hostile critics would in this case have said that the fineness of the day and the excitement of the pageant had merely caused a hundred thousand persons to come out for a holiday. Now, however, the depth, reality, and intensity of the popular feeling was about to be keenly tested. The subjoined account of this memorable demonstration is summarized from the Dublin daily papers of the next ensuing publication, the report of the *Freeman's Journal* being chiefly used :—

As early as ten o'clock crowds began to gather in Beresford-place, and in an hour about ten thousand men were present. The morning had succeeded to the hopeless humidity of the night, and the drizzling rain fell with almost pitiless persistence. The early trains from Kingstown and Dalkey, and all the citerior townlands, brought large numbers into Dublin; and Westland-row, Brunswick, D'Olier, and Sackville-streets, streamed with masses of humanity. A great number of the processionists met in Earlsfort-terrace, all round the Exhibition, and at twelve o'clock some thousands had collected. It was not easy to learn the object of this gathering; it may have been a mistake, and most probably it was, as they fell in with the great body in the course of half an hour. The space from the quays, including the great sweep in front of the Custom-house, was swarming with men, and women, and small children, and the big, ungainly crowd bulged out in Gardiner-street, and the broad space leading up Talbot-street. The ranks began to be formed at eleven o'clock amid a down-pour of cold rain. The mud was deep and aqueous, and great pools ran through the streets almost level with the paths. Some of the more prominent of the men and several of the committee rode about directing and organizing the crowd, which presented a most extraordinary appearance. A couple of thousand young children stood quietly in the rain and slush for over an hour; while behind them, in close-packed numbers, were over two thousand young women. Not the least blame can be attached to those who managed the affairs of the day, inasmuch as the throng must have far exceeded even their most sanguine expectations. Every moment some overwhelming accession rolled down Abbey-street or Eden-quay, and swelled the already surging multitude waiting for the start. Long before twelve o'clock, the streets, converging on the square, were packed with spectators or intending processionists. Cabs struggled hopelessly to yield up the large number of highly respectable and well-attired ladies who had come to walk. Those who had hired vehicles for the day to join the procession were convinced of the impracticable character of their intention; and many delicate old men who would not give up the design, braved the terrors of asthma and bronchitis, and joined the rain-defying throng. Right across the spacious ground was one unmoving mass, constantly being enlarged by ever-coming crowds. All the windows in Beresford-place were filled with spectators, and the rain and cold seemed to have no saddening effect on the numerous multitude. The various bands of the trade were being disposed in their respective positions, and the hearses were a long way off and altogether in the background, when, at a quarter to twelve, the first rank of men moved forward. Almost every one had an umbrella, but they were thoroughly saturated with the never-ceasing down-pour. As the steady, well-kept, twelve-deep ranks moved slowly out, some ease was given to those pent up behind; and it was really wonderful to see the facility with which the people adapted themselves to the orders of their directors. Every chance of falling in was seized, and soon the procession was in motion. The first five hundred men were of the artisan class. They were dressed very respectably, and each man wore upon his left shoulder a green rosette, and on his left arm a band of crape. Numbers had hatbands depending to the shoulder; others had close crape intertwined carefully with green ribbon around their hats; and the great majority of the better sort adhered to this plan, which was executed with a skill unmistakably feminine. Here and there a man appeared with a broad, green scarf around his shoulders, some embroidered with shamrocks, and others decorated with harps. There was not a man throughout the procession but was conspicuous by some emblem of nationality. Appointed officers walked at the sides with wands in their hands, and gently kept back the curious and interested crowd whose sympathy was certainly demonstrative. Behind the five hundred men came a couple of thousand of young children. These excited, perhaps, the most considerable interest amongst the bystanders, whether sympathetic, neutral, or opposite. Of tender age and innocent of opinions on any subject, they were being marshalled by their parents in a demonstration which will probably give a tone to their career hereafter; and seeds in the juvenile mind ever bear fruit in due season. The presence of these shivering little ones gave a serious significance to the procession—they were hostages to the party who had organized the demonstration. Earnestness must, indeed, have been strong in the mind of the parent who directed his little son or daughter to walk in saturating rain and painful cold through five or six miles of mud and water, and all this merely to say, "I and my children were there." It portends something more than sentiment. It is national education with a vengeance. Comment on this remarkable constituent was very frequent throughout the day, and when, towards evening, this band of boys sang out with lusty unanimity a popular Yankee air, spectators were satisfied of their culture and training. After the children came about one hundred young women who had been unable to gain their proper position, and accepted the place which chance assigned them. They were succeeded by a band dressed very respectably, with crape and green ribbons round their caps. These were followed by a number of rather elderly men, probably the parents of the children far ahead. At this portion of the procession, a mile from the point, they marched four deep, there having been a gradual decline from the front. Next came the bricklayers' band all dressed in green caps, a very superior-looking body of men. Then followed a very imposing well-kept line, composed of young men of the better class, well attired and respectable-looking. These wore crape hatbands, and green rosettes with harps in the centre. Several had broad, green body-scarfs, with gold-tinsel shamrocks and harps interwined. As this portion of the procession marched, they attracted very considerable attention by their orderly, measured tread, and the almost soldierly precision with which they maintained the line. They numbered about four or five thousand, and there were few who were not young, sinewy, stalwart fellows. When they had reached the further end of Abbey-street, the ground about Beresford-place was gradually becoming clear, and the spectator had some opportunity afforded of glancing more closely at the component parts of the great crowd. All round the Custom-house was still packed a dense throng, and large streams were flowing from the northern districts, Cloutarf, the strand, and the quays. The shipping was gaily decorated, and many of the masts were filled with young tars, wearing green bands on their hats. At half-past twelve o'clock, the most interesting portion of the procession left the Custom-house. About two thousand young women, who, in attire, demeanor, and general appearance, certainly justified their title to be called ladies, walked in six-deep ranks. The general public kept pace with them for a great distance. The green was most demonstrative; every lady having shawl, bonnet, veil, dress, or mantle of the national hue. The mud made sad havoc of their attire, but, notwithstanding all mishaps, they maintained good order and regularity. They stretched for over half a mile, and added very notably to the imposing appearance of the procession. So great was the pressure in Abbey-street, that, for a very long time, there were no less than three processions walking side by side. These halted at the end of the street, and followed as they were afforded opportunity. One of the bands was about to play near the Abbey-street Wesleyan House, but, when a policeman told them of the proximity of the place of worship, they immediately desisted. The first was a very long way back in the line, and the foremost men must have been near the Ormond-quays, when the four horses moved into Abbey-street. They were draped with black cloths, and white plumes were at their heads. The hearse also had white plumes, and was covered with black palls. On the side was "William P. Allen." A number of men followed, and then came a band. In the earlier portion of the day there were seen but two hearses, the second one bearing Larkin's name. It was succeeded by four mourning coaches, drawn by two horses each. A large number of young men from the monster houses followed in admirable order. In this throng were very many men of business, large employers, and members of the professions. Several of the trades were in great force. It had been arranged to have the trade banners carried in front of the artisans of every calling, but, at the suggestion of the chairman, this design was abandoned. The men walked, however, in considerable strength. They marched from their various committee-rooms to the Custom-house. The quay porters were present to the number of 500, and presented a very orderly, cleanly appearance. They were comfortably dressed, and walked close after the hearse bearing Larkin's name. Around this bier were a number of men bearing in their hands long and waving palms—emblems of martyrdom. The trades came next, and were led off by the various branches of the association known as the Amalgamated Trades. The plasterers made about 300, the painters 350, the boot and shoemakers mustered 1,000, the bricklayers 500, the carpenters 300, the slaters 450, the sawyers 200, and the skinners, coopers, tailors, bakers, and the other trades, made a very respectable show, both as to numbers and appearance. Each of these had representatives in the front of the procession, amongst the fine body of men who marched eight deep. The whole ground near the starting-place was clear at half-past one, and by that time the demonstration was seen to a greater advantage than previously. All down Abbey-street, and, in fact, throughout the procession, the pathways were crowded by persons who were practically of it, though not in it. Very many young girls, naturally enough, preferred to stand on the pathways than to be saturated with mud and water. But it may be truly said that every second man and woman of the crowds in almost every street were of the procession. Cabs filled with ladies and gentlemen remained at the waysides all day watching the march. The horses' heads were gaily decorated with green ribbons, while every Jehu in the city wore a rosette or a crape band. Nothing of special note occurred until the procession turned into Dame-street. The appearance of the demonstration was here far greater than at any other portion of the city. Both sides of the street, and as far as Carlisle-bridge, were lined with cabs and carriages filled with spectators, who were prevented by the bitter inclemency of the day from taking an active part in the proceedings. The procession was here grandly imposing, and after Larkin's hearse were no less than nine carriages, and several cabs. It is stated that Mrs. Luby and Miss Mulcahy occupied one of the vehicles, and relatives of others, now in confinement, were alleged to have been present. One circumstance, which was generally remarked as having great significance, was the presence in one line of ten soldiers of the 86th regiment. They were dressed in their great overcoats, which they wore open so as to show the scarlet tunic. These men may have been on leave,

Inasmuch as the great military force were confined to barracks, and kept under arms from six o'clock A.M. The cavalry were in readiness for action, if necessary. Mounted military and police orderlies were stationed at various points of the city, to convey any requisite intelligence to the authorities; and the constabulary at the depot, Phœnix Park, were also prepared, if their services should be required. At the police stations throughout the city, large numbers of men were kept all day under arms. It is pleasant to state that no interference was necessary, as the great demonstration terminated without the slightest disturbance. The public houses generally remained closed until five o'clock, and the sobriety of the crowds was the subject of general comment.

From an early hour in the morning every possible position along the quays, that afforded a good view of the procession, was taken advantage of; and, despite the inclemency of the weather, the parapets of the various bridges, commencing at Capel-street, were crowded with adventurous youths, who seemed to think nothing of the risks they ran in comparison with the opportunities they had of seeing the great sight in all its splendor. From eleven until twelve o'clock the greatest efforts were made to secure good places. The side-walks were crowded and impassable. The lower windows of the houses were made the most of by men who clutched the shutters and bars, whilst the upper windows were, as a general rule, filled with the fair sex; and it is almost unnecessary to add that almost every man, woman, and child displayed some emblem suitable to the occasion. Indeed, the originality of the designs was a striking feature. The women wore green ribbons and veils, and many, entire dresses of the favorite color. The numerous windows of the Four Courts accommodated hundreds of ladies, and we may mention that within the building were two pieces of artillery, a plentiful supply of rockets, and a number of policemen. It was arranged that the rockets should be fired from the roof in case military assistance was required. Contrary to the general expectation, the head of the procession appeared at Essex-bridge shortly before twelve o'clock. As it was expected to leave Beresford-place about that time, and as such gigantic arrangements are seldom carried out punctually, the thousands of people who congregated in this locality were pleasantly disappointed when a society band turned the corner of Mary-street and came towards the quays, with the processionists marching in slow and regular time. The order that prevailed was almost marvellous—not a sound was heard but the mournful strains of the music, and the prevalent feeling was expressed, no doubt, by one or two of the processionists, who said in answer to an inquiry, "We will be our own police to day." They certainly were their own police, for those who carried white wands did not spare themselves in their endeavors to maintain order in the ranks. As we have mentioned already, the first part of the procession reached Capel-street shortly before twelve o'clock, and some idea of the extent of the demonstration may be formed from the fact that the hearses did not come in view until a quarter-past one o'clock. They appeared at intervals of a quarter of an hour, and were received by a general cry of "hush." The number of fine, well-dressed young women in the procession here was the subject of general remark, whilst the assemblage of boys astonished all who witnessed it on account of its extent. The variety of the tokens of mourning, too, was remarkable. Numbers of the women carried laurel branches in addition to green ribbons and veils, and many of the men wore shamrocks in their hats. The procession passed along the quays as far as King's-bridge, and it there crossed and passed up Stevens'-lane. The windows of all the houses en route were crowded chiefly with women, and the railings at the Esplanade and at King's-bridge were crowded with spectators.

About one o'clock the head of the procession, which had been compressed into a dense mass in Stephens'-lane, burst like confined water when relieved of restraint, on entering James's-street, where every window and doorstep was crowded Along the line of footway, extending at either side from the old fountain up to James's-gate, was literally tented over with umbrellas of every hue and shade, held up as protection against the cold rain that fell in drizzling showers and made the street-way on which the vast numbers stood, ankle-deep in the slushy mud. The music of the "Dead March in Saul," heard in the distance, caused the people to break from the lines in which they had partially stood awaiting the arrival of the procession, which now, for the first time, began to assume its full proportions. As it moved along the quays at the north side of the river, every street, bridge, and laneway served to obstruct to a considerable extent its progress and its order, owing to interruption from carriage traffic and from the crowds that poured into it and swelled it in its onward course. In the vast multitude that lined this great western artery of the city, the greatest order and propriety were observed, and all seemed to be impressed with the one solemn and all-pervading idea that they were assembled to express their deep sympathy with the fate of three men who, they believed, had been condemned and had suffered death unjustly. Even amongst the young there was not to be recognized the slightest approach to levity, and the old characteristics of a great Irish gathering were not to be perceived anywhere. The wrong. whether real or imaginary, done to Allen, O'Brien, and Larkin, made their memory sacred with the thousands that stood for hours in the December cold and wet of yesterday, to testify by their presence their feelings and their sympathies. The horsemen, wearing green rosettes, trimmed with crape, who rode in advance of the procession, kept back the crowds at either side that encroached on the space in the centre of the street required for the vast coming mass to move through. On it came, the advance with measured tread, to the music of the band in front, and, notwithstanding the mire which had to be waded through, the line went on at quick pace, and with admirable order, but there was no effort at anything like semi military swagger or pompous demonstration. Every window along the route of the procession was fully occupied by male and female spectators, all wearing green ribbons and crape, and in front of several of the houses black drapery was suspended. The tide of men, women, and children continued to roll on in the drenching rain, but nearly all the fair processionists carried umbrellas. It was not till the head of the vast moving throng had reached James's-gate that any thing like a just conception could be formed of its magnitude, as it was only now that it was beginning to get into regular shape and find room to extend itself. The persons whose duty it was to keep the several parts of the procession well together had no easy part to play, as the line had to be repeatedly broken to permit the ordinary carriage traffic of the streets to go on with as little delay as possible. The *cortége* at this point looked grand and solemn in the extreme because of its vastness, and, also, because of all present appearing to be impressed with the one idea. The gloomy, wet, and cheerless weather was quite in keeping with the funeral march of 35,000 people. The bands were placed at such proper distances that the playing of one did not interfere with the other. After passing James's-gate the band in front ceased to perform, and on passing the house 151 Thomas-street every head was uncovered in honor of Lord Edward Fitzgerald, who was arrested and mortally wounded by Major Sirr and his assistants in the front bedroom of the second floor of that house. Such was the length of the procession, that an hour had elapsed from the time its head entered James's-street before the first hearse turned the corner of Stevens'-lane. In the neighborhood of St. Catherine's Church a vast crowd of spectators had settled down, and every available elevation was taken possession of. At this point a large portion of the streetway was broken up for the purpose of laying down waterpipes, and on the lifting-crane and the heaps of earth the people wedged and packed themselves, which showed at once that this was a great centre of attraction—and it was, for here was executed the young and enthusiastic Robert Emmet sixty-four years ago. When Allen, O'Brien, and Larkin were condemned to death as political offenders, some of the highest and the noblest in the land warned the government to pause before the extreme penalty pronounced on the condemned men would be carried into effect; but all remonstrance was in vain, and, on last Saturday fortnight, three comparatively unknown men in their death passed into the ranks of heroes and martyrs, because it was believed, and believed generally, that their lives were sacrificed to expediency, and not to satisfy justice. The spot where Robert Emmet closed his young life on a bloody scaffold was yesterday regarded by thousands upon thousands of his countrymen and women as a holy place, and all looked upon his fate as similar to that of the three men whose memory they had assembled to honor, and whose death they pronounced to be unjust. It would be hard to give a just conception of the scene here, as the procession advanced and divided, as it were, into two great channels, owing to the breaking-up of the streetway. On the advance of the *cortége* reaching the top of Bridgefoot-street every head was uncovered, and nothing was to be heard but the measured tread of the vast mass, but, as if by some secret and uncontrollable impulse, a mighty, ringing, and enthusiastic cheer broke from the moving throng as the angle of the footway at the eastern end of St. Catherine's Church, where the scaffold on which Emmet was executed stood, was passed. In that cheer there appeared to be no fiction, as it evidently came straight from the hearts of thousands, who waved their hats and handkerchiefs, as did also the groups that clustered in the windows of the houses in the neighborhood. As the procession moved on, from every part of it the cheers rose again and again; men holding up their children, and pointing out the place where one who loved Ireland, "not wisely but too well," rendered up his life. When the hearse with white plumes came up bearing on the side draperies the words, "William P. Allen," all the enthusiasm and excitement ceased, and along the lines of spectators prayers for the repose of the soul of the departed man passed from mouth to mouth, and a sense of deep sadness seemed to settle down on the swaying multitude as the procession rolled along on its way. After this hearse came large numbers of females walking on bravely, apparently heedless of the muddy streets and the unceasing rain that came down without a moment's intermission. When the second hearse, bearing white plumes and the name of "Michael O'Brien" on the side pendants, came up, again all heads were uncovered, and prayers were recited by the people for the everlasting rest of the departed. Still onward rolled the mighty mass, young and old, and in the entire assemblage was not to be observed a single person under the influence of drink, or requiring the slightest interference on the part of the police, whose exertions were altogether confined to keeping the general thoroughfare clear of obstruction. Indeed, justly speaking, the people required no supervision, as they seemed to feel that they had a solemn duty to discharge. Fathers were to be seen bearing in their arms children dressed in white and decorated with green ribbons, and here, as elsewhere, was observed unmistakable evidence of the deep sympathy of the people with the executed men. This was, perhaps, more strikingly illustrated as the third hearse, with sable plumes, came up, bearing at either side the name of "Michael Larkin;" prayers for his soul's welfare were mingled with expressions of commiseration for his widow and children. At the entrance to Cornmarket, where the streetway narrows, the crushing became very great, but still the procession kept its onward course. On passing the shop of Hayburne, who, it will be remembered, was convicted of being connected with the Fenian conspiracy, a large number of persons in the procession uncovered and cheered. In the house of Roantree, in High-street, who was also convicted of treason-felony, a harp was displayed in one of the drawing-room windows by a lady dressed in deep mourning, and the procession loudly cheered as it passed on its route.

Standing at the corner of Christchurch-place a fine view could be had of the procession as it approached Winetavern-street from High-street. The compact mass moved on at a regular pace, while from the windows on either side of the streets the well-dressed citizens, who preferred to witness the demonstration from an elevated position rather than undergo the fatigues and unpleasantness of a walk through the city in such weather, eagerly watched the approach of the procession. Under the guidance of the horsemen and those whose wands showed it was their duty to marshal the immense throng, the procession moved at an orderly pace down Winetavern-street, which, spacious as it is, was in a few minutes absolutely filled with the vast crowds. The procession again reached the quays, and moved along Wood-quay and Essex-quay, and into Parliament-street, which it reached at twenty minutes to two o'clock. Passing down Parliament-street, and approaching the O'Connell statue, a number of persons began to cheer, but this was promptly suppressed by the leaders, who galloped in advance for some distance with a view to the preservation of the mournful silence that had prevailed. This was strictly enjoined, and the instruction was generally observed by the processionists. The reverential manner in which the many thousands of the people passed the statue of the Liberator, was very observable. A rather heavy rain was falling at the time, yet there were thousands who uncovered their heads as they looked up to the statue which expressed the noble attitude and features of O'Connell. As the procession moved along through Dame-street the footways became blocked up, and lines of cabs took up places in the middle of the carriage-way, and the police exercised a wise discretion in preventing vehicles from the surrounding streets driving in amongst the crowds. By this means the danger of serious accident was prevented without any public inconvenience being occasioned, as a line parallel to that which the procession was taking was kept clear for all horse conveyances. Owing to the hour growing late, and a considerable distance still to be gone over, the procession moved at a quick pace. In anticipation of its arrival, great crowds collected in the vicinity of the Bank of Ireland and Trinity College, where the *cortége* was kept well together, notwithstanding the difficulty of such a vast mass passing on through the heart of the city filled at this point with immense masses of spectators. On passing the old Parliament-house numbers of men in the procession took off their hats, but the disposition to cheer was suppressed, as it was at several other points along the route. Turning down Westmoreland-street, the procession, marshalled by Dr. Waters on horseback, passed slowly along between the thick files of people on each side, most of whom displayed the mourning and national symbols, black and green. The spacious thoroughfare in a few minutes was filled with the dense array, which in close, compact ranks pressed on, the women, youths, and children bearing bravely the privations of the day ; the bands, preceding and following the hearses playing the Dead March ; the solemn notes filling the air with mournful cadence. The windows of the houses on each side of the street were filled with groups of spectators of the strange and significant spectacle below. With the dark masses of men, broken at intervals by the groups of females and children, still stretched lengthily in the rear, the first section of the procession crossed Carlisle-bridge, the footways and parapets of which were thronged with people, nearly all of whom wore the usual tokens of sympathy. Passing the bridge, a glance to the right, down the river, revealed the fact that the ships, almost without exception, had their flags flying half-mast high; and that the rigging of several were filled with seamen, who chose this elevated position to get a glimpse of the procession as it emerged into Sackville-street. Here the sight was imposing. A throng of spectators lined each side of the magnificent thoroughfare, and the lofty houses had their windows on each side occupied with spectators. Pressing onwards with measured, steady pace, regardless of the heavy rain, the cold wind, and the gloomy sky, the procession soon filled Sackville-street from end to end with its dense, dark mass, which, stretching away over Carlisle-bridge, seemed motionless in the distance. The procession defiled to the left of the site of the O'Connell monument, at the head of the street, and the national associations connected with this spot were acknowledged by the large numbers of the processionists, who, with uncovered heads, marched past, some expressing their feelings with a subdued cheer. The foremost ranks were nearing Glasnevin when the first of the hearses entered Sackville-street, which, at this moment, held a numberless throng of people, processionists and spectators, the latter, as at all the other points of the route, exhibiting prominently the sable and green emblems, which evidenced their approval of the demonstration. The hearses slowly passed along, followed by the mourning carriages, the bands playing alternately "*Adeste Fideles*" and the "Dead March," and then followed the deep column of the processionists, still marching onwards with unflagging spirit, thousands seeming to be thoroughly soaked with the rain, which was falling all the morning. Sackville-street was perhaps the best point from which to get a correct notion of the enormous length of the procession, and of the great numbers that accompanied it on its way without actually entering the ranks. The base of the Nelson monument was covered with spectators, and at the corners of Earl-street and Henry-street there were stationary crowds, who chose these positions to get a good view of the great display as it progressed towards Cavendish-row. Through this comparatively narrow thorougfare the procession passed along into North Frederick-street and Blessington-street, and thence by Upper Berkeley-street to the Circular-road. Along this part of the route there were crowds of spectators, male and female, most of whom wore the crape and green ribbons, all hurrying forward to the cemetery, the last stage of the long and fatiguing journey of the procession. As the first part of the array passed the Mater Misericordiae Hospital, and came in sight of the Mountjoy Prison, they gave a cheer, which was caught up by those behind, and, as file after file passed the prison, the cheers were repeated. With unbroken and undiminished ranks the procession pressed on towards Glasnevin; but when the head had reached the cemetery, the closing section must have been far away in the city. The first part of the procession halted outside the gate of the cemetery, the spacious area in front of which was in a few moments completely filled by the dense masses who came up. A move then became necessary, and accordingly the procession recommenced its journey by passing through the open gates of the cemetery down the pathways leading to the M'Manus grave, followed by some of the bands playing the "*Adeste Fideles.*" As fast as the files passed through, others marched up, and, when, after some time, the carriage containing Mr. John Martin arrived, the open ground fronting the cemetery was one enormous mass of the processionists; while behind, on the road leading up to this point, thousands were to be seen moving slowly forward to the strains of the "Dead March" given out by the bands immediately in front of the hearses.

MR. MARTIN'S ADDRESS.

On the arrival of the procession at the cemetery Mr. Martin was hailed with loud applause. It being understood he would make some observations, the multitude gathered together to hear him. He addressed the vast multitude from the window of a house overlooking the great open space in front of the cemetery. On presenting himself he was received with enthusiastic cheering. When silence was obtained, he said :—

"Fellow-countrymen:—This is a strange kind of funeral procession in which we are engaged to-day. We are here, a vast multitude of men, women, and children, in a very inclement season of the year, under rain and through mud. We are here escorting three empty hearses to the consecrated last resting-place of those who die in the Lord (cheers). The three bodies that we would tenderly bear to the churchyard, and would bury in consecrated ground with all the solemn rites of religion, are not here. They are away in a foreign and hostile land (hear, hear), where they have been thrown into unconsecrated ground, branded by the triumphant hatred of our enemies as the vile remains of murderers (cries of 'No murderers,' and cheers). Those three men whose memories we are here to-day to honor—Allen, O'Brien, and Larkin—they were not murderers (great cheering). (A Voice—Lord, have mercy on them.) These men were pious men, virtuous men—they were men who feared God and loved their country. They sorrowed for the sorrows of the dear old native land of their love (hear, hear). They wished, if possible, to save her, and for that love and for that wish they were doomed to an ignominious death at the hands of the British hangman (hear, hear). It was as Irish patriots that these men were doomed to death (cheers). And it was as patriots that they met their death (cheers). For these reasons, my countrymen, we here to-day have joined this solemn procession to honor their memories (cheers). For that reason we say from our hearts, 'May their souls rest in peace' (cries of Amen, and cheers). For that reason, my countrymen, we join in their last prayer, 'God save Ireland' (enthusiastic cheering). The death of these three men was an act of English policy. (Here there was some interruption caused by the fresh arrivals and the pushing forward.) I beg of all within reach of my voice to end this demonstration as we have carried it through to the present time, with admirable patience, in the best spirit, with respect, silence, and solemnity, to the end (cheers, and cries of 'We will'). I say the death of these men was a legal murder, and that legal murder was an act of English policy (cheers)—of the policy of that nation which, through jealousy and hatred of our nation, destroyed by fraud and force our just government sixty-seven years ago (cheers). They have been sixty-seven sad years of insult and robbery—of impoverishment—of extermination—of suffering beyond what any other subject people but ours have ever endured from the malignity of foreign masters (cheers). Nearly through all these years the Irish people continued to pray for the restoration of their Irish national rule. They offered their forgiveness to England. They offered even their friendship to England, if she would only give up her usurped power to tyrannize over us, and leave us to live in peace as honorable neighbors. But in vain. England felt herself strong enough to continue to insult and rob us, and she was too greedy and too insolent to cease from robbing and insulting us (cheers). Now it has come to pass as a consequence of that malignant policy pursued for so many long years—it has come to pass that the great body of the Irish people despair of obtaining peaceful restitution of our national rights (cheers). And it has also come to pass that vast numbers of Irishmen, whom the oppression of English rule forbade to live by honest industry in their own country, have in America learned to become soldiers (cheers). And those Irish soldiers seem resolved to make war against England (cheers). And England is in a panic of rage and fear in consequence of this (loud cheers). And being in a panic about Fenianism, she hopes to strike terror into her Irish malcontents by a legal murder (loud cheers). England wanted to show that she was not afraid of Fenianism. (A Voice—'She will be.') And she has only shown that she is not afraid to do injustice in the face of Heaven and of man. Many a wicked statute has she framed—many a jury has she packed, in order to dispose of her Irish political offenders: but, in the case of Allen, O'Brien, and Larkin, she has committed such an outrage on justice and decency as to make even many Englishmen stand aghast. I shall not detain you with entering into details, with which you are all well acquainted, as to the shameful scenes of the handcuffing of the untried prisoners—as to the shameful scenes of the trial up to the last moment, when the three men, our dearly beloved Irish brethren, were forced to give up their innocent lives as a sacrifice for the cause of Ireland (loud cheers); and, fellow-countrymen, these three humble Irishmen who represented Ireland on that sad occasion demeaned themselves as Christians, as patriots, modestly, courageously, piously, nobly (loud cheers). We need not blush for them. They bore themselves all through with a courage worthy of the greatest heroes that ever obtained glory upon earth. They behaved through all the trying scenes I referred to with Christian patience—with resignation to the will of God—(hear, hear)—with modest, yet proud and firm adherence to principle (cheers). They showed their love to Ireland and their fear of God from the first to the last (cheers). It is vain for me to attempt to detain you with many words upon this matter. I will say this, that all who are here do not approve of the schemes for the relief of Ireland that these men were supposed to have contemplated; but all who love Ireland, all generous, Christian men, and women, and children of Ireland—all the children growing up to be men and women of Ireland (hear, hear)—all those feel an intense sympathy, an intense love, for the memories of these three men whom England has murdered in form of law by way of striking terror into her Irish subjects. Fellow-countrymen, it is idle almost for me to persist in addressing weak words of mine to you—for your presence here to-day—your demeanor all through—the solemn conduct of the vast multitude assembled directly under the terrorism of a hostile government—say more than the words of the greatest orator—more than the words of a Meagher could say for you (cheers). You have behaved yourselves all through this day with most admirable spirit as good Irishmen and women—as good boys and girls of holy Ireland ought to do (cheers), and I am sure you will behave so to the end (cries of, Yes, yes). This demonstration is mainly one of mourning for the fate of these three good Irishmen (cheers), but fellow-countrymen, and women, and boys, and girls, it is also one of protest and indignation against the conduct of our rulers (hear, hear, and cheers). Your attendance here to-day is a sufficient protest. Your orderly behavior—your good temper all through this wretched weather—your attendance here in such vast numbers for such a purpose—avowedly and in the face of the terrorism of the government, which falls most directly upon the metropolis—that is enough for protest. You in your multitudes, men, women, and children, have to-day made that protest. Your conduct has been admirable for patience, for good-nature, for fine spirit, for solemn sense of that great duty you were resolved to do. You will return home with the same good order and inoffensiveness. You will join with me now in repeating the prayer of the three martyrs whom we mourn—'God save Ireland!' And all of you, men, women, and boys and girls that are to be men and women of holy Ireland, will ever keep the sentiment of that prayer in your heart of hearts." Mr. Martin concluded amid enthusiastic cheering.

At the conclusion of his address, Mr. Martin, accompanied by a large body of the processionists, proceeded to the cemetery, where Mr. Martin visited the grave of Terence Bellew M'Manus. The crowds walked around the grave as a mark of respect for the memory of M'Manus. Mr. Martin left the cemetery soon after, and went to his carriage; the people gathered about him and thanked him, and cheered him loudly. The vast assemblage dispersed in the most orderly and peaceful manner, and returned to their homes. They had suffered much from the severity of the day, but they exhibited to the end the most creditable endurance and patience. In the course of an hour the roads were cleared, and the city soon resumed its wonted quiet aspect.*

Of the number in the procession, "An Eye-witness," writing in the *Freeman*, says :—

The procession took one hour and forty minutes to pass the Four Courts. Let us assume that as the average time in which it would pass any given point, and deduct ten minutes for delays during that time. If, then, it moved at the rate of two and a-half miles per hour, we find that its length, with those suppositions, would be three and three-quarter miles. From this deduct a quarter of a mile for breaks or discrepancies, and we find the length of the column, if it moved in a continuous line, to be three and a-half miles. We may now suppose the ranks to be three feet apart, and consisting of ten in each, at an average. The total number is therefore easily obtained by dividing the product of $3\frac{1}{2}$ and 5,280 by 3, and multiplying the quotient by 10. This will give as a result 61,600, which, I think, is a fair approximation to the number of people in the procession alone.

Even in the columns of the *Irish Times* a letter appeared giving an honest estimate of the number in the procession. It was signed " T. M. G.," and said :—

I believe there were not fewer than 60,000 persons taking part in the procession on Sunday. My point of observation was one of the best in the city, seeing, as I could, from the entrance to the Lower Castle Yard to the College Gates. I was as careful in my calculation as an almost quick march would allow. There were also a few horsemen, three hearses, and sixty-one hired carriages, cabs, and cars. A correspondent in your columns this morning speaks of rows of from four to nine deep; I saw very many of from ten to sixteen deep, especially among the boys. The procession took exactly eighty minutes to pass this. There were several thousand on-lookers within my view.

Of the ladies in the procession the *Freeman's Journal*

---

*In consequence of some vile misstatements in the government press, which represented the crowd to have not only behaved recklessly, but to have done considerable damage to the graves, tombs, shrubs and fences in the cemetery, Mr. Coyle, secretary to the Cemetery Board, published in the *Freeman* an official contradiction, stating that not one sixpence worth of damage had been done. It is furthermore worthy of note, that, at the city police offices next morning, not one case arising out of the procession was before the magistrates, and the charges for drunkenness were one-fourth below the average on Monday!

bore the following testimony, not more generous than truthful:—

The most important physical feature was not, however, the respectable dress, the manly bearing, the order, discipline, and solemnity of the men, but the large bodies of ladies who, in rich and costly attire, marched the whole length of the long route, often ankle-deep in mud, utterly regardless of the incessant down-pour of rain which deluged their silks and satins, and melted the mourning crape till it seemed incorporated with the very substance of the velvet mantles or rich shawls in which so many of the fair processionists were enveloped. In vain did well-gloved hands hold thousands of green parasols and umbrellas over their heads as they walked four and five deep through the leading thoroughfares yesterday. The bonnets with their "green and crape" were alone defensible: velvets and Paisleys, silks and satins, met one common fate—thorough saturation. Yet all this and more was borne without a murmur. These ladies, and there were many hundreds of them, mingled with thousands in less rich attire, went out to coöperate with their fathers, brothers, and sweethearts in honoring three men who died upon the ignominious gallows, and they never flinched before the torrents, or swerved for an instant from the ranks. There must be some deep and powerful influence underlying this movement that could induce thousands of matrons and girls of from eighteen to two-and twenty, full of the blushing modesty that distinguishes Irishwomen, to lay aside their retiring characteristics, and march to the sound of martial music through every thoroughfare in the metropolis of this country decked in green and crape.

The Dublin correspondent of the *Tipperary Free Press* referred to the demonstration as follows:—

Arrived in Sackville-street, we were obliged to leave our cab and endeavor, on foot, to force our way to our destination. This magnificent street was crowded to repletion, and the approaches to Beresford-place were 'black with people.' It was found necessary, owing to the overwhelming numbers that assembled, to start the procession before the hour named for its setting forth, and so it was commenced in wonderful order, considering the masses that had to be welded into shape. Marshals on foot and on horseback proceeded by the side of those in rank and file, and they certainly were successful in preserving regularity of procedure. Mourning-coaches and cabs followed, and after each was a procession of women, at least a thousand in number. Young and old were there—all decked in some shape or other with green; many green dresses—some had green feathers in their hats, but all had green ribbons prominently displayed. The girls bore all the disagreeability of the long route with wonderful endurance; it was bitterly cold—a sleety rain fell during the entire day, and the roads were almost ankle-deep in mud—yet, when they passed me on the return route, they were apparently as unwearied as when I saw them hours before. As the procession trooped by—thousand after thousand—there was not a drunken man to be seen—all were calm and orderly ; and if they were, as many of them were, soaked through—wet to the skin—they endured the discomfort resolutely. The numbers in the procession have been variously estimated, but in my opinion there could not have been less than 50,000. But the demonstration was not confined to the processionists alone; they walked through living walls, for along the entire route a mass of people lined the way, the great majority of whom wore some emblem of mourning, and every window of every house was thronged with ladies and children, nearly all of whom were decorated. All semblance of authority was withdrawn from sight, but every preparation had been made under the personal direction of Lord Strathnairn, the commander-in-chief, for the instant intervention of the military, had any disturbances taken place. The troops were confined to barracks since Saturday evening; they were kept in readiness to march at a moment's notice; the horses of the cavalry were saddled all day long, and those of the artillery were in harness. A battery of guns was in the rear yard of the Four Courts, and mounted orderlies were stationed at arranged points so as to convey orders to the different barracks as speedily as possible. But, thanks to Providence, all passed off quietly; the people seemed to feel the responsibility of their position, and accordingly not even an angry word was to be heard throughout the vast assemblage that for hours surged through the highways of the city.

The *Ulster Observer*, in the course of a beautiful and sympathetic article, touched on the great theme as follows :—

The main incidents of the singular and impressive event are worthy of reflection. On a cold December morning, wet and dreary as any morning in December might be, vast crowds assembled in the heart of Dublin to follow to consecrated ground the empty hearses which bore the names of the Irishmen whom England doomed to the gallows as murderers. The air was piercingly chill, the rain poured down in torrents, the streets were almost impassable from the accumulated pools of mingled water and mud, yet 80,000 people braved the inclemency of the weather, and unfalteringly carried out the programme so fervently adopted. Amongst the vast multitude there were, not only stalwart men, capable of facing the difficulties of the day, but old men who struggled through and defied them; and, strangest of all, "young ladies, clothed in silk and velvet," and women with tender children by their sides, all of whom continued to the last to form a part of the *cortége*, although the distance over which it passed must have taxed the strongest physical energy. What a unanimity of feeling, or rather what a naturalness of sentiment does not this wonderful demonstration exhibit! It seems as if the "God save Ireland" of the humble successors of Emmet awoke in even the breast of infancy the thrill which must have vibrated sternly and strongly in the heart of manhood. Without exalting into classical grandeur the simple and affectionate devotion of a simple and unsophisticated people, we might compare this spectacle to that which ancient Rome witnessed, when the ashes of Germanicus were borne in solemn state within her portals. There were there the attendant crowd of female mourners, and the bowed heads and sorrowing hearts of strong men. If the Irish throngs had no hero to lament, who sustained their glory in the field, and gained for them fresh laurels of victory, theirs was at least a more disinterested tribute of grief, since it was paid to the unpretending merit which laid down life with the simple prayer of "God save Ireland!" Amidst all the numerous thousands who proceeded to Glasnevin. there was not, probably, one who would have sympathized with any criminal offence, much less with the hideous one of murder. And yet these thousands honored and revered the memory of the men condemned in England as assassins, and ignominiously buried in felons' graves.

This mighty demonstration—at once so unique, so solemn, so impressive, so portentous—was an event which the rulers of Ireland felt to be of critical importance. Following upon the Requiem Masses and the other processions, it amounted to a great public verdict which changed beyond all resistance the moral character of the Manchester trial and execution. If the procession could only have been called a "Fenian" demonstration, then, indeed, the government might hope to detract from its significance and importance. The sympathy of "conspirators" with fallen companions could not well be claimed as an index of general *public opinion.* But here was a demonstration, notoriously apart from Fenianism, and it showed that a moral, a peaceable, a virtuous, a religious people, moved by the most virtuous and religious instincts, felt themselves coerced to execrate as a cowardly and revolting crime the act of state policy consummated on the Manchester gibbet. In fine, the country was up in moral revolt against a deed which the perpetrators themselves already felt to be of evil character, and one which they fain would blot forever from public recollection.

What was to be done? For the next ensuing Sunday

similar demonstrations were announced in Killarney, Kilkenny, Drogheda, Ennis, Clonmel, Queenstown, Youghal, and Fermoy—the preparations in the first-named town being under the direction of, and the procession about to be led by, a member of parliament, one of the most distinguished and influential of the Irish popular representatives—The O'Donoghue. What was to be done? Obviously, as the men had been hanged, there could be no halting half-way now. Having gone so far, the government seemed to feel that it must needs go the whole way, and choke off, at all hazards, these inconvenient, these damnatory public protests. No man must be allowed to speak the unutterable words, which, like the handwriting on the wall in the banqueting hall of Belshazzar, seemed ever to be appearing before the affrighted conscience of Ireland's rulers. Be it right or be it wrong, be it justice or be it murder, the act must now be upheld—in fact, must not be alluded to. There must be *silence*, by law, on what had been done beneath the Manchester gallows-tree.

But here there presented itself a difficulty. Before the government had any idea that the public revulsion would become so alarmingly extensive, the responsible ministers of the Crown, specifically interrogated on the point, had, as we have seen, declared the funeral processions not to be illegal, and how, now, could the government interpose to prevent them? It certainly was a difficulty which there was no way of surmounting save by a proceeding which, in any country constitutionally governed, would cost its chief authors their lives on impeachment. The government, notwithstanding the words of its own responsible chiefs—*on the faith of which the Dublin procession was held, and numerous others were announced*—decided to treat as illegal the proceedings they had but a week before declared to be *not* illegal; decided to prosecute the processionists who had acted on the government declarations; and decided to prevent, by sabre and cannon—by slaughter, if necessary—the further processions announced in Killarney, Clonmel, Kilkenny, and elsewhere!

On the evening of Thursday, the 12th December,

Dublin city was flung into the most intense excitement by the issue of the following Government Proclamation:—

BY THE LORD LIEUTENANT AND COUNCIL OF IRELAND.

A PROCLAMATION.

ABERCORN.

Whereas it has been publicly announced that a meeting is to assemble in the city of *Kilkenny*, and that a procession is to take place there on Sunday, 15th of December instant:

And whereas placards of the said intended meeting and procession have been printed and circulated, stating that the said intended procession is to take place in honor of certain men lately executed in Manchester for the crime of murder, and calling upon Irishmen to assemble in thousands for the said procession :

And whereas meetings and processions of large numbers of persons have been already held and have taken place in different parts of the United Kingdom of Great Britain and Ireland under the like pretence, at some of which, and particularly at a meeting and procession in the city of Dublin, language of a seditious and inflammatory character has been used, calculated to excite discontent and disaffection in the minds of her Majesty's subjects, and to create ill-will and animosity amongst them, and to bring into hatred and contempt the government and constitution of the country as by law established :

And whereas the said intended meeting and procession, and the objects of the persons to be assembled, and take part therein, are not legal or constitutional, but are calculated to bring into hatred and contempt the government of the United Kingdom as by law established, and to impede the administration of justice by intimidation and the demonstration of physical force.

Now, we, the Lord Lieutenant and General Governor of Ireland, by and with the advice of her Majesty's Privy Council in Ireland, being satisfied that such meetings and processions as aforesaid can only tend to serve the ends of factious, seditious, and traitorous persons, and to the violation of the public peace, do hereby caution and forewarn all persons whomsoever that they do abstain from assembling at any such meeting, and from joining or taking part in any such procession.

And we do hereby order and enjoin all magistrates and officers intrusted with the preservation of the public peace, and others whom it may concern, to aid and assist the execution of the law, in preventing the said intended meeting and procession, and in the effectual suppression of the same.

Given at the Council Chamber in Dublin, this twelfth day of December, 1867.

RICHARD C. DUBLIN.	R. KEATINGE.
A. BREWSTER, C.	WILLIAM KEOGH.
MAYO.	JOHN E. WALSH.
STRATHNAIRN.	HEDGES EYRE CHATTERTON.
FRED. SHAW.	ROBERT R. WARREN.

Everybody knew what this proclamation meant. It plainly enough announced that not only would the further demonstrations be prevented, but that the Dublin processionists were to feel "the vengeance of the law"— that is, the vengeance of the Manchester executioners. Next day the city was beset with the wildest rumors as to the arrests to be made or the prosecutions to be commenced. Everyone seemed to conclude, of course, that Mr. John Martin, Mr. A. M. Sullivan, and the Honorary Secretaries of the Procession Committee, were on the Crown Prosecutor's list; but, besides these, the names of dozens of gentlemen who had been on the committee, or who had acted as stewards, marshals, etc., at the funeral, were likewise mentioned. On Saturday it became known that, late on the previous evening, crown summonses had been served on Mr. J. J. Lalor, Dr. J. C. Waters, and Mr. James Scanlan, requiring them to attend on the following Tuesday at the head police office to answer informations sworn against them for taking part in an "illegal procession" and a "seditious assembly." A summons had been taken out also against Mr. Martin; but, as he had left Dublin for home on Friday, the police officers proceeded after him to Kilbroney, and "served" him there on Saturday evening.

Beside and behind this open move was a secret Castle plot, so utterly disreputable that, as we shall see, the Attorney-General, startled by the shout of universal execration which it elicited, sent his official representative into public court to repudiate it as far as *he* was concerned, and to offer a public apology to the gentlemen aggrieved by it. The history of that scandalous proceeding will appear in what follows.

On Monday, 16th December, 1867, the head police office, Exchange-court, Dublin, presented an excited scene. The daily papers of the day report the proceedings as follows:—

At one o'clock, the hour appointed by the summons, the defendants attended in court, accompanied by their professional advisers and a number of friends, including Alderman Plunkett, Mr. Butler, T. C.; the Rev. P. Langan, P. P., Ardcath; A. M. Sullivan, T. C.; T. D. Sullivan, J. J. Lalor, etc. Mr. Dix and Mr. Allen, divisional magistrates, presided. Mr. James Murphy, Q. C., instructed by Mr. Anderson, represented the Crown. Mr. Heron, Q. C., and Mr. Molloy appeared for J. J. Lalor. Mr. Crean appeared for Dr. Waters. Mr. Scallan appeared as solicitor for J. J. Lalor and for Dr. Waters.

It was generally understood, on arrival at the head office, that the cases would be heard in the usual court upstairs, and, accordingly, the defendants and the professional gentlemen waited in the court for a considerable time after one o'clock. It was then stated that the magistrates would sit in another court downstairs, and all the parties moved towards the door for the purpose of going there. Then another arrangement was made, that the change would not take place, and the parties concerned thereupon returned to their places. But in a few minutes it was again announced that the proceedings would be in the court downstairs. A general movement was made again by defendants, by counsel, by solicitors, and others towards that court, but, on arriving at the entrances, they were guarded by detectives and police. The benches, which ought to have been reserved for the bar and solicitors, and also for the press, were occupied by detectives, and for a considerable time great difficulty was experienced in getting places.

Mr. George M'Dermott, barrister, applied to the magistrates to assign a place for the members of the bar.

Mr. Dix:—I don't know that the bar, unless they are engaged in the cases, have any greater privilege than any one else. We have a wretched court here.

Mr. M'Dermott said the bar was entitled to have room made for them when it could be done.

Mr. W. L. Hackett:—All the seats should not be occupied by policemen to the exclusion of the bar.

Mr. Scallan, solicitor, who spoke from the end of the table, said: —Your worships, I am solicitor for one of the traversers, and I cannot get near my counsel to communicate with him. The court is filled with detectives.

Mr. Molloy:—My solicitor has a right to be here; I want my solicitor to be near me.

Mr. Dix:—Certainly: how can men defend their clients if they are inconvenienced?

An appeal was then made to the detectives, who occupied the side bar behind the counsel, to make way.

Mr. Murphy, Q. C., said one was a policeman who was summoned.

Mr. Dix:—The police have no right to take seats.

The detectives then yielded, and the professional gentlemen and the reporters were accommodated.

Mr. Dix then called the cases.

Mr. Molloy:—I appear with Mr. Heron, Q. C., on behalf of J. J. Lalor.

Mr. Crean:—I appear for Dr. Waters.

Mr. John Martin:—I appear on behalf of myself.

Mr. Crean:—I understand there is an impression that Dr. Waters has been summoned, but he has not.

Mr. Dix :—If he appears, that cures any defect.
Mr. Crean :—I appear on his behalf, but I believe his personal attendance is necessary.
Mr. Dix :—Does any one appear for Mr. Scanlan ?
There was no answer.
Mr. Murphy, Q. C.:—I ask whether Dr. Waters and Mr. Lalor appear in court.
Mr. Molloy :—My client Mr. Lalor is in court.
Mr. Crean:—I believe my client is not in court.
Mr. Murphy, Q. C.:—I will prove the service of the summons against Dr. Waters. If there is any defect in the summons, it can be remedied. I will not proceed against any person who does not appear.
Mr. Dix :—Am I to take it there is no appearance for Dr. Waters or Mr. Scanlan ?
Mr. Crean : —I appear for Dr. Waters. I believe he is not in court. It was stated in the newspapers that he was summoned, but I am instructed he has not been summoned at all.

Mr. Murphy, Q. C., then proceeded in a careful and precise address to state the case for the Crown. When he had concluded, and was about calling evidence, the following singular episode took place :—

Mr. Dix:—You only proceed against two parties ?
Mr. Murphy:—I shall only proceed against the parties who attend. Against those who do not attend, I shall not give evidence.
Mr. John Martin :—If I am in order I would say, to save the time of the court and to save the public money, that I would be very glad to offer every facility to the Crown. I believe, sir, you (to Mr. Murphy) are the Crown ?
Mr. Murphy : —I represent the Crown.
Mr. Martin :—I will offer every facility to the Crown for establishing the facts both as to my conduct and my words.
Mr. A. M. Sullivan :—I also will help you to put up some one, as you seem scarce of the accused. I have been summoned myself——
Mr. Dix :—Who are you ?
Mr. Sullivan :—My name is Alexander M. Sullivan, and, meaning no disrespect to either of the magistrates, I publicly refuse even to be sworn. I was present at the funeral procession—I participated in it openly, deliberately, heartily—and I denounce as a personal and public outrage the endeavor to degrade the national press of this country by attempting to place in the light of——
Mr. Dix :—I cannot allow this. This is not a place for making speeches. I understand you are not summoned here at all.
Mr. Murphy :—He is only summoned as a witness.
Mr. Dix :—When you (to Mr. Sullivan) are called on will be the time to hear you ; not now.
Mr. Sullivan :—I ask your worship, with your usual courtesy, to

hear me while I complain publicly of endeavoring to place the editor of a national journal on the list of crown witnesses in this court as a public and personal indignity—and as an endeavor to destroy the influence of that national press, whose power they feel and fear, but which they dare not prosecute. I personally complain——

Mr. Murphy :—I don't know that this should be permitted.

Mr. Sullivan : —Don't interrupt me for a moment.

Mr. Dix :— Mr. Sullivan wants to have himself included in the summons and charge.

Mr. Murphy :—That cannot be done at present.

Mr. Sullivan :—With one sentence I will conclude.

Mr. Murphy :—I don't intend to have you called as a witness——

Mr. Sullivan :—It is an endeavor to accomplish my imprisonment for contempt, when the government, "willing to wound, afraid to strike," know that they dare not accuse me as a Fenian——

Mr. Dix :—You are not here as a Fenian.

Mr. Sullivan :—For a moment. Knowing well, your worship, that they could not get in all Ireland a jury to convict me, to secure my imprisonment openly and fairly, they do this. I now declare that I participated in that funeral, and I defy those who were guilty of such cowardice as to subpœna me as a crown witness (applause).

Mr. Crean :—I perceive that my client. Dr. C. Waters, is now in court. In order to facilitate business, I shall offer no further objection ; but, as a matter of fact, he was not summoned.

Then the case proceeded, the police giving their evidence, on the whole, very fairly, and testifying that the procession was one of the most peaceable, orderly, solemn, and impressive public demonstrations ever seen in Dublin. Against Mr. Martin it was testified that he marched at the head of the procession arm-in-arm with Mr. A. M. Sullivan and another gentleman ; and that he delivered the memorable speech at the cemetery gate. Against Dr. Waters and Mr. Lalor it was advanced that they were honorary secretaries of the funeral committee, and had moreover acted, the former as a marshal, the latter as a steward, in the procession. It was found, however, that the case could not be closed that day ; and accordingly, late in the evening, the magistrates intimated that they would adjourn over to next morning. Suddenly, from the body of the court, is heard a stentorian voice:

Mr. Bracken:—I am summoned here as a crown witness. My name is Thomas Bracken. I went, heart and soul, into that procession (applause)——

Mr. Anderson, Junior :—I don't know this gentleman.

Mr. Bracken :—I am very proud that neither you nor any one like you knows me (applause).

Mr. Dix :—I cannot hear you.

Mr. Bracken :—I have been brought here as a crown witness away from my business, and am losing my time here.

Mr. Donal Sullivan :—I am another, and I avow myself in the same way.

Several voices :—So am I.

Mr. Bracken :—I want to know why I should be taken from my business, by which I have to support my family, and put me before the eyes of my countrymen as a crown witness (applause). I went heart and soul into the procession, and I am ready to do the same to-morrow, and abide by the consequences (applause). It is curious that the government should point me out as a witness.

Mr. Murphy :—I ask for an adjournment till to-morrow.

Mr. Dix :—It is more convenient to adjourn now.

Mr. Martin :—I don't want to make any insinuations against the gentlemen who represent the Crown, nor against the police, but I mention the fact, in order that they may relieve themselves from the odium which would attach to them if they cannot explain it. This morning a paragraph appears in one of the principal Dublin daily papers, the *Irish Times*, in which it is said that I, John Martin, have absconded : I must presume that the information was supplied to that paper either by the crown representatives or by the police.

Mr. Murphy, Q. C. :—It is right to state, so far as I am informed, that an endeavor was made to serve Mr. Martin in Dublin. When the summonses were issued he was not in Dublin, but had gone down to the country, either to his own or the house of his brother, or——

Mr. Ross Todd, who sat beside Mr. Martin, here jumped up and said :—To his own house, sir, to his own house.

Mr. Murphy :—Very well. A constable was sent down there, and saw Mr. Martin, and he reported that Mr. Martin said he would attend forthwith.

Mr. Dix :—And he has done so?

Mr. Murphy :—I have no other knowledge. It was briefed to me that Mr. Martin said he would attend forthwith.

Mr. Martin :—I am glad I have given the representatives of the Crown an opportunity of making that statement. But I cannot understand how, when the representatives of the Crown had the information, and when I told the constables I would attend—as I have done at great inconvenience and expense to myself—I cannot understand how a newspaper should come to say I had absconded.

Mr. Murphy :—I cannot understand it either; I can only tell the facts within my own knowledge.

Mr. Molloy said it seemed very extraordinary that witnesses should be summoned, and the Crown say they were not.

Mr. Sullivan wished his summons to be examined. Did the magistrates sign it?

Mr. Dix:—Unless I saw the original I could not say.

Mr. J. J. Lalor:—Sir John Gray has been summoned as a witness, too It is monstrous.

Sir John Gray, M.P.:—I wish to state to your worship the unpleasant circumstances under which I find myself placed. At an advanced hour on Saturday I learned that the Crown intended to summon as witnesses for the prosecution some of the gentlemen connected with my establishment. I immediately communicated with the Crown Prosecutor, and said it was unfair towards these gentlemen to have them placed in such an odious position, and that their refusal to act as crown witnesses might subject them to serious personal consequences ; I said it would not be right of me to allow any of the gentlemen of my establishment to subject themselves to the consequences of such refusal, as I knew well they would all refuse. I suggested, if any unpleasant consequences should follow, they should fall on the head of the establishment alone (applause). I said, " Summon me, and deal with me." I am here now, sir, to show my respect for you personally and for this court ; but I wish to state most distinctly that I will never consent to be examined as a crown witness (applause).

Mr. Anderson, Jun., here interposed.

Sir John Gray:—I beg your pardon. I am addressing the bench, and I hope I won't be interrupted. Some of my family are going to-night to England to spend the Christmas with my son. I intend to escort them. I will not be here to-morrow. I wish distinctly to state so. If I were here, my respect for you and the bench would induce me to be present, but I would be present only to declare what I have already stated, that I would not consent to be sworn or to give any evidence whatever in this prosecution. I think it right to add that I attach no blame whatever to the police authorities in this transaction. They have, I am sure, performed their duty in this case with that propriety which has always characterized their conduct. Neither do I attach any blame to the Crown Prosecutor. I simply desire to state, with the most profound respect for the bench and the court, that I will not be a witness (loud applause).

Mr. Anderson:—We don't intend to examine Sir John Gray, but I wish to say that, if the police believed any one could give important evidence, it is a new proposition to me that it is an indignity upon a man to summon him as a crown witness——

Mr. A. M. Sullivan:—I say it is an indignity, and that the Crown Solicitor should not seek to shift the responsibility on the police, who only do what they are told.

Mr. Anderson:—I am not trying to shift anything.

Mr. Sullivan:—You are. You are trying to shift the responsibility of having committed a gross indignity upon a member of parliament, upon myself, and upon many honest men here.

Several persons holding up summonses said, " Hear, hear," and " Yes."

Mr. Sullivan:—This I charge to have been done by Mr. Anderson as his base revenge upon honest men who bade him defiance. Mr. Anderson must answer for this conduct. It is a vile conspiracy—a plot against honest men, who here now to his face tell him they scorn and defy him (applause).

Mr. Dix:—I adjourn the case till one o'clock to-morrow.

The proceedings were then adjourned.

So far have we quoted from the *Freeman's Journal.* Of the closing scene *Saunders's News-Letter,* grieving sorely over such a fiasco, gives the following account:—

The adjournment of the court was attended with a scene of tumult and disorder that was rarely, or never, witnessed in a police court, in presence of the magistrates and a large number of police—both inspectors and detectives. The crowd of unwilling witnesses who had been summoned to give evidence against the defendants, clamorously protested against being brought there as crown witnesses, avowed that they were present taking part in the procession, and loudly declared that they would not attend at any subsequent hearing of the case. The latter part of the case, indeed, was marked with frequent interruptions and declarations of a similar kind, often very vociferously uttered. The proceedings terminated amid the greatest and unchecked disorder.

In plain words, " Scene I, Act I," in what was meant to be a most solemn, awe-inspiring government function, turned out an unmistakable farce, if not a disastrous break-down. Even the government journals themselves, without waiting for " Scene II," (though coming off immediately), raised a shout of condemnation at the discreditable bungle, and demanded that it should be forthwith abandoned. Considering the course ultimately taken by the government, these utterances of the government organs themselves have a serious meaning, and are of peculiar importance. The ultra-conservative *Evening Mail* (Tuesday, 17th December) said:—

THE POLICE COURT SCENE.

The scenes of yesterday in the Dublin police-court will cause an astonished public to put the question, Is the government insane? They suppress the processions one day, and on the next proceed with deliberation to destroy all possible effect from such an act by inviting the magistrates' court to be used as a platform from which a fresh roar of defiance may be uttered. The originators of the seditious demonstrations are charged with having brought the government of the kingdom into hatred and contempt; but what step taken, or word spoken or written, from the date of the first procession to the last, brought the government into anything like the "contempt" into which it plunged itself yesterday? The prosecutions now instituted are in themselves an act of utter weakness. We so declared when we imagined that they would be at least rationally conducted; but what is to be said now? It is literally impossible to give any sane explanation of the course taken in summoning as a crown witness one who must have been known to be prepared to boast of his participation in the procession. Mr. Sullivan boldly bearded the prosecutors of his brethren. It was a splendid opportunity for him. "I was present," he said, "at that funeral procession. I participated in it, deliberately and heartily. I call this a personal and public outrage, to endeavor to drag the national press of this country——" Timid and ineffectual attempts were made by the magistrate to protect his court and position from insult, but Mr. Sullivan had the field, and would hold it. "He might help the Crown to put some one else up," he said, "as they are scarce, perhaps, in accused." The summoning of him was, he resumed, an "attempt to destroy the national press, whose power the Crown feels and fears, but which they dare not prosecute." Mr. Sullivan was suffered to describe the conduct of the crown prosecutors at another stage as an "infamous plot." The government desired "to accomplish his imprisonment; they were willing to wound, but afraid to strike." "They knew," he added, "that they would not get a jury in all Ireland to agree to convict me; and I now characterize the conduct of the Crown as base and cowardly." Another witness, in a halting way, entered a like protest against being supposed to have sympathy with the Crown in the case; and the net result was a very remarkable triumph for what Mr. Sullivan calls the "national press"—a title wholly misapplied and grossly abused. Are we to have a succession of these "scenes in court"?

Saunders's News-Letter of the same date dealt with the subject as follows :—

The first step in what appears to be a very doubtful proceeding was taken yesterday by the law-advisers of the Crown. We refer to the prosecution instituted against the leaders and organizers of the Fenian procession which took place in this city on Sunday, the 8th instant, in honor of the memories of the men executed at Manchester for murder. As to the character of that demonstration we never entertained any doubt. But it must be remembered that similar demonstrations had taken place a week previously in London, in Manchester, and in Cork, and that not only did the authorities not interfere to prevent them, but that the prime minister declared in the House of Lords that they were not illegal. Lord Derby, doubtless, intended to limit his observations to the violation of the Party Processions Act, without pronouncing any opinion as to the legality or illegality of the processions, viewed under another aspect, as seditious assemblies. But his language was calculated to mislead, and, as a matter of fact, was taken by the Fenian sympathizers as an admission that their mock-funeral processions were not unlawful. It is not to be wondered at, therefore, however much to be deplored, that the disaffected portion of the population should have eagerly taken advantage of Lord Derby's declaration to make a safe display of their sympathies and of their strength. They were encouraged to do so by the toleration already extended towards their fellows in England and in Cork, as well as by the statement of the prime-minister. Under these circumstances the prosecution of persons who took part in the Dublin procession, even as organizers of that proceeding, appears to us to be a matter of doubtful policy. Mr. John Martin, the leader of the movement, stands in a different position from his companions. They confined themselves to walking in the procession; he delivered an inflammatory and seditious speech, for which he alone is responsible, and which might have been made the subject of a separate proceeding against him. To do Mr. Martin justice, he showed no desire to shirk the responsibility he has incurred. At the police-court, yesterday, he frankly avowed the part he had taken in the procession, and offered to acknowledge the speech which he delivered on that occasion. If, however, the policy which dictated the prosecution be questionable, there can be no doubt at all as to the objectionable manner in which some of the persons engaged in it have acted—assuming the statement to be true that Mr. Sullivan, proprietor and editor of the *Nation* newspaper, and Sir John Gray, proprietor of the *Freeman's Journal*, have been summoned as crown witnesses. Who is responsible for this extraordinary proceeding, it is at present impossible to say. Mr. Murphy, Q. C., the counsel for the Crown, declared that he did not intend to examine Mr. Sullivan ; Mr. Anderson, the son of the Crown Solicitor, who appears to be intrusted with the management of these prosecutions, denied that he had directed the summonses to be served, and Mr. Dix, the magistrate, stated that he had not signed them. Yet Mr. Sullivan produced the summons requiring him to attend as a witness, and in the strongest manner denounced the proceeding as a base and cowardly attempt on the part of the government to imprison for contempt of court a "national journalist" whom they dared not prosecute. Sir John Gray, in less violent language, complained of an effort having been made to place some of the gentlemen in his employment in the "odious position of crown witnesses," and stated that he himself had been subpœnaed, but would decline to give evidence. We have not concealed our opinion as to the proper way of dealing with Mr. Sullivan. As the weekly disseminator of most exciting and inflammatory articles, he is doing much to promote disaffection and encourage Fenianism. In no other country in the world would such writing be tolerated for a day ; and assuredly it ought not to be permitted in Ireland in perilous and exciting times like the present. But if Mr. Sullivan has offended against the law, let him be proceeded against boldly, openly, and fairly. He has, we think, a right to complain of being summoned as a witness for the Crown; but the government have even more reason to complain of the conduct of their servants in exposing them by their blunders to ridicule and contempt. It is too bad that, with a large and highly-paid staff of lawyers and attorneys, the government prosecutions should be conducted in a loose and slovenly manner. When a state prosecution has been determined upon, every step ought to be carefully and anxiously considered, and subordinate officials should not be permitted by acts of officious zeal to compromise their superiors and bring discredit on the administration of the law.

The Liberal-Conservative *Irish Times* was still more outspoken:—

While all commend the recent action of the government, and give the executive full credit for the repression by proclamation of processions avowedly intended to be protests against authority and law, it is generally regretted that prosecutions should have been instituted against some of those who had taken part in these processions. Had these menacing assemblages been held after the proclamations were issued, or in defiance of the authorities, the utmost power should have been exerted to put them down, and the terrors of the law would properly have been invoked to punish the guilty. But, bearing in mind the fact that these processions had been declared by the head of the government—expressing, no doubt, the opinion entertained at that time by the law officers of the Crown—that these processions were "not illegal;" remembering, too, that similar processions had been already held without the slightest intimation of opposition on the part of the government; and recollecting, also, that the proclamation was everywhere implicitly obeyed, and without the least wish to dispute it, we cannot avoid regretting that the government should have been advised, at the last hour, to institute prosecutions of such a nature. Once, however, it was determined to vindicate the law in this way, the utmost care should have been taken to maintain the dignity of the proceedings, and to avoid everything calculated to create annoyance, irritation, or offence. If we except the moderate and very able speech of Mr. Murphy, Q. C., there is no one part of the proceedings in the police-court which merits commendation. Some of the witnesses utterly broke down; opportunity was given for utterances not calculated to increase respect for the law; and disloyal sentiments were boldly expressed and cheered until the court rang again. Great and serious as was the mistake in not obtaining an accurate legal opinion respecting the character of these meetings at the first, and then prohibiting them, a far greater mistake is now, we think, committed in instituting *these retrospective prosecutions*. For this mistake the law-officers of the Crown must, we infer, be held responsible. Were they men of energy and vigor, with the necessary knowledge of the world, they would not have suffered the executive to permit processions first, and then prohibit them, and at the same time try men for participating in what had been pronounced not to be illegal. We exonerate the Attorney-General from the error of summoning to give evidence persons who openly gloried in the part they had taken in these meetings. To command the presence of such witnesses was of the nature of an offence. There was no ground, for instance, for supposing that Mr. Sullivan would have played the informer against the friends who had walked with him in the procession—such is not his character, his feeling, or his sense of honor. The summoning of those who had moved with, and as part of, the multitude, to give evidence against their fellows, was not only a most injudicious, but a futile expedient, and naturally has caused very great dissatisfaction and annoyance. The circumstance, however, proves that the prosecution was instituted without that exact care and minute attention to all particulars which are necessary in a case of this kind.

Even the *Daily Express*, the organ of the ultra-Orange section of the Irish administration, had to own the discomfiture of its patrons :—

Are our police offices to become a kind of national journals' court? Is the "national press of Ireland" then and there to bid for the support immediately of the gallery, and more remotely of that portion of the population which is humorously called the Irish Nation? These speculations are suggested by a curious scene which took place at the inquiry at the police office yesterday, and which will be found detailed in another column. Mr. Sullivan, the editor of the *Nation*, seized the opportunity of being summoned as a witness, to denounce the government for not including him in the prosecution. He complained "of endeavoring to place the editor of a national journal on the list of crown witnesses in this court as a public and personal indignity," and as an endeavor to destroy the influence of the national press. It is certainly an open avowal to declare that the mere placing of the name of the editor of a "national" journal upon the list of crown witnesses is an unparalleled wrong. But Sir John Gray was still more instructive. From him we learn that a witness summoned to assist the Crown in the prosecution of sedition is placed in an "odious position." Odious it may be, but in the eyes of whom? Surely not of any loyal subject. A paid informer, or professional spy, may be personally odious in the eyes of those who make use of his services. But we have yet to learn how a subject who is summoned to come forward to assist the government fills an odious position in the opinion of his loyal fellow-subjects. We should rather have supposed him to be entitled to their gratitude. However that may be, Sir John Gray came gallantly to the rescue of several "gentlemen connected with his establishment," whom, he was informed, the government intended to summon as witnesses. This, he knew, they would all refuse. "I suggested, if any unpleasant consequences should follow, that they should fall on the head of the establishment alone." He called upon the authorities to summon him. We do complain of our police-courts being made the scenes of open avowals of determination to thwart, or, at least, not to assist the government in their endeavors to prosecute treason and sedition. We can imagine no principle on which a subject could object to assisting the Crown as a witness, which, if followed to its logical consequences, would not justify open rebellion. It is certainly a dangerous doctrine to preach that it is allowable, nay, even praiseworthy in a subject to refuse to give evidence when called upon to do so by the Crown. There is a disposition too prevalent in this country to regard the law as an enemy, and opposition to it, either by passive obstruction or active rebellion, as a praiseworthy and patriotic act. Can we wonder at this when we hear opposition to constituted authority openly preached by the instructors of "the nation," and witness the eagerness of the "national press" to free itself from the terrible suspicion of coming to the assistance, even involuntarily, of the government in its struggle with sedition and treason?

It was amidst such an outburst of vexation and indignation as this, even from the government journals themselves, that the curtain rose next morning on Act II, in the head police office. A very unique episode commenced the proceedings on this day also. At the resumption of the case, Mr. Murphy, Q. C., on behalf of the Crown, said :—

Mr. Sullivan and some other gentlemen complained yesterday of having been served with summonses to give evidence in those cases. I am directed by the Attorney-General to state that he regrets it, and that it was done without his authority. He never gave any directions to have those persons summoned, nor was it done by any one acting under his directions. It occurred in this way. General directions were given to the police to summon parties to give evidence, in order to establish the charge against those four gentlemen who are summoned for taking an active part in the procession. The police, in the exercise of their discretion, thought it might be necessary to summon parties who took part in the procession, but there was no intention, on the part of those aiding on behalf of the Crown, to summon partiest to give evidence who themselves took part in the procession, and I am sorry it occurred.

Mr. Dix :—I may mention that a magistrate when signing a summons knows nothing of the witnesses. If they were all living in Jamaica, he merely signs it as a matter of form.

Mr. A. M. Sullivan :—I thank your worship and Mr. Murphy, and

I think it will be seen that, had your worship not allowed me yesterday to make the protest I did, the Attorney-General would not have the opportunity of making the disclaimer which it became the dignity of the government to make. The aspect of the case yesterday was very adverse towards Sir John Gray, myself, and other gentlemen. Although my brother signed his name to the notice, he was not summoned as principal but as a witness, but, if necessary, he was determined to stand side by side in the dock with Mr. Martin.

Mr. Allen :—I am very glad of the explanation, because I was blamed for allowing persons making speeches here yesterday. I think, if a man has any ground of complaint, the sooner it is set right the better.

Mr. Sullivan :—I have to thank the bench.

Mr. Allen :—I am glad that a satisfactory arrangement has been come to by all parties, because there is an objection entertained by some persons to be brought into court as witnesses for the Crown.

Mr. Sullivan :—Especially a public journalist.

Mr. Allen : —Quite so.

Mr. Heron then proceeded to cross-examine the witness.

It was elicited from the government reporter that, by a process which he called "throwing in the vowels," he was able to make Mr. Martin's speech read sufficiently seditious. Mr. D. C. Heron, Q. C., then addressed the court on behalf of Mr. J. J. Lalor; and Mr. Michael Crean, barrister, on behalf of Dr. Waters. Mr. Martin, on his own behalf, then spoke as follows:—

I admit I attended the procession. I admit also that I spoke words which I consider very grave and serious words upon that occasion. For my acts on that occasion, for the sense and intention of the words I spoke on that occasion, I am perfectly willing to be put upon my country. Not only for all my acts on that occasion— not only for the words which I spoke on that occasion ; but for all my acts, and all the words I ever spoke or wrote, publicly or privately, upon Irish politics, I am perfectly willing to be put upon my country. In any free country that has real constitutional institutions to guarantee the liberty of the subject—to guarantee the free trial of the subject charged with an offence against either the state or his neighbor, it would be quite absurd to expect a man could be put upon his country and convicted of a crime for doing that and using such words as the vast majority of his fellow-countrymen approve. In this case I believe that a vast majority of my fellow-countrymen do not disapprove of the acts I acknowledge on that occasion, and that they sympathize in the sentiment of the words I then spoke. Therefore the mere fact that a prosecution is preferred against me for that act and for those words, is evidence, in my opinion, that this country does not at present enjoy real constitutional institutions, guaranteeing a free trial—guaranteeing that the man accused shall be really put upon his country. Because it is absurd to think that any twelve honest men, my neighbors, put upon their oaths, would declare that to be a crime which it is probable that, at least, four-fifths of them believe to be right—right both constitutionally and morally. I am aware—we are all aware—that the gentlemen who represent the Crown in this country, have very powerful means at their disposal for obtaining convictions, in the form of law and in the form of justice, of any person they think proper to accuse; and, without meaning either to sneer or to joke in this matter, I acknowledge the moderation of the gentlemen who represent the government, since they chose to trouble themselves with me at all. I acknowledge their moderation in proposing to indict me only for sedition, for the language which they say I used, because it is possible for them, with the means at their disposal, to have me convicted for murder, or burglary, or bigamy (laughter). I am sorry to say what seems like a sneer, but I use the words in deep and solemn seriousness, and I say no more than I am perfectly ready to be tried fairly or foully (applause in court).

The magistrates reserved their decision till next day; so that there might be decent and seemly pause for the purpose of looking up and pondering the legal precedents, as the legal fiction would have it; and on next day, they announced that they would send all the accused for trial to the next Commission at Green-street, to open on the 10th February, 1868. The several traversers, however, were required to enter merely into their own recognizances in £500 each to appear for trial.

In this police-court proceeding the government, confessedly, were morally worsted—utterly humiliated, in fact. So far from creating awe or striking terror, the prosecution had evoked general contempt, scorn, and indignation. To such an extent was this fact recognized, that the government journals themselves, as we have seen, were amongst the loudest in censuring the whole proceeding, and in supporting the general expectation that there was an end of the prosecution.

Not so, however, was it to be. The very bitterness of the mortification inflicted upon them by their "roll in the dust" on their first legal encounter with the processionists, seemed to render the crown officials more and more vindictive. It was too galling to lie under the public challenge hurled at them by Mr. Bracken, Mr. O'Reilly, and Mr. Sullivan. After twelve days' cogitation, the government made up its mind to strike.

On Saturday, 28th December, 1867—just as every one in Ireland seemed to have concluded that, as the conservative journals said, there was "an end" of the foolish and ill-advised funeral prosecutions—Mr. Sullivan, Mr. Bracken (one of the funeral stewards), Mr. Jennings, of Kingstown (one of the best known and most trusted of the nationalists of "Dunleary" district), Mr. O'Reilly (one of the mounted marshals at the procession), and some others, were served with citations to appear, on Monday the 30th, at the head police office, to answer charges identical with those preferred on the 16th against Mr. Martin, Dr. Waters, and Mr. Lalor.

Preliminary prosecution No. 2 very much resembled No. 1. Mr. Murphy, Q. C., stated the crown case with fairness and moderation; and the police, as before, gave their evidence like men who felt "duty" and "conscience" in sore disagreement on such an occasion. Mr. Jennings and Mr. O'Reilly were defended, respectively, by Mr. Molloy and Mr. Crean; two advocates whose selection from the junior bar for these critical and important public cases was triumphantly vindicated by their conduct from the first to the last scene of the drama. Mr. Sullivan, Mr. Bracken, and the other accused, were not represented by counsel. On the first-named gentleman (Mr. Sullivan) being formally called on, he addressed the court at some length. He said:—

Please your worship, had the officials of the Crown adopted towards me, in the first instance, the course which they have taken upon the present occasion, and had they not adopted the singular course which they pursued in my regard when I last appeared in this court, I should trouble you with no observations. For, as one of the 50,000 persons who, on the 8th of December, in this city, publicly, lawfully, and peacefully demonstrated their protest against what they believed to have been a denial of law and an outrage on justice, I should certainly waste no public time in this preliminary investigation, but rather admit the facts as you perceive I have done to-day, and hasten the final decision on the issues really knit between us and the Crown. What was the course adopted by the Crown in the first instance against me? They had before them, on the 9th, just as well as on the 29th—it is in evidence that they had—the fact that I, openly and publicly, took part in that demonstration—that sorrowful and sad protest against injustice (applause). They had before them then as much as they have before them to-day, or as much as they will ever have affecting me. For, whatever course I take in public affairs in this country, I conceal nothing; I take it publicly, openly, and deliberately. If I err, I am satisfied to abide the consequences; and, whenever it may suit the weathercock judgment of Lord Mayo, and his vacillating law-advisers, to characterize my acts or my opinions as illegal, seditious, heretical, idolatrous, or treasonable, I must, like every other subject, be content to take my chance of their being able to find a jury sufficiently facile or sufficiently stupid to carry out their behests against me. But they did not choose that course at first. They did not summon me as a principal, but they subpœnaed me as a witness—as a crown witness—against some of my dearest personal and public friends. The Attorney-General, whose word I most fully and frankly accept in the matter—for I would not charge him with being wanting in personal truthfulness—denied having had any complicity in the course of conduct pursued towards me; but where does he lay the responsibility? On "the police." What is the meaning of that phrase, "the police"? He surely does not mean that the members of the force, who parade our streets, exercise viceregal functions (laughter). Who was this person thus called the "police"? How many degrees above or below the Attorney-General are we to look for this functionary described as "the police," who has the authority to have a "seditious" man—that is the allegation—a seditious man, exempted from prosecution? The police cannot do that. Who, then? Who was he that could draw the line between John Martin and his friend, A. M. Sullivan—exempt the one, prosecute the other—summon the former as a defendant and subpœna the latter as a crown witness? What was the object? It is plain. There are at this moment, I am convinced—who doubts it?—throughout Ireland, as yet unfound out, Talbots and Corridons in the pay of the Crown acting as Fenian Centres, who, next day, would receive from their employers directions to spread amongst my countrymen the intelligence that I had been here to betray my associate, John Martin (applause). But their plot recoiled—their device was exposed; public opinion expressed its reprobation of the unsuccessful trick; and now they come to mend their hand. The men who were exempted before are prosecuted to-day. Now, your worships, on this whole case—on this entire procedure—I deliberately charge that not we, but the government, have violated the law. I charge that the government are well aware that the law is against them—that they are irresistibly driven upon this attempt to strain and break the law against the constitutional right and liberty of the subject by their mere party exigencies and necessities.

He then reviewed at length the bearing of the Party Processions Act upon the present case, and next proceeded to deal with the subject of the Manchester executions; maintaining that the men were hanged, as were others before them, in like moments of national passion and frenzy, on a false evidence and a rotten verdict. Mr. Sullivan proceeded :—

It is because the people love justice and abhor injustice—because the real crime of those three victims is believed to have been devotion to native land—that the Catholic churches of Ireland resound with prayers and requiem hymns, and the public highways were lined with sympathizing thousands, until the guilty fears of the executioners proclaimed it illegal to mourn. Think you, sir, if the crown-view of this matter were the true one, would the Catholic clergy of Ireland—they who braved fierce and bitter unpopularity in reprehending the Fenian conspiracy at a time when Lord Mayo's organ was patting it on the back for its " fine Sardinian spirit"—would these ministers of religion drape their churches for three common murderers ? I repel as a calumnious and slanderous accusation against the Catholic clergy of Ireland this charge, that, by their mourning for these three martyred Irishmen, they expressed sympathy, directly or indirectly, with murder or life-taking. If an act be seditious, it is not the less illegal in the church than in the graveyard, or on the road to the cemetery. Are we, then, to understand that our churches are to be invaded by bands of soldiery, and our priests dragged from the altars, for the seditious crime of proclaiming aloud their belief in the innocence of Allen, Larkin, and O'Brien ? This, sir, is what depends on the decision in this case, here or elsewhere. All this and more. It is to be decided whether, in their capacity of Privy Councillors, the judges of the land shall put forth a proclamation, the legality or binding force of which they will afterwards sit as judges to try. It is whether, there being no constitution now allowed to exist in the country, there is to be no law save what a Castle proclamation will construct, permit, or decree ; no mourning save what the police will license ; no demonstration of opinion save whatever accords with the government views. We hear much of the liberties enjoyed in this country. No doubt, we have fine constitutional rights and securities until the very time they are most required. When we have no need to invoke them, they are permitted to us ; but at the only time when they might be of substantial value, they are, as the phrase goes, "suspended." Who, unless in times of governmental panic, need apprehend unwarranted arrest ? When else is the *Habeas Corpus* Act of such considerable protection to the subject ? When, unless when the Crown seeks to invade public liberty, is the purity and integrity of trial by jury of such value and importance in political cases ? Yet all the world knows that the

British government, whenever such a conflict arises, juggles and packs the jury——

Mr. Dix :—I really cannot allow that language to be used in this court, Mr. Sullivan, with every disposition to accord you, as an accused person, the amplest limits in your observations. Such language goes beyond what I can permit——

Mr. Sullivan :—I, at once, in respect for your worship, retract the word juggle. I will say the Crown manipulates the jury.

Mr. Dix :—I can't, at all, allow this line of comment to be pursued——

Mr. Sullivan :—With all respect for your worship, and, while I am ready to use any phrase most suitable for utterance here, I will not give up my right to state and proclaim the fact, however unpalatable, when it is notoriously true. I stand upon my rights to say that you have all the greater reasons to pause, ere you send me, or any other citizen, for trial before a jury in a crown prosecution at a moment like the present, when trial by jury, as the theory of the constitution supposes it, does not exist in the land. I say there is now, notoriously, no fair trial by jury to be had in this country, as between the subject and the Crown. Never yet, in an important political case, have the government in this country dared to allow twelve men, indifferently chosen, to pass into the jury-box to try the issue between the subject and the Crown. And now, sir, if you send the case for trial, and suppose the government succeed by the juries they are able to empanel here, with " Fenian" ticketed on the backs of the accused by the real governors of the country—the Heygates and the Bruces—and if it is declared by you that in this land of mourning it has become, at last, criminal even to mourn—what a victory for the Crown! Oh, sir, they have been for years winning such victories, and thereby manufacturing conspiracies--driving people from the open and legitimate expression of their sentiments into corners to conspire and to hide. I stand here as a man against whom some clamor has been raised for my efforts to save my countrymen from the courses into which the government conduct has been driving them, and I say that there is no more revolutionary agent in the land than that persecution of authority which says to the people, " When we strike you, we forbid you to weep." We meet the Crown, foot to foot, on its case here. We say we have committed no offence, but that the prosecution against us has been instituted to subserve their party exigencies, and that the government is straining and violating the law. We challenge them to the issue ; and even should they succeed in obtaining from a crown jury a verdict against us, we have a wider tribunal to appeal to—the decision of our own consciences and the judgment of humanity (applause).

Mr. Murphy, Q. C.. briefly replied. He asked his worship not to decide that the procession was illegal, but that this case was one for a court of law and a jury.

On this occasion it was unnecessary for Mr. Dix to

take any "time to consider his decision." All the accused were bound over in their own recognizances to stand their trials at the forthcoming Commission in Green-street court, on the 10th of February, 1868.

The plunge, before attempting which, the crown officials had shivered so long, had now been taken, and they determined to go through with the work, *à l'outrance*. In the interval between the last police-court scene described above, and the opening of the Green-street Commission, in February, 1868, prosecutions were directly commenced against the *Irishman* and the *Weekly News* for seditious writing. In the case of the former journal, the proprietor tried some skilfully-devised preparatory legal moves and manœuvres, not one of which, of course, succeeded, though their justice and legality were apparent enough. In the case of the latter journal—the *Weekly News*—the proprietor raised no legal point whatsoever. The fact was that when he found the Crown, not content with *one* state prosecution against him (that for the funeral procession), coming upon him with *a second*, he knew his doom was sealed. He very correctly judged that legal moves would be all in vain—that his conviction *per fas aut nefas* was to be obtained—that a jury would be packed against him—and that, consequently, the briefest and most dignified course for him would be to go straight to the conflict and meet it boldly.

On Monday, 10th February, 1868, the Commission was opened in Green-street, Dublin, before Mr. Justice Fitzgerald and Baron Deasy. Soon a cunning and unworthy legal trick on the part of the Crown was revealed. The prosecuted processionists and journalists had been indicted in the *city* venue, and had been returned for trial to the *city* commission by a *city* jury. But the government at the last moment mistrusted a city jury in this instance—even a *packed* city jury—and without any notice to the traversers, sent the indictments before the *county* grand jury, so that they might be tried by a jury picked and packed from the anti-Irish oligarchy of the Pale. It was an act of gross illegality, hardship, and oppression. The illegality of such a course had been ruled and decided in the case of Mr. Gavan Duffy in 1848. But the point was raised vainly now. When Mr. Pigott, of the *Irishman*, was called to plead, his counsel, Mr. Heron, Q. C., insisted that he, the traverser, was now in custody of the *city* sheriff in accordance with his recognizances, and could not without legal process be removed to the county venue. An exciting encounter ensued between Mr. Heron and the crown counsel, and the court took till next day to decide the point. Next morning it was decided in favor of the Crown, and Mr. Pigott was about being arraigned, when, in order that he might not be prejudiced by having attended pending decision, the Attorney-General said " he would shut his eyes to the fact that that gentleman was now in court," and would have him called immediately—an intimation that Mr. Pigott might, if advised, try the course of refusing to appear He did so refuse. When next called, Mr. Pigott was not forthcoming, and on the police proceeding to his office and residence that gentleman was not to be found—having, as the Attorney-General spitefully expressed it, " fled from justice." Mr. Sullivan's case, had, of necessity, then to be called ; and this was exactly what the Crown had desired to avoid, and what Mr. Heron had aimed to secure. It was the secret of all the skirmishing: A very general impression prevailed that the Crown would fail in getting a jury to convict Mr. Sullivan on any indictment tinctured even ever so faintly with " Fenianism ; " and it was deemed of great importance to Mr. Pigott's case to force the Crown to begin with the one in which failure was expected—Mr. Sullivan having intimated his perfect willingness to be either pushed to the front or kept till the last, according as might best promise to secure the discomfiture of the government. Mr. Heron had therefore so far outmanœuvred the Crown. Mr. Sullivan appeared in court and announced himself ready for trial, and the next morning was fixed for his arraignment. Up to this moment, that gentleman had expressed his determination not only to discard legal points, but to decline ordinary professional defence, and to address the jury in his own behalf. Now, however, deferring to considerations strongly pressed on him (set forth in his speech to the jury in the funeral procession case), he relinquished this resolution; and, late on the night preceding his trial, intrusted to Mr. Heron, Q. C., Mr. Crean, and Mr. Molloy, his defence on this first prosecution.

Next morning, Saturday, 15th February, 1868, the trial commenced; a jury was duly packed by the "stand-by" process, and notwithstanding a charge by Justice Fitzgerald, which was, on the whole, one of the fairest heard in Ireland in a political case for many years, Mr. Sullivan was duly convicted of having, by pictures and writings in his journal, the *Weekly News*, seditiously brought the Crown and government into hatred and contempt.

The government officials were jubilant. Mr. Pigott was next arraigned, and, after an exceedingly able defence by Mr. Heron, was likewise convicted.

It was now very generally concluded that the government would be satisfied with these convictions, and would not proceed with the funeral procession cases. At all events, it was universally regarded as certain that Mr. Sullivan would not be arraigned on the second or funeral procession indictment, as he now stood convicted on the other—the press charge. But it was not to be so. Elated with their success, the crown officials thought they might even discard their doubts of a city jury; and, on Thursday morning, 20th February, 1868, John Martin, Alexander M. Sullivan, Thomas Bracken, and J. J. Lalor,* were formally arraigned in the *city* venue.

It was a scene to be long remembered, that which was presented in the Green-street court-house on that Thursday morning. The dogged vindictiveness of the crown officials, in persisting with this second prosecution, seemed to have excited intense feeling throughout the city, and, long before the proceedings opened, the court was crowded in every part with anxious spectators.

---

* Dr. Waters, in the interval since his committal on this charge, had been arrested, and was now imprisoned, under the Suspension of the *Habeas Corpus* Act. He was not brought to trial on the procession charge.

When Mr. Martin entered, accompanied by his brother-in-law, Dr. Simpson, and Mr. Ross Todd, and took his seat at the traversers' bar, a low murmur of respectful sympathy, amounting to applause, ran through the building. And surely it was a sight to move the heart to see this patriot—this man of pure and stainless life; this man of exalted character, of noble soul, and glorious principles—standing once more in that spot where, twenty years before, he stood confronting the same foe in the same righteous and holy cause—standing once more at that bar whence, twenty years before, he was led off, manacled, to a felon's doom for the crime of loving Ireland! Many changes had taken place in the interval, but over the stern integrity of *his* soul time had wrought no change. He himself seemed to recall at this moment his last "trial" scene on this spot, and, as he cast his gaze around, one could detect on his calm, thoughtful face something of sadness, yet of pride, as memory doubtless pictured the spectacle of twenty years ago.

Mr. Sullivan, Mr. Bracken, and Mr. Lalor, arrived soon after, and immediately after the judges appeared on the bench, the proceedings began.

On their lordships, Mr. Justice Fitzgerald and Mr. Baron Deasy, taking their seats upon the bench, Mr. Smartt, deputy clerk of the Crown, called upon John Martin, Alexander M. Sullivan, James J. Lalor, and Thomas Bracken, to come and appear as they were bound to do in discharge of their recognizances.

All the traversers answered.

Mr. Smartt then proceeded to arraign the traversers under an indictment charging in the first count:—"That John Martin, John C. Waters, James J. Lalor, Alexander M. Sullivan, and Thomas Bracken, being malicious, seditious, and ill-disposed persons, and intending to disturb the peace and tranquillity of the realm, and to excite discontent and disaffection, and to excite the subjects of our Lady the Queen, in Ireland, to hatred and dislike of the government, the laws, and the administration of the laws of this realm, on the 8th day of December, in the year of our Lord, 1867, unlawfully did assemble and meet together with divers other persons, amounting to a large number—to wit, fifteen thousand persons—for the purpose of exciting discontent and disaffection, and for the purpose of exciting her Majesty's subjects in Ireland to hatred of her government and the laws of this realm, in contempt of our Lady the Queen, in open violation of the laws of this realm, and against the peace of our Lady the Queen, her crown and dignity." The second count charged that the defendants intended " to cause it to be believed that the three men who had been duly tried, found guilty, and sentenced, according to law, for murder, at Manchester, in England, had been illegally and unjustly executed ; and to excite hatred, dislike, and disaffection against the administration of justice, and the laws of this realm, for and in respect of the execution of the said three men." A third count charged the publication at the unlawful assembly, laid in the first and second counts, of the false and seditious words contained in Mr. John Martin's speech. A fourth and last count was framed under the Party Processions Act, and charged that the defendants " did unlawfully meet, assemble, and parade together, and were present at and did join in a procession with divers others, and did bear, wear, and have amongst them, in said procession, certain emblems and symbols, the display whereof was calculated to and did tend to provoke animosity between different classes of her Majesty's subjects, against the form of the statute in such case made and provided, and against the peace of our Lady the Queen, her crown and dignity."

The traversers severally pleaded not guilty.

The Attorney-General, the Solicitor-General. Dr. Ball, Q. C. ; Mr. Charles Shaw, Q. C. ; Mr. James Murphy, Q. C.; Mr. R. H. Owen, Q. C., and Mr. Edward Beytagh, instructed by Mr. Anderson, Crown Solicitor, appeared to prosecute.

Mr. Martin, Mr. Sullivan, and Mr. Bracken were not professionally assisted.

Mr. Michael T. Crean, instructed by Mr. John T. Scallan, appeared for Mr. Lalor.

And now came the critical stage of the case. *Would the crown pack the jury ?* The Clerk of the Crown began to call the panel, when——

John Keegan was called and ordered to stand by on the part of the Crown.

Mr. Sullivan : —My lord, have I any right to challenge?

Mr. Justice Fitzgerald :—You have, Mr. Sullivan, for cause.

Mr. Sullivan :—And can the Crown order a juror to stand by without a cause assigned ?

Mr. Justice Fitzgerald :—The Crown has a right to exercise that privilege.

Mr. Sullivan :—Well, I will exercise no challenge, for cause or without cause. Let the Crown select a jury now as it pleases.

Subsequently, George M'Cartney was called, and directed to stand by.

Patrick Ryan was also ordered to stand by.

Mr. Martin :—I protest against this manner of selecting a jury. I do so publicly.

J. J. Lalor :—I also protest against it.

Thomas Bracken :—And I also.

The sensation produced by this scene embarrassed the crown officials not a little. It dragged to light the true character of their proceeding. Eventually the following twelve gentlemen were suffered by the crown to pass into the box as a "jury"*—

SAMUEL EAKINS, Foreman. JOSEPH PURSER.
WILLIAM DOWNES GRIFFITH. THOMAS PAUL.
EDWARD GATCHELL. JAMES REILLY.
THOMAS MAXWELL HUTTON. JOHN GEORGE SHIELS.
MAURICE KERR. WILLIAM O'BRIEN SMYTH.
WILLIAM LONGFIELD. GEORGE WALSH.

The Solicitor-General, Mr. Harrison, stated the case for the prosecution. Next the police repeated their evidence—their description of the procession—as given before the magistrate, and the government short-hand writer proved Mr. Martin's speech. The only witnesses now produced, who had not testified at the preliminary stage, were a Manchester policeman named Seth Bromley, who had been one of the van escort on the day of the rescue, and the degraded and infamous crown-spy, Corridon. The former—eager as a beagle on the scent to run down the prey before him—left the table amidst murmurs of derision and indignation evoked by his over-eagerness on his direct examination, and his "fencing" and evasion on cross-examination. The spy Corridon was produced "to prove the existence of the Fenian conspiracy." Little notice was taken of him. Mr. Crean asked him barely a trivial question or two. Mr. Martin and Mr. Sullivan, when asked if they desired to cross-examine him, replied silently by gestures of loathing; and the wretch left the table—crawled from it—like a crippled murderer from the scene of his crime.

This closed the case for the Crown, and Mr. Crean, counsel for Mr. Lalor, rose to address the jury on behalf of his client. His speech was argumentative, terse, forcible, and eloquent, and seemed to please and astonish, not only the auditors, but the judges themselves, who

---

* Not one Catholic was allowed to pass into the box. Every Catholic who came to the box was ordered to "*stand by.*"

evidently had not looked for so much ability and vigor in the young advocate before them. Although the speeches of professional advocates do not come within the scope of this publication, Mr. Crean's vindication of the national color of Ireland—probably the most telling passage in his address—has an importance which warrants its quotation here :—

Gentlemen, it is attempted in this case to make the traversers amenable under the Party Processions Act, because those in the procession wore green ribbons. Gentlemen, this is the first time, in the history of Irish State Prosecutions, which mark the periods of gloom and peril in this country, that the wearing of a green ribbon has been formally indicted ; and, I may say, it is no good sign of the times that an offence which has been hitherto unknown to the law should now crop up for the first time in this year of grace, one thousand eight hundred and sixty-eight. Not even in the worst days of Lord Castlereagh's ill omened *régime* was such an attempt as this made to degrade the green of Ireland into a party color, and to make that, which has long been regarded as a national emblem, the symbol of a faction. Gentlemen, there is no right-minded or right-hearted man—looking back upon the ruinous dissensions and bitter conflicts which have been the curse and bane of this country—who will not reprobate any effort to revive and perpetuate them. There is no well-disposed man in the community who will not condemn and crush those persons—no matter on what side they may stand—who make religion, which should be the fountain and mother of all peace and blessings, the cause of rancor and animosity. We have had, unhappily, gentlemen, too much of this in Ireland. We have been too long the victims of that wayward fate of which the poet wrote, when he said :—

"Whilst our tyrants join in hate,
We never joined in love."

But, gentlemen, I will ask of you if you ever before heard, until this time, that the green of Ireland was the peculiar color of any particular sect, creed, or faction, or that any of the people of this country wore it as the peculiar emblem of their party, and for the purpose of giving annoyance and of offering insult to some other portion of their fellow-countrymen. I must say that I never heard before that Catholic or Protestant, or Quaker or Moravian, laid claim to this color as a symbol of party. I thought all Irishmen, no matter what altar they bowed before, regarded the green as the national color of Ireland. If it is illegal to wear the green, all I can say is that the constabulary are guilty of a constant and continuing breach of the law. The Lord and the Lady Lieutenant will probably appear on next Patrick's Day, decorated with large bunches of green shamrock. Many of the highest officials of the government will do the same; and is it to be thought, for one moment, that they, by wearing this green emblem of Ireland and of Irish nationality, are violating the law of the land? Gentlemen, it is perfectly absurd to think so. I hope this country has not yet so fallen as that it has become a crime to wear the green. I trust we have not yet come to that pass of national degradation, that a jury of Irishmen can be found so forgetful of their country's dignity and of their own as to brand with a mark of infamy a color which is associated with so many recollections, not of party triumphs, but of national glories—not with any sect, or creed, or party, but with a nation and a race whose children, whether they were the exiled soldiers of a foreign state, or the soldiers of Great Britain—whether at Fontenoy or on the plains of Waterloo, or on the heights of Fredericksburgh—have nobly vindicated the chivalry and fame of Ireland! It is for them that the green has its true meaning. It is to the Irishman in a distant land this emblem is so dear, for it is entwined in his memory, not with any miserable faction, but with the home and the country which gave him birth. I do hope that Irishmen will never be ashamed in this country to wear the green; and I hope an attempt will never again be made in an Irish court of justice to punish Irishmen for wearing that which is a national color, and of which every man, who values his country, should feel proud.

When Mr. Crean resumed his seat—which he did amidst strong manifestations of applause—it was past three o'clock in the afternoon. It was not expected that the case would have proceeded so far by that hour, and Mr. Martin and Mr. Sullivan, who intended each to speak in his own behalf, did not expect to rise for that purpose before next day, when it was arranged that Mr. Martin would speak first, and Mr. Sullivan follow him. Now, however, it was necessary some one of them should rise to his defence, and Mr. Martin urged that Mr. Sullivan should begin.

By this time the attendance in court, which, during the Solicitor-General's speech and the crown evidence, thinned down considerably, had once more grown too great for the fair capacity of the building. There was a crush within, and a crowd without. When Mr. Sullivan was seen to rise, after a moment's hurried consultation with Mr. Martin, who sat beside him, there was a buzz, followed by an anxious silence. For a moment the accused paused, almost overcome (as well he might have been) by a sense of the responsibility of this novel and dangerous course. But he quickly addressed himself to the critical task he had undertaken, and spoke as follows :—*

My lords and gentlemen of the jury :—I rise to address you under circumstances of embarrassment which will, I hope, secure for me a little consideration and indulgence at your hands. I have to ask you at the outset to banish any prejudice that might arise in your minds against a man who adopts the singular course—who undertakes the serious responsibility—of pleading his own defence. Such a proceeding might be thought to be dictated either by disparagement of the ordinary legal advocacy, by some poor idea of personal vanity, or by way of reflection on the tribunal before which the defence is made. My conduct is dictated by neither of these considerations or influences. Last of all men living should I reflect upon the ability, zeal, and fidelity of the Bar of Ireland, represented as it has been in my own behalf, within the past two days, by a man whose heart and genius are, thank God, still left to the service of our country, and represented, too, as it has been here this day by that gifted young advocate, the echoes of whose eloquence still resound in this court, and place me at disadvantage in immediately following him. And, assuredly, I design no disrespect to this court ; either to tribunal in the abstract, or to the individual judges who preside ; from one of whom I heard two days ago, delivered in my own case, a charge of which I shall say—though followed by a verdict which already consigns me to prison—that it was, judging it as a whole, the fairest, the clearest, the most just and impartial ever given, to my knowledge, in a political case of this kind in Ireland between the subject and the Crown. No ; I stand here in my own defence to-day, because long since I formed the opinion that, on many grounds, in such a prosecution as this, such a course would be the most fair and most consistent for a man like me. That resolution I was, for the sake of others, induced to depart from on Saturday last, in the first prosecution against me. When it came to be seen that I was the first to be tried out of two journalists prosecuted, it was strongly urged on me that my course and the result of my trial might largely affect the case of the other journalists to be tried after me ; and that I ought to waive my individual views and feelings, and have the utmost legal ability brought to bear in behalf of the case of the national press at the first point of conflict. I did so. I was defended by a bar not to be surpassed in the kingdom for ability and earnest zeal ; yet the

---

* As Mr. Sullivan delivered this speech without even the ordinary assistance of written notes or memoranda, the report here quoted is that which was published in the newspapers of the time. Some few inaccuracies which he was precluded from correcting then (being a prisoner when this speech was first published), have been corrected for this publication.

result was what I anticipated. For I knew, as I had held all along, that, in a case like this. where law and fact are left to the jury, legal ability is of no avail if the Crown comes in with its arbitrary power of moulding the jury. In that case, as in this one, I openly, publicly, and distinctly announced that I for my part would challenge no one, whether with cause or without cause. Yet the Crown —in the face of this fact—and in a case where they knew that, at least, the accused had no like power of peremptory challenge—did not venture to meet me on equal footing—did not venture to abstain from their practice of absolute challenge ; in fine, did not dare to trust their case to twelve men "indifferently chosen," as the constitution supposes a jury to be. Now, gentlemen, before I enter further upon this jury question, let me say that with me this is no complaint merely against "the Tories." On this, as well as on numerous other subjects, it is well known that it has been my unfortunate lot to arraign both Whigs and Tories. I say further, that I care not a jot whether the twelve men selected or permitted by the Crown to try me, or rather to convict me, be twelve of my own co-religionists and political compatriots, or twelve Protestants, Conservatives, Tories, or "Orangemen." Understand me clearly on this. My objection is not to the individuals comprising the jury. You may be all Catholics, or you may be all Protestants, for aught that affects my protest, which is against the mode by which you are selected—selected by the Crown—their choice for their own ends—and not "indifferently chosen" between the Crown and the accused. You may disappoint or you may justify the calculations of the crown official who has picked you out from the panel, by negative or positive choice (I being silent and powerless)—you may or may not be all he supposes—the outrage on the spirit of the constitution is the same. I say, by such a system of picking a jury by the Crown, I am not put upon my country. Gentlemen, from the first moment these proceedings were commenced against me, I think it will be admitted that I endeavored to meet them fairly and squarely, promptly and directly. I have never once turned to the right or to the left, but gone straight to the issue. I have from the outset declared my perfect readiness to meet the charges of the Crown. I did not care when or where they tried me. I said I would avail of no technicality—that I would object to no juror—Catholic, Protestant, or Dissenter. All I asked— all I demanded—was to be "put upon my country" in the real, fair, and full sense and spirit of the constitution. All I asked was that the Crown would keep its hand off the panel, as I would keep off mine. I had lived fifteen years in this c ty ; and I should have lived in vain, if, amongst the men that knew me in that time, whatever might be their political or religious creed, I feared to have my acts, my conduct, or principles tried. It is the first and most original condition of society that a man shall subordinate his public acts to the welfare of the community, or, at least, acknowledge the right of those amongst whom his lot is cast, to judge him on such an issue as this. Freely I acknowledged that right. Readily have I responded to the call to submit to the judgment of my country the question whether, in demonstrating my sorrow and sympathy for misfortune, my admiration for fortitude, my vehement indignation against what I considered to be injustice, I had gone too far and invaded the rights of the community. Gentlemen, I desire, in all that I have to say, to keep or be kept within what is regular and seemly, and above all to utter nothing wanting in respect for the court; but I do say, and I do protest, that I have not got trial by jury according to the spirit and meaning of the constitution. It is as representatives of the general community, not as representatives of the crown officials, the constitution supposes you to sit in that box. If you do not fairly represent the community, and if you are not empanelled indifferently in that sense, you are no jury in the spirit of the constitution. I care not how the crown practice may be within the technical letter of the law, it violates the intent and meaning of the constitution, and it is not "trial by jury." Let us suppose the scene removed, say, to France. A hundred names are returned on what is called a panel by a state functionary for the trial of a journalist charged with sedition. The accused is powerless to remove any name from the list unless for over-age or non-residence. But the imperial prosecutor has the arbitrary power of ordering as many as he pleases to "stand aside." By this means he puts or allows on the jury only whomsoever he pleases. He can, beforehand, select the twelve, and, by wiping out, if it suits him, the eighty-eight other names, put the twelve of his own choosing into the box. Can this be called trial by jury? Would not it be the same thing, in a more straightforward way, to let the Crown-Solicitor send out a policeman and collect twelve well-accredited persons of his own mind and opinion? For my own part, I would prefer this plain-dealing, and consider far preferable the more rude but honest hostility of a drumhead court-martial (applause in the court). Again I say, understand me well, I am objecting to the principle, the system, the practice, and not to the twelve gentlemen now before me as individuals. Personally, I am confident that, being citizens of Dublin, whatever your views or opinions, you are honorable and conscientious men. You may have strong prejudices against me or my principles in public life—very likely you have; but I doubt not that, though these may unconsciously tinge your judgment and influence your verdict, you will not consciously violate the obligations of your oath. And I care not whether the Crown, in permitting you to be the twelve, ordered three, or thirteen, or thirty others to " stand by"—or whether those thus arbitrarily put aside were Catholics or Protestants, Liberals, Conservatives, or Nationalists—the moment the Crown put its finger at all on the panel, in a case where the accused has no equal right, the essential character of the jury was changed, and the spirit of the constitution was outraged. And now, what is the charge against my fellow-traversers and myself? The Solicitor-General put it very pithily awhile ago when he said our crime was, "glorifying the cause of murder." The story of the Crown is a very terrible, a very startling one. It alleges a state of things which could hardly be supposed to exist amongst the Thugs of India. It depicts a population so hideously depraved that thirty thousand of them in one place, and tens of thousands of them in various other places, arrayed themselves publicly in procession to honor and glorify murder—to sympathize with murderers as murderers. Yes, gentlemen, that is the crown case, or they have no case at all—that the funeral procession in Dublin, on the 8th December last, was a demonstration of sympathy with murder as murder. For you will have noted that never once, in his smart narration of the crown story, did Mr. Harrison allow even the faintest glimmer to appear of any other possible complexion or construction of our conduct. Why, I could have imagined it easy for him not merely to state his own case, but to state ours too, and show where we failed, and where his own side prevailed. I could easily imagine Mr. Harrison stating our view of the matter—and combating it. But he never once dared to even mention our case. His whole aim was to hide it from you, and to fasten, as best such efforts of his could fasten, in your minds this one miserable refrain—"They glorified the cause of murder and assassination." But this is no new trick. It is the old story of the maligners of our people. They call the Irish a turbulent, riotous, crime-loving, law-hating race. They are forever pointing to the unhappy fact—for, gentlemen, it is a fact—that, between the Irish people and the laws under which they now live, there is little or no sympathy, but bitter estrangement and hostility of feeling or of action. Bear with me if I examine this charge, since an understanding of it is necessary in order to judge our conduct on the 8th December last. I am driven upon this extent of defence by the singular conduct of the Solicitor-General, who, with a temerity which he will repent, actually opened the page of Irish history, going back upon it just so far as it served his own purpose, and no farther. Ah! fatal hour for my prosecutors when they appealed to history! For, assuredly, that is the tribunal that will vindicate the Irish people, and confound those who malign them as sympathizers with assassination and glorifiers of murder——

Solicitor-General:—My lord, I must really call upon you—I deny that I ever——

Mr. Justice Fitzgerald:—Proceed, Mr. Sullivan.

Mr. Sullivan:—My lord, I took down the Solicitor-General's words. I quote them accurately as he spoke them, and he cannot get rid of them now. "Glorifiers of the cause of murder" was his designation of my fellow-traversers and myself, and our fifty thousand fellow-mourners in the funeral procession; and before I sit down I will make him rue the utterance. Gentlemen of the jury, if British law be held in "disesteem"—as the crown prosecutors phrase it—here in Ireland, there is an explanation for that fact other than that supplied by the Solicitor-General, namely, the wickedness of seditious persons like myself, and the criminal sympathies of a people ever ready to "glorify the cause of murder."

Mournful, most mournful, is the lot of that land where the laws are not respected—nay, revered by the people. No greater curse could befall a country than to have the laws estranged from popular esteem, or in antagonism with the national sentiment. Everything goes wrong under such a state of things. The ivy will cling to the oak, and the tendrils of the vine reach forth towards strong support. But more anxiously and naturally still does the human heart instinctively seek an object of reverence and love, as well as of protection and support, in law, authority, sovereignty. At least, among a virtuous people like ours, there is ever a yearning for those relations which are, and ought to be, as natural between a people and their government as between the children and the parent. I say for myself, and I firmly believe I speak the sentiments of most Irishmen when I say, that, so far from experiencing satisfaction, we experience pain in our present relations with the law and governing power; and we long for the day when happier relations may be restored between the laws and the national sentiment in Ireland. We Irish are no race of assassins or "glorifiers of murder." From the most remote ages, in all centuries, it has been told of our people that they were preëminently a justice-loving people. Two hundred and fifty years ago the predecessor of the Solicitor-General—an English Attorney-General—it may be necessary to tell the learned gentleman that his name was Sir John Davis (for historical as well as geographical * knowledge seems to be rather scarce amongst the present law-officers of the Crown) (laughter)—held a very different opinion of them from that put forth to-day by the Solicitor-General. Sir John Davis said no people in the world loved equal justice more than the Irish, even where the decision was against themselves. That character the Irish have ever borne and bear still. But, if you want the explanation of this "disesteem" and hostility for British law, you must trace effect to cause. It will not do to stand by the river-side near where it flows into the sea, and wonder why the water continues to run by. Not I—not my fellow traversers—not my fellow-countrymen—are accountable for the antagonism between law and popular sentiment in this country. Take up the sad story where you will—yesterday, last month, last year, last century, two centuries ago, three centuries, five centuries, six centuries—and what will you find? English law presenting itself to the Irish people in a guise forbidding sympathy or respect, and evoking fear and resentment. Take it at its birth in this country. Shake your minds free of legal theories and legal fictions, and deal with facts. This court where I now stand is the legal and political heir, descendant, and representative of the first law-court of the Pale six or seven centuries ago. Within that Pale were a few thousand

---

* On Mr. Sullivan's first trial the Solicitor-General, until stopped and corrected by the court, was suggesting to the jury that there was no such place as Knockrochery, and that a Fenian proclamation which had been published in the *Weekly News* as having been posted at that place, was, in fact, composed in Mr. Sullivan's office. Mr. Justice Deasy, however, pointedly corrected and reproved this blunder on the part of Mr. Harrison.

English settlers, and of them alone did the law take cognizance. The Irish nation—the millions outside the Pale—were known only as "the King's Irish enemie." The law classed them with the wild beasts of nature whom it was lawful to slay. Later on in our history, we find the Irish near the Pale sometimes asking to be admitted to the benefits of English law, since they were forbidden to have any of their own; but their petitions were refused. Gentlemen, this was English law as it stood towards the Irish people for centuries; and wonder, if you will, that the Irish people held it in "disesteem:"—

"The Irish were denied the right of bringing actions in any of the English courts in Ireland for trespasses to their lands or for assaults and batteries to their persons. Accordingly, it was answer enough to the action in such a case to say that the plaintiff was an Irishman, unless he could produce a special charter giving him the rights of an Englishman. If he sought damage against an Englishman for turning him out of his land, for the seduction of his daughter Nora, or for the beating of his wife Devorgil, or for the driving off of his cattle, it was a good defence to say he was a mere Irishman. And if an Englishman was indicted for manslaughter, if the man slain was an Irishman, he pleaded that the deceased was of the Irish nation, and that it was no felony to kill an Irishman. For this, however, there was a fine of five marks payable to the King; but mostly they killed us for nothing. If it happened that the man killed was a servant of an Englishman, he added to the plea of the deceased being an Irishman, that, if the master should ever demand damages, he would be ready to satisfy him."

That was the egg of English law in Ireland. That was the seed—that was the plant—do you wonder if the tree is not now esteemed and loved? If you poison a stream at its source, will you marvel if down through all its courses the deadly element is present? Now trace from this, its birth, English law in Ireland—trace down to this hour—and examine when or where it ever set itself to a reconciliation with the Irish people. Observe the plain relevancy of this to my case. I and men like me are held accountable for bringing law into hatred and contempt in Ireland, and, in presenting this charge against me, the Solicitor-General appealed to history. I retort the charge on my accusers, and I will trace down to our own day the relations of hostility which English law itself established between itself and the people of Ireland. Gentlemen, for four hundred years—down to 1607—the Irish people had no existence in the eye of the law; or rather, much worse, were viewed by it as "the King's Irish enemie." But even within the Pale, how did it recommend itself to popular reverence and affection? Ah! gentlemen, I will show that in those days, just as there have been in our own, there were executions and scaffold-scenes which evoked popular horror and resentment, though they were all "according to law," and not to be questioned unless by "seditionists." The scaffold streamed with the blood of those whom the people loved and revered—how could they love and revere the scaffold? Yet, 'twas all "according to law." The sanctuary was profaned and rifled; the priest was slain or banished: 'twas all "according to law," no doubt, and to hold law in "disesteem" is "sedition." Men were convicted and executed "according to law;" yet the people demonstrated sympathy for them, and resentment against their executioners—most perversely, as a Solicitor-General, doubtless, would say. And, indeed, the state papers contain accounts of those demonstrations written by crown officials which sound very like the Solicitor-General's speech to-day. Take, for instance, the execution—"according to law"—of the "popish bishop" O'Hurley. Here is the letter of a state functionary on the subject:—

"I could not before now so impart to her Majesty as to know her mind touching the same for your lordship's direction. Wherefore she having at length resolved, I have, accordingly, by her commandment, to signify her Majesty's pleasure unto you touching Hurley, which is this:—That the man being so notorious and ill a subject, as appeareth by all the circumstances of his cause he is, you proceed, if it may be, to his execution by ordinary trial of him for it. How be it, in case you shall find the effect of his course DOUBTFUL by reason of the affection of such as shall be on his jury, and by reason of the supposal conceived by the lawyers of that country, that he can hardly be found guilty for his treason committed in foreign parts against her Majesty; then her pleasure is you take A SHORTER WAY WITH HIM by martial law. So, as you may see, it is referred to your discretion, whether of those two ways your lordship will take with him, and the man being so resolute to reveal no more matter, it is thought best to have NO FURTHER TORTURES used against him, but that you proceed FORTHWITH TO HIS EXECUTION in manner aforesaid. As for her Majesty's good acceptation of your careful travail in this matter of Hurley, you need nothing to doubt, and, for your better assurance thereof, she has commanded me to let your lordship understand that, as well as in all others the like, as in the case of Hurley, she cannot but greatly allow and commend YOUR DOINGS."

Well, they put his feet into tin boots filled with oil, and then placed him standing in the fire. Eventually they cut off his head, tore out his bowels, and cut the limbs from his body. Gentlemen, 'twas all "according to law;" and to demonstrate sympathy for him and "disesteem" of that law was "sedition." But do you wonder greatly that law of that complexion failed to secure popular sympathy and respect? One more illustration, gentlemen, taken from a period somewhat later on. It is the execution—"according to law," gentlemen, entirely "according to law"—of another popish bishop named O'Devany. The account is that of a crown official of the time—some most worthy predecessor of the Solicitor-General. I read it from the recently published work of the Rev. C. P. Meehan:—"On the 28th of January, the bishop and priest, being arraigned at the King's Bench, were each condemned of treason, and adjudged to be executed the Saturday following; which day being come, a priest or two of the Pope's brood, with holy water and other holy stuffs"—(no sneer was that, at all, gentlemen; no sneer at Catholic practices, for a crown official never sneers at Catholic practices)—"were sent to sanctify the gallows whereon they were to die. About two o'clock P. M., the traitors were delivered to the sheriffs of Dublin, who placed them in a small car. which was followed by a great multitude. As the car progressed the spectators knelt down, but the bishop, sitting still like a block, would not vouchsafe them a word, or turn his head aside. The multitude, however, following the car, made such a dole and lamentation after him, as the heavens themselves resounded the echoes of their outcries." (Actually a seditious funeral procession—made up of the ancestors of those thirty thousand men, women, and children, who, according to the Solicitor-General, glorified the cause of murder on the 8th of last December.) "Being come to the gallows, whither they were followed by troops of the citizens, men and women of all classes, most of the best being present, the latter kept up such a shrieking, such a howling, and such a hallooing, as if St. Patrick himself had been gone to the gallows, could not have made greater signs of grief; but when they saw him turned from off the gallows, they raised the *whobub* with such a maine cry, as if the rebels had come to rifle the city. Being ready to mount the ladder, when he was pressed by some of the bystanders to speak, he repeated frequently, *Sine me quæso*. The executioners had no sooner taken off the bishop's head, but the townsmen of Dublin began to flock about him, some taking up the head with pitying aspect, accompanied with sobs and sighs; some kissed it with as religious an appetite as ever they kissed the Pax; some cut away all the hair from the head, which they preserved for a relic; some others were practisers to steal the head away, but the executioner gave notice to the sheriffs. Now, when he began to quarter the body, the women thronged about him, and happy was she that could get but her handkerchief dipped in the blood of the traitor; and the body being once dissevered in four quarters, they neither left finger nor toe, but they cut them off and carried them away; and some others that could get no holy monuments that appertained to his person, with their knives they shaved off chips from the hallowed gallows; neither could they omit the halter wherewith he was hanged, but it was rescued for holy uses. The same night after the execution, a great crowd flocked about the gallows, and there spent the fore part of the night in heathenish howling, and performing many popish ceremonies; and after midnight, being then Candlemas-day, in the morning having their priest present in readiness, they had Mass after Mass till, daylight being come, they departed to their own houses." There was "sympathy with sedition" for you, gentlemen. No wonder the crown official who tells the story—some worthy predecessor of Mr. Harrison—should be horrified at such a demonstration. I will sadden you with no further illustrations of English law, but I think it would be admitted that, after centuries of such law, one need not wonder if the people hold it in "hatred and contempt." With the opening of the seventeenth century, however, came a golden and glorious opportunity for ending that melancholy—that terrible state of things. In the reign of James I, English law, for the first time, extended to every corner of this kingdom. The Irish came into the new order of things frankly and in good faith; and if wise counsels prevailed then amongst our rulers, oh, what a blessed ending there might have been to the bloody feud of centuries! The Irish submitted to the Gaelic King, to whom had come the English crown. In their eyes he was of a friendly, nay, of a kindred race. He was of a line of Gaelic Kings that had often befriended Ireland. Submitting to him was not yielding to the brutal Tudor. Yes, that was the hour, the blessed opportunity for laying the foundation of a real union between the three kingdoms : a union of equal national rights under the one crown. This was what the Irish expected ; and in this sense they, in that hour, accepted the new dynasty. And it is remarkable that, from that day to this, though England has seen bloody revolutions and violent changes of rulers, Ireland has ever held faithfully—too faithfully —to the sovereignty thus adopted. But how were they received ? How were their expectations met ? By persecution, proscription, and wholesale plunder, even by that miserable Stuart. His son came to the throne. Disaffection broke out in England and Scotland. Scottish Protestant Fenians, called " Covenanters," took the field against him, because of the attempt to establish Episcopalian Protestantism as a state church. By armed rebellion against their lawful king, I regret to say it, they won rights which now most largely tend to make Scotland contented and loyal. I say it is to be regretted that those rights were thus won ; for I say that, even at best, it is a good largely mixed with evil where rights are won by resort to violence or revolution. His concessions to the Calvinist Fenians in Scotland did not save Charles. The English Fenians, under their Head Centre Cromwell, drove him from the throne, and murdered him on a scaffold in London. How did the Irish meanwhile act ? They stood true to their allegiance. They took the field for the King. What was the result ? They were given over to slaughter and plunder by the brutal soldiery of the English Fenians. Their nobles and gentry were beggared and proscribed ; their children were sold as white slaves to West Indian planters ; and their gallant struggles for the King, their sympathy for the royalist cause, was actually denounced by the English Fenians as "sedition," "rebellion," "lawlessness," "sympathy with crime." Ah ! gentlemen, the evils thus planted in our midst will survive, and work their influence ; yet some men wonder the English law is held in "disesteem" in Ireland. Time went on, gentlemen ; time went on. Another James sat on the throne ; and again English Protestant Fenianism conspired for the overthrow of their sovereign. They invited "foreign emissaries" to come over from Holland and Sweden to begin the revolution for them. They drove their legitimate King from the throne—never more to return. How did the Irish act in that hour ? Alas ! Ever too loyal—ever only too ready to stand by the throne and laws, if only treated with justice or kindliness—they took the field for the King, not against him. He landed on our shores ; and had the English Fenians rested content with rebelling themselves, and allowed us to remain loyal as we desired to be, we might now be a neighboring but friendly and independent kingdom under the ancient Stuart line. King James came here and opened his Irish parliament in person. Oh, who will say in that brief hour, at least, the Irish nation was not reconciled to the throne and laws ? King, parliament, and people, were blended in one element of enthusiasm, joy and hope, the first time for ages Ireland had known such a joy. Yes——

> " We, too, had our day—it was brief, it is ended—
> When a King dwelt among us—no strange King—but OURS;
> When the shout of a people delivered ascended,
> And shook the green banner that hung on yon towers.
> We saw it like leaves in the summer-time shiver;
> We read the gold legend that blazoned it o'er—
> 'To-day—now or never; to-day and forever'—
> O God! have we seen it to see it no more?"

(Applause in court.) Once more the Irish people bled and sacrificed for their loyalty to the throne and laws. Once more confiscation devastated the land, and the blood of the loyal and true was poured like rain. The English Fenians and the foreign emissaries triumphed, aided by the brave Protestant rebels of Ulster. King William came to the throne—a prince whose character is greatly misunderstood in Ireland: a brave, courageous soldier, and a tolerant man, could he have had his way. The Irish who had fought and lost, submitted on terms; and had law even now been just or tolerant, it was open to the revolutionary *régime* to have made the Irish good subjects. But what took place? The penal code came, in all its horror, to fill the Irish heart with hatred and resistance. I will read for you what a Protestant historian—a man of learning and ability—who is now listening to me in this court—has written of that code. I quote "Godkin's History," published by Cassell of London:—

"The eighteenth century," says Mr. Godkin, "was the era of persecution, in which the law did the work of the sword more effectually and more safely. Then was established a code framed with almost diabolical ingenuity to extinguish natural affection—to foster perfidy and hypocrisy · to petrify conscience —to perpetuate brutal ignorance—to facilitate the work of tyranny—by rendering the vices of slavery inherent and natural in the Irish character, and to make Protestantism almost irredeemably odious as the monstrous incarnation of all moral perversions."

Gentlemen, in that fell spirit English law addressed itself to a dreadful purpose here in Ireland; and, mark you, that code prevailed down to our own time—down to this very generation. "Law" called on the son to sell his father; called on the flock to betray the pastor. "Law" forbade us to educate—forbade us to worship God in the faith of our fathers. "Law" made us outcasts, scourged us, trampled us, plundered us—do you marvel that, amongst the Irish people, law has been held in "disesteem"? Do you think this feeling arises from "sympathy with assassination or murder"? Yet, if we had been let alone, I doubt not that time would have fused the conquerors and the conquered, here in Ireland as elsewhere. Even while the millions of the people were kept outside the constitution, the spirit of nationality began to appear and under its blessed influence toleration touched the heart of the Irish-born

Protestant. Yes, thank God—thank God, for the sake of our poor country, where sectarian bitterness has wrought such wrong—it was an Irish Protestant parliament that struck off the first link of the penal chain. And lo! once more, for a bright brief day, Irish national sentiment was in warm sympathy and heart-felt accord with the laws. "Eighty-two" came. Irish Protestant patriotism, backed by the hearty sympathy of the Catholic millions, raised up Ireland to a proud and glorious position; lifted our country from the ground, where she lay prostrate under the sword of England--but what do I say? This is "sedition." It has this week been decreed sedition to picture Ireland thus. * Well, then they rescued her from what I will call the loving embrace of her dear sister Britannia, and enthroned her in her rightful place, a queen among the nations. Had the brightness of that era been prolonged—picture it, think of it--what a country would ours be now! Think of it! And contrast what we are with what we might be! Compare a population, filled with burning memories—disaffected, sullen, hostile, vengeful—with a people loyal, devoted, happy, contented; and England, too, all the happier, the more secure, the more great and free. But sad is the story. Our independent national legislature was torn from us by means, the iniquity of which, even among English writers, is now proclaimed and execrated. By fraud and by force that outrage on law, on right, and justice, was consummated. In speaking thus I speak "sedition." No one can write the facts of Irish history without committing sedition. Yet every writer and speaker now will tell you that the overthrow of our national constitution, sixty-seven years ago, was an iniquitous and revolting scheme. But do you, then, marvel that the laws imposed on us by the power that perpetrated that deed are not revered, loved, and respected? Do you believe that that want of respect arises from the "seditions" of men like my fellow-traversers and myself? Is it wonderful to see estrangement between a people and laws imposed on them by the over-ruling influence of another nation? Look at the lessons—unhappy lessons—taught our people by that London legislature where their own will is overborne. Concessions refused and resisted as long as they durst be withheld; and when granted at all, granted only after passion has been aroused and the whole nation been embittered. The Irish people sought Emancipation. Their great leader was dogged at every step by hostile government proclamations and crown prosecutions. Coercion act over coercion act was rained upon us; yet O'Connell triumphed. But how and in what spirit was Emancipation granted? Ah! there never was a speech more pregnant with mischief, with sedition, with revolutionary teaching—never words tended more to bring law and government into contempt—than the words of the English premier when he declared Emancipation must, sorely against his will, be granted if

---

*For publishing an illustration in the *Weekly News* thus picturing England's policy of coercion, Mr. Sullivan had been found guilty of seditious libel on the previous trial.

England would not face a civil war. That was a bad lesson to teach Irishmen. Worse still was taught them. O'Connell, the great constitutional leader, a man with whom loyalty and respect for the laws was a fundamental principle of action, led the people towards further liberation—the liberation, not of a creed, but a nation. What did he seek? To bring once more the laws and the national will into accord; to reconcile the people and the laws by restoring the constitution of Queen, Lords, and Commons. How was he met by the government? By the flourish of the sword; by the drawn sabre and the shotted gun, in the market-place and the highway. "Law" finally grasped him as a conspirator, and a picked jury gave the Crown then, as now, such verdict as was required. The venerable apostle of constitutional doctrine was consigned to prison, while a sorrowing, aye, a maddened nation wept for him outside. Do you marvel that they held in "disesteem" the law and government that acted thus? Do you marvel that to-day, in Ireland, as in every century of all those through which I have traced this state of things, the people and the law scowl upon each other? Gentlemen, do not misunderstand the purport of my argument. It is not for the purpose—it would be censurable—of merely opening the wounds of the past that I have gone back upon history somewhat farther than the Solicitor-General found it advantageous to go. I have done it to demonstrate that there is a truer reason than that alleged by the Crown in this case for the state of war—for, unhappily, that is what it is—which prevails between the people of Ireland and the laws under which they now live. And now apply all this to the present case, and judge you my guilt—judge you the guilt of those whose crime, indeed, is that they do not love and respect law and government as they are now administered in Ireland. Gentlemen, the present prosecution arises directly out of what is known as the Manchester tragedy. The Solicitor-General gave you his version, his fanciful sketch, of that sad affair; but it will be my duty to give you the true facts, which differ considerably from the crown story. The Solicitor-General began with telling us about "the broad summer's sun of the 18th September" (laughter). Gentlemen, it seems very clear that the summer goes far into the year for those who enjoy the sweets of office; nay, I am sure it is summer "all the year round" with the Solicitor-General while the present ministry remain in. A goodly golden harvest he and his colleagues are making in this summer of prosecutions ; and they seem very well inclined to get up enough of them (laughter). Well, gentlemen, I'm not complaining of that, but I will tell you who complain loudly—the "outs," with whom it is midwinter, while the Solicitor-General and his friends are enjoying this summer (renewed laughter). Well, gentlemen, some time, last September, two prominent leaders of the Fenian movement—alleged to be so at least—named Kelly and Deasy, were arrested in Manchester. In Manchester there is a considerable Irish population, and amongst them it was known those men had sympathizers. They were brought up at the police court—and now, gentlemen, pray attentively mark this. The Irish executive that morning telegraphed to the Manchester authorities a strong warning of an attempted rescue. The Manchester police had full notice—how did they treat the timely warning sent from Dublin—a warning which, if heeded, would have averted all this sad and terrible business which followed upon that day? Gentlemen, the Manchester police authorities scoffed at the warning. They derided it as a "Hirish" alarm. What! The idea of low "Hirish" hodmen or laborers rescuing prisoners from them, the valiant and the brave! Why, gentlemen, the Seth Bromleys of the "force" in Manchester waxed hilarious and derisive over the idea. They would not ask even a truncheon to put to flight even a thousand of those despised "Hirish;" and so, despite specific warning from Dublin, the van containing the two Fenian leaders, guarded by eleven police officers, set out from the police office to the jail. Now, gentlemen, I charge on the stolid vaingloriousness in the first instance, and the contemptible pusillanimity in the second instance, of the Manchester police—the valiant Seth Bromleys—all that followed. On the skirts of the city the van was attacked by some eighteen Irish youths, having three revolvers—three revolvers, gentlemen, and no more—amongst them. The valor of the Manchester eleven vanished at the sight of those three revolvers—some of them, it seems, loaded with blank cartridge! The Seth Bromleys took to their heels. They abandoned the van. Now, gentlemen, do not understand me to call those policemen cowards. It is hard to blame an unarmed man who runs away from a pointed revolver, which, whether loaded or unloaded, is a powerful persuasion to—depart. But I do say that I believe in my soul that, if that had occurred here in Dublin, eleven men of our metropolitan police would have taken those three revolvers or perished in the attempt (applause). Oh, if eleven Irish policemen had run away like that from a few poor English lads with barely three revolvers, how the press of England would yell in fierce denunciation—why, they would trample to scorn the name of Irishman—(applause in the court, which the officials vainly tried to silence).

Mr. Justice Fitzgerald:—If these interruptions continue, the parties so offending must be removed.

Mr. Sullivan:—I am sorry, my lord, for the interruption; though not sorry the people should endorse my estimate of the police. Well, gentlemen, the van was abandoned by its valiant guard; but there remained inside one brave and faithful fellow, Brett by name. I am now giving you the facts as I in my conscience and soul believe they occurred—and as millions of my countrymen—aye, and thousands of Englishmen, too—solemnly believe them to have occurred, though they differ in one item widely from the crown version. Brett refused to give up the key of the van which he held; and the attacking party commenced various endeavors to break it open. At length one of them called out to fire a pistol into the lock, and thus burst it open. The unfortunate Brett at that moment was looking through the keyhole, endeavoring to get a view of the inexplicable scene outside, when he received the bullet and fell dead. Gentlemen, that may be the true, or it may be the mistaken version. You may hold to the other, or you may hold to this. But whether I be mistaken therein or otherwise, I say here, as I would say if I stood now before my eternal Judge on the Last Day, I solemnly believe the mournful episode to have happened thus—I solemnly believe that the man Brett was shot by accident, and not by design. But even suppose your view differs sincerely from mine, will you, can you, hold that I, thus conscientiously persuaded, sympathize with murder, because I sympathize with men hanged for that which I contend was accident, and not murder? That is exactly the issue in this case. Well, the rescued Fenian leaders got away; and then, when all was over—when the danger was passed—valor tremendous returned to the fleet-of-foot Manchester police. Oh, but they wreaked their vengeance that night on the houses of the poor Irish in Manchester! By a savage razzia they soon filled the jails with our poor countrymen seized on suspicion. And then broke forth all over England that shout of anger and passion which none of us will ever forget. The national pride had been sorely wounded; the national power had been openly and humiliatingly defied; the national fury was aroused. On all sides resounded the hoarse shout for vengeance, swift and strong. Then was seen a sight the most shameful of its kind that this century has exhibited—a sight at thought of which Englishmen yet will hang their heads for shame, and which the English historian will chronicle with reddened cheek—those poor and humble Irish youths led into the Manchester dock in chains! In chains! Yes; iron fetters festering wrist and ankle! Oh! gentlemen, it was a fearful sight: for no one can pretend that in the heart of powerful England there could be danger those poor Irish youths would overcome the authorities and capture Manchester. For what, then, were those chains put on untried prisoners? Gentlemen, it was at this point exactly that Irish sympathy came to the side of those prisoners. It was when we saw them thus used, and saw that, innocent or guilty, they would be immolated—sacrificed to glut the passion of the hour—that our feelings rose high and strong in their behalf. Even in England there were men —noble-hearted Englishmen, for England is never without such men—who saw that, if tried in the midst of this national frenzy, those victims would be sacrificed; and accordingly efforts were made for a postponement of the trial. But the roar of passion carried its way. Not even till the ordinary assizes would the trial be postponed. A special commission was sped to do the work while Manchester jurors were in a white heat of panic, indignation, and fury. Then came the trial, which was just what might be expected. Witnesses swore ahead without compunction, and jurors believed them without hesitation. Five men arraigned together as principals—Allen, Larkin, O'Brien, Shore, and Maguire—were found guilty, and, the judge concurring in the verdict, were sentenced to death. Five men—not three men, gentlemen—five men in the one verdict, not five separate verdicts. Five men by the same evidence and the same jury in the same verdict. Was that a just verdict? The case of the Crown here to-day is that it was—that it is "sedition" to impeach that verdict. A copy of that conviction is handed in here as evidence to convict me of sedition for charging, as I do, that that was a wrong verdict, a bad verdict, a rotten and a false verdict. But what is the fact? That her Majesty's ministers themselves admit and proclaim that it was a wrong verdict, a false verdict. The very evening those men were sentenced, thirty newspaper reporters sent up to the Home Secretary a petition protesting that—the evidence of the witnesses and the verdict of the jury notwithstanding—there was at least one innocent man thus marked for execution. The government felt that the reporters were right and the jurors wrong. They pardoned Maguire as an innocent man—that same Maguire whose legal conviction is here put in as evidence that he and four others were truly murderers, to sympathize with whom is to commit sedition—nay, "to glorify the cause of murder." Well, after that, our minds were easy. We considered it out of the question any man would be hanged on a verdict thus ruined, blasted, and abandoned; and believing those men innocent of murder, though guilty of another most serious legal crime—rescue with violence, and incidental, though not intentional loss of life—we rejoiced that a terrible mistake was, as we thought, averted. But now arose in redoubled fury the savage cry for blood. In vain, good men, noble and humane men, in England tried to save the national honor by breasting this horrible outburst of passion. They were overborne. Petitioners for mercy were mobbed and hooted in the streets. We saw all this—we saw all this; and think you it did not sink into our hearts? Fancy, if you can, our feelings when we heard that yet another man out of five was respited—ah! he was an American gentleman—an American, not an Irishman—but that the three Irishmen, Allen, Larkin, and O'Brien, were to die—were to be put to death on a verdict and on evidence that would not hang a dog in England! We refused to the last to credit it; and thus incredulous, deemed it idle to make any effort to save their lives. But it was true; it was deadly true. And then, gentlemen, the doomed three appeared in a new character. Then they rose into the dignity and heroism of martyrs. The manner in which they bore themselves through the dreadful ordeal ennobled them forever. It was then we all learned to love and revere them as patriots and Christians. Oh! gentlemen, it is only at this point I feel my difficulty in addressing you whose religious faith is not that which is mine. For it is only Catholics who can understand the emotions aroused in Catholic hearts by conduct such as theirs in that dreadful hour. Catholics alone can understand how the last solemn declarations of such men, after receiving the last sacraments of the Church, and about to meet their great Judge face to face, can outweigh the reckless evidence of Manchester thieves and pickpockets. Yes; in that hour they told us they were innocent, but were ready to die; and we believed them. We believe them still. Aye, do we! They did not go to meet their God with a falsehood on their lips. On that night before their execution, oh, what a scene! What a picture did England present at the foot of the Manchester scaffold! The brutal populace thronged thither in tens of thousands. They danced; they sang; they blasphemed: they chorused "Rule Britannia," and "God save the Queen," by way of taunt and defiance of the men whose death agonies they had come to see! Their shouts and brutal cries disturbed the doomed victims inside the prison as in their cells they prepared in prayer and meditation to meet their Creator and their God. Twice the police had to remove the crowd from around that wing of the prison; so that our poor brothers might in peace go through their last preparations for eternity, undisturbed by the yells of the multitude outside. Oh, gentlemen, gentlemen—that scene! That scene in the grey cold morning when those innocent men were led out to die—to die an ignominious death before the wolfish mob! With blood on fire—with bursting hearts—we read the dreadful story here in Ireland. We knew that these men would never have been thus sacrificed had not their offence been political, and had it not been that in their own way they represented the old struggle of the Irish race. We felt that, if time had but been permitted for English passion to cool down, English good feeling and right justice would have prevailed; and they never would have been put to death on such a verdict. All this we felt, yet we were silent till we heard the press, that had hounded those men to death, falsely declaring that our silence was acquiescence in the deed that consigned them to murderers' graves. Of this I have personal knowledge, that, here in Dublin at least, nothing was done or intended, until the *Evening Mail* declared that popular feeling, which had had ample time to declare itself, if it felt otherwise, quite recognized the justice of the execution. Then we resolved to make answer. Then Ireland made answer. For what monarch, the loftiest in the world, would such demonstrations be made, the voluntary offerings of a people's grief? Think you it was "sympathy for murder" called us forth, or caused the priests of the Catholic Church to drape their churches? It is a libel to utter the base charge. No, no. Of the acts of those men at that rescue we had naught to say. Of their innocence of murder we were convinced. Their patriotic feelings, their religious devotion, we saw proved in the noble, the edifying manner of their death. We believed them to have been unjustly sacrificed in a moment of national passion; and we resolved to rescue their memory from the foul stains of their maligners, and make it a proud one forever with Irishmen. Sympathy with murder, indeed! What I am about to say will be believed—for I think I have shown no fear of consequences in standing by my acts and principles: I say for myself, and for the priests and people of Ireland, who are affected by this case, that sooner would we burn our right hands to cinders than express, directly or indirectly, sympathy with murder; and that our sympathy for Allen, Larkin, and O'Brien is based upon the conviction that they were innocent of any such crime. Gentlemen, having regard to all the circumstances of this sad business, having regard to the feelings under which we acted, think you, is it a true charge that we had for our intent and object the bringing of the administration of justice into contempt? Does a man, by protesting, ever so vehemently, against an act of a not infallible tribunal, incur the charge of attempting its overthrow? What evidence can be shown to you that we uttered a word against the general character of the administration of justice in this country, while denouncing this particular proceeding, which we say was a fearful failure of justice—a horrible blunder, a terrible act of passion! None— none. I say, for myself, I sincerely believe that in this country of ours justice is administered by the judges of the Irish Bench with a purity and impartiality between man and man not to be surpassed in the universal world. Let me not be thought to cast reflection on this court, or the learned judges before whom I now stand, if I except in a certain sense, and on some occasions, political trials between the subject and the Crown. Apart from this, I fearlessly say the bench of justice in Ireland fully enjoys, and is worthy of, respect and homage. I care not from what political party its members be drawn, I say that, with hardly an exception, when robed with the ermine, they become dead to the world of politics, and sink the politician in the loftier character of representative of sacred Justice. Yet, gentlemen, holding those views, I would, nevertheless, protest against and denounce such a trial as that in Manchester, if it had taken place in Ireland. For, what we contend is that the men in Manchester would never have been found guilty on such evidence, would never have been executed on such a verdict, if time had been given to let panic and passion pass away— time to let English good sense and calm reason and sense of justice have sway. Now, gentlemen, judge ye me on this whole case; for I have done. I have spoken at great length, but I plead not merely my own cause, but the cause of my country. For myself I care little. I stand before you here with the manacles, I might say, on my hands. Already a prison cell awaits me in Kilmainham. My doom, in any event, is sealed. Already a conviction has been obtained against me for my opinions on this same event; for it is not one arrow alone that has been shot from the crown-office quiver at me—at my reputation, my property, my liberty. In a few hours more my voice will be silenced; but, before the world is shut out from me for a term, I appeal to your verdict—to the verdict of my fellow-citizens—of my fellow-countrymen—to judge my life, my conduct, my acts, my principles, and say am I a criminal. Sedition, in a rightly ordered community, is indeed a crime. But who is it that challenges me? Who is it that demands my loyalty? Who is it that calls out to me, "O ingrate son! where is the filial affection, the respect, the obedience, the support, that is my due? Unnatural, seditious, and rebellious child, a dungeon shall punish your crime!" I look in the face of my accuser, who thus holds me to the duty of a son. I turn to see if there I can recognize the features of that mother, whom indeed I love, my own dear Ireland. I look into that accusing face, and there I see a scowl, and not a smile. I miss the soft, fond voice, the tender clasp, the loving word. I look upon the hands reached out to grasp me—to punish me; and lo! great stains, blood-red, upon those hands; and my sad heart tells me it is the blood of my widowed mother. Ireland. Then I answer to my accuser—"You have no claim on me—on my love, my duty, my allegiance. You are not my mother. You sit indeed in the place where she should reign. You wear the regal garments torn from her limbs, while she now sits in the dust, uncrowned and overthrown, and bleeding from many a wound. But my heart is with her still. Her claim alone is recognized by me. She still commands my love, my duty, my allegiance; and whatever the penalty may be, be it prison, chains, be it exile or death, to her I will be true" (applause). But, gentlemen of the jury, what is that Irish nation to which my allegiance turns? Do I thereby mean a party, or a class, or creed? Do I mean only those who think and feel as I do on public questions? Oh, no. It is the whole people of this land—the nobles, the peasants, the clergy, the merchants, the gentry, the traders, the professions—the Catholic, the Protestant, the Dissenter. Yes, I am loyal to all that a good and patriotic citizen should be loyal to; I am ready, not merely to obey, but to support with heart-felt allegiance, the constitution of my own country—the Queen, as Queen of Ireland, and the free parliament of Ireland once more reconstituted in our national senate-house in College-green. And reconstituted once more it will be. In that hour the laws will again be reconciled with the national feeling and popular reverence. In that hour there will be no more disesteem, or hatred or contempt for the laws : for, howsoever a people may dislike and resent laws imposed upon them against their will by a subjugating power, no nation disesteems the laws of its own making. That day, that blessed day, of peace and reconciliation, and joy, and liberty, I hope to see. And when it comes, as come it will, in that hour it will be remembered for me that I stood here to face the trying ordeal, ready to suffer for my country—walking with bared feet over red-hot ploughshares like the victims of old. Yes; in that day it will be remembered for me, though a prison awaits me now, that I was one of those journalists of the people who, through constant sacrifice and self-immolation. fought the battle of the people, and won every vestige of liberty remaining in the land. (As Mr. Sullivan resumed his seat, the entire audience burst into applause, again and again renewed, despite all efforts at repression.)

The effect of this speech, certainly, was very considerable. Mr. Sullivan spoke for upwards of two hours and forty minutes, or until nearly a quarter past six o'clock. During the delivery of his address, twilight had succeeded daylight; the court attendants, later still, with silent steps and taper in hand, stole around and lit the chandeliers, whose glare upon the thousand anxious faces below seemed to lend a still more impressive aspect to the scene. The painful idea of the speaker's peril, which was all-apparent at first amongst the densely-packed audience, seemed to fade away by degrees, giving place to a feeling of triumph, as they listened to the historical narrative of British misrule in Ireland, by which Irish "disesteem" for British law was explained and justified, and later on to the story of the Manchester tragedy by which Irish sympathy with the martyrs was completely vindicated. Again and again, in the course of the speech, they burst into applause, regardless of threatened penalties; and, at the close, gave vent to their feelings in a manner that for a time defied all repression.

When silence was restored, the court was formally adjourned to next day, Friday, at 10 o'clock, A. M.

The morning came, and with it another throng; for it was known Mr. Martin would now speak in his turn. In order, however, that his speech, which was sure to be an important one, might close the case against the Crown, Mr. Bracken, on the court resuming, put in *his* defence very effectively as follows :—

> My lords :—I would say a word or two, but, after Mr. Sullivan's grand and noble speech of last evening, I think it now needless on my part. I went to the procession of the 8th December, assured that it was right from reading a speech of the Earl of Derby in the newspapers. There was a sitting of the Privy Council in Dublin on the day before, and I sat in my shop that night till twelve o'clock, to see if the procession would be forbidden by government. They, however, permitted it to take place, and I attended it, fully believing I was right. That is all I have to say.

This short speech, delivered in a clear, musical, and manly voice, put the whole case against the Crown in a nutshell. The appearance of the speaker too—a fine, handsome, robust, and well-built man, in the prime of life, with the unmistakable stamp of honest sincerity on his countenance and in his eye—gave his words greater effect with the audience ; and it was very audibly murmured on all sides that he had given the government a home-thrust in his brief but telling speech.

Then Mr. Martin rose. After leaving court the previous evening, he had decided to commit to writing what he intended to say; and he now read from manuscript his address to the jury. The speech, however, lost nothing in effect by this; for any auditor, out of view, would have believed it to have been spoken, as he usually speaks *extempore,* so admirably was it delivered. Mr. Martin said :—

My lords and gentlemen of the jury :—I am going to trouble this court with some reply to the charge made against me in this indictment. But I am sorry that I must begin by protesting that I do not consider myself as being now put upon my country to be tried as the constitution directs—as the spirit of the constitution requires—and, therefore, I do not address you for my legal defence, but for my vindication before the tribunal of conscience—a far more awful tribunal, to my mind, than this. Gentlemen, I regard you as twelve of my fellow-countrymen, known or believed by my prosecutors to be my political opponents, and selected for that reason for the purpose of obtaining a conviction against me in form of law. Gentlemen, I have not the smallest purpose of casting an imputation against your honesty or the honesty of my prosecutors who have selected you. This is a political trial, and in this country political trials are always conducted in this way. It is considered by the crown prosecutors to be their duty to exclude from the jury-box every juror known or suspected to hold or agree with the accused in political sentiments. Now, gentlemen, I have not the least objection to see men of the most opposite political sentiments to mine placed in the jury-box to try me, provided they be placed there as the constitution commands—provided they are twelve of my neighbors indifferently chosen. As a loyal citizen I am willing and desirous to be put upon my country, and fairly tried before any twelve of my countrymen, no matter what may happen to be the political sentiments of any of them. But I am sorry and indignant that this is not such a trial. This system by which, over and over again, loyal subjects of the Queen in Ireland are condemned in form of law for seeking, by such means as the constitution warrants, to restore her Majesty's kingdom of Ireland to the enjoyment of its national rights—this system of selecting anti-Repealers and excluding Repealers from the jury-box, when a Repealer like me is to be tried, is calculated to bring the administration of justice into disesteem, disrepute, and hatred. I here protest against it. My lords and gentlemen of the jury, before I offer any reply to the charges in this indictment, and the further development of those charges made yesterday by the learned gentleman whose official duty it was to argue the government's case against me, I wish to apologize to the court for declining to avail myself of the professional assistance of the bar upon this occasion.

It is not through any want of respect for the noble profession of the bar that I decline that assistance. I regard the duties of a lawyer as among the most respectable that a citizen can undertake. His education has taught him to investigate the origin, and to understand the principles, of law, and the true nature of loyalty. He has had to consider how the interests of individual citizens may harmonize with the interests of the community, how justice and liberty may be united, how the state may have both order and contentment. The application of the knowledge which he has gained from the study of law to the daily facts of human society, sharpens and strengthens all his faculties, clears his judgment, helps him to distinguish true from false, and right from wrong. It is no wonder, gentlemen, that an accomplished and virtuous lawyer holds a high place in the aristocracy of merit in every free country. Like all things human, the legal profession has its dark as well as its bright side, has in it germs of decay and rotten foulness as well as of health and beauty; but yet it is a noble profession, and one which I admire and respect. But, above all, I would desire to respect the bar of my own country, and the Irish bar—the bar made illustrious by such memories as those of Grattan and Flood, and the Emmets, and Curran, and Plunket, and Saurin, and Holmes, and Shiel, and O'Connell. I may add, too, of Burke and of Sheridan, for they were Irish in all that made them great. The bar of Ireland wants this day only the ennobling inspirations of national freedom to raise it to a level with the world. Under the Union very few lawyers have been produced whose names can rank in history with any of the great names I have mentioned. But still, even in the present times of decay, and when the Union is preparing to carry away our superior courts and the remains of our bar to Westminster, and to turn that beautiful building upon the quay into a barrack like the Linen Hall, or an English taxgather's office like the Custom House, there are many learned, accomplished, and respectable lawyers at the Irish bar; and far be it from me to doubt but that any Irish lawyer, who might undertake my defence, would loyally exert himself, as the lofty idea of professional honor commands, to save me from a conviction. But to this attack upon my character as a good citizen and upon my liberty, my lords and gentlemen, the only defence I could permit to be offered would be a full justification of my political conduct, morally, constitutionally, legally—a complete vindication of my acts and words alleged to be seditious and disloyal, and to retort against my accusers the charge of sedition and disloyalty. Not, indeed, that I would desire to prosecute these gentlemen upon that charge, if I could count upon convicting them and sending them to the dungeon instead of myself. I don't desire to silence them, or to hurt a hair of their wigs, because their political opinions differ from mine. Gentlemen, this prosecution against me, like the prosecutions just accomplished against two national newspapers, is part of a scheme of the ministers of the Crown for suppressing all voice of protest against the Union, for suppressing all public complaint against the deadly results of the Union, and all advocacy by act, speech, or writing for Repeal of the Union. Now I am a Repealer so long as I have been a politician at all— that is, for at least twenty-four years past. Until the national self-government of my own country be first restored, there appears to me to be no place, no *locus standi* (as lawyers say), for any other Irish political question, and I consider it to be my duty, as a patriotic and loyal citizen, to endeavor by all honorable and prudent means to procure the Repeal of the Act of the Union, and the restoration of the independent Irish government, of which my country was (as I have said in my prosecuted speech), "by fraud and force," and against the will of the vast majority of its people of every race, creed, and class, though under false form of law, deprived sixty-seven years ago. Certainly, I do not dispute the right of you, gentlemen, or of any man in this court, or in all Ireland, to approve of the Union, to praise it, if you think right, as being wise and beneficent, and to advocate its continuance openly by act, speech, and writing. But I naturally think that my convictions in this matter of the Union ought to be shared by you, also, gentlemen, and by the learned judges, and the lawyers, both crown lawyers and all others, and by the policemen and soldiers, and all faithful subjects of her Majesty in Ireland. Now, gentlemen, such being my convictions, were I to intrust my defence in this court to a lawyer, he must speak as a Repealer, not only for me, but for himself; not only as a professional advocate, but as a man, and from the heart. I cannot doubt but that there are very many Irish lawyers who privately share my convictions about Repeal. Believing as I do in my heart and conscience, and with all the force of the mind that God has given me, that Repeal is the right and the only right policy for Ireland—for healing all the wounds of our community, all our sectarian feuds, all our national shame, suffering, and peril—for making our country peaceful, industrious, prosperous, respectable and happy—I cannot doubt but that in the enlightened profession of the bar there must be very many Irishmen who, like me, consider Repeal to be right, and best, and necessary for the public good. But, gentlemen, ever since the Union, by fraud and force and against the will of the Irish people, was enacted—ever since that act of usurpation by the English parliament of the sovereign rights of the Queen, Lords, and Commons of Ireland—ever since this country was thereby rendered the subject instead of the sister of England—ever since the Union, but especially for about twenty years past, it has been the policy of those who have got possession of the sovereign rights of the Irish crown to appoint to all places of public trust, emolument, or honor in Ireland only such men as would submit, whether by parole or by tacit understanding, to suppress all public utterance of their desire for the Repeal of the Union. Such has been the persistent policy towards this country of those who command all the patronage of Irish officers, paid and unpaid—the policy of all English ministers, whether Whig or Tory. Combined with the disposal of the public forces—such a policy is naturally very effective in not really reconciling, but in keeping

Ireland quietly subject to the Union. It is a hard trial of men's patriotism to be debarred from every career of profitable and honorable distinction in the public service of their own country. I do not wonder that few Irish lawyers, in presence of the mighty power of England, dare sacrifice personal ambition and interest to what may seem a vain protest against accomplished facts. I do not wish to attack or offend them—as this court expresses it, to impute improper motives to them—by thus simply stating the sad facts which are relevant to my own case in this prosecution, and explaining that I decline professional assistance, because few lawyers would be so rash as to adopt my political convictions, and vindicate my political conduct as their own; and because, if any lawyer were so bold as to offer me his aid on my own terms, I am too generous to permit him to ruin his professional career for my sake. Such are the reasons, gentlemen of the jury and my lords, why I am now going through this trial, not *secundum artem*, but, like an eccentric patient, who won't be treated by the doctors, but will quack himself. Perhaps I would be safer if I did not say a word about the legal character of the charge made against me in this indictment. There are legal matters as dangerous to handle as any drugs in the pharmacopœia. Yet I shall trouble you for a short time longer, while I endeavor to show that I have not acted in a way unbecoming a good citizen. The charge against me in this indictment is that I took part in an illegal procession, and violated the statute entitled the Party Processions Act. His lordship enumerated seven conditions, the violation of some one of which is necessary to render an assembly illegal at common law. Those seven conditions are:—1. That the persons forming the assembly met to carry out an unlawful purpose. 2. That the numbers in which the persons met endangered the public peace. 3. That the assembly caused alarm to the peaceful subjects of the Queen. 4. That the assembly created disaffection. 5. That the assembly incited her Majesty's Irish subjects to hate her Majesty's English subjects—his lordship did not say anything of the case of an assembly inciting the Queen's English subjects to hate the Queen's Irish subjects, but no such case is likely to be tried here. 6. That the assembly intended to asperse the right and constitutional administration of justice; and 7. That the assembly intended to impair the functions of justice, and to bring the administration of justice into disrepute. I say that the procession of the 8th December did not violate any one of these conditions:—1. In the first place, the persons forming that procession did not meet to carry out any unlawful purpose—their purpose was peaceably to express their opinion upon a public act of the public servants of the Crown. 2. In the second place, the numbers in which those persons met did not endanger the public peace. None of those persons carried arms. Thousands of those persons were women and children. There was no injury or offence attempted to be committed against anybody, and no disturbance of the peace took place. 3. In the third place, the assembly caused no alarm to the peaceable subjects of the Queen—there is not a tittle of evidence to that effect. 4. In the fourth place, the assembly did not create disaffection, neither was it intended or calculated to create disaffection. On the contrary, the assembly served to give peaceful expression to the opinion entertained by vast numbers of her Majesty's peaceful subjects upon a public act of the servants of the Crown,—an act which vast numbers of the Queen's subjects regretted and condemned. And thus the assembly was calculated to prevent or remove disaffection. For such open and peaceful manifestation of the real opinions of the Queen's subjects upon public affairs is the proper, safe, and constitutional way in which they may aid to prevent disaffection. 5. In the fifth place, the assembly did not incite the Irish subjects of the Queen to hate her Majesty's English subjects. On the contrary, it was a proper constitutional way of bringing about a right understanding upon a transaction which, if not fairly and fully explained and set right, must produce hatred between the two peoples. That transaction was calculated to produce hatred. But those who protest peaceably against such a transaction are not the party to be blamed, but those responsible for the transaction. 6. In the sixth place, the assembly had no purpose of aspersing the right and constitutional administration of justice. Its tendency was peaceably to point out faults in the conduct of the servants of the Crown, charged with the administration of justice, which faults were calculated to bring the administration of justice into disrepute. 7. Nor, in the seventh place, did the assembly impair the functions of justice, or intend or tend to do so. Even my prosecutors do not allege that judicial tribunals are infallible. It would be too absurd to make such an allegation in plain words. It is admitted on all hands that judges have sometimes given wrong directions, that juries have given wrong verdicts, that courts of justice have wrongfully appreciated the whole matter for trial. When millions of the Queen's subjects think that such wrong has been done, is it sedition for them to say so peaceably and publicly? On the contrary, the constitutional way for good citizens to act in striving to keep the administration of justice pure and above suspicion of unfairness, is by such open and peaceable protests. Thus, and thus only, may the functions of justice be saved from being impaired. In this case wrong had been done. Five men had been tried together upon the same evidence, and convicted together upon that evidence, and, while one of the five was acknowledged by the Crown to be innocent, and the whole conviction was thus acknowledged to be wrong and invalid, three of the five men were hanged upon that conviction. My friend, Mr. Sullivan, in his eloquent and unanswerable speech of yesterday, has so clearly demonstrated the facts of that unhappy and disgraceful affair of Manchester, that I shall merely say of it that I adopt every word he spoke upon the subject for mine, and to justify the sentiment and purpose with which I engaged in the procession of the 8th December. I say the persons responsible for that transaction are fairly liable to the charge of acting so as bring the administration of justice into contempt, unless, gentlemen, you hold those persons to be infallible, and hold that they can do no wrong. But, gentlemen, the constitution does not say that the servants of the Crown can do no wrong. According to the constitution the Sovereign can do no wrong, but her servants may. In this case they have done wrong. And, gentlemen, you cannot right that wrong, nor save the administration of justice from the disrepute into which such proceedings are calculated to bring it, by giving a verdict to put my comrades and myself into jail for saying openly and peaceably that we believe the administration of justice in that unhappy affair did do wrong. But further, gentlemen, let us suppose that you twelve jurors, as well as the servants of the Crown who are prosecuting me, and the two judges, consider me to be mistaken in my opinion upon that judicial proceeding, yet you have no right under the constitution to convict me of a misdemeanor for openly and peaceably expressing my opinion. You have no such right; and as to the wisdom of treating my differences of opinion and the peaceable expression of it as a penal offence—and the wisdom of a political act ought to be a serious question with all good and loyal citizens—consider that the opinion you are invited by the crown prosecutors to pronounce to be a penal offence is not mine alone, nor that alone of the five men herein indicated, but is the opinion of all the 30,000 persons estimated by the crown evidence to have taken part in the assembly of the 8th of December; is the opinion, besides, of the 90,000 or 100,000 others who, standing in the streets of this city, or at the open windows overlooking the streets traversed by the procession that day, manifested their sympathy with the objects of the procession; is the opinion, as you are morally certain, of some millions of your Irish fellow-subjects. By indicting me for the expression of that opinion, the public prosecutors virtually indict some millions of the Queen's peaceable Irish subjects. It is only the convenience of this court—which could not hold the millions in one batch of traversers, and which would require daily sittings for several successive years to go through the proper formalities for duly trying all those millions; it is only the convenience of this court that can be pretended to relieve the crown prosecutors from the duty of trying and convicting all those millions, if it is their duty to try and convict me. The right principles of law do not allow the servants of the Crown to evade or neglect their duty of bringing to justice all offenders against the law. I suppose these gentlemen may allege that it is at their discretion what offenders against the law they will prosecute. I deny that the principles of law allow them, or allow the Queen, such discretion. The Queen, at her coronation services, swears to do justice to all her subjects, according to the law. The Queen, certainly, has the right by the constitution to pardon any offenders against the law. She has the prerogative of mercy. But there can be no pardon, no mercy, till after an offence be proved in due course of law by accusation of the alleged offenders before the proper tribunals, followed by their plea of guilty or the jurors' verdict of guilty. And to select one man or six men for trial, condemnation, and punishment, out of, say, four millions who have really participated in the same alleged wicked, malicious, seditious, evil-disposed, and unlawful proceeding, is unfair to the six men, and unfair to the other 3,999,994 men—is a dereliction of duty on the part of the officers of the law, and is calculated to bring the administration of justice into disrepute. Equal justice is what the constitution demands. Under military authority an army may be decimated, and a few offenders may properly be punished, while the rest are left unpunished. But under a free constitution it is not so. Whoever breaks the law must be made amenable to punishment, or equal justice is not rendered to the subjects of the Queen. Is it not pertinent, therefore, gentlemen, for me to say to you this is an unwise proceeding which my prosecutors bid you to sanction by a verdict? I have heard it asked by a lawyer addressing this court as a question that must be answered in the negative—Can you indict a whole nation? If such a proceeding as this prosecution against the peaceable procession of the 8th of December receives the sanction of your verdict, that question must be answered in the affirmative. It will need only a crown prosecutor. an Attorney-General, and a Solicitor-General, two judges, and twelve jurors, all of the one mind. while all the other subjects of the Queen in Ireland are of a different mind, and the five millions and a-half of the Queen's subjects in Ireland outside that circle of seventeen of her Majestys' subjects, may be indicted, convicted, and consigned to penal imprisonment in due form of law—as law is understood in political trials in Ireland. Gentlemen, I have thus far endeavored to argue from the common-sense of mankind, with which the principles of law must be in accord, that the peaceable procession of the 8th of December—that peaceable demonstration of the sentiment of millions of the Queen's subjects in Ireland—did not violate any of the seven conditions of the learned judge to the grand jury in defining what constitutes an illegal assembly at common law ; and I have also argued that the prosecution is unwise, and calculated to excite discontent. Gentlemen, I shall now endeavor to show you that the procession of the 8th of December did not violate the statute entitled the Party Processions Act. The learned judge in his charge told the grand jury that under this act all processions are illegal which carry weapons of offence, or which carry symbols calculated to promote the animosity of some other class of her Majesty's subjects. Applying the law to this case, his lordship remarked that the processions of the 8th of December had something of military array—that is, they went in regular order with a regular step. But, gentlemen, there were no arms in that procession, there were no symbols in that procession intended or calculated to provoke animosity in any other class of the Queen's subjects, or in any human creature. There was neither symbol, nor deed, nor word, intended to provoke animosity. As to the military array—is it not absurd to attribute a warlike character to an unarmed and perfectly peaceful assemblage, in which there were some thousands of women and children? No offence was given or offered any human being. The authorities were so assured of the peacefulness and inoffensiveness of the assemblage that the police were withdrawn in a great measure from their ordinary duties of preventing disorders. And as to the remark that the people walked with a regular step, I need only say that was done for the sake of order and decorum. It would be merely to doubt whether you are men of common-sense if I argued any further to satisfy you that the procession did not violate the Party Processions Act, as defined by the learned judge. The speech delivered on that occasion is an important element in forming a judgment upon the character and object of the procession. The speech declared the procession to be a peaceable expression of the opinion of those who composed it upon an important public transaction—an expression of sorrow and indignation at an act of the ministers of the government. It was a protest against that act—a protest which those who disapproved of it were entitled by the constitution to make, and which they made, peaceably and legitimately. Has not every individual of the millions of the Queen's subjects the right to say openly whether he approves or disapproves of any public act of the Queen's ministers? Have not all the Queen's subjects the right to say so together, if they can, without disturbance of the Queen's peace? The procession enabled many thousands to do that without the least inconvenience or danger to themselves, and with no injury or offence to their neighbors. To prohibit or punish peaceful, inoffensive, orderly, and perfectly innocent processions upon pretence that they are constructively unlawful, is unconstitutional tyranny. Was that done because the ministers discovered that the terror of suspended *Habeas Corpus* had not in this matter stifled public opinion? Of course, if anything be prohibited by government, the people obey—of course I obey. I would not have held the procession had I not understood that it was permitted. But understanding that it was permitted, and so believing that it might serve the people for a safe and useful expression of their sentiment, I held the procession. I did not hold the procession because I believed it to be illegal, but because I believed it to be legal and understood it to be permitted. In this country it is not law that must rule a loyal citizen's conduct, but the caprice of the English ministers. For myself, I acknowledge that I submit to such system of government unwillingly, and with constant hope for the restoration of the reign of law, but I do submit. Why at first did the ministers of the Crown permit an expression of censure upon that judicial proceeding at Manchester by a procession—why did they not warn her Majesty's subjects against the danger of breaking the law? Was it not because they thought that the terrors of the suspended *Habeas Corpus* would be enough to prevent the people from coming openly forward at all to express their real sentiments? Was it because they found that so vehement and so general was the feeling of indignation at that unhappy transaction at Manchester that they did venture to come openly forward, with perfect and most careful observance of the peace, to express their real sentiments—that the ministry proclaimed down the procession, and now prosecute us in order to stifle public opinion ? Gentlemen of the jury, I have said enough to convince any twelve reasonable men that there was nothing in my conduct in the matter of that procession which you can declare on your oaths to be "malicious, seditious, ill-disposed, and intended to disturb the peace and tranquillity of the realm." I shall trouble you no further, except by asking you to listen to the summing up of the indictment, and, while you listen, to judge between me and the Attorney-General. I shall read you my words and his comment. Judge, Irish jurors, which of us two is guilty :—"Let us, therefore, conclude this proceeding by joining heartily, with hat soff, in the prayer of those three men, 'God save Ireland.'" "Thereby," says the Attorney-General in his indictment, "meaning, and intending to excite hatred, dislike, and animosity against her Majesty and the government, and bring into contempt the administration of justice and the laws of this realm, and cause strife and hatred between her Majesty's subjects in Ireland and in England, and to excite discontent and disaffection against her Majesty's government." Gentlemen, I have now done.

Mr. Martin sat down amidst loud and prolonged applause.

This splendid argument, close, searching, irresistible, gave the *coup de grace* to the crown case. The prisoners having called no evidence, according to honorable custom having almost the force of law, the prosecution was disentitled to any rejoinder. Nevertheless, the Crown put up its ablest speaker, a man far surpassing in attainments as a lawyer and an orator both the Attorney and Solicitor-General, Mr. Ball, Q. C., to press against the accused that technical right which honorable usage reprehended as unfair ! No doubt the crown authorities felt it was not a moment in which they could afford to be squeamish or scrupulous. The speeches of Mr. Sullivan and Mr. Martin had had a visible effect upon the jury—had, in fact, made shreds of the crown case; and so Mr. Ball was put up as the last hope of averting the "disaster" of a failure. He spoke with his accustomed ability and dignity, and made a powerful appeal in behalf of the Crown. Then Mr. Justice Fitzgerald proceeded to charge the jury, which he did in his own peculiarly calm, precise, and perspicuous style. At the outset, referring to the protest of the accused against the conduct of the Crown in the jury challenges, he administered a keen rebuke to the government officials. It was, he said, no doubt the strict legal *right* of the Crown to act as it had done; yet, considering that this was a case in which the accused was accorded no corresponding privilege, the exercise of that right in such a manner by the Crown certainly was, in his, Mr. Justice Fitzgerald's estimation, *a subject for grave objection.*

Here there was what the newspaper reporters call "sensation in court." What! Had it come to this, that one of the chief institutions of the land—a very pillar of the Crown and government—namely, *jury-packing*, was to be reflected upon from the bench itself. Monstrous!

The charge, though mild in language, was pretty sharp on the "criminality" of such conduct as was *imputed* to the accused, yet certainly left some margin to the jury for the exercise of their opinion upon "the law and the facts."

At two o'clock in the afternoon the jury retired to consider their verdict, and as the judges at the same moment withdrew to their chamber, the pent-up feelings of the crowded audience instantly found vent in loud Babel-like expressions and interchange of comments on the charge, and conjectures as to the result. "Waiting for the verdict" is a scene that has often been described and painted. Every one of course concluded that half-an-hour would, in any case, elapse before the anxiously-watched jury-room door would open; but, when the clock hands neared three, suspense, intense and painful, became more and more visible in every countenance. It seemed to be only now that men fully realized all that was at stake, all that was in peril, on this trial! *A conviction in this case rendered the national color of Ireland forevermore an illegal and forbidden emblem!* A conviction in this case would degrade the symbol of nationality into a badge of faction! To every fevered, anxious mind at this moment rose the troubled memories of gloomy times—the "dark and evil days" chronicled in that popular ballad, the music and words of which now seemed to haunt the watchers in the court:—

"O Patrick dear! and did you hear
The news that's going round?
The shamrock is by law forbid
To grow on Irish ground.
No more St. Patrick's day we'll keep—
His color can't be seen,
For there's a bloody law agen
The wearing of the Green."

But hark! There is a noise at the jury-room door! It opens—the jury enter the box. A murmur, swelling to almost a roar, from the crowded audience is instantly followed by a death-like stillness. The judges are called; but by this time it is noticed that the foreman has not the "issue-paper" ready to hand down; and a buzz goes round—"A question; a question!" It is even so. The foreman asks:—

Whether, if they believed the speech of Mr. Martin to be in itself seditious, should they come to the conclusion that the assemblage was seditious?

Mr. Justice Fitzgerald answers *in the negative*, and a thrill goes through the audience. Nor is this all. One of the jurors declares that there is no chance whatever of their agreeing to a verdict! Almost a cheer breaks out. The judge, however, declares they must retire again; which the jury do, very reluctantly and doggedly; in a word, very unlike men likely to "persuade one another."

When the judges again leave the bench for their chamber, the crowd in court give way outright to joy. Every face is bright; every heart is light; jokes go round, and there is great "chaff" of the crown officials, and of the "polis," who, poor fellows, to tell the truth, seem to be as glad as the gladdest in the throng. Five o'clock arrives—half-past five—the jury must surely be out soon now. At a quarter to six they come; and, for an instant, the joke is hushed, and cheeks suddenly grow pale with fear lest, by any chance, it might be evil news. But the faces of the jurymen tell plainly, "No verdict." The judges again are seated. The usual questions in such cases: the usual answers. "No hope whatever of an agreement." Then, after a reference to the Solicitor-General, who, in a sepulchral tone, "supposes" there is "nothing for it" but to discharge the jury, his lordship declares the jury discharged.

Like a volley there burst a wild cheer, a shout, that shook the building! Again and again it was renewed; and, being caught up by the crowd outside, sent the tidings of victory with electrical rapidity through the city. Then there was a rush at Mr. Martin and Mr. Sullivan. The former especially was clasped, embraced, and borne about by the surging throng, wild with joy. It was with considerable difficulty any of the traversers could get away, so demonstrative was the multitude in the streets. Throughout the city the event was hailed with rejoicing, and the names of the jurymen, "good and bad," were vowed to perpetual benediction. For once, at least, justice had triumphed; or rather, injustice had been baulked. For once, at least, the people had won the day; and the British government had received a signal overthrow in its endeavor to proscribe—

"THE WEARING OF THE GREEN."

For one of the actors in the above-described memorable scene, the victory purchased but a few hours' safety. Next morning, Mr. A. M. Sullivan was placed again at the bar to hear his sentence—that following upon the first of the prosecutions hurled against him (the *press* prosecution), on which he had been found guilty. Again the court was crowded—this time with anxious faces devoid of hope. It was a brief scene. Mr. Justice Fitzgerald announced the sentence—six months in Richmond Prison; and, amidst a farewell demonstration that compelled the business of the court to be temporarily suspended, the officials led away in custody the only one of the prosecuted processionists who expiated by punishment his sympathy with the fate of the Martyred Three of Manchester.

www.ingramcontent.com/pod-product-compliance
Lightning Source LLC
Chambersburg PA
CBHW051728300426
44115CB00007B/507